# The background of ecology
Concept and theory

# CAMBRIDGE STUDIES IN ECOLOGY

EDITORS:

E. Beck   *Department of Plant Physiology,
University of Bayreuth*
H. J. B. Birks   *Department of Botany,
University of Cambridge*
E. F. Connor   *Department of Environmental Science,
University of Virginia*

ALSO IN THE SERIES

Hugh G. Gauch, Jr.   *Multivariate analysis in community
ecology*
Robert Henry Peters   *The ecological implications of body
size*
C. S. Reynolds   *The ecology of freshwater phytoplankton*
K. A. Kershaw   *Physiological ecology of lichens*

# The background of ecology
## Concept and theory

ROBERT P. McINTOSH

*University of Notre Dame*

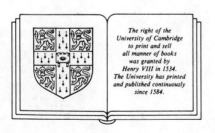

The right of the
University of Cambridge
to print and sell
all manner of books
was granted by
Henry VIII in 1534.
The University has printed
and published continuously
since 1584.

CAMBRIDGE UNIVERSITY PRESS

*Cambridge*
*London   New York   New Rochelle*
*Sydney   Melbourne*

Published by the Press Syndicate of the University of Cambridge
The Pitt Building, Trumpington Street, Cambridge CB2 1RP
32 East 57th Street, New York, NY 10022, USA
10 Stamford Road, Oakleigh, Melbourne 3166, Australia

First published 1985

Printed in the United States of America

*Library of Congress Cataloging in Publication Data*
McIntosh, Robert P. (Robert Patrick)
The background of ecology.
(Cambridge studies in ecology)
Bibliography: p.
Includes index.
1. Ecology.  I. Title.  II. Series.
QH541.M386   1985   574.5   84-27490
ISBN 0 521 24935 X

For Joan

# Contents

# Preface

An attempt to write a general account of the origins, development, and current problems of ecology, even within the constraints noted below, might well be thought foolhardy. Ecology built upon traditions of natural history beginning in classical antiquity but developed as a science in the context of late 19th-century biology, natural history surveys, and conservation. It became widely known to the general public, often in distorted forms, only in the 1960s. It has been called polymorphic because it appeared and continues in numerous and different forms appropriate to the enormous variability and complexity of the things studied by ecologists. Until recently, ecology has not excited the interest of historians of science, and detailed historical studies of ecology or biographical works about ecologists are few. This volume was not, however written to fill the need for careful historical analyses of ecology and its relation to biology and to environmental concerns, although it leans heavily on those now available. It is an attempt to provide an account of the background of ecology and suggest its relevance to current problems of ecology as a science. It has an underlying assumption that some of the difficulties and conflicts now manifest in ecology can be better resolved if ecologists, particularly younger ecologists, become familiar with what went before them and their mentors and outside their immediate interests. Ecologists should be free of what one ecologist described as the "tyranny of the present," not simply because knowledge of past events is interesting but because ignorance of the past makes for redundance at best and confusion at worst. It is likely that the hope of enhancing understanding of current ecology influenced my selection of materials and contributes to the shortcomings of this book from a historian's viewpoint.

Because of limitations of space, sources, and the author, the present account of ecology is largely that which has been called Anglo-American ecology. Continental sources, influences, and parallels are noted, particularly where they were cited by British and American ecologists. However, it would be vainglorious to attempt an overview of ecology at large. At best, it may be hoped that the present volume will achieve a beginning of a general account of ecology and its sources. It does not pretend to be definitive even within its geographical boundaries. Because ecology developed from rather separate traditions of plant, animal, freshwater, and marine ecology, the organization of the book is, in some degree, comparative. It attempts to follow developments in each of these somewhat isolated areas and, where possible, to identify parallels or convergences. The aim is to consider methodological, conceptual, and theoretical attributes developed in, or shared by, the several disparate sources of ecology, and no effort is made to review the enormous body of empirical ecological work.

The several chapters have a rough chronology, although strict chronology is not consistently followed. In the hope of suggesting the connectedness of ideas and different times, reference may be made, on occasion, to earlier or later events and comments. Chapter 1 is essentially a review of ideas expressed about the sources of ecology before it became a recognized science. Chapter 2 considers the emergence of ecology from the 1890s to 1915, ending with the creation of formal ecological societies. Chapters 3, 4, and 5 backtrack to the largely 19th-century beginnings of their respective topics and extend to the 1950s. Chapters 6 and 7 include more recent developments of ecology and extend from the 1920s and 1930s nearly to the present. Chapter 8 links ecology and the conservation movement of the early 1900s and ecology and the environmental movement of the 1960s and 1970s. Because the subject matters of the chapters overlap, some redundancy is unavoidable.

The scope of the book required that it be based almost entirely on published material. An effort has been made to cite and quote references where ecologists, and others, comment about ecology and their views of ecology as a science and its methodological and epistemological problems rather than the empirical substance of ecology. Unfortunately, it was not generally possible to provide extensive biographical data or the fascinating personal and anecdotal material which normally enlivens or disgraces scientific discourse. It may be hoped that ecologists will find in the book, and in the literature cited, materials useful in gaining an understanding of the sources and nature of ecology and its relation to other aspects of biology and environmental concerns. If the book also leads ecologists to identification with their predecessors and to their contemporaries in other aspects of ecology, so much the better. It will be sheer lagniappe if historians, sociologists, and philosophers of science find in it some points of departure which encourage them to extend their own investigations to include ecology.

*Notre Dame, Indiana*                                    Robert P. McIntosh

# Acknowledgments

The completion of the manuscript owes much to the unstinting assistance of my colleague Ronald Hellenthal for his comments and computer skills which made possible its entry in multiple drafts into the word processor and its composition from a computer disk. Entry was achieved by the care and skill exercised by Victoria S. Harman in typing and meticulously correcting the many errors in the early drafts. Laura Gibson worked assiduously checking citations and literature cited. The manuscript benefited greatly by the substantive and editorial comments of Susan and Stephen Carpenter, who read it in its entirety, some parts more than once. Members of the graduate seminar in ecology also read early drafts of the complete manuscript and by a complex of commentary, expressed confusion, and unexpressed ennui stimulated its improvement. Historians of science, among them notable contributors to the history of ecology, were kind enough to read and comment on individual chapters. These include Eugene Cittadino, Frank Egerton, Sharon Kingsland, Malcolm Nicolson, Francesco M. Scudo, Philip Sloan, and Ronald Tobey. None, I am sure, endorses any historical views expressed, but all saved me from some errors of an ecologist dabbling in history of science. Philosophers of science John Lyon and Mark Sagoff, and sociologists Chung Lin Kwa and Jacqueline Cramer, read chapters and offered helpful comments. I am greatly indebted to the camaraderie among ecologists, some friends for many years, others whom I have never met, who read and commented on one or more chapters. Not all agreed with me or with each other in their commentary, but all were uniformly and kindly critical, to my benefit. My gratitude is extended to T. F. H. Allen, W. Dwight Billings, F. Herbert Bormann, Robert L. Burgess, James T. Callahan, Grant Cottam, Paul Dayton, Francis Evans, Peter Greig-Smith, Frances James, Gene E. Likens, Orie Loucks, Brian Moss, Jerry Olson, Robert V. O'Neill, Robert K. Peet, L. B. Slobodkin, F. E. Smith, and James White. Other ecologists, among them Robert E. Cook, Jerry Franklin, Robert A. McCabe, Frank A. Pitelka, and Earl

Werner, offered helpful responses to specific inquiries. Peter Rich and James MacMahon read the final draft to warn of residual flaws. Countless others, too many to name, have given critical and helpful comments, often unwittingly, in adding to my file of the lore of ecology. Completion of the work in reasonable time was allowed by the helpfulness of T. Crovello in arranging, and the University of Notre Dame in granting, a part-time leave during 1982–3. I am particularly thankful to J. H. B. Birks, who invited me to undertake this book and paid for his kindness with having to read the whole thing in draft.

R. P. McI.

# 1

## Antecedents of ecology

Ecology in its early years was sometimes decried as not a science at all but merely a point of view. After nearly a century of trying to erect a conceptual, methodological, and theoretical framework for the most complex phenomena encountered in nature, ecology was familiar only to a relatively small number of academic biologists and applied biologists, range managers, foresters, and fishery and game managers. These shared an overlapping, but not coincident, network of concepts, methodologies, professional associations, publications, funding sources, and concerns about the relations of organisms as populations and communities to their environment. In the wake of widespread recognition, in the 1960s, of the "environmental crisis," ecology was abruptly thrust into the public arena and widely hailed as an appropriate guide to the relation of humans, as well as other forms of life, to their environment. Strikingly, ecology became a watchword, even in high political circles, just when Paul B. Sears, one of its most articulate practitioners and expositors, described ecology as "a subversive subject" (Sears 1964). Sears's point was that the view of nature derived from ecological studies called into question some of the cultural and economic premises widely accepted by Western societies. Chief among these premises was that human civilizations, particularly of advanced technological cultures, were above or outside the limitations, or "laws," of nature (Dunlap 1980b).

Although ecologists had long asserted that ecological science was significant in offering insight about, and to, human societies, they were ill prepared to cope with the abrupt seizure of the name and its extension to include all aspects of environmental concern, often leaving behind ecological concepts and canons of evidence which had been developed over the decades. Ecology was, and is, a science which does not fit readily into the familiar mold of science erected on the model of classical physics, and it deals with phenomena which frequently touch very close to the quick of human sensibilities, including aesthetics, morality, ethics, and, even worse in some minds, economics. Ecology

1

suffered more from some of its admirers and friends who sometimes misinterpreted or overextended its competence than from its critics. The concepts and methods of ecology, at best a polymorphic science, were often lost in the extension of the term to incorporate almost any idea, or ideal, concerning the environment taken as meritorious by some group. The large body of hard-won knowledge gained by ecologists which afforded some of the best evidence of the environmental crisis and promising guides for dealing with it was often bypassed, or even distorted, to support ill-founded "ecological" panaceas. Ecology was not, and is not, a predictive science, but ecologists knew a lot more than they were able to bring to the attention of those who made major decisions affecting the environment of humans and other organisms. One of the continuing difficulties of ecology is that its sources and boundaries are difficult to specify and this problem has been exacerbated in recent years. One ecologist, perhaps in desperation, wrote that ecology is what ecologists do. Examination of what ecologists do, or even what "protoecologists" (Voorhees 1983) did and thought, before there was a name for them, may lead to a better understanding of what ecology is, whence it came, and what it may become.

The term *ecology* shares with the word *biology* the distinction of first appearing obscurely in a 19th-century treatise and only gradually becoming accepted as a name for a distinct and respectable science. Ecology, like biology, came to include a wide range of phenomena which had been pursued since antiquity under different rubrics and philosophies of nature. The coinage of *biology* is variously attributed, Karl Friedrich Burdach apparently being the earliest to use it in 1800 (Baron 1966; Coleman 1977; Farber 1982). Lamarck, another of the earliest users of *biology* in 1802, believed that it was a new theory of living organisms (Farber 1982); and Treviranus, who used *biology* in 1802, described it as "the philosophy of living nature" (Burdon-Sanderson 1893). Ecology was similarly to be regarded as having portent for life and philosophy. Coleman (1977) wrote that it took a century for biology to progress from "a hopeful term" to a "vigorous and autonomous science by 1900." Ecology progressed slowly from the coining of the word by the eminent German zoologist Ernst Haeckel in 1866 to a recognized and vigorous science (ca. 1920), although it took a century for ecology to become widely familiar outside professional circles in the 1960s, and questions about its autonomy and maturity as a science persist today (McIntosh 1976, 1980a).

Some historians of science regarded 19th-century biology as distinctly different from, and more significant than, natural history or as even excluding it (Coleman 1977). Biology, in this view, concentrated on functional aspects of individual living organisms and became, according to Coleman, essentially synonymous with physiology in the 19th century. It may come as a surprise to many biologists that Farber (1982) believed it necessary to urge historians of science to recognize that natural history did not fade away in the 19th century. In fact, as Farber and most biologists know, natural history proliferated in the 19th century, fragmenting into separate disciplines to accommodate the deluge of new information about the kinds and properties of living organisms, their activities, and distribution. Darwinian evolutionary theory, largely a product of natural history, was the major intellectual achievement of 19th-century biology. Farber wisely urged parity in the significance of the developments of physiology and natural history in the 19th century and their continuance into 20th-century biology. This is certainly appropriate for ecology, which is an amalgam of both.

The terminological problems of biology and ecology are evident in the various interpretations given them. Biology had, late in the 19th century, acquired what Stauffer (1957) described as an "arbitrarily restricted" usage. Instead of being equivalent to physiology, as Coleman (1977) stated, biology had come to mean "what is now included under ecology," a usage commonly deplored by biologists (Boerker 1916). Haeckel, according to Stauffer, introduced the word *ecology* as a substitute for this limited meaning of biology, freeing *biology* for its more appropriate use as a general term including botany and zoology in all their forms. Ecology was described by Haeckel as a part of physiology (Smit 1967) and, as late as 1891, he felt it necessary to specify that "the terms biology and œcology are not interchangeable" (Haeckel 1891). J. S. Burdon-Sanderson (1893), in his presidential address to the British Association for the Advancement of Science, made ecological history by elevating "œcology" to one of three natural divisions of biology, equivalent in rank to physiology and morphology. He added that "œcology" represented, more than other branches of biology, Treviranus's "philosophy of living nature."

Ecology was seen by Haeckel and many 19th-century biologists as simply a branch of physiology; and two of the founders of American plant ecology, F. E. Clements and H. C. Cowles, perhaps for reasons of academic politics, described it as identical with physiology (Cittadino 1980; McIntosh 1983a). Other early animal ecologists described ecology as the "new natural history" (Adams 1917) or "scientific natural history" (Elton 1927). Many ecologists regarded their science as an extension of traditional natural history, which emphasized study of whole organisms in the field, in contrast to the emphasis on laboratory studies, which developed in 19th-century biology. Some of the newer breed of ecologist deplore the continuing blend of natural history in current ecology, which they believe makes it unnecessarily complex and necessarily unscientific (Peters 1980). Other ecologists assert that it is the very complexity of the natural phenomena it studies which is the essence of ecology and question the desirability, or feasibility, of molding ecology in the tradition of the mechanistic, reductionist science of the 19th century (Odum 1977).

## A transformed natural history

Natural history in the 17th and early 18th centuries had been concerned with description of naturally occurring phenomena. It was defined by John Harris in *Lexicon Technicum,* a reference current in the early 1700s:

> Natural history is a Description of any of the Natural Products of the Earth, Water or Air, such as Beasts, Birds, Fishes, Metals, Minerals, Fossils, together with such Phenomena as at any time appear in the material world; such as Meteors etc. (Lyon and Sloan 1981:2)

Natural history in the Baconian and Aristotelian tradition consisted of describing individual facts of nature, forming a systematic classification of these facts, and from this generating empirical laws. Ecology, as it developed in the late 19th and early 20th centuries, was commonly criticized for adhering to observation, description, and an inductive approach to science. V. M. Spalding (1903), for example, stated an extreme inductionist position:

> At present it is really the main business of the ecological student to ascertain and record fully, definitely, perfectly and for all time the facts. He is not bound to tell us what they mean.

Other ecologists, such as W. F. Ganong (1904), acknowledged the criticisms of ecology as descriptive and emphasizing observation and facts. He called for a new method of experimental study and logical proof in place of "speculative yokings of conspicuous effects with prominent possible causes."

Some historians of science believe that descriptive natural history had already been transformed in the 18th century into "history of nature"

(Lyon and Sloan 1981). According to Lyon and Sloan, the initiation of a new scientific program by this transformation provided an alternative to the physical sciences, which had dominated 17th- and 18th-century science, and had "profound implications for the philosophical directions of 19th-century science." This transformed natural history, they argued, was the "historical root of modern evolutionary biology, biogeography, ecology." That root, they said, was imbedded in the attributes of "quality," "process," "historicity," and "concreteness" as opposed to "quantification," "mechanism," "rigorous deductive analysis," and "mathematical abstraction," the latter being the attributes which characterized the scientific revolution of the 17th century. Natural history was changed from "mere" description of facts into a set of scientific disciplines with their own methodology, ontology, and epistemology, distinct from the physical sciences, as the result of the work of natural scientists, such as Buffon, Hutton, and Lamarck, among a complex of other figures of 18th-century philosophy and science. Lyon and Sloan described this transformation as "in many respects as great an intellectual event as the scientific revolution of the seventeenth century." This assessment of the origin of a group of disciplines including ecology and its major associates evolutionary biology and biogeography as being "away from the physicist's paradigm" contrasts sharply with recent widespread assertions that ecology must move to conform to the 20th-century paradigm of science, erected on the "hard" physical sciences, if it is to attain "maturity" as a rigorous, deductive, mathematical, theoretical science (McIntosh 1976, 1980a; Cannon 1978; Rehbock 1983).

Lyon and Sloan (1981) asserted that the transformation from description of nature to a genuine historical understanding of nature as a temporal process, interpreting nature as a dynamic process rather than a static, nontemporal mechanism, was initiated by a radical change in natural history in the late 18th century, notably in the work of Buffon. Not all historians of science concur in this interpretation of the role of Buffon in the transformation. Oldroyd (1980) wrote of the work of Linnaeus and Buffon, "Although temporal change was envisaged, there was no historical inquiry into the earth's past, and its former organisms." It is striking that the qualities listed by Lyon and Sloan as distinguishing the new natural history of the late 18th century – quality vs. quantification, process vs. mechanism, concreteness vs. deductive abstract analysis, and historical vs. ahistorical explanation – are essentially those which are at the heart of much discussion about recent ecology in its own transformation following World War II.

Coleman (1977:160) said that 19th-century biologists lost interest in historical explanation:

> As biologists focused even more intently on problems of organic function they transferred their allegiance from the ideal of historical explanation . . . to the promise extended by the experimental investigation of vital processes.

The antipathy of some current ecologists to historical explanations and the reciprocal antipathy of others to a reductionist experimental approach in ecology is anticipated in the transfer Coleman suggests in 19th-century biologists, but the difference Coleman describes was more a separation of interest among biologists than a transfer (Mayr 1982). The distinction between historical and ahistorical explanation in ecology is still evident in current discussions of ecology. R. C. Lewontin (1969a), for example, recognized two groups of ecologists: (1) those who study ergodic[1] properties which are invariant and involve no historical considerations, and (2) those who study properties which are not invariant in time and which involve historical considerations. Some current theoretical ecologists introduced mathematical models, such as the Markov chain, which involve an assumption of time invariance and the absence of historical effects. Traditional ecologists generally assumed historical sequence to be the essence of ecology. Cowles (1901) wrote, "A plant society is not a product of present conditions alone, but the past is involved as well"; and Spalding (1903) urged Charles Darwin as the model for ecologists: "He would formulate a law not so much to express a present reaction as a habit and a history." *Ergodic* came into the ecological lexicon with the flush of theoretical ecology in the 1960s and even then was used sparingly. The question for ecologists is: Are there any ergodic properties in ecological phenomena?

## What is ecology?

As ecology achieved high visibility and even notoriety in the mid-20th century, it was frequently confounded with any concern for, or ideology about, the environment. Diverse interpretations were offered for its origins or roots, often predicated on very different ideas of what ecology is. I have chosen the neutral term *antecedents* for the title of this chapter rather than *roots* (Worster 1977), *origins,* or even *history*

---

[1]Ergodic: having every sizable sample statistically the same; therefore, each sample is representative of the whole.

(Klaauw 1936; Brewer 1960; Kormondy 1969; Egerton 1977b), all of which may imply direct lineal connections which are rarely demonstrated. *Antecedent* in its familiar usage simply indicates what has gone before without intimating that what has gone before necessarily gave rise to what came later. Coleman (1977) warned of the pitfalls of the assumption that temporal sequence equals causal explanation, a problem familiar to students of ecological succession. The historical connections or, in biological parlance, phylogeny of ecology is seen very differently by ecologists past and present and recently by historians of science following different canons of historiography.

After decades of benign neglect by historians, philosophers (cf. Lindeman 1940, as a rare and transient exception), and commentators on intellectual history, detailed study of the history of ecology is limited. Histories of science, even histories of biology, give it passing mention at best. Allee et al. (1949) began their discussion in *The History of Ecology* by "giving warning" of the lack of knowledge of ecology among scholars and philosophers. The intrinsically polymorphic nature of ecology as a science, the widespread distortion of its content and competence which accompanied its meteoric rise in public awareness during the period of environmental concern, or crisis, of the 1960s and 1970s, and the lack of historical studies combined to allow diverse, even contradictory, opinions to persist about the roots or origins of ecology. Hence, what I call *retrospective* ecology encounters problems in identifying roots simply because ecology is, to continue the botanical metaphor, more a bush with multiple stems and a diffuse rootstock than a tree with a single, well-defined trunk and roots. Kuhn (1970) suggested that a developing scientific discipline may represent a fusion of several separate trunks lacking a common initial rootstock, and ecology fits that model.

Ecology shares with biology, in addition to its 19th-century origin, difficulty of concise definition, although definitions are myriad. Haeckel in 1870 elaborated on his brief mention of the word in 1866 and defined *ecology* as follows:

> By ecology we mean the body of knowledge concerning the economy of nature – the investigation of the total relations of the animal both to its inorganic and to its organic environment; including above all, its friendly and inimical relations with those animals and plants with which it comes directly or indirectly into contact – in a word, ecology is the study of all those complex interrelations referred to by Darwin as the con-

ditions of the struggle for existence. (Trans. in Allee et al.
1949:frontispiece)

This definition illustrates the common and continuing tendency of zoologists and botanists to arrogate the whole of ecology to animals or
plants, respectively. Haeckel's emphasis on the relation of ecology to
Darwinian evolutionary theory was explicit in the title of the work
(Haeckel 1866) in which the word first appeared, and he stated the
connection in the mechanistic mode of 19th-century physiology:

Thus, the theory of evolution explains the housekeeping relations of organisms mechanistically as the necessary consequences of effectual causes and so forms the monistic groundwork of ecology. (Trans. in Stauffer 1957)

Haeckel's definition is commonly abbreviated in ecology references
and textbooks as the study of the interrelations of plants and animals
with their environments. The modifiers *scientific study* or *under natural
conditions* are sometimes added. These succinct definitions are generally satisfactory until one pursues the specific meaning of *environment,
scientific,* or *natural* as applied by diverse ecologists. Some definitions
are more elusive or even "strange and interesting" (Egler 1982). A
leading textbook of general ecology stated, "What constitutes 'modern' ecology depends upon the ecologist or group of ecologists to
whom the question is addressed" (Smith 1980). If definitions of ecology were confined to ecologists, this might be tractable, but ecology no
longer can "develop outside the distorting influences often accompanying high popularity" (Allee et al. 1949), and it is difficult to confine its
use to a professional group of ecologists. One of my favorite definitions, by a psychiatrist, is this:

Ecology may be defined as that inter-intra confrontation of
biological, social and historical factors that embrace one's
family, school, neighborhood, and the many overlapping communities that teach values, defenses, and offenses, the meaning of oneself and one's existence. (Hedgpeth, 1969)

Cowles (1904) had commented, "No one at this time is . . . prepared
to define or delimit ecology." The same difficulty was apparent to
C. C. Adams (1913:16), who wrote:

There are also so many degrees and kinds of work that go by
the name ecological, which may or may not be, and so many
also which are truly ecological but which do not go under that
name, that it is necessary that the student shall be able to see
through its diverse guises and recognize its essential character.

The "essential character" of ecology remained unclear. Definitions proliferated as its area of interest expanded. When animal populations became a focus, ecology was simply the study of the distribution and abundance of animals (Andrewartha and Birch 1954). Later, when ecosystems came to the fore, ecology became the study of the structure and function of ecosystems (E. P. Odum 1971). It seems that since the rise of ecology to high popularity in the 1960s, almost everyone is prepared to define or delimit ecology and, having done so, to say whence it came and to answer the question frequently raised in the early years of ecology, What good is ecology?

## Sources of ecology seen by biologists

Some biologists and early ecologists looked to classical natural history for the beginnings of ecology even as they disputed the choice of a name. Lankester (1889) asserted that Buffon called attention to "bionomics" or the interrelations of organisms (Chapman 1931). Bionomics, like "ethology," lost out to ecology in the last decade of the 19th century in the choice of a name for the then rising young science. That several names were suggested for the unformed discipline having to do with organisms and their environment indicates that the time was ripe for a new science. W. M. Wheeler (1902) (later the first vice-president of the Ecological Society of America), although he preferred the word *ethology* to *œcology* for the nascent discipline, claimed that zoological *œcology* began with Aristotle. He included Pliny and a host of pre-19th-century figures up to Buffon among "œcologists." Cowles (1904) cited as ecology Theophrastus' recognition of mangroves, their salt-water habitat, and species relationships as well as his physiognomic conception of vegetation antedating such use by Alexander von Humboldt in the 19th century. H. S. Reed (1905), in what is probably the first history of ecological work, started with Andreas Caesalpino in the 17th century and continued with Linnaeus, C. K. Sprengel's work on flower structure and pollination, and Humboldt's geographical studies of vegetation. E. L. Greene (1909), the major American student of the history of classical botany, claimed expansively, "Even from primitive times every botanist was an ecologist." He specifically credited Theophrastus with beginning synecology, because he distinguished habitat groups or communities and he described Tragus as the first autecologist and phenologist because he recognized the ecological properties of plant populations. N. Taylor (1912) examined some modern trends in ecology which, even then, he described as "that much used and sadly misunderstood word," but looked back only to the early 19th century, as he put it, "without unearthing the more-or-less apocryphal progenitors of the idea." C. E. Moss (1913) was critical of those who linked ecology with Lamarckian ideas of evolution and vigorously denied that A. P. DeCandolle was the first ecologist because this ignored Humboldt, Linnaeus, and Tournefort. He asserted, "It is hyperbolic" to describe Darwin as "the true premier ecologist." R. Ramaley (1940) wrote, contrary to Wheeler, that Aristotle "hardly takes a place in ecology," but Theophrastus "may well be called the first ecologist in history, for he wrote, and quite sensibly too, of the communities in which plants are associated, the relation of plants to each other and to their lifeless environment." Allee et al. (1949) commented that Aristotle's efforts are not yet ecology "but do constitute good natural history, . . . a part of the study from which ecology has developed." They saw the "modern" aspect of ecology taking form in the 18th century in the work of Linnaeus and Buffon. G. E. Du Reitz (1957) cited Linnaeus for recognizing succession and producing the first real vegetation profile in the botanical literature. E. P. Odum (1964) identified multiple roots of ecology, which, he said, remained largely divergent with little theory to connect them. Andrewartha and Birch (1973) wrote, "The laws governing communities and ecosystems were thoroughly discussed . . . and much was agreed on in the writings of Reamur, Buffon and Haeckel." This would have been a notable achievement indeed, since laws, if any, governing communities are not established even today.

Many early ecologists joined Haeckel in attributing ecology to evolution by natural selection and Charles Darwin. Spalding (1903) described Darwin as "the great exponent of ecology before it had a name." Cowles (1904) also voiced this belief: "If ecology has a place in modern biology, certainly one of its great tasks is to unravel the mysteries of adaptation." Concern with evolution and adaptation was a logical extension of the Darwinian emphasis on the environment, and many ecologists stressed the effect of the environment on the development, distribution, and morphology of organisms (McIntosh 1976, 1980a).

The essential relationship of evolution and ecology is evident in current ecology. Kiester (1982) suggested that a science of evolutionary ecology provides ecology "with needed theoretical help and would advance the unity of science." Orians (1980) similarly described ecosystem ecology as aided by "basic evolutionary principles," a proposition which was the basis of S. A. Forbes's (1880a) "a priori" approach to ecological systems. Bormann and Likens (1979a) commented on a reciprocal relation in which "theories of ecosystem development are beginning to play a major role in studies of evolution." A major aspect of current ecology hopes to develop ecological theory from the life history properties of species. The species is a critical entity of evolutionary concern, and speciation is central to most evolutionary theory. Some ecologists, however, suggest that the species is not necessarily the ecological functional unit, as is often assumed (Harper 1980). Other ecologists have sought properties of organisms other than specific distinctions, even using aggregate or "macro" variables of ecological entities on which to base ecological theory.

Ecology did not, however, converge with its very nearly twin science of genetics, and many years were to pass before a hybrid science of ecological genetics came into being. John Harper (1967) complained that ecology had abandoned evolution to genetics and that theoretical genetics developed with little concern for ecology. L. B. Slobodkin's (1961) hope that the resolution of many problems would be based on "amplifications of the existing theories of population dynamics, population genetics and interspecific competition" has yet to be realized. Although E. O. Wilson (1978) claimed that ecology had been transformed by natural selection "by stark reduction," the merger of ecology, with its concern with the environment, and genetics, with its concern with variation, into a unified science remains a prospect for the future.

## Sources of ecology seen by historians

Historians who considered ecology at all were similarly divided in their views of its origins and orginators. One of the first historians to comment was R. C. Stauffer (1957), who wrote, "As a source for a vital stimulus to the continuing development of ecology we must look rather to the work of Charles Darwin." Vorzimmer (1965), however, stated, "It is even slightly ironical that most modern ecologists look back to Darwin as the Father of Ecology," because, he said, Darwin had ignored the significance of his contributions to ecology. Limoges (1971) argued that an ecological viewpoint was impossible before the Darwinian concept of nature and that ecology arose when Haeckel, stimulated by Darwin, coined the word in 1866. This attitude was recently stated

emphatically by Oldroyd (1980): "Ecology in the modern sense became possible only after the establishment of the Darwinian theory."
Lynn White (1967) wrote, "The crystallization of the novel concept of
ecology" (ca. 1850) was forced by "the emergence in widespread practice of the Baconian creed that scientific knowledge means technological power over nature" and that it was a "union of the theoretical and
the empirical approaches to our natural environment." White, like
many nonscientists discussing ecology, confounded it with general environmental impacts in his comment that the first cannon manufac-
tured in the early 14th century "affected ecology" by precipitating
cutting of forests. This linkage of ecology and technology is developed
in detail by Tobey (1976, 1981) in his studies of the emergence of plant
ecology.

Interest in the environment and the relation of humans to it permeates mythology, history, literature, and art. A continuing problem is
discerning the relation of ecology to this ubiquitous interest. Glacken
saw the end of the 18th century bringing in an entirely different concept of humans' relationship to nature influenced by incipient evolutionary thought. He wrote:

> It is no accident that ecological theory which is the basis of so
> much research in the study of plant and animal populations,
> conservation, preservation of nature, wildlife and land use
> management, and which has become the basic concept for a
> holistic view of nature has behind it the long preoccupation in
> Western civilization with interpreting the nature of earthly en-
> vironments, trying to see them as wholes, as manifestations of
> order. (Glacken 1967:706)

Glacken identified three major questions of Western thought: (1) Is
the earth purposefully made or designed? (2) Has the environment
influenced humankind? (3) Has humankind changed the earth from its
pristine condition? The search for answers to these questions was
based on the yearning for order and purpose in nature which pervades
much of Western religion and philosophy. Throughout the 18th century, order and purpose were linked in diverse religious and philosophical traditions having in common a belief that there is a Divine
Creator and/or Manager who designed and operated the cosmic order
after some eternal ideal. Evidence for design and purpose was commonly seen in natural history in the order observable in celestial events
and natural phenomena, including relationships among organisms, humans among them, and between organisms and their environment

(Lovejoy 1936; McIntosh 1960). Caveats such as that of Theophrastus, who suggested there is disorder in the universe and that order must be proven, not assumed, or of Epicurean philosophers who wondered about inhospitable places such as desert or Arctic wastes, were not usually heeded in the widespread acceptance of a providential view of nature or in physico-theology, which saw evidence of design in nature (Glacken 1967). Glacken's (1967) book, *Traces on the Rhodian Shore*, is a mine of observations which are clearly antecedent to ecology and which strike a chord with any ecologist. These are attributed to persons from diverse times and cultures: Herodotus on predators, St. Basil on forest succession, Jose de Acosta on the biogeographical conundrums posed by the New World, and Benjamin Franklin on control of insect pests by birds. The balance of nature, described by Egerton (1976) as "the oldest ecological theory," was evident in the writing of St. Thomas Aquinas, who in an early comment on species diversity and stability wrote, "It is better to have a multiplicity of species than a multiplicity of individuals of one species." Such observations are not roots of ecology in the biological sense of that metaphor, for it is not clear that ecology grew from them in any direct way.

Glacken identified two pervasive views of nature which were evident in traditional natural history and persist in current discussions of ecological theory (McIntosh 1976, 1980a):

1. *Mechanical:* Actions of individual parts of a whole are explained by known laws, and the whole is the sum of the parts and their interaction.
2. *Organic:* The whole exists first and its design explains the action of the parts.

Glacken also reviewed post-Renaissance conceptions of nature and saw design concepts of nature as spawning ecological theory. He wrote:

> I am convinced that modern ecological theory, so important in our attitudes toward nature and man's interference with it, owes its origin to the design argument. The wisdom of the creator is self-evident, everything in the creation is interrelated, no living thing is useless, and all are related one to the other. (Glacken 1967:243)

It is this notion of interrelatedness that Stauffer (1960) described as "Darwin's fundamental ecological insight" which permeates ecology. What differs is the explanation for interrelatedness.

Naturalists, theologians, and philosophers before and well into the

19th century commonly concurred that there is order in nature based on a divinely created harmony. The differences were largely between those who were concerned with final causes and those who would allow the possibility of secondary causes of order in nature. Buffon, for example, rejected concern with final causes in the study of nature. Natural history, he said, was concerned with secondary causes – *how* nature acts, not *why* (Lyon and Sloan 1981). Burdon-Sanderson (1893) stated that the function of the physiologist was to investigate processes, not to inquire into final causes: "His question is ever How rather than Why." Current ecologists generally avoid anything described as final cause but not "how" and "why." Calow and Townsend (1981), for example, stated that the "physiological question is *how* organisms work and the ecological and evolutionary question is *why* they work in the way they do." W. D. Billings (1980), however, saw physiology considering *why* organisms grow where they do. Application of ideas of cause in ecology has proven extremely difficult, and the classic interpretations of cause-and-effect relationships are commonly questioned (Whittaker 1953). Some present-day ecologists speak, paradoxically, of "future" causes (Allen and Starr 1982).

Glacken's book is an admirable history of the views expressed in Western culture about the environment and "man's" relationship to it. But are these to be considered ecology, and can these philosophical and natural history observations be seen as giving rise in some continuous way to ecology qualified as "modern" or "self-conscious?" Clearly these traditions were antecedent to 20th-century ecology. In what way can it be said that ecology is rooted in them? If, as Glacken suggested, pre-19th century conceptions of humankind's relation to nature were of an entirely different order than those influenced by theories of evolution, what was the nature of the transformation in 19th-century science which gave rise to ecology as a distinctive aspect of biological science (Coleman 1977)? Identifying the origins of ecology is difficult in that all definitions specify that it has to do with the relation of organisms and their environment. Humans are clearly organisms. Glacken commented that the design argument explaining the nature of environments incorporated a number of ideas and added:

> In exploring the history of these ideas from the fifth century B.C. to the end of the eighteenth century, it is a striking fact that virtually every great thinker who lived within this 2300-year period had something to say about one of these ideas, and many had something to say about all of them. (Glacken 1967:713)

It is not surprising, then, that one frequently encounters assertions that ecology, or some aspect of it, began with diverse protoecologists from classical antiquity up to the Enlightenment (Liebetrau 1973; Egerton 1976; Worster 1977). The term *protoecologist* was coined in Voorhees (1983) to describe those who had ecological insights before a formal science of ecology was formulated.

The word *ecology* and the genesis of ecology as a recognized science are clearly products of the last third of the 19th century. Several ecologists and historians converged on ecology as a logical, even necessary, consequence of Darwinian evolutionary thought and on Darwin as the premier ecologist. But Donald Worster (1977), an intellectual historian seeking the "roots of ecology" in "nature's economy," described the idea of ecology as much older than the name, and he began "its modern history" in the 18th century, before it had a name. What he saw beginning was not, however, the field of science which is professional ecology but what he described as the "larger penumbra of ecological thought," which is very difficult to define, as shadows often are. The breadth of Worster's scope of ecology is indicated by his suggestion that John Wesley wrote a volume on ecology. This elastic view of ecology is also evident in Worster's assertion that "the Age of Ecology began on the desert outside of Alamogordo, New Mexico on July 16, 1945." Such an extended vision of who is an ecologist, whence ecology came, and when it began derives from Worster's definition of ecology and conception of historical scholarship.

Worster entitled the first section of his book "Ecology in the Eighteenth Century" and wrote, "Like a stranger who has just blown into town, ecology seems a presence without a past." Worster provided that past in the form of dual origins of ecology in the eighteenth century. One source he categorized as "arcadian": the holistic organismic views represented by Gilbert White's prescient observations in his parish at Selborne, which others, including myself (McIntosh 1958a), have seen as "anticipation of ecology." Worster described this tradition as continued in the 19th century by Henry David Thoreau and John Burroughs and linked in the 20th century to the philosophical views of Alfred North Whitehead and Ludwig von Bertalanffy, the last sometimes acclaimed as the intellectual source of current work in systems ecology. Worster's alternate source was "imperial," "anti-arcadian," mechanistic ecology, which he attributed to Francis Bacon but saw primarily exemplified by the "businesslike, ambitious and enterprising Swede" Linnaeus.

Worster's typology of ecology and ecologists is criticized adversely by some historians of science (Egerton 1979b; Tobey 1981), although reviews by ecologists are more favorable (Kormondy 1978; Smith 1978). Egerton regarded Worster's types as existing only in his mind and Worster's point of view as making a good story but not conveying objective history of ecology. R. Tobey (1981:1) wrote:

> Popular writers today assume that ecology sprang from the transcendental naturalism of Emerson and Thoreau or from the preservation movement represented by John Muir and John Burroughs. Historians know this is not true.

Since Thoreau and Burroughs are among those cited by Worster as typifying his "arcadian" ecology, Worster is a popular writer but not a historian by Tobey's classification, which Worster, no doubt, would dispute. Worster assigned apparently equal significance to his "arcadian" and "imperial" sources of ecology, but gives the nod to the "arcadian" root as dominant in current ecological thought. Tobey, conversely, described "key insights making possible the scientific paradigm of the first generation of ecological research" as deriving from "utilitarian and scientific problems," clearly meaning the "imperial," hard-nosed, scientific source described by Worster.

A more detailed analysis of Worster's case for the 18th-century roots of ecology is made by Nicolson (1982a pers. commun.) and serves as a review of the meanings given *ecology*. Nicolson's critique is directed at Worster's tripartite use of the meaning of ecology and his sliding from one meaning to the other. According to Nicolson, ecology can refer to (1) the professional science of ecology in a variety of guises – marine, terrestrial, etc.; (2) the political movement or philosophy broadly incorporating a variety of environmental concerns; or (3) the relation of any organism to the environment (i.e., "its ecology"). Nicolson asserted that Worster's analysis of the roots of ecology fails because of this semantic slipperiness. The other failing which Nicolson attributed to Worster, and to Egerton (1976), is that they ignored two opposing trends in historical scholarship. Although Worster asserted that "ideas grow out of specific cultural conditions," Nicolson claimed that he traced ideas independently of their context, as if ideas transcend the circumstances of their generation. This, Nicolson said, ignores a trend in history of science stemming from T. S. Kuhn's (1970) *The Structure of Scientific Revolutions,* which emphasizes "contextural historiography" or knowledge understood within its cultural context. Linking Linnaean ideas of economy of nature, founded on a static, nonhistorical, divinely ordered system of nature, and "modern" post-Darwinian, ecological thought is unjustified in the view of Nicolson and of such other historians as Oldroyd (1980). Nicolson and Oldroyd argue that the Darwinian "revolution" places the complex of pre-Darwinian natural history observations in a completely different context than post-Darwinian ecology. S. A. Forbes (1880a, 1887), a major proponent of scientific ecology in its formative years, emphatically expressed a post-Darwinian, balance-of-nature concept, but it is not to be placed according to the views of Nicolson and Oldroyd, in the same class as Linnaeus's economy of nature even though some of the terminology is similar. Stauffer (1960), however, saw in Linnaeus's economy of nature "a crude but meaningful presentation of ecology in its eighteenth century guise." This primitive theme, he said, reappears in Lyell and was "transmuted by Darwin into vital elements of his theory of evolution." Nicolson's advice is, nevertheless: "Do not believe there was a science of ecology in the eighteenth century, even if a historian of ecology tells you so" – counsel which makes things difficult for ecologists.

It is perhaps unfair to marshal the several criticisms of Worster's account. It is, after all, a first effort to examine the intellectual tradition of which ecology may or may not be a lineal descendant. The point is not simply to criticize a notable effort which Egerton (1979b), in spite of his own assertion that Worster's thesis "seems simplistic and wrong headed," described as "clearly an important contribution to the history of ecology." Ecologists such as F. E. Smith (1978) derived "new perceptions about ecology and ecologists" from Worster's book, and Kormondy (1978) described it as a "very worthwhile guide" to ecologists. Ecologists sorely need a guide to understanding the background of their science, but it is unfortunate if the science of ecology is conflated with diverse historical concerns with the relation between humanity and the environment and if things that have simply "gone before" are linked as if they are in a direct line of development to ecology. Worster's "arcadian" and "imperial" categories, as different ways of looking at nature in the 18th century, are acceptable on their own grounds; his argument that the "arcadian," holistic natural history of Gilbert White is continuous with, and represented by, ecology in the present needs to be proven. Current ecology, even in its limited scientific context, is a battleground between those urging a "hard science," reductionist, "imperial" approach and those arguing a holistic, organismic, if not truly "arcadian," approach. The real modern counterpart of Worster's "arcadian" ecology lies outside scientific ecology, in that "larger penumbra of ecological thought" which came to the fore with the surge of the environmental movement in the 1960s and subjected ecology to the distorting influence of high popularity of which Allee et al. (1949) warned.

The most diligent and productive historian of ecology is Frank Egerton. In addition to numerous publications on pre-Haeckelian ventures into ecological subjects, Egerton has edited or written several salient guides to the history of ecology which are essential to anyone entering that field. Egerton (1976) wrote the most detailed outline available on protoecological studies and observations before 1900, when ecology flowered as a science. He edited (Egerton 1977a) a collection of reprinted volumes and articles ranging from the 18th-century works of William Derham (*Physico-Theology*, 1716), John Ray (*The Wisdom of God Manifested in the Works of the Creation*, 1717), Linnaeus, including his essay *Economy of Nature*, (1762), and abridged selections from Buffon's *Natural History* (1780–85), to works of 20th-century ecology such as Victor Shelford's (1913) *Animal Communities in Temperate America*, Robert Whittaker's (1962) *Classification of Natural Communities*, and his own *History of American Ecology* (Egerton 1977a), a collection of articles about the history of ecology. He also wrote *A Bibliographical Guide to the History of General Ecology and Population Ecology* (1977b), and his *History of Ecology* (1983) expands the bibliographical coverage to include plant, marine, and animal ecology, limnology, and applied ecology. The more recent bibliography is restricted to the 19th and 20th centuries, whereas the earlier one begins with ancient times.

Egerton, like Worster, takes a comprehensive view of ecology, reaching back to antiquity in his reviews, bibliographies, and articles on demography and other ecological topics. He cited as ecologists included in the *Dictionary of Scientific Biography* Leeuwenhoek, Ray, Reamur, Linnaeus, Peter Kalm, and Gilbert White. Egerton (1976) construed ecology, before its formal period, as "similar to but not identical with the history of natural history." He interpreted the Hippocratic treatise *Airs, Waters, and Places* as "opening with an explicitly ecological program of correlations between environmental conditions and sickness." Egerton described naturalists in the 18th and 19th centuries as beginning "to grope toward the organization of an ecological science." He said phenology was an early, failed candidate for the framework of an ecological theory but that "in 1749, Linnaeus had outlined an ecological science based on the economy of nature." The identification of pre-Darwinian observations of nature as ecology is disputed by such historians of ecology as Limoges (1971), Oldroyd (1980), and Nicolson (1982a pers. commun.), as we have seen. This makes it difficult for an ecologist, who is hardly in a position to ajudicate the scholarly dispute among historians. Clearly, there are substantial discontinuities and Kuhn-type paradigm changes in 19th-century biology, but just as clearly, many natural history traditions were transmitted from Linnaeus, Buffon, and Humboldt, reassembled by Darwin in his evolutionary thought, and later integrated into scientific ecology by recognized professional ecologists. Tracing the detailed links between 18th-century natural history and 19th-century biology, as well as those among 19th-century biologists, is manifestly beyond the scope of this volume.

## Who founded ecology?

One by-product of the search for the origins or roots of ecology is the frequent designation of various individuals as the founder, father, or mother of ecology or some aspect of it. Sometimes this has had a nationalistic basis, particularly as ecology came to be a highly visible aspect of science, even suggesting a new ethical approach to the relations of humans with their environment (McIntosh 1976). As Worster (1977) put it, "In our time ecology has come to represent the arcadian mood that would return man to a garden of natural peace and piety." Many would claim parentage of such an ideal.

Credit for the origin of the word *ecology* was, erroneously as it turned out, transferred from the scientist Haeckel to the "arcadian" naturalist, poet, and philosopher Henry David Thoreau. The hold that such attributions have is seen in the resurrection of this reputed coinage in *Science* magazine after it had previously been reported to be an erroneous attribution in that journal (McIntosh 1975b). Even the *Oxford English Dictionary* contains the attribution to Thoreau. Thoreau was also credited with being the father of phenology, the aspect of ecology dealing with the chronology of biological events (Whitford and Whitford 1951), although Egerton (1976) disputed this parentage. E. S. Deevey (1942) described Thoreau as being an insightful and eloquent limnologist before the term was provided by Forel. V. Gendron (1961) claimed that Humboldt "single handed created the science of ecology." He attributed Humboldt's priority to his idea of vertical zonation of vegetation based on his ascent of the peak of Tenerife "because these observations were the ones on which he founded the science of ecology." Daniel Drake, described as "a pioneer in modern ecology" by A. E. Waller (1947), was interested in phenology, but Waller's claim is bolstered largely by Drake's consideration of disease and environment in the 1830s. Titus Smith was described by Gorham (1955) as a "pioneer" of plant ecology based on his travels in Nova Scotia in 1801-2 and his recognition of different and changing forest types. J. C. Arthur (1895) wrote, "We may call Darwin the father of vegetable ecology." H. S. Conard (1950), in the foreword to his translation of Kerner von Marilaun's book *Plant Life of the Danube Basin,* said it was "the immediate and direct parent of all later works on plant ecology." Taylor (1980) identified Victor Hensen, a German physiologist and marine biologist, as the "father of quantitative plankton ecology." George Perkins Marsh was said to be the father of American ecology for recognizing the impact of human actions on the earth in his book *Man and Nature in America* (Marx 1970). An even broader claim was made by Robert Clarke (1973), who subtitled his book on Ellen Swallow *"The Woman Who Founded Ecology."*

Ellen Swallow (Mrs. Richards) recognized many problems of the environment in an era when industrialization and modern technology were just developing some of the basis of air and water pollution and rural and urban decay which are the bane of modern environmentalists. She was a crusader for establishing a scientific basis for bettering human life. According to Swallow:

> For this knowledge of right living we have sought a new name. . . . as theology is the science of religious life, and biology the science of life, . . . so let Œkology be hence the worthiest of all the applied sciences which teaches the principles on which to found healthy . . . and happy life. (Quoted in Clarke 1973:120)

The *Boston Globe* announced in November 1892, "Mrs. Richards names it Œkology," perhaps the first appearance in the public press of Haeckel's word (Clarke 1973). Despite this promising beginning, human ecology – or sociology, as it was alternately called – was not firmly incorporated in the young science.

Maycock (1967) described the Polish botanist Jozef Paczoski as the "founder of phytosociology," a distinctive branch of ecology. Morton (1981), following the lead of many plant ecologists, including H. C. Cowles and Arthur Tansley, wrote, "Plant ecology is usually considered to begin with the publication of E. Warming's *Plantesamfund* in 1895." Warming's claim to paternity was reopened recently by Goodland (1975), who claimed that "his contribution remains unacknowledged." Actually, Warming's seminal contributions to plant ecology and the priority of his work *Plantesamfund* are probably the most widely asserted recognition of parentage for plant ecology by his contemporaries and subsequent commentators (cf. Waller 1947), and Warming needs no latter-day justification.

According to the ecologists Kormondy and McCormick (1981), "historians of science" mark the rise of "modern ecology" with the introduction of the ecosystem concept. They do not specify which historians do so. The difficulties of identifying ecology or its founders are compounded by the use of the modifier *modern* by ecologists and historians alike. Allee et al. (1949) in their encyclopedic work on animal ecology wrote that "modern aspects of ecology did not begin to take form until early in the 18th century," citing the work of Linnaeus and Buffon. The historian of science Oldroyd (1980), however, argued that ecology in the "modern" sense existed only after Darwinian theory, which eliminates Linnaeus and Buffon, at least, as "modern" ecologists. Taylor (1912) cited Warming as the father of "modern" plant ecology, whereas Boerker (1916) and Godwin (1977) preferred C. Schröter. Waller (1947) saw "modern" ecology arising in the medical sciences early in the 19th century, thus warranting his citation of the Cincinnati physician Daniel Drake as a pioneer of ecology. Egerton (1976) commented that phenology is not an important part of "modern" ecology, which he contrasted with that of the 18th and 19th centuries, implying that "modern" means 20th-century ecology. Ecologists recently are prone to restrict the realm of "modern" ecology to post-World War II developments in quantitative or theoretical ecology or, even further, to systems ecology.

## Self-conscious ecology

Clearly, historians of science and ecologists who have commented on the history of ecology do not offer unequivocal guides to the origins of ecology, nor do they provide explicit criteria for determining when ecology came to be "modern" or "mature," who may be said to be founders of ecology, or what its lineage may be. One problem is that the roots of ecology are commonly sought using some perception of what it has become, and current perceptions of ecology differ greatly. One of the favorite lecture topics of ecologists through the years has been the nature of ecology, or "What is ecology?" (Moore 1920; Taylor 1936; Dice 1955). If that question had ever been successfully answered, either by reference to the various definitions of ecology or by close analysis of what ecologists do, better consensus might have been achieved concerning the roots of ecology. The lack of consensus is due to the fact that seeking roots implies some idea of what it is you are seeking roots for. It is necessary to distinguish between retrospective ecology and what Allee et al. (1949) called "self-conscious" ecology. Retrospective ecology focuses on what I call the antecedents of ecology – that is, on seeing that someone was doing something similar to what later came to be recognized as an aspect of ecological science. It is looking backward rather than following the development of something, and unless it turns up hidden linkages it does not expose roots. Egerton (1976) commented, "The transmission of a man's work establishes his place in the history of science, but it should not be assumed that publication is automatic assurance of this transmission." What is lacking in many retrospective views of ecology before the 19th century is evidence that the work was connected with, or led to, that of later workers. That brilliant ideas have been amply studied, elegantly expressed, and even published without having influenced the work of contemporary scientists is familiar in the history of Gregor Mendel's lonely efforts.

F. E. Clements (1905, 1916) prefaced some of his early volumes on various aspects of ecology with historical summaries, but he gave little indication that these are anything but retrospective searches through the natural history literature for sharp insights which could be seen in hindsight as ecological. Ecologists looking retrospectively into the background of their science are generally innocent of the historiographic concerns which are of primary interest to historians of science. The crux of the present volume is the rise of self-conscious ecology and the establishment of ecology as a science, particularly its identification of distinctive concepts and questions and the various efforts to establish a theoretical framework. It is clear that ecology did not emerge fully formed from the head of Haeckel any more than biology emerged from Burdach, Treviranus, and Lamarck or genetics from Mendel. Haeckel's coinage of *ecology* in 1866 did not provoke a rash of ecological studies or prompt the identification of biologists as ecologists; in fact, hardly anyone noticed the new term for over two decades. Some have even accused Haeckel of neglecting his neologism and not pursuing ecology effectively himself (Egerton 1977b). Haeckel's biographer (Bolsche 1909) does not index *ecology*.

Ecology and genetics both surfaced as distinctive sciences around the turn of the century. Ecology, as early ecologists and later historians recognized, was stimulated by, and in some respects anticipated by, Darwin and his concept of evolution by natural selection (Stauffer 1957, 1960; Ghiselin 1969). Haeckel (1866) specifically attributed ecology to Darwinian evolution as early as 1866, but neither he nor anyone else developed the idea until the 1890s, when numerous biologists seized on the relationship and began to treat ecology as a formal discipline. Haeckel provided a name but little substance for the new science. Mendel, almost simultaneously (1865), supplied the substance of genetics without a name. His insights similarly lay fallow until their multiple rediscovery in 1900. Haeckel rose to worldwide notoriety and Mendel retired to scientific obscurity, yet both are acclaimed as the founders of major developments of 20th-century biology which, many assert, should combine to resolve the "great mystery" recognized by Darwin.

During the last decades of the 19th century, four quite independent aspects of biological science were developing – oceanography: its biological component, limnology, the freshwater analog of oceanography; plant ecology; and animal ecology (Egerton 1976). Oceanography (Deacon 1971; 1978; Schlee 1973; Sears and Merriam 1980) and, more recently, aspects of ecology (Cox 1979; Cittadino 1980, Tobey 1981; Kingsland 1981) have been the subjects of detailed historical studies. Their affinity as ecological sciences was not always recognized by their early practitioners. They developed with considerable redundancy and even today retain discrete institutional organization and publication outlets in spite of basically common ecological concerns.

The history of the emergence of ecology is relatively poorly known, in part, because historians of science have substantially ignored it in favor of following the dramatic development of physiology and genetics. Coleman (1977) asserted that late 19th-century biologists switched from historical explanation to experimental investigation. Mayr (1982) is critical of historians who do not understand there are two biologies – that of function (physiology) and that of evolutionary and historical causation (ecology, genetics, and evolution). Coleman was perfectly clear that there are two biologies, but denied that the transition from natural history to the history of nature, as suggested by Lyon and Sloan (1981), was a successful revolution in science. Specifically, he attacked the possibility that the history of nature constitutes an explanation or genuine understanding, an opinion shared by some current ecologists. Coleman saw the historical ideal as occupying a lesser position, displaced by experimental physiology, which "offered little encouragement to the historian of life." Cravens (1978) similarly saw practitioners of experimental biology supplanting those he called "natural historians" and overshadowing them in terms of university and research institute appointments, journal space, prestige, "limelight," and glory. Some historians may understand that there are "two biologies" but commonly see experimental and functional biology as leading the pack, and their statements sometimes suggest that experimental-functional biology and biology are one. Coleman described "biologists" as "transferring their allegiance" to experimental biology. Allen (1979) described naturalists and experimentalists as being at war in the 19th century, the fray continuing into the 20th century as the ecologists entered the lists, not clearly knowing which side to join.

Ecology at the turn of the century was pursuing in some ways what Cannon (1978:105) characterized as "Humboldtian science," which was

> the great new thing in professional science in the first half of the 19th century, . . . the accurate measured study of wide-spread but interconnected real phenomena in order to find a definite law and a dynamical cause.

Cannon (1978:105) described the limited view held by some of 19th-century biology:

> It was only toward the end of the 19th century, after physics and laboratory physiology had risen to their position of dogmatic self-assurance, that this kind of activity was in its turn seen as old-fashioned, that Gauss's theory of terrestrial magnetism was judged not to be a theory at all, and Darwin not a professional biologist.

Cannon's "Humboldtian Science," in its biological aspects, exemplified the qualities Lyon and Sloan (1981) ascribed to the transformed natural history of the 18th century. Cannon identified the quality of "Humboldtian Science" which made it kin to ecology and distinct from experimental physiology as the presumed zenith of 19th-century biology – the concern of ecology for the complexity of "interconnected real phenomena." She wrote:

> Compared to this, the study of nature in the laboratory or the perfection of differential equations was old-fashioned, was simple science concerned with easy variables. (Cannon 1978:105)

What she might have added is that concern with single variables one at a time rather than with multiple variables in the full context of their interactions in nature was not satisfying to many 19th-century biologists, although some pursued "single-factor" ecology (Egler 1951). This distinction may be seen as the hub of current discussions of a theoretical ecology split between those urging a holistic approach to the complexity of nature via simplifying "macrovariables" and a reductionist approach in the mold of the ideal of late 19th-century physiology. Peculiarly, ecology was initially described as a branch of, or even equivalent to, physiology by turn-of-the-century ecologists, and the ideal of function and experiment of 19th-century physiology was urged on ecology (Cittadino 1980; McIntosh 1983a). The utility and merits of experimental approaches were heralded by some early ecologists and many of their successors (Ganong 1904; Clements 1905; Tansley 1914a; Antonovics 1976). Manipulation of organisms in controlled situations or seizing on "natural experiments" is still urged as an essential, if not the only, way to achieve understanding of ecology. Other ecologists doubted the possibility of gaining understanding of organisms in nature from controlled experiments, and some questioned the meaning of "natural experiments" (Cowles 1904; Redfield 1958).

One of the difficulties in assessing ecology is that it is commonly described as a synthetic science, which, depending on one's definition of *synthetic,* can mean it integrates diverse materials to gain a new level of insight or it is artificial and not a science at all. Both definitions have been used. After decades of quietly trying to develop an academic and scientific identity, ecology was propelled into the limelight when the environmental crisis was widely perceived in the 1960s. What does a hitherto unheralded science do when the following is said?

> Ecology provides a model to philosophy and to the other human sciences of a new way of viewing the interrelationships between the phenomena of Nature. Central to its perspective is the idea of ecosystem analysis and the concepts of the balance of nature. . . . The answer to the value question then from an ecological point of view is this: human values are founded in objectively determinable ecological relations within Nature. (Colwell 1970)

This volume examines the background of some of the basic concepts and the attempts at theory of ecology which purport to define it as a science. It is evident from the forays of historians of science into ecology that some of the general concepts of ecology are not unique to it but come from the long traditions of intellectual concern with nature expressed by Aristotle, Kant, Spencer, Whitehead, and a host of others interested in natural history in its broadest sense. Ecology shares such intellectual ancestors with other sciences, and it is necessary to separate it from its distinguished ancestry and distinguished relatives if it is to have an identity.

Self-conscious ecology grew from a complex interaction of 19th-century natural history and 19th-century physiology. The natural history was not, however, the much maligned and misrepresented "stamp collecting," as it is sometimes described. Simple-minded collectors of plants, animals, and observations no doubt persisted, but natural history was not confined to such. Ecology grew from natural history transformed by Buffon and Humboldt, which held that "observations are not really interesting, except when we can dispose their results in such a manner as to lead to general ideas" (Cannon 1978:95). Such natural history in the form of "Humboldtian Science" involved accurate measurement of what could be measured, questioning of past theory, development or adoption of new tools to study natural phenomena, and applications, not in the laboratory but to a variety of phenomena in the field, all of which required a new approach. This change was exemplified in the report of the Second Decennial of the Botanical Seminar which was organized by C. E. Bessey at the University of Nebraska in 1886. The report commented that the report of the first decade (1886–96) focused on laboratory methods, whereas that of the second decade (1896–1906) was largely on field methods ("The Second Decennial . . ." 1906). Some 19th-century physiologists returned to the field to accomplish the type of study required to meet the needs of ecology (Cowles 1909). Ecology took up problems not considered by physiology at all. It sought reasons for the distributions of organisms in nature, it extended Malthus's ideas on human populations to populations at large, and it continued the development of community concepts begun by 19th-century biogeographers. A major difficulty of ecology has been developing a body of theory to accommodate the vagaries of the phenomena it purports to explain (McIntosh 1980a). Ecology was split, historically, and remains torn between different conceptions of science in general and biology in particular (Saarinen 1982; Rehbock 1983). The conventional criteria of science, devised largely by philosophers and physicists, have been difficult to apply to ecological phenomena.

Examination of the diverse views of the roots or origins of ecology reveals great differences of opinion. What is clear is that in the last decade of the 19th century several facets of natural history and physiology combined and emerged quite suddenly as a recognizable discipline of ecology.

# 2

## The crystallization of ecology

The rapid, even "revolutionary," emergence of self-conscious ecology from the amorphous body of classical natural history and the overshadowing presence of experimental laboratory-based physiology, which was the dominant aspect of late 19th century biology, is a remarkable, and poorly studied, phase in the history of biology (Frey 1963a; Coleman 1977; Egerton 1976; Lowe 1976; McIntosh 1976, 1983a; Cox 1979; Cittadino 1980, 1981; Tobey 1981). Oscar Drude, an eminent German plant geographer and a major influence on the development of plant ecology in America, aptly described the sudden recognition of ecology at the Congress of Arts and Sciences meeting at the Universal Exposition in St. Louis in 1904:

> If at a Congress fifteen years ago, ecology had been spoken of as a branch of natural science, the equal in importance of plant morphology and physiology, no one would have understood the term. (Drude 1906)

In spite of the fact that *ecology* was coined in 1866 and had been, unnoticed, in the literature since then, it was, as Drude stated, essentially unknown in 1890.

Whatever may be said of the origins of ecology in the Greek science of Hippocrates, Aristotle, and Theophrastus, or in 18th-century natural history as exemplified by Linnaeus and Buffon, or even in Darwinian evolutionary biology, its rise as a named and "self-conscious" discipline with its own practitioners was essentially in the last decade of the 19th century (Allee et al. 1949). Ecologists began to define ecology by doing it and recognizing that they were doing it. "Crystallization" seems an appropriate metaphor for the abrupt appearance of ecology as a recognized scientific discipline. Trass (1976) described the development of plant ecology ("geobotany") in the United States as "invasive" and wrote that ecology, "appearing in American botany, instantaneously gained recognition and expanded with unusual rapidity." It is not clear what caused many biologists, particularly botanists, in the last decade of the 19th century to feel the need for a word to describe an activity just then becoming a significant part of biology – a need which had been felt by the zoologists I. G. St. Hilaire and Ernst Haeckel over two decades earlier. It seems clear that Haeckel's term *ecology* caught the fancy of botanists first. W. M. Wheeler (1902), a major American entomologist, deplored the botanists' usurpation of Haeckel's word and expressed his preference for St. Hilaire's *ethology* (Wheeler 1902, 1926; Adams 1913). Others, such as Spalding (1903), preferred Patrick Geddes's *bionomics,* but *ecology* was spontaneously adopted in the botanical literature.

The first appearance of *ecology* in a book title was in 1885 in a work by Hans Reiter, *Die Consolidation der Physiognomik als Versuch einer Œkologie der Gewaechse* (Egerton 1977b). As early as 1887 Georg Volkens, a German physiological anatomist, claimed that his work on Egyptian-Arabian flora "called forth an entire literature and thereby helped found and develop a special discipline of botany, the ecology of plants" (Cittadino 1981). However, credit for stimulating the rapid development of plant ecology was given to others. L. H. Pammel (1893) published *Flower Ecology,* apparently the first book in English with *ecology* in its title. In the same year, Stanley Coulter (1893) noted, without explanation, the desirability of "œcological notes" to accompany taxonomic collections. The year 1893 was a banner year for ecology, for the president of the British Association for the Advancement of Science, J. S. Burdon-Sanderson (1893), described "œcology" as a branch of biology coequal with morphology and physiology and "by far the most attractive." Also, in 1893, the Madison Botanical Congress, (Madison Botanical Congress 1894) acted on the recommendation of a Committee on Terminology of Physiology and adopted *ecology,* omitting the diphthong *œ,* a decision which Wheeler (1902) thought unwise simply to save a letter (or *only* half a letter). Arthur (1895) hailed the rise of the "new" botany, meaning experimental and physiological botany, and traced the development of ecology as a "department" of physiology. Arthur mentioned (but did not cite) books by the German plant physiologists J. Weisner and F. Ludwig as the first independent treatises on ecology and said a similar work in English was to be desired. Later ecologists, however, chose other works as the early influential works on plant ecology, and Weisner and Ludwig have not subsequently been credited as being among the founders of ecology. A significant distinction that an article by MacMillan (1897) was "purely ecological not phytogeographical" was made in a review by the young Nebraska ecologists Roscoe Pound and F. E.

Clements (1897). In the same year a chair of ecological botany was established at Uppsala University, starting a distinguished tradition. That Robert Smith (1899), a seminal figure in the initiation of British plant ecology, used *œcology* "at least four times" in an article on plant associations was a response to an inquiry about this strange word (Ganong 1902). Ecology had been originally described as a part of physiology by Haeckel and by some early ecologists (Cittadino 1980; McIntosh 1983a) but apparently it filled a special need not met by physiology as it evolved in the 19th century. In any event, the word and the subject quickly became current in the 1890s.

Egerton (1976) noted that one of the important questions which historians of ecology should consider is why the formal organization of science did not begin until the 1890s. No comprehensive answer to this question has been suggested, but it is clear that ecology flourished in that decade. C. E. Bessey (1902) commented that ecology had been in general use for eight years and lamented, in a letter to Conway Mac-Millan, that it was becoming a fad (Tobey 1981). Ganong (1902) said that every schoolboy, if taught by a modern teacher, knows something of ecology. The Carnegie Institution of Washington in 1902 was considering funding work in plant ecology (McIntosh 1983a). Spalding (1903) described ecology as "having the double burden of a popular fad and oftentimes the cold shoulder of those who sit in judgement." Arthur Tansley (1904a) reported the same attitudes in Britain, where ecology was "almost a fashionable study" but where some botanists "tacitly distrust" it and have a "hostile" attitude. Nevertheless, by 1904, ecology was dignified as Section E of the Congress of Arts and Sciences.

One of the consistent difficulties of ecology is that, like beauty, it is in the eye of the beholder. Most of these early references to ecology, although unqualified, refer to ecology of plants. Plant and animal ecologists tended to use the term generically, without the appropriate modifier; and the common result, then as now, was sweeping generalities about ecology based on either plants or animals but not always clearly relevant to both. Turn-of-the-century ecology was not an internally consistent intellectual discipline. It was a loose amalgam of concepts, often separately arrived at and heavily influenced by the taxonomic, habitat, or geographical distribution of the organisms studied. Egerton (1976, 1983) described four "semidistinct ecological sciences," as distinct from natural history, developing in the latter part of the 19th century – oceanography, limnology, plant ecology, and animal ecology. This four-part classification falls into the classical aquatic versus terrestrial distinction based on habitat used by Aristotle and, within the terrestrial class, was divided on taxonomic lines – animals versus plants. Oceanography and limnology, the aquatic sciences, were, to a much larger extent than terrestrial ecology, dominated by considerations of the physical environment. Although plants as well as animals are present in both oceans and lakes, most early marine biology and limnology was done by zoologists, and they trained students who continued to dominate aquatic studies (Frey 1963b). Early terrestrial ecological studies were largely botanical. It was only later that students of these several disciplines recognized that they had much in common; these common interests made headway with difficulty against the inertia of established traditions of marine, freshwater, animal, and plant ecology and the institutions and societies in which they had become enmeshed. Even today ecology is hardly a unified science, and these initial distinctions based on habitat, taxon, and tradition are still evident.

One of the earlier commentators on the history of ecology (Ramaley 1940) asserted, "It is always true that ecology of plants is in advance of animal ecology." This leadership of botanists in the early years of ecology was recognized by the major British and American animal ecologists Charles Elton, C. C. Adams, R. N. Chapman, and W. C. Allee (McIntosh 1976). It was also commonly asserted by early plant ecologists, although the plant physiologist Arthur (1895) saw new life breathed into floras and plant geography by "the biological method" inspired by zoologists. The "biological method" involved explanation of distribution of organisms by environmental factors which promoted or restricted development, including "the reciprocal influence of proximity." It is not clear why terrestrial zoologists lagged behind botanists in seizing upon ecology as a distinct branch of biology and segregating it from physiology and natural history. Certainly there were general works, such as Semper's (1881) *Animal Life as Affected by the Natural Conditions of Existence,* which were substantially ecological in content if not in name. Studies of geographical distribution and recognition of community concepts, which were distinctive elements distinguishing ecologists from physiologists, were familiar in marine zoological studies; and Möbius's (1877) famous definition of the oyster bed "biocœnosis" is commonly recognized as one of the earliest statements of community. Cox (1979) suggested that studies of terrestrial animal communities lagged behind plant community ecology because, as Elton

(1927) said, animals were not readily visible and rushed away when ecologists tried to catch them. Yet zoologists studied aquatic communities as early as botanists studied terrestrial plant communities. The entomologist-limnologist S. A. Forbes was a more sophisticated ecologist than most plant ecologists, or anyone else, in 1880 when he wrote "On Some Interactions of Organisms" (1880a), which anticipated many ecological concepts not formalized until decades later. Forbes (1896) was one of the first zoologists to take cognizance of the embryo science and described ecology as "lately distinguished as a separate subject" and economic entomology as "a division of this science of œcology." Forbes notwithstanding, contemporary comments agreed that animal ecology lagged behind plant ecology. Wheeler (1902), however, disputed unspecified allegations that zoologists had neglected ecology. Nevertheless, the accusations continued, sometimes taking the form of jibes at zoologists:

> It is a matter of congratulations that zoologists are entering this field [ecology] with enthusiasm and well-defined aims. We extend to them our hearty greetings for the new year and the new era of biological work. (Spalding 1903)

C. H. Shaw (1909) wrote, "Rumors have been heard that zoologists are beginning to study ecology and looking to botanical methods for hints of developing their own." F. E. Lutz (1909) commented, "Zoologists have been rather behind the botanists in ecological work, but the zoological school of ecology is growing." The zoologist C. C. Adams (1917) said of ecology, "The botanical side has perhaps grown more rapidly than the zoological, at least consciously." The last phrase is suggestive of the distinction of "self-conscious" ecology used by Allee et al. (1949). Some biologists were becoming "self-conscious" ecologists, others were still cryptoecologists. Some were doing ecology but either failing, or refusing, to recognize that fact, labeling themselves physiologists, perhaps, because ecology was new, only dubiously respectable, and not a good prospect to hitch one's career to in the professional climate of the day.

There is no general account of the development of fin-de-siècle ecology. Conventional histories of biology of the 19th century, even those considering 20th-century biology, do not usually recognize ecology. Only a few historians of science or ecologists have considered the phenomenal rise of ecology or aspects of it in this era (Frey 1963a; Egerton 1976; Lowe 1976; Trass 1976; Cox 1979; Cittadino 1981; Tobey 1981; Engel 1983; McIntosh 1983a). Many accounts of the emergence of ecology are by ecologists as amateur historians (Coleman 1977; Cook 1977). Cook commented on the lack of studies of the history of ecology and suggested a number of significant questions for historical studies which are germane to consideration of its early years:

1. Why, since Darwin was, and is, commonly recognized as the prototype ecologist, was the evolutionary side of ecology not pursued more effectively?
2. Why did ecology first emerge from a somewhat Lamarckian conception of plant communities, and how did animal ecology fit in?
3. Why did most early American ecologists live and work in the midwest? Put conversely, where, before 1970, was the "Princeton-Imperial College-Harvard axis of ecology that Harper (1977a) described?
4. When did theoretical ecology arise in the tradition of empirical and field studies?
5. What was, and is, the relation between the abstractions of scientific ecology and the impact of humans on their environment (and it may be added, vice versa)?

These and other questions have not been seriously considered or answered. They need to be raised and considered to enhance understanding of the development of ecology in its early decades.

Ecology crystallized, as a good crystal should, by accretion, layer upon layer; but unlike a crystal, the successive layers were not alike and its growth was not symmetrical. Nor were the components of the science of ecology formed from a homogeneous solution of elemental facts of natural history of the different habitats (marine, freshwater, terrestrial) or taxonomic (animal, plant) sources. Students of each of these usually made progress independently in formulating ecological concepts about natural phenomena based on very different sets of natural history, morphological, and physiological observations, forming different, if overlapping, conceptual, methodological, ontological, and terminological assemblies. These separately forged assemblies were not easily combined into a unified science of ecology even when it became apparent that they had much in common and shared many of the same problems. It seems desirable to examine the states of the semiindependent progenitors of ecology circa 1900 to determine what, if any, common denominator they may have had in stimulating their convergence on ecology.

**Nuclei for ecology.**

Students of plant geography were prominent among 19th-century biologists who produced a substantial body of research as self-conscious
ecology, identifying it as a new, distinctive, and significant approach to
biology (Egerton 1976, 1979a; Lowe 1976; McIntosh 1976; Tobey
1976, 1981; Cittadino 1980). The specific impetus to the abrupt rise of
ecology is variously interpreted. Some historians see it as a consequence of technology (White 1967; Tobey 1976, 1981). Tobey (1976)
argued that the problems faced by agriculture, expanding from the
forest into the grasslands of North America, were a major stimulus for
the development of scientific plant ecology. Problems of agricultural
technology and weed control, he said, initiated a response from professional botanists, notably Bessey and his famous Botanical Seminar at
the University of Nebraska (Stieber 1980). Tobey recounted the development of grassland ecology and the spin-off development of the profession of range management at a number of midwestern institutions.
He believed the institutional link was the agricultural experiment stations established at the land-grant universities, fulfilling a hope expressed earlier by Arthur (1895). Arthur saw ecology in the future as
holding a "commanding position in the curriculum of the agricultural
and general science courses" of the agricultural colleges and other
land-grant institutions, although he admitted that at the time ecology
was a "nomen incognitum" to curriculum makers at those institutions.
Spalding (1903) similarly anticipated that ecology would provide the
substrate of scientific principles for applied sciences such as agriculture, horticulture, and forestry. Spalding was a realist, however, in his
hopes for ecology, saying that if ecology survived it would be because
of its inherent fitness and vitality, not because of patronage. A few
institutions in Kansas and Nebraska produced a large volume of ecological research and numerous ecologists in the early 20th century.
Some were employed in agricultural experiment stations. Some plant
ecologists, such as John Weaver and F. E. Clements, continued a
lifelong interest in agricultural problems. Agricultural scientists and
ecologists, however, did not develop strong ties. The hopes of Arthur
and Spalding for ecology were not fulfilled, at least in typical agricultural college curricula, and even general science programs were laggard in introducing ecology in most universities. It was not, for example, until the late 1940s that the University of Wisconsin had a
full-time teacher of plant ecology, J. T. Curtis, in the Botany Depart-

ment, and plant ecology, as such, was not taught in the agriculture college. The university created a special chair in 1933 and, in 1939, a Department of Game Management for Aldo Leopold, located administratively in the Department of Agricultural Economics (Flader 1974), but with little effect on the agricultural curriculum at large. Harper (1967), the eminent British plant population ecologist, has often in recent years criticized ecologists for failing to recognize the extensive, experimental population studies of crop and weed plants accomplished at agricultural institutions, so the lack of interest may be reciprocal.

The several categories of land management, for example, agriculture, range management, forestry, and game management, which are commonly recognized as applied ecology have quite different connections with ecology. Tobey (1981) followed in detail the development of the profession of range management, which he described as an outgrowth of the community of grassland ecologists which appeared in Nebraska, Kansas, and Iowa. Professional forestry, however, developed earlier than, and largely independently of, ecology (Boerker 1916). B. E. Fernow (1903) recognized that although silviculture had preceded ecology in practice, it was applied ecology, and he observed that "for ecology has come the time to direct the practice." Forty-three foresters were among the 307 charter members of the Ecological Society of America. A forester, Barrington Moore, was its fourth president, the only one to serve two terms, in addition to editing the society's journal. A number of professional foresters made notable contributions to ecology, among them G. Pearson, C. F. Korstian, J. W. Toumey, and Raphael Zon, who were all charter members of the Ecological Society. H. J. Lutz and Joseph Kittredge continued this distinguished tradition. Professional foresters and ecologists have largely diverged, and the percentage of foresters in the society is probably now smaller than the 14 percent of the charter members. Aldo Leopold, trained as a forester, is commonly described as the "father" of game management. Author in 1933 of the first book entitled *Game Management,* Leopold was, according to his biographer, more concerned with the conservation movement than "the intracacies of ecology." Nevertheless, the biographer said, he "integrated the new functional concepts of ecology" advanced by Charles Elton into his book *Game Management,* although the word *ecology* scarcely appeared (Flader 1974).

Cittadino (1980), in contrast to Tobey, saw plant ecology in America as not so much a response to the technological needs of agriculture or to the recognition of the limitations of natural resources as a response to the professional development of the science of botany.

In this view ecology was an inherent product of the intellectual development of biology, especially evolution and its major problem, adaptation to the environment. It was, Cittadino said, a consequence of the "maturation and professionalization" of botany, especially the development of physiology, in the last decades of the 19th century. Plant ecology in Britain was described as initiated in part as "a response to the social situation and organization of local natural history and the social relationship between amateur and professional practitioners" (Lowe 1976), a thesis in keeping with Cittadino's. Tobey (1981) agreed with Cittadino that the pioneers of ecology at the University of Chicago followed the orientation of their university and pursued a "purely academic route" in contrast to the applied emphasis at Nebraska and some other land-grant universities. The "Chicago school" produced a diffuse group of ecologists, both plant and animal, who pursued divergent interests. Thus even in the midwestern cradle of ecology in the United States, the impetus to develop an ecological science differed, and the nuclei and stimuli were not identical. British and American plant ecologists acknowledged a debt to German plant geographers as pioneers of ecology.

The rapid development of German botany in the 19th century produced many capable younger botanists trained in the concepts of Darwinian evolution; and by the 1880s, many were studying morphology and physiology with respect to the environment and geographical distribution of plants. Although its major tenet of natural selection was not always accepted, Darwin's theory provided the stimulus for examining structure and function of plants in relation to the environment (Cittadino 1981). Cittadino suggested that the salient change in German botany was a shift of emphasis from the laboratory-based mechanistic-reductionist approach to botany to a holistic approach that emphasized the plant in its natural setting—a return-to-the-field or natural history context—but that brought to it ideas and techniques developed in the laboratory. Stauffer (1957) noted that Haeckel's coinage of *ecology* was due to his recognition that Darwin's theory of evolution "explained simply and consistently" and "mechano-causally" the relations of organisms to their environment. Haeckel regarded ecology as a branch of physiology, which, he said, had concentrated on the individual and the relation of its parts to the whole. Haeckel was critical of this type of physiology, however, and wrote:

> Physiology has largely neglected the relations of the organisms
> to the environment, the place each organism takes in the house-
> hold of nature, in the economy of all nature, and has aban-
> doned the gathering of the relevant facts to an uncritical "nat-
> ural history," without making an attempt to explain them
> mechanistically. (Trans. in Stauffer 1957)

This failure of physiology, stated in 1866, apparently went largely unnoticed until the 1880s, but much German botany in the last two
decades of the 19th century was directed at the relation of the plant to
its environment and the conflicting Darwinian and Lamarckian explanations of adaptation (Cittadino 1980).

Cittadino (1981) commented that an important reason for the turn in
German botany from laboratory studies to questions of adaptation to
the natural environment was the development of German colonies in
the tropics and opportunities for young German botanists to travel to
exotic places. He also noted that almost all significant ecological work
of German botanists of the time was based on their tropical field
experience and very little on their European experience. The impetus
to travel was in part due to limited academic openings in the home-
land. Goodland (1975) reviewed the impact of tropical experience on
19th-century biologists and specifically attributed Eugen Warming's
pivotal position in plant ecology to three years spent in Brazil as a
young student working as an assistant in anthropological studies.
Warming, a Dane, subsequently published his famous *Plantesamfund:
Grundtrak af den Okologiska Plantegeografi* (1895). Goodland, in fact,
accused Schimper (1898) of using extensive parts of Warming's work
without acknowledgment. Cittadino (1981) concurred with Goodland's
assertion that Schimper's book added no new methods or points of
view of ecology, attributing most advances to Warming's earlier work.
He believed, however, that Schimper's book summarized an important
tradition of plant adaptation and influenced subsequent development
of plant ecology.

Whatever his sources, Schimper's interest in botany, like Warming's,
was stimulated by extensive tropical travels to study morphology and
physiology of plants rather than the traditional purpose of adding collections of new species. He anticipated later studies of plant-animal
interaction and coevolution by studies of a tree species inhabited by an
ant which protected it from other herbivores. The stimulus to initiating
plant ecology provided by travels in the tropics in the 1890s did not
markedly influence its later content, as most of the tradition of subse-

quent plant ecology was based on work in the Arctic and the temperate zone of the northern hemisphere. Although Schimper and others of his contemporaries had stressed the significance of the rich tropical vegetation for studies of plant geography and physiology, ecologists in the 1950s were lamenting that concepts of vegetation were distorted by being based largely on the relative poverty of temperate-zone vegetation. The principal 20th-century American textbooks of plant ecology reviewed by Egler (1951) barely mentioned tropical forests. Paul Richards's (1952) book *The Tropical Rainforest* was an eye-opener to most ecologists, since few had experience in the tropics (Janzen 1977). It was not until the mid-1960s that studies of tropical ecology became common and the tropics became the standard to which other regions were compared and in which ecological theories were generated and, where possible, tested.

Protoecologists and ecologists of the turn of the century agreed with Haeckel about the central relation of evolution and adaptation to ecology (McIntosh 1976), although there was a substantial element of Lamarckism which lingered into the 20th century (Cittadino 1980, 1981; McIntosh 1983a). Cittadino (1980) commented that Ghiselin (1974) asserted that ecology developed much of its conceptual base during the interval when Darwinian natural selection was out of favor. The early emphasis of ecologists on adaptation was not solely a product of Darwinian concepts of natural selection. Traditional natural history had a concept of "natural place," meaning the adjustment of organic structure and function to their physical and biological environment as a consequence of divine foresight (Coleman 1977). Evolutionary ideas transformed the ultimate cause from divine design to a natural cause of adaptation; but early in the rise of self-conscious ecology, the mechanism of adaptation was hotly disputed. In the development of German plant physiology in the latter part of the 19th century, Darwinian evolution was popular and influential, but natural selection was viewed by some with suspicion as a return to an earlier speculative botany (Cittadino 1981). Cowles (1909) quoted Schimper as expressing concern about "dilettantism and anthropomorphic trifling" which threatened to bring studies of adaptation into "complete discredit." Schimper's antidote was "experimental physiology," and this recommendation is still offered by some plant physiologists (Osmond et al. 1980).

One of the consequences of the Darwinian impact was to place environment in the fore. This directed attention of biologists to the relation of organisms to the environment. Commonly attention centered on the physical environment, although Darwin, Haeckel, and some other early ecologists emphasized the importance of other organisms, or what later came to be called the *biotic* environment. Pound and Clements (1897), for example, while generally praising MacMillan's (1897) pioneer paper on ecological phytogeography, criticized it for considering only the physical environment and not the biological environment, which, Pound and Clements stated, "often proves of no less moment." Clements, Tansley, and other early plant ecologists were acutely aware of the impact, often controlling, of animals on vegetation, and both recognized vegetation states established and maintained by animals. Clements, much criticized for his tendency to create new terminology, even had a name, "therium," for a sere due to animals. Environment and adaptation were concepts crucial to the formulation of ecological science, as they were for evolutionary biology. Both turn out to be less easily defined in what came to be called operational terms than appeared to be the case in the early years of ecology. Disputes concerning the meaning and utility of environment and adaptation persist in recent ecology, particularly in the effort to merge it with evolutionary biology (Gould and Lewontin 1979).

## Plant ecology, physiology, and plant geography

Many turn-of-the-century ecologists agreed with Haeckel that ecology was part of physiology and shared his concern that physiology had failed to address questions concerning the relations of organisms to the environment. Burdon-Sanderson (1893), the Madison Botanical Congress of 1893, and the Congress of Arts and Sciences meeting at St. Louis in 1904 recognized ecology as of equal rank with morphology, and physiology. Cowles (1899b) described "the impetus to a study of ecology as an integral part of biology coordinate with morphology and physiology" as stemming from Eugen Warming's (1895) *Plantesamfund*. Physiologists who turned into ecologists and ecologists from other sources differed in their recognition of the relationship between physiology and its bastard offspring ecology. Burdon-Sanderson considered physiology as dealing with the internal actions of the organism and its parts, using the methods of physics and chemistry; ecology, he said, explored the external relations of animals and plants under natural conditions. Arthur (1895) substantially concurred, describing ecology as the "external or sociological economy of the adult plant," which is more limiting than common ecological practice, which included the entire life cycle of an organism.

Plant ecology as it emerged at the turn of the century was torn conceptually, methodologically, and terminologically between traditional botany, floristics, and plant geography, descended from natural history, and what was then commonly called the "new botany," which had created a methodology based on experimental physiological studies in the laboratory. Plant physiology developed primarily in Germany in the mid-19th century. In early 19th-century botany, summarized in Sachs's (1874) famous textbook, only morphology and physiology were specified and there was no mention of plant distribution or environment (Cittadino 1981). By the 1880s and 1890s Schimper, along with other German physiologists, began to study plant physiology in relation to plant distribution and its relation to the environment. Their contemporary, the Danish botanist Warming, was doing the same. These physiologists, trained in the new botany, turned away from the laboratory restrictions of earlier physiology to the examination of plants in the field, but they differed from the floristic focus of other contemporary botanists. Cittadino (1981) noted that Schimper differed from his predecessor A. Grisebach (1872) in looking at vegetation with an evolutionary and physiological perspective, whereas Grisebach had a static and floristic view with little reference to physiological processes. Many physiologists turned from restricted laboratory studies to the whole plant and its environment. This was lauded by Cowles (1909), who wrote:

> The increasing sanity of physiological problems is due in large measure to the wholesome influence of ecology. In the old days when physiology was a mere laboratory science, and therefore artificial, no experimental test could be too bizarre to be applied to plants.

Cowles and his contemporary Clements both commented on the interdependence and even the identity of physiology and ecology, although they apparently had quite different things in mind. Clements even anticipated an ultimate merging of ecology and physiology, under the name *physiology*, which did not come to pass (McIntosh 1983a).

William H. Howell (1906), a prominent physiologist, described physiologists as the "flower of the army, the imperial guard" of biology; but he allowed that "the varied and important reactions between the organism and the environment should be included under ecology" in default of physiological study. A historian of science (Cravens 1978) concurred with Howell about the superiority of laboratory experimental biology and wrote that by 1910, experimentalists overshadowed natural historians. One of the products of this, according to Cravens, was that the environment was considered of little importance. But just in this era many biologists were, in fact, turning their attention to the environment, and assigning it major importance in the distribution, growth, and evolution of organisms. Drude (1906), a major influence on Clements, claimed for ecology "the life-history of the plant and animal worlds." Drude wrote:

> Whoever wishes to pursue the study of the physiology and development of organs in order to understand the weapons used in the struggle for space on land or in water; whoever wishes to study the mutual relations of species, rather than their inherited characteristics, or to consider the flora and fauna not only as they determine the characteristic appearance of the country they inhabited, but also as being the external, vital result of the effect of geographical factors, which is capable in its turn of influencing the aspect of nature, had to be called an ecologist, whether he wished to be so designated or not.

The ambivalent relations of physiology and ecology were evident in much of the ecological literature of the early 20th century, and hybrid names such as *ecological* and *physiological plant geography* arose and were used interchangeably (McIntosh 1983a). *Physiological ecology* and *ecological physiology* or *ecophysiology* persist to indicate the natal link of ecology with physiology before it became clear that ecology addressed questions different from those addressed by physiology and in ways not conventionally used by physiologists. Consensus about the content of these hybrids has not been achieved (Billings 1957, 1980; Calow and Townsend 1981; Tracy and Turner 1982).

Tobey (1981) commented that we do not know much about the rise of ecology, and he developed a scenario which traced the origins of the two primary centers of plant ecology in America from European sources, which he said were based on quite different philosophical and scientific traditions. Tobey identified the two early centers of American plant ecology as the new land-grant University of Nebraska and the similarly new but privately funded University of Chicago. Nebraska, under the leadership of C. E. Bessey, responded to the technological demands of prairie agriculture, whereas ecology at Chicago, initiated by J. M. Coulter, was more a product of the inherent development of botanical science (Sears 1956; Cittadino 1981). However, Bessey and Coulter shared an interest, along with many contemporary biologists, in the concerns of biological survey of their respective areas. Tobey also made the relevant point that a reasonable narrative history of events is necessary before it is possible to test any of the current theories about how a science develops, whether they be sociological, historical, or philosophical theories. The crystallization of ecology was a complex concatenation of events, and distilling it into a reasonably succinct narrative is difficult enough without demonstrating the validity of a particular theoretical framework.

In the rather disorganized mixture of late 19th century plant geography the most distinctive works which served as nuclei for the science of plant ecology were the writings of Kerner von Marilaun (1863), Drude (1890, 1896), Warming (1895), and Schimper (1898). The works of Drude, particularly his *Handbuch der Pflanzengeographie* (1890) and *Deutschlands Pflanzengeographie* (1896), greatly influenced the young American ecologist Clements and his associates at the University of Nebraska (Pound 1896; Tobey 1981). Clements wrote to Drude, "You will recall that I obtained my first clear view of our field through your *Deutschlands Pflanzengeographie*" acknowledging transmission, via Drude, of the tradition of German plant geography (Tobey 1981). Warming's major work, *Plantesamfund* (1895), was originally published in Danish and was the first textbook of plant ecology labeled as such, based on a course he taught. The German translation of 1896 was more accessible to most scientists and was important in stimulating ecological studies in Britain and the United States. Cowles (1899b) (who learned Danish to read the original) wrote: "The impetus to a study of ecology as an integral part of botany, coordinate with morphology and physiology, dates back to Warming's *Ecological Plant Geography* published only four years ago." Tansley (1947), reviewing the history of plant ecology in Britain, said the modern meaning of ecology was fixed by Warming's book.

The citations of Drude and Warming identify not only two significant individuals in the development of plant ecology but also two different philosophical traditions in early ecology which some see as persisting to the present (Simberloff 1980; Tobey 1981). Tobey traced the source of concepts of vegetation advanced by the influential American ecologist F. E. Clements to Drude. Clements was early recognized and often acclaimed, even by his critics, as the formulator of the first logical system of vegetation commonly described as theory or, more recently, paradigm *(sensu* Kuhn 1970). Clements's theories were extremely controversial, and the persistence, intensity, and inconclusiveness of much of the controversy suggests a philosophical as well as an empirical problem (McIntosh 1976, 1980a, 1981). Clements formalized ideas about the holistic nature of communities as organisms which were widespread, if not universal, among other progenitors of animal ecology, oceanography, and limnology. Their philosophical origins are particularly interesting. Clements was committed to a theory of the plant formation as a holistic superorganism, developing to a climax stable state controlled by the climate, in which it was self-maintaining (Clements 1905). Tobey (1981) asserted that Clements's ecological thought was primarily influenced by German idealism transmitted by Drude from the German philosophical tradition of Kant and Goethe and the biogeography of Humboldt and Grisebach. Clements's concept of vegetation as an organism was also influenced by Herbert Spencer, a source he shared with the premier American animal ecologist S. A. Forbes (Egerton 1976; Tobey 1981; Nicolson 1983 pers. commun.).

In contrast to this holistic organismic tradition, Tobey (1981) suggested a tradition influencing H. C. Cowles at the University of Chicago which stemmed from the Swiss botanist and plant geographer A. P. DeCandolle and the Danish plant geographer Warming, who espoused a different philosophical position from the German tradition of Humboldt and Drude. Warming's emphasis was on the individual plant, and he was critical of higher-level units, such as formations, or causes which could be applied to such entities. According to Tobey, Charles Darwin followed DeCandolle in developing his ecological ideas, and this framework was adopted by Warming in his ecological plant geography. Darwin was acknowledged by German plant ecologists as a major influence on their own ecological studies, but apparently Darwin's philosophical position was replaced, in some cases, by German nature philosophy. Warming, however, was more reductionist and mechanistic, and his ideas of community and succession lacked the organismic and directional emphasis which characterized the thought of Drude and Clements. Thus, at the very onset of ecology in America Tobey described two distinct approaches in which very different philosophical positions were evident. Their differences were apparent to the principals, and Cowles (1898) wrote, in a review of Pound and Clements's (1898) early statement of the ecology of the Nebraska school:

> It may be too early as yet to predict whether the direction to
> future work in plant geography will be given by Warming or by

Drude; and so whether we shall speak of ecology or phytogeography, or life forms or of vegetational forms, or plant societies or formations is yet to be decided.

As usual in ecology, dichotomy is an oversimplification, for a third, powerful force in plant ecology was developing on the Continent, although its influence on Anglo-American ecology was small (Weadock and Dansereau 1960; Van der Maarel 1975). Clements and Cowles both explicitly described ecology as a branch of physiology, even identical to it and destined to merge with it. The Zurich-Montpellier school, or SIGMATIST school, as it came to be known, followed the taxonomic tradition of natural history. The school originated in the 1890s in the work of C. Schröter and Charles Flahault, but its major persona became J. Braun-Blanquet, whose dominance continued from circa 1915 until his death in 1980. The crux of this school, in several variants, was that composition of character species was the basis of characterizing community rather than physiognomy or dominant species. Nicolson (1982b pers. commun.) distinguished it from the tradition exemplified by Clements largely by its emphasis on floristic description of the vegetation unit and the nature of the vegetational entity which both called "association." The emphasis of the Braun-Blanquet school was on classification of vegetation parallel to that in manuals on flora; and its long-term aim, still pursued today, was to produce a "prodromus," or classification of vegetation. Nicolson described the Zurich-Montpellier tradition as a continuation of traditional botany or natural history – collecting and classifying – and the Nebraska (Clements) tradition as an offshoot of the "new" physiological botany to which the Chicago (Cowles) tradition could be added. Contemporary ecologists, like the British ecologist Moss (1910), however, did not see plant ecology as properly linked with either. In his view,

> the study of vegetation touches on physiology at many points, but at present there is not and cannot be any essential identity between them: it needs the systematist, but it is in no sense a branch of Taxonomy.

British plant ecology was associated with the rising professionalism of science and changes in natural history in the last half of the 19th century (Tansley 1904a,b, 1947; Salisbury 1964; Lowe 1976; Godwin 1977; Allen 1979; White 1982; Gimingham et. al. 1983; Rehbock 1983). According to Lowe, professionalization of the sciences came later in Britain than on the Continent. Physics and chemistry developed early as specialized sciences, withdrawing from the general rubric of natural history, leaving it largely the domain of field investigators. The term *naturalist* took on a pejorative tone. *Scientist* had been coined only in the 1830s, and the snobbish ideas about "real" science and natural history, suggested by Cannon (1978), developed along with the professionalization of science generally and of biology largely in the form of morphology and physiology.

British plant ecology derived largely from botanical surveys instituted by amateur naturalists who were informally trained in botany owing to their membership in local natural history societies which proliferated in Britain in the 1870s and 1880s. By 1900 there were some 500 such societies with nearly 100,000 members. During the 1890s the chief activity of these societies was changing from classical "botanizing" and collecting, or "floristic" botany, to survey of vegetation aimed at describing and mapping plant communities. This type of work was stimulated by the more scientifically trained members of these societies. According to Tansley (1947), Robert Smith and his brother William "were the original pioneers of modern ecology in Britain." The brothers had studied with Patrick Geddes at Dundee. Geddes in 1898 was urging a regional survey of diverse aspects of the environment of Britain (Gimingham et al. 1983). Robert Smith also learned the latest continental ideas on vegetation from Flahault at Montpellier. He began mapping the vegetation of Scotland, a task William Smith took up after Robert's untimely death in 1900. The young Tansley, recently returned from the Far East in 1901, learned of Smith's studies. In 1904, he suggested, in his newly founded journal *The New Phytologist,* the formation of the "the Central Committee for the Survey and Study of British Vegetation." This unwieldy title was later shortened to the British Vegetation Committee (Tansley 1904b, 1947; Lowe 1976).

The British Vegetation Committee brought together much of the scientifically trained leadership of the natural history societies. Three of four members at the original meeting were one-time students of Geddes. An interesting instance in the transformation of British plant ecology from floristic botany to vegetation survey, and from amateur to professional, is evident in the career of R. L. Praeger (Lowe 1976; White 1982). Praeger learned his botany as a boy as a member of a local natural history society and became the leading student of the floristic botany of Ireland by 1900. He had read extensively in the early literature of plant ecology and became a member of the British Vegetation Committee. In 1905 he began studying vegetation in addition to floristics. In 1922 Praeger was elected president of the British Ecological Society. In his presidential address he voiced his concern that as an amateur, lacking university and laboratory training in science, he was "somewhat of an imposter" (quoted in Lowe 1976). Praeger was employed as a librarian, and in the development of British plant ecology he represents the highly competent, if nonprofessional, contributor to ecology in contrast to the university-trained professionals William Smith and Arthur Tansley. The British Vegetation Committee included these diverse individuals and had the advantage of their connections with the extensive network of regional federations of natural history societies in developing and coordinating vegetation surveys. It also had scholarly connections with continental ecologists. Moss (1910), one of the committee's founding members, reviewed the disputatious problem in his vegetation survey *The Fundamental Units of Vegetation*. He analyzed the units and terminology advanced by the several schools of continental plant ecology which had developed. Moss voiced a familiar and persistent problem of ecology:

> The subject of ecological plant geography has suffered and still suffers very considerably from lack of uniformity in the use of its principal terms. (Moss 1910)

In 1911 Tansley edited *Types of British Vegetation,* which incorporated the surveys to that date. The continental stimulus to British plant ecology was recognized in the dedication of that volume to Warming as "the father of modern plant ecology" and the Swiss Flahault, "who through his pupil Robert Smith inspired the botanical survey of this country" (Pearsall 1964). The international status of nascent plant ecology was also indicated in the fact that the volume was prepared for the First International Phytogeographical Excursion of 1911, which brought together Clements and Cowles of the United States, Drude and P. Graebner from Germany, E. Rubel and Schröter of Switzerland, and Tansley, among other notable British ecologists. Warming and Flahault were, unfortunately, unable to attend. Tansley (1947) described the excursion an "outstanding success, both floristically and ecologically." It marked, symbolically, the extension of phytogeography from a purely floristic enterprise to an ecological one with the vegetation and its units as the center of attention. The British Vegetation Committee was significant in that it decided in 1912 to form a British Ecological Society.

Plant ecology, in its formative years, was split in several ways. There was widespread agreement that there was some sort of basic unit of vegetation but very little agreement on how to define it. Botanists who were primarily influenced by traditional natural history with a floristic emphasis aiming to produce a taxonomy of vegetation, did not see eye to eye with those primarily influenced by the physiological emphasis of the "new" botany, who wanted to study the structure and function of vegetation and its relation to the environment in a manner analogous to the physiology of the individual organism. Cittadino (1980) described the rise of ecology in America as a consequence of the professionalization of botany in America, paralleling Lowe's (1976) view of professionalism in Britain. He characterized the pioneer ecologists as midwesterners, young (the oldest 36, mean age 30), and mostly employed as professional botanists, a sharp break from traditional taxonomy and morphology largely accomplished by persons trained as physicians and rarely employed as botanists. Cittadino noted that professional botanists in the post-Civil War era numbered only a half-dozen but that their numbers increased rapidly in the latter decades of the 19th century, although Cattell (1906) listed only 53 botany professors in American universities circa 1900.

It is not clear that there was a similar relationship in America and Britain between the rise of plant ecology, the professionalization of botany, and the activity of amateur devotees of natural history. Although local natural history societies flourished in the United States as in Britain, they were more ephemeral and less prevalent. Societies were formed in several cities of the Midwest (Louisville, Grand Rapids, Milwaukee, Chicago) in the 1850s. Natural history surveys proliferated in America in the 1880s and the 1890s but were commonly institutionalized as state agencies. None was more famous or more productive than the Illinois Natural History Survey, which grew out of a Natural History Society chartered in 1861 (Forbes 1907c; Mills 1958). S. A. Forbes (1907c) reviewed the history of one such organization, noting its formation in the period of exploration and discovery of the "scientific contents and economic resources of our territory." Almost none of the participants, he commented, had a scientific education, yet it included some eminent figures in the study of natural history in the period, such as the explorer Major J. W. Powell, the botanists George Vasey and M. S. Bebb, and the first state entomologist of Illinois, Benjamin D. Walsh. This society was absorbed by the state of Illinois in 1867 and subsequently funded Major Powell's famous expeditions to the Far West. In 1879 a new organization was founded, as Forbes noted, "in the period of the return to nature in the study of science" following the influence of the evolutionists Darwin and Huxley and the antievolutionist Louis Agassiz. By 1885 this society passed out of existence due to lack of interest. The Illinois Natural History Survey, under a series of names, had a distinctive connection with the emergence of ecology in America because several key figures in plant and animal ecology and in limnology were associated with it. Literally "Chief" among these, was S. A. Forbes, who was largely self-educated, one of the first zoologists to take formal cognizance of ecology, and the author of several of the most advanced ecological papers published before 1900. C. A. Kofoid published the earliest studies of plankton in rivers done before the turn of the century, which he conducted at a biological station on the Illinois River which was established by Forbes. C. C. Adams, later the author of the first manual on animal ecology, was employed by the survey during 1896–8. T. J. Burrill, a botanist associated with the survey (1885–92), stimulated the young H. A. Gleason's interest in prairies. Gleason's (1910) early publication in ecology was done under the aegis of the survey, although he is not listed as an employee. Arthur Vestal, briefly, and Victor Shelford, for an extended period, were also associated with the survey. J. M. Coulter and H. C. Cowles of the University of Chicago were members of the board of the survey.

The common link of state natural history surveys with "self-conscious" ecology is also evident in the Botanical Survey of Nebraska, organized by C. E. Bessey, which produced the premier work of Pound and Clements (1898b) on the *Phytogeography of Nebraska.* MacMillan (1897) wrote his important work on Minnesota phytogeography while he was a part-time state botanist. J. M. Coulter and his brother, Stanley initiated the botanical survey in Indiana. C. C. Adams moved from Illinois to the Natural History Museum of the University of Michigan and later to that of New York State. E. A. Birge, a pioneer limnologist, was director of the Natural History Division of Wisconsin formed in 1897. There is a parallel in the widespread interest in botanical or biological surveys between America and Britain. In the United States the postbellum westward expansion involved extended surveys of the poorly known trans-Mississippi region for railroads and other purposes and incorporated biological surveys. Many biologists who later became prominent whetted their appetites for natural history by reading about, or taking part in, the various federal or state surveys of biological resources. F. V. Coville's interest in desert plants was stimulated by his experience in 1881 on the Death Valley Expedition, lead by C. H. Merriam. This experience influenced Coville's proposal to the Carnegie Institution in 1902 that it fund physiological and ecological research at a Desert Laboratory (McIntosh 1983a). T. H. Kearney, an agrostologist who later published significant early studies on the ecology of the southeastern United States, accompanied Coville on an expedition to Alaska in 1899. In the United States, a considerable number of the biologists identified as significant contributors to the emergence of ecology were linked in various ways with federal or state biological surveys of the late 19th and early 20th centuries. Individual biologists employed by such agencies made notable contributions to ecology in its early years, although ecology per se was not formally institutionalized as the science basic to these surveys and their successor agencies. The applied aspects of ecology all too commonly were not closely integrated with the academic. This was notably true in the development of oceanography and marine biology.

## Marine ecology

Oceanography, like ecology, is a youthful science, although interest in the sea and its life goes back to antiquity. The study of marine organisms was, until the 19th century, largely incidental to other purposes, such as coastal surveys, exploration, and fishery management. Much of this work was still largely collection, description, and classification of new organisms and, in the 19th century, examination of their morphological and embryological characteristics. Throughout much of this time emphasis was on physical and chemical properties of the seas – currents, waves, depth, temperature, salinity – and this dominance persisted into the 19th century. Deacon (1978), for example, offered a collection of salient articles on the history of oceanography; ten are on circulation of the ocean, seven on tides, five on waves, five on water chemistry, seven on depth and the seabed. Only three are on biology of marine organisms, the earliest of these published in 1844. This emphasis may be justified by the fact that marine systems are in most respects dominated by the physical environment more than terrestrial environments, where organisms are characteristically more conspicuous and in many areas exercise rather obvious control over the physical environment. Oceanography is an even more hybrid science than terrestrial ecology. It includes marine biology or, more generally, hydrobiology, and even these terms require qualification before they become comparable to terrestrial ecology. Marine ecology proper relates to the larger body of data concerning the marine environment in a way analogous to the relation of terrestrial ecology to meteorology (Allee et al. 1949). The point of ecology is not only the relation of the organisms, individually and collectively, to the physical environment but their relationships to other organisms and their reciprocal effect on the physical environment. These are less conspicuous in the ocean than on land but are nonetheless significant. Terrestrial biologists, in large part, examined the clearly visible and, in the case of plants, largely stationary organisms. Aquatic biologists, particularly marine biologists, were dealing with organisms that commonly were motile, often not visible, or were seen only after laborious efforts at collection, removed from their immediate habitat. One aspect of marine ecology which has recently linked concepts and theories of terrestrial and marine biologists consists of studies of the marine littoral, where the dominant animals are readily visible and often sessile (Connell 1978).

Oceanography like forestry differs from ecology in that there has been a much greater awareness of its history. Several volumes on the history of oceanography are available (Bigelow 1931; Deacon 1971, 1978; Schlee 1973; Sears and Merriam 1980), whereas there have been none of ecology in its general sense. Oceanography differs from traditional ecology in another respect in that, by virtue of its methods, it is inherently a more expensive science. Quite early on it enlisted large-scale funding from scientific societies, governments, and royal patrons to undertake extended voyages for research and to publish the results of these voyages.

Paradoxically, the earliest studies of marine organisms which took on an ecological flavor were not of conspicuous and economically valuable fishes but of inconspicuous animals of the seabed (benthos). Historians of oceanography focus on Edward Forbes, a British naturalist. Forbes's biogeographical ideas were influenced by the botanists A. P. DeCandolle and H. Watson, and his early studies were on terrestrial molluscs (Rehbock 1983). Forbes persuaded the newly formed British Association for the Advancement of Science to establish a Dredging Committee in 1839 and to provide funds for dredging of the seabed for a decade thereafter (Rice and Wilson 1980; Rehbock 1979,1983). The Dredging Committee was instrumental in developing systematic surveys of the sea bottom, including recording the location and depth of collections, and numbers of organisms, in lieu of the usual naturalists' practice of swelling the collections of museums and records of species. On the basis of studies along British coasts and other studies in the Aegean Sea, Forbes defined zones of characteristic fauna of the sea bottom, noting that species occurred in the same faunal assemblage and range of depth. Forbes's work was credited with supporting the idea that below 300 meters there was an azoic zone. This was derivative of the "azoic theory," which held that the ocean depths were static and lacked oxygen and hence were sterile. This "theory" persisted until the *Challenger* expedition of 1873, even in the face of evidence of living organisms dredged up from deep water. Dredging continues into the modern era supplemented by increasingly sophisticated and expensive diving mechanisms which allow direct observation of limited areas of the sea bottom.

Dredging is a blind grabbing of a portion of the unseen ocean bottom; and early marine biologists, perforce, dealt only with the collection of organisms brought up in the dredge hauls. They can have had no illusions of subjective judgments or direct evaluations of species associations or community boundaries which pervaded terrestrial studies. The idea of community recognition as an art form based on the knowledge and insight gained by experience, the "*phytosociologischer Blick*" of the terrestrial plant ecologist, was impossible for the dredger. The significance of the sample or "quadrat" as representing the community, which slowly dawned on terrestrial ecologists and which was seized on by F. E. Clements in developing his theories of vegetation, was an immediate necessity to the dredger. Dredgers had nothing but the hard-won sample of an unseen universe which could be tabulated as the number of species and, if they were patient, the total number of individuals of each species. Dredgers dealt only with the sample and the numerical representations from it to infer the larger whole of the unseen bottom. The advantages of immediate sense perceptions enjoyed by some plant ecologists (Stout 1981) were not for them and, willy-nilly, they necessarily compared the samples to recognize similarities and differences from place to place. The emphasis on the sample or quadrat and the elementary mathematization it imposed was what Tobey (1981) saw as revolutionary in the terrestrial plant ecology of Clements at the turn of the century. Marine ecologists were forced to accept what Thorson (1957) later described as the statistical community unit, which became the standard for subsequent generations of dredgers. There are interesting parallels in the problems of community recognition in marine and terrestrial ecology, later recognized by Jones (1950), Sanders (1968), Mills (1969), and Stephenson (1973).

A significant aspect of marine benthic studies was relating organisms to the nature of the bottom sediments and the studies of communities (Verrill 1874; Allee 1934a). The earliest mention of the marine animal community is commonly attributed to the German zoologist Karl Möbius (1877) in a study of oyster culture which was precipitated by impoverishment of natural oyster beds. Appropriately, the early dredging studies of Edward Forbes used oystermen's dredges, and Möbius's community was based on extensive dredging records of natural oyster beds. In Möbius's words:

> Every oyster-bed is thus, to a certain degree, a community of living beings, a collection of species, and a massing of individuals, which find here everything necessary for their growth and continuance, such as suitable soil, sufficient food, the requisite percentage of salt, and a temperature favorable to their development. Each species which lives here is represented by the greatest number of individuals which can grow to maturity subject to the conditions which surround them, for among all species the number of individuals which arrive at maturity at each breeding period is much smaller than the number of germs produced at that time. The total number of mature individuals of all the species living together in any region is the sum of the survivors of all the germs which have been produced at all breeding or brood periods; and this sum of matured germs represents a certain quantum of life which enters into a certain number of individuals, and which, as does all life, gains permanence by means of transmission. Science possesses, as yet, no word by which such a community of living beings may be designated; no word for a community where the sum of species and individuals, being mutually limited and selected under the average external conditions of life, have, by means of transmission, continued in possession of a certain definite territory. I propose the word *Biocœnosis* for such a community. Any change in any of the relative factors of a biocönose produces changes in other factors of the same. If, at any time, one of the external conditions of life should deviate for a long time from its ordinary mean, the entire biocönose, or community, would be transformed. It would also be transformed, if the number of individuals of a particular species increased or diminished through the instrumentality of man, or if one species entirely disappeared from, or a new species entered into, the community. (Möbius 1877:41 in translation)

Edward Forbes, in addition to his bottom-dredging studies, collected minute free-floating organisms in the Aegean Sea and found characteristic groups of organisms at different depths (Deacon 1971). Scientists on the *Challenger* expedition related the nature of the bottom sediment to the minute organisms found in the upper waters which settled to the bottom in enormous quantity. The name *plankton* was given to these organisms by the German zoologist Victor Hensen. Hensen, like his contemporaries in German plant ecology, was trained in physiology, and in 1865 he was named director of the Physiological Institute of Kiel, also the academic home of Möbius, who joined the faculty in 1868. Hensen had worked on physiology using marine organisms, but about 1867 he became interested in problems of fisheries, particularly the problem of judging the productivity of the ocean (Lussenhop 1974). Like his counterparts in benthic studies, Hensen had to develop methods of sampling the invisible and, in this case, mobile organisms. Hensen transformed the study of plankton by developing a sampling method of drawing a fine-meshed silk net vertically through a water column 200 meters long and 1 meter square. This enabled him to estimate the plankton populations of the top 200 meters of the ocean and earned him the appellation "father of quantitative plankton ecology" (Taylor 1980). Hensen was a pioneer in statistical estimates of the populations of organisms and faced the problem which continues to plague both empirical and theoretical ecologists to the present – the heterogeneous distribution of organisms in space, or pattern. Hensen, like Darwin, also attempted to study the effects of earthworms and calculated the number of earthworms, assuming that their burrows were uniformly distributed. In studies of fish eggs and plankton he assumed that these were also uniformly distributed in space, and he calculated the number of organisms in one of the first efforts to use statistical methods on natural populations (Lussenhop 1974; Damkaer and Mrozek-Dahl 1980; Taylor 1980). The problem of spatial distribution of organisms, and particularly the problem of pattern, remains the key to modern ecological studies and theories, frustrating both empiricists and theorists. It pervades all aspects of ecology, and its traditional segregation is evidenced by a marine ecologist recently stating, "It surprised me to find, for instance, that patchiness problems are not much different in other ecosystems" (Reeve 1979).

Hensen's results, methods, assumptions, and scientific acumen were vigorously attacked by the coiner of *ecology*, Haeckel (1891). Haeckel lamented, probably incorrectly, that the study of distribution of marine organisms lagged behind that of terrestrial plants and animals. Although Haeckel reasserted that ecology is a part of physiology, Hensen attributed part of Haeckel's criticism of his work to the fact that he (Hensen) was "only a physiologist" and presumably not competent to pronounce on the study of plankton (Damkaer and Mrozek-Dahl 1980). Haeckel distrusted Hensen's then unusual application of population statistics and described Hensen's results as "remarkably negative" and "utterly worthless." He further deplored the laborious counting of the microscopic organisms necessary to Hensen's method as having the potential for "ruin of mind and body" (Taylor 1980). Haeckel disputed the merits of Hensen's counts of numbers of individuals, insisting that the only useful method was to determine weights and substance – later called *biomass*. He disputed the merits of Hensen's counts on the grounds that plankton were not uniformly distributed, as Hensen assumed, but were clumped. Although Haeckel urged the merit of exact quantitative methods in physiology, the problems of ecology, he argued, are too complicated "or not even susceptible to exact definition." Appropriate use of sampling and statistics in ecology is still plagued by these problems.

Hensen's other major contribution was his effort in the 1890s to estimate the chemical composition of plankton and the productivity of ocean water. His startling conclusion that cold Arctic oceans produced more than warm tropical oceans was contrary to the intuitive expectations of biologists, including Haeckel, and therefore difficult to sell (Damkaer and Mrozek-Dahl 1980; Taylor 1980). Parsons (1980) described Hensen's motives as pure science, not management, contradicting Lussenhop's (1974) opinion that Hensen's interest derived from the economic importance of fishing to Germany. Subsequent work on plankton by Hensen's associates Friedrich and Maria Dahl identified plankton faunal districts related to environmental conditions, primarily salinity (Damkaer and Mrozek-Dahl 1980). Hensen's leadership in quantitative sampling and studies of the productivity and trophic structure of aquatic systems was influential in aquatic ecology, and the primacy of studies in aquatic systems in analysis of trophic and ecosystem relations persists in current ecology (Lindeman 1942; Kozlovski 1968).

The last decades of the 19th century marked the rise of marine biology and distinctive elements recognizable as ecology, although the word *ecology* was not widely applied to marine studies. Damkaer and Mrozek-Dahl (1980) refer to the "glorious decade" of 1870–80, and many of the early organizations for studying the biology of the sea appeared in that decade, along with the fabled *Challenger* expedition. In the last decades of the 19th century it was becoming apparent that fish stocks were diminishing, and fishermen had to go farther and work longer to fill their holds. This brought governments even more into the marine sciences. The first major marine biological station was established at Naples in 1873, and Britain and Germany expanded their support for marine studies around this time. Hensen's plankton work was the product of Germany's first major oceanographic exploration, the famous "Plankton-Expedition of 1889." The U.S. Fish Commission.was formed in 1872, its laboratory at Woods Hole, Massachusetts, was established in 1885; and, in 1888, the famous Marine Biological Laboratory, a private foundation, was established (Redfield 1945). The major person behind the establishment of the U.S. Fish Commission was Spencer Fullerton Baird (Allard 1967), who hoped to initiate basic ecological studies of American waters, but the government wished to keep out of "basic scientific investigations except in an incidental way"–fish hatching was the commission's major function (Schlee 1973). By 1902 an International Council for the Exploration of the Sea (ICES) had been formed, but Parsons (1980) commented that Hensen, almost alone, showed more "of how the ecology of the ocean worked than all the committees of the ICES together."

The significance of understanding ecological relations among marine organisms was apparent but not effectively pursued. Parsons (1980) quoted M. MacDonald, a U.S. commissioner of fisheries, as saying, "A knowledge of life in its relation to the environment is an important subject which biological investigators have not heretofore sufficiently dealt with," thus putting his finger on ecology. Nevertheless, marine ecology did not flourish at Woods Hole. Schlee (1973) wrote that only in the 1950s did the Board of Directors of the Marine Biological Laboratory decide to reemphasize marine ecology, and only in 1962 did it establish a program of year-round studies in ecology. Redfield (1958) explained this by noting that the interest of naturalists who came to Woods Hole early in the 20th century was diverted from problems of marine biology in the ocean to experimentation on marine organisms in the laboratory. He described the consequence for marine biology:

> I believe that in the United States the progress of marine biology was retarded for fifty years by the introduction of experimental methods in biology.

The dual problem of ecology is evident in the preeminence gained by experimental biology in the 19th century, which was seen as retarding ecology, and the difficulty of applying, in ecology, the methods which had proven so effective in the physical sciences and in physiology.

Oceanography, or that part of it designated as hydrobiology or marine biology, followed a pattern of development similar to that of plant ecology. A long tradition of natural history studies and collections emphasizing taxonomy and classification and, in the mid-19th century, morphology, embryology, and physiology of organisms was followed in the latter decades of the 19th century by studies of the biogeography or regional distribution of organisms and, increasingly, their relations to the physical environment. The formal concepts of the community exemplified in the "formation" of Grisebach and the biocœnose of Möbius and the recognition of interactions among organisms became established in the last quarter of the 19th century. The significance of the statistical unit or sample was forced on students of benthic and plankton communities and later dawned upon terrestrial ecologists. By 1900 elementary descriptive statistics was being used, and the major problems of homogeneity and pattern were recognized. Even Haeckel, although expressing doubt of the merits of statistics, recognized, in 1890, "monotonic" communities if one species comprised more than 50 percent of the individuals and "polymixic" communities if no single species exceeded 50 percent (Taylor 1980). Plant ecologists in this era similarly distinguished communities by the ubiquity of certain species, usually using frequency, or percentage of samples in which a species occurred (commonly 50 or 60 percent), rather than number of individuals. In any event, Haeckel was making a distinction of diversity, or number of species in an area or a community, a topic which has engaged quantitative ecologists to the present. Marine ecologists also developed productivity and trophic concepts, which persist as major concerns in current ecology.

What is not evident in turn-of-the-century oceanography is the rapid acceptance of the term *ecology*, which was so evident in plant ecology. Although ecology was clearly being practiced, it was not as self-conscious as that of terrestrial ecologists. Marine biologists were largely zoologists, whereas terrestrial ecologists were largely, at this time, botanists. Parsons (1980) lists Johnstone's (1908) *Conditions of Life in the Sea* as the earliest classic work on ecology of the seas. This was sandwiched between Clements's (1905) *Research Methods in Ecology* and Adams's (1913) *Guide to the Study of Animal Ecology,* the first general works in America on terrestrial plant and animal ecology, respectively.

It was not until the 1970s that it became conventional to use *ecology* in the titles of books on marine conditions, although one of the early textbooks of general ecology was by a marine biologist (Clarke 1954). Biological Oceanography was transferred to a division of the U.S. National Science Foundation other than the division which included the rest of ecology, including limnology.

## Limnology

Limnology is the part of hydrobiology, or aquatic biology, which deals with inland waters, normally freshwaters. Although the word *limnology* was coined by F. A. Forel in 1892, it appeared after over two decades of Forel's studies of Lac Léman (Lake Geneva) in Switzerland (Needham 1941; Berg 1951; Egerton 1962). Forel's studies began early in 1869, and he provided a list of what a program of lake studies should include (Forel 1871). Berg commented, without equivocation, "Forel was an ecologist," although Forel himself did not use the term. Elster (1974) addressed the question which is germane to this discussion, "What was the approach to studies of inland waters before they became limnology?" His answer was that geologists, geographers, physicists, and chemists studied light, temperature, and evaporation, and lakes were classified on their geological origin, but not much attention was given to the biology of lakes, an emphasis parallel to that in oceanography. Forel (1892) described limnology as the oceanography of lakes; and Elster noted the influence on Forel of the *Challenger* expedition, of Möbius's concept of biocœnosis, and of Hensen's plankton studies in the late 1880s and 1890s (cf. Egerton 1976). Forel, like many of his contemporaries in biology, was trained in medicine (at the University of Würzburg) and taught anatomy and physiology much of his professional life. He did not retire from teaching and devote full time to limnology until 1895.

Allee et al. (1949) commented that Forel's importance for ecology lies not in the priority of his observations but in the significance of his work. Unlike Haeckel, who coined the word *ecology* but was not himself a notable contributor to the science he christened, Forel both named and created limnology (Berg 1951; Egerton 1962). Egerton wrote:

> A few times in its history, science has reached a point of development at which one man with comprehensive abilities has been able to carry out investigations resulting in the estab-

lishment of a new field of study. Francois Alphonse Forel was such a man; the branch of science he created is limnology. He even formally christened it. (Egerton, 1962)

Berg (1951), criticizing an article which implied that the "peculiarity" of limnology was not recognized until the 1920s, strongly asserted the primacy of Forel as the founder of limnology. Berg also noted that limnology and terrestrial plant ecology were linked in the work of C. Schröter, a Swiss phytogeographer, who published on the association concept in terrestrial plants and wrote on limnology. Schröter examined the plants of lakes in respect to the environment and as plant formations (Schröter and Kirchner 1896, 1902). The link with ecology is apparent in that Schröter introduced new, specificially ecological terms – for example, *synecology* and *autecology* – into the limnological lexicon in the context of his studies of plant plankton (Chapman 1931; Berg 1951).

Limnology from its beginnings shared with oceanography an emphasis on the physical environment, which seems appropriate to an entity defined more explicitly by its physical than its biological qualities. Faegri (1954) commented, "Limnology is part of ecology"; but he added, "A lake is not a community, a lake is a habitat." Symbolically, G. E. Hutchinson (1957b) began his multivolume *Treatise on Limnology* with the volume on geography, physics, and chemistry. Geologists (including notably Louis Agassiz), geographers, physicists, and chemists in the 19th century provided extensive analysis of physical properties such as temperature, and by the 1890s the generality of temperature stratification in northern temperate lakes was established, and oxygen determinations made even in deep waters. Early terrestrial, especially plant, ecologists were also concerned with the physical environment and its relations to the organisms, but the organisms were much more in evidence and exerted more obvious influence on the physical environment in most terrestrial situations than in lakes. The internal physical qualities of the lake, such as the physical properties of water, its temperature, and its chemical characteristics were studied earlier, in more detail, and seemed to lend themselves more readily to integration with the biological factors than physical attributes in terrestrial habitats. Limnologists, even before they were called such, treated lakes, as Hutchinson (1957b) put it, "as more or less closed systems" or, in 19th-century terms, as "microcosms" (S. A. Forbes 1887). S. A. Forbes earlier (1883b) emphasized the regularity and stability of plants and animals in lakes as "favorable to an exact and economical balance of supply and demand," in the classic phraseology of economics. In his more famous article "The Lake as a Microcosm" (1887) he wrote:

> The lake is an old and relatively primitive system, isolated from its surroundings. Within it matter circulates, and controls operate to produce an equilibrium comparable with that in a similar area of land. In this microcosm nothing can be fully understood until its relationship to the whole is clearly seen.

Forbes's explicitly organismic conception of the lake parallels Clements's organismic concept of plant formation, which appeared in its earliest detailed statement in 1905.

Forbes, in 1872 became curator of Illinois's Museum of the State Natural History Society, in 1875 professor of zoology at Illinois State Normal University, in 1877 director of the State Laboratory of Natural History, and in 1885 professor and chairman of the Department of Zoology at the University of Illinois, all without benefit of a doctoral degree. Forbes became interested in the food of fishes and food supply in lakes as early as 1878, and his "Lake as a Microcosm" (1887) is commonly described as a classic of limnology and ecology. In this essay he described the lake as a microcosm stressing its holistic nature and "the necessity for taking a comprehensive survey of the whole as a condition to a satisfactory understanding of any part." True to his ideal he studied plants and animals, benthos and plankton organisms, invertebrates and vertebrates, and compared these with those of European lakes. He developed detailed ideas of trophic structure, even including the insectivorous plant, the bladderwort. Elster (1974) suggested that the theory of evolution, an important stimulus to the establishment of ecology, was less significant as a stimulus to limnology. However, Forbes is explicit in advancing an idea of the balance of nature – a "beneficent order" promoted by the process of natural selection through competition and predation. These "laws of life," Forbes believed, established an equilibrium that "is steadily maintained and that actually accomplished for all the parties involved the greatest good which the circumstances will at all permit." Forbes's holistic conception of the lake permeated limnology and was later formalized by Thienemann in his conception of the lake as "super-organism" (Rodhe 1979). Forbes was notable also in that he established in 1894 the first American river laboratory at Havana, Illinois, on the Illinois River. At the Havana Station, Charles Kofoid, from 1895 to 1900, conducted his pioneer studies of river plankton. For many years limnologists were primarily concerned with lakes, to the point where the more encompassing meaning of the term *limnology* to include all inland waters was nearly lost. Only in recent decades has the study of the ecology of running waters excited interest comparable to the study of lakes.

The other major early contributor to limnology in the United States was E. A. Birge, more familiarly encountered as part of the team of Birge and Juday because of his later long-term collaboration with Chancey Juday (Mortimer 1956; Sellery 1956). Birge started his interest in lakes with studies of Cladocera in 1877 and continued to conduct systematic and faunistic studies of zooplankton and their distribution. Like Forbes, Birge served as director of a state natural history survey in Wisconsin and its Natural History Division, and he was able to develop limnological studies through the survey and to appoint Juday as biologist in 1900. Juday came from another early center for limnology in Indiana, established by Carl H. Eigenmann, who in 1895 began the earliest lake biological station in the United States (Eigenmann 1895). Frey (1963b) described Birge's interest in the plankton group of crustaceans as shifting from systematics to ecology in 1894, when he encountered a paper on their daily vertical migration. Birge started studying this phenomenon in Lake Mendota, Wisconsin and, because it involved water temperature, he became interested in thermal attributes of lakes and developed detailed analyses of the annual thermal regime of Lake Mendota (Birge 1898). Frey saw this as Birge's shift from systematist to limnologist examining the distribution of plankton in the context of the physical and chemical properties of the lake, which Birge himself noted began in 1897 (Birge and Juday 1911). Birge had done postgraduate work in Germany, although not in limnology. However, it seems likely that he was aware of contemporary activities in limnology on the Continent. The emphasis in limnology, as in plant ecology and oceanography, on studying organisms in their natural environment is clear in Birge and Juday's (1911) statement:

> It is evident that, if we wish to understand the physiology of some of these lake-inhabiting organisms, we must study them in their natural environment and not merely in the laboratory where they are subjected to a purely artificial environment. . . . The results obtained under the former conditions may differ materially from those obtained under the latter.

The general increase in activity in limnology in the last decade of the 19th century is evident in the establishment of enough freshwater biological stations in that interval to have warranted assembling a list of these (Ward 1899a) and enough investigations to have warranted compiling a bibliography for 1895–99 (Ward 1899b). The point to be emphasized was well made by Berg (1951). Limnology was not only "né[e] dans le dernier tiers du XIX siècle," but limnologists were well aware of this fact. Limnology, like ecology, had become "self-conscious," although limnologists' recognition of their affinity was not always explicit; and limnologists, marine biologists, and terrestrial ecologists largely pursued their separate ways. In Britain, the first surveys of lakes were begun in 1897 and concentrated on bathymetrical measures, although incidental biological collections were also made (Murray and Pullar 1910; Maitland 1983). Although plankton surveys were made of small lakes before the turn of the century, extended studies comparable to those of Birge and Juday did not begin until later. The first freshwater station was founded on Lake Windemere in 1930 by the Freshwater Biological Association (Macan 1970; Le Cren 1979; Maitland 1983). Subsequent limnologists clearly recognized that limnology is a branch of ecology (Faegri 1954; Rodhe 1975, 1979), although ingrained institutionalization of academic centers, laboratories, societies and journals persisted.

## Terrestrial animal ecology

Although the term *ecology* was coined by a zoologist, neither the term nor the discipline was adopted as readily by terrestrial zoologists as by botanists. Animal ecologists commonly recognized that botanists developed the science of ecology (Adams 1913; Shelford 1913; Chapman 1931; Elton 1933; Allee et al. 1949). Zoologists were the principal contributors to limnology (Frey 1963b), but in terrestrial ecology they lagged behind botanists.

Elton (1927:5) wrote:

> Preliminary biological surveys have been undertaken in most civilized countries except England and China, where animal ecology lags behind in a peculiar way.

It does seem odd that in a nation where gamekeeping and hunting were notable traditions and where plant ecology had been formed on a base of botanical surveys that animal ecology should lag, but Elton offers no explanation. Elton (1933) also noted the contributions of natural history societies, but they were not significant in the same way as in plant ecology. The earliest ecological surveys of animals that Elton mentions were of aquatic organisms in the 1890s. Elton (1927) and Chapman (1931) attributed the more rapid advance of plant ecology to the fact that plants are sessile and thus their distribution is more easily studied than that of animals. It is likely that the early emphasis on the plant community as the basis of ecology was not as easy for terrestrial animal ecologists because of problems of identification as well as capture. Macan (1963), for example, made the point that the notable distinction between Arthur Tansley's book on British vegetation and Charles Elton's book on animal ecology was the lack of accounts of community composition in the latter. The ideal of ecological surveys, although not easily achieved, was expressed by S. A. Forbes:

> I cannot too strongly emphasize the fact . . . that a comprehensive survey of our entire natural history is absolutely essential to a good working knowledge of those parts of it which chiefly attract popular attention, – that is, its edible fishes, its injurious and beneficial insects, and its parasitic plants. Such a survey, however, should not stop with a study of the dead forms of nature, ending in mere lists and descriptions. To have an applicable value, it must treat the life of the region as an organic unit, must study it in action, and direct principal attention to the laws of its activity. (Forbes 1883a)

Shelford (1913) made a notable start in animal community studies, although his example was not widely followed by animal ecologists. Allee et al. (1949), in one of the few commentaries on the general history of ecology, traced the background of "self-conscious ecology" from several sources beginning with Aristotle. They described the relations of ecology to physiology as "environmental physiology," or the physiological responses of organisms to the physical environment, and "response physiology," the behavorial responses of organisms to the physical environment. Relationship of populations to the environment, and their growth and distribution, was another source of ecological thought growing out of economic biology. Evolutionary biology, they noted, was closely linked in the rise of ecology to the Darwinian "struggle for existence," tempered by recognition of cooperation in nature, which was developed in some detail by Allee (1931). They round out with a discussion of oceanography and limnology, what they call the substrate of self-conscious ecology. Allee et al. (1949) and Adams (1913:xii) both quoted from W. K. Brooks, a prominent zoologist at Johns Hopkins University, who called for study of the environmental relations of organisms.

> To study life we must consider three things: first, the orderly sequence of external nature; second, the living organism and

the changes which take place in it; and, third, that continuous adjustment between the two sets of phenomena which constitutes life.

The physical sciences deal with the external world, and in the laboratory we study the structure and activities of organisms by very similar methods; but if we stop there, neglecting the relation of the living being to its environment, our study is not biology or the science of life.

Brooks expressed an idea which was "already old" in 1899, according to Allee et al., and extensively pursued in limnology, oceanography, and plant ecology, but which was less familiar in terrestrial zoology in spite of the notable ecological work of S. A. Forbes. The widely recognized return to interest in the organism in its natural environment and disaffection with the product of laboratory studies became apparent in biology in the late 19th century and persisted in the 20th (Redfield 1958). The impetus given by Darwin to the study of organisms and their relations with their environment in the field clearly was paramount, although some who studied such aspects of biology (e.g., Louis Agassiz) were not committed to, or were even opposed to, natural selection. The core of ecology described by Burdon-Sanderson (1893) as the external relations of the whole organism to its external environment had been stated earlier by the zoologist Karl Semper (1881) in his book *Animal Life as Affected by the Natural Conditions of Existence*. Semper set in opposition to the then current view of physiology – the internal physiology of organs – the "almost unworked" branch of biology,

> which regards the species of animals as actualities and investigates the reciprocal relations which adjust the balance between the existence of any species and the natural, external conditions of its existence, in the widest sense of the term. (Semper 1881:33)

He called it "universal physiology or the physiology of organisms." Semper's volume certainly addressed ecological concerns, although not using the term *ecology*. According to Cox (1979), the ecological treatment of animals in textbooks did not appear until 1901 (Jordan and Kellogg) and 1913 (Adams). Jordan and Kellogg introduced their book as "an elementary account of animal ecology." None appeared in Britain until Elton's (1927) famous primer *Animal Ecology,* which, however, had a much greater impact on ecology. Concern for distribution of organisms in relation to the environment was not entirely new. Karl Bergman had developed, in the 1830s, the well-known and still debated "Bergman's rule," which related the body size of animals to temperature (Coleman 1979). Perhaps the most frequently cited "laws" of pre-1900 ecology were C. Hart Merriam's "Laws of temperature control of geographic distribution," which recognized and named zones of distribution on the premise that "animals and plants are restricted in northward distribution by the total quantity of heat during the season of growth and reproduction." Rules and laws were sometimes seen in the irregularities of the actions and distributions of organisms, but few, if any, have survived careful scrutiny (McIntosh 1980a).

If there was a missed opportunity to develop an integrated science of animal ecology it was surely that no school of ecology seized on the polymathic work of S. A. Forbes (Howard 1932; Egerton 1976). Forbes was, perhaps, closer to the "compleat" ecologist than any figure of the 19th century. He examined terrestrial as well as aquatic organisms and ranged widely over the major taxonomic groups. More notable were his keen insights into salient ecological problems and methods. His most cited paper (Forbes 1887), "The Lake as a Microcosm," was described by Hutchinson (1963) as "the first important theoretical ecological construct to develop in American limnology. The idea has become a guiding principle of limnologists ever since."

Forbes first advanced education consisted of one antebellum year (1860) at Beloit Academy and an unfinished course (1866-7) at Rush Medical School in Chicago. Forbes discontinued his medical training when his savings from his service in the Civil War were exhausted and he left college and turned to teaching. He later studied one year (1871) at Illinois State Normal University. He pursued his interest in natural history, however, and became sufficiently known so that when the famous naturalist-explorer J. W. Powell resigned, in 1872, as curator of the Museum of the State Natural History Society, Forbes succeeded him. Forbes earliest published papers were largely pedagogical, but in 1877 he turned his attention to food of birds and fishes and to the relationships of organisms. These studies are full of shrewd insights, many anticipating ideas which reappeared much later. The relation of morphology and behavior to feeding or what came to be called resource partitioning is clearly stated in his early fish studies. He commented on competition between birds and fishes, recognizing what later came to be known as *diffuse competition*—common use of a resource by quite unrelated organisms. A dramatic example of his insight is seen in his article "On Some Interactions of Organisms" (1880a), which stated some prescient ideas concerning the relations of organisms in communities and provided some maxims concerning their study. Forbes anticipated ideas of competitive exclusion, population oscillation, and predator-prey interactions, among other concerns of later ecologists. Forbes noted the inadequacy of inductive approaches to ecology, traveling, as he said, by the "a priori road," and he urged the need for exhaustive inquiry. Forbes wrote:

> Reasoning unwarranted by facts, and facts not correctly, and sufficiently reasoned out, are equally worthless and dangerous for practical use. (Forbes 1880a)

Forbes himself, and the Natural History Survey he directed, gathered facts using quantitative sampling methods well before such methods characterized terrestrial ecology. If botanists were ahead of zoologists in ecology, as commonly asserted, Forbes was clearly an exception. He postulated "as an accepted Law of Nature" that "the rate of reproduction is in inverse ratio to the grade of individual development and activity." This concept, which he attributed to Herbert Spencer, sounds like an ancient version of the current rationale of "allocation of resources." In addition to assembling voluminous statistical data, Forbes (1907a) developed one of the first statistical methods of showing relationships between species and between species and environment, an approach not explored in ecology until the 1920s.

A most surprising aspect of early animal ecology was the virtual exclusion of the intrinsically ecological study of parasitology from ecology. The role of insects as vectors of disease was clearly established in the last decades of the 19th century, and their importance to agriculture and human health were patent. Students of insect parasites made notable contributions to ecological concepts. However, parasitology as a discipline went its own way. Kennedy (1976) commented:

> The realization that it [parasitology] could be approached from an ecological standpoint initially grew slowly, but now, largely as a result of the pioneer studies of V. A. Dogiel and his colleagues, is widely accepted, to the extent that many people consider parasitology as only a special branch of ecology.

The Dogiel references cited were from the 1960s. It is not clear what turned parasitology from its apparently natural affinity with ecology. Certainly ecologists have done little to remedy the breach, for their attention to interspecific relations has been almost entirely directed at competition and predation; references to parasites and parasitism in ecological texts, for example, are rare. It may be that a reconciliation is in the offing. Gross (1982) wrote:

> Now parasitology is once again a frontier subject. . . . This is not so much because it lies at the useful edge of molecular biology, but because it lies between molecular biology and the extended research of modern ecology.

## The institutionalization of ecology

Institutionalization in the format of the science of the late 19th and 20th centuries followed soon after the crystallization of self-conscious ecology. The British Vegetation Committee, which had been founded to further the survey of British vegetation, moved to establish a British Ecological Society (BES) in 1912. It was formally organized on 12 April 1913, and the first issue of its first publication, the *Journal of Ecology,* was printed in time for its first meeting. Arthur Tansley, its first president, was elected as fellow of the Royal Society in 1915, although he was not appointed to a university chair until 1927 (Tansley 1947; Godwin 1977). Evans (1976) makes the point that Tansley's presidential address to the society in 1914 was the first presidential address ever given to any ecological society. Although Tansley (1947) wrote that the intention was that the society and journal "should include animal ecology," both were dominated by plant ecologists in the early years. The first animal ecologist to serve as president was A. E. Boycott in 1929. Charles Elton was president in 1932, and in 1933 he established the *Journal of Animal Ecology,* a segregation which continues to the present. World War I slowed the growth of ecology and the BES. In 1918 the Society had 114 members. After the war, ecology, the society, and its journals prospered. By 1932 the members numbered 250, a surprisingly small group for the quality and quantity of ecological work produced. By 1914 American ecologists decided the time was ripe to establish an Ecological Society of America (ESA), which they did in 1915 (Cowles 1915; Ecological Society of America 1916; Shelford 1917; Burgess 1977). Charter members of the ESA ranged from Charles Adams, an animal ecologist, to Raphael Zon, then chief of investigations of the U.S. Forest Service. Approximately equal numbers of the 307 charter members described themselves as interested in plant ecology (88) or animal ecology (86). Applied ecology was represented by foresters (43), entomologists (39), and agriculturists (12). Marine ecology was the major interest of 14, but no one classified their major interest as limnology, although E. A. Birge, Chancey Juday, and Charles Kofoid were among those listed. Only three parasitologists were included. The first president of the society was the zoologist Victor Shelford, and the first vice-president was the entomologist W. M. Wheeler. The second president was the noted climatologist and human ecologist Ellsworth Huntington, but human ecology and sociology did not develop as a substantial part of American ecology (Dogan and Rokkan 1969). Fuchs (1967), however, described ecological theory developing in geography in this period, 1900–30. For many years, the initial mix of animal and plant ecologists was incorporated in a tradition of alternating a zoologist and botanist as president of the society. The Oceanographic Society of the Pacific was not established until 1935, nor the Limnological Society of America until 1936. These merged in 1948 to form the American Society of Limnology and Oceanography (Lauff 1963), and its journal, *Limnology and Oceanography,* began publication in 1956. Although the leadership and membership of the Ecological Society of America and the Society of Limnology and Oceanography overlapped extensively, the institutionalization of the traditional habitat distinction of ecology inhibits interchange.

Self-conscious ecology implies formation of an image among a group of biologists of a distinctive scientific activity and a community of scientists who share some level of interest. This clearly occurred in the last decade of the 19th century and the first decade of the 20th. The concept, current among sociologists and historians of science, of the scientific community as the basis of scientific activity poses the problem of the emergence of scientific disciplines (Lemaine et al. 1977). The 1960s and 1970s saw the development of a historical view (Kuhn 1970) and a sociological view (Crane 1972) of how a science or scientific specialty develops. Commentaries on ecology have recently become liberally sprinkled with "paradigm," but only very loosely applied in the sense of Kuhn (Woodwell 1976; Regier and Rapport 1978; McIntosh 1980a; Simberloff 1980). Much more detailed study of the emergence of ecology will be required to determine which, if any, of these conceptions of the rise of scientific disciplines provide a best fit. About the only detailed effort to apply either approach to ecology is Tobey's (1981) consideration of the rise of grassland ecology, or the Clementsian school at Nebraska. This is a limited part of the crystallization of plant ecology, and there is no intention of considering these ideas in detail here as applied to ecology at large. The present effort is primarily directed at developing a narrative history of the several aspects of ecology as they converged on the concepts, questions, theories, or possibly "invisible colleges" or "paradigms" which brought them into the loose amalgam of activities now called ecology.

It is not entirely clear when a science, such as ecology, may be said to have metamorphosed from a developmental stage, such as natural history, or from an established discipline, such as physiology, or when it becomes "modern" or "mature." What seems clear is that the succession of 19th-century biology in the guise of physiology as described by Coleman (1977) did not produce a biology which was synonymous with physiology, as hoped by Clements and Cowles. Physiology "budded," in good biological parlance, and in part produced ecology. Although laboratory and experimental biology, as Cravens (1978) noted, secured the best and most university appointments, dominated the leading scientific societies and journals, controlled the major research institutes, and got the bulk of limelight, prestige, and glory, it was not, in the view of some biologists, getting all the job done. In fact, it was evading many of the most significant biological questions. The oversight called forth ecology. Drude (1906) stated the basis of ecology in surprisingly modern rhetoric:

> Ecology has arisen from the need to unite originally separate branches of science in a new and natural doctrine; it is characterized by the breadth of its aims, and its peculiar power and strength in its ability to unite knowledge of organic life with knowledge of its home, our earth. It assumes the solution of that most difficult as well as most fascinating problem which occupies the minds of philosophers and theologians alike, namely, the life history of the plant and animal worlds under the influences of space and time.

# 3

# Dynamic ecology

The 18th century produced at least the beginning of a change in natural history from a view of nature as a divinely ordered, essentially static system following a providential mandate to a dynamic "historically changing" entity endowed with "self-activating" and "self-realizing" powers (Lyon and Sloan 1981). This conception of natural history persisted in the early 19th century in "Humboldtian science" (Cannon 1978). Its canon of "accurate measured study of widespread but interconnected phenomena . . . to find a definite law and a dynamical cause" was continued by the rising science of ecology in the late 19th century. A major theme of functional, experimental biology as it developed in the 19th century was its emphasis on progressive change as the most significant characteristic of natural phenomena (Coleman 1977). Whether ecology is seen as emerging from 18th- or 19th-century natural history, from 19th-century mechanistic physiology, or some amalgam of these, the conception sometimes encountered of early self-conscious ecology as descending from and embodying a static, typological, descriptive progenitor needs to be reconsidered. Certainly in the view of most of its early proponents and practitioners, the key word for ecology was *dynamic*. This was explicit in the writings of the leading figures of ecology as it became a self-conscious science. If they or lesser ecologists failed immediately to emphasize all of the ideas that later came to typify the "new" dynamic or functional ecology, it should not be assumed that first-generation ecologists were content with description as the aim of ecology.

Traditional natural history had as a central theme the concept of balance of nature, of things interconnected to preserve an order, which for centuries had been described in Western thought as divinely ordained. Randomness and extinction were not usually considered possibilities (Lovejoy 1936; McIntosh 1960; Glacken 1967; Egerton 1973), and variation and change were largely ignored. The somewhat waggish current statement about ecology as being everything connected to everything else was specifically stated by Richard Bradley in 1721:

> All Bodies have some Dependance upon one another; and . . . every distinct Part of Nature's works is necessary for the Support of the rest; and . . . if any one was wanting all the rest must consequently be out of Order. (Quoted in Egerton 1973)

Egerton specified that the traditional balance-of-nature concept assumed approximate stability of populations in a similarly stable environment. The concept of balance of nature or economy of nature incorporated the three distinct theoretical viewpoints which came to characterize ecology – population ecology, community ecology, and systems ecology (Cittadino 1981).

Speculation about populations and reproduction began in antiquity. Aristotle was concerned with the number of offspring required to maintain a population and the relation between number of offspring and size of organism (Egerton 1973). References to population phenomena dot the natural history literature before the 19th century, but the clearest statements on population antedating, and influencing, protoecology are those of Thomas Malthus at the end of the 18th century (Hutchinson 1978). Malthus suggested that human populations are limited by natural checks, and it was this idea which provided Charles Darwin with "a theory by which to work" (Barlow 1958) and led Alfred Russell Wallace to the same theory. Struggle for existence, natural selection, and their evolutionary implications were clearly a stimulus for many biologists who were the founders of ecology. Harper (1967) stated unequivocally, in retrospect, that Darwin's theory of natural selection is an ecological theory. Malthus's emphasis was on the relation of population growth to availability of a resource, food supply, a current ecological theme. Darwin's ideas on competition and resulting mortality as the basis of natural selection are commonly cited as his major contribution to stimulating ecological thought.

That populations of organisms are members of aggregations of different kinds of organisms and influenced by these, as well as by the physical environment, was also familiar to early 19th-century naturalists. Coleman (1977:68) quoted Lyell as writing in 1832:

> The possibility of the existence of a certain species in a given locality or of its thriving more or less therein, is determined not merely by temperature, humidity, soil, elevation or other circumstances of the like kind, but also by the existence or non-existence, the abundance or scarcity of a particular assemblage of other plants and animals in the same region.

The change of aggregations of plants and animals from place to place, and the reasons thereof, had been the concern of many 19th-century biogeographers following the example and precept of Humboldt and A. P. DeCandolle. That communities also changed temporally, sometimes in dramatic ways, had been noted by biogeographers and naturalists, among them Wallace. Nevertheless, the concept of nature as essentially stable, or balanced, and of species populations as forming assemblages or communities which functioned as orderly integrated units to establish and maintain an equilibrium was nearly universal in the 19th century. Darwin wrote "In the long-run the forces are so nicely balanced that the face of nature remains uniform for long periods of time" (quoted by Stauffer 1957).

**Early community and equilibrium concepts**

Möbius's (1877) definition of his neologism *biocœnosis* as a community incorporated this equilibrium concept, describing each area of a biocenosis as supporting a "certain quantum of life which enters into a certain number of individuals." Favorable conditions, he added, might produce an excessive number of offspring, but since space and food were limited, "the sum of individuals in the community soon returned to its former mean," a theme reminiscent of Malthus's propositions concerning human populations and their limitation by resources. Decrease in the number of one species, Möbius wrote, would be compensated by increase in the numbers of another, because "every biocœnotic territory has during each period of generation the highest measure of life which can be produced and maintained there," an idea rediscovered by recent theoretical ecologists. Möbius noted that yield or productivity of an area was increased by augmenting natural forces with human labor, not only directly by tillers of the soil but indirectly by "mechanics and opticians" who enhanced the efforts of the tillers. Such augmentation, he said, was necessary to maintain artificial communities, created by human energies, against the tendency of nature to restore its own communities. Möbius described changes in communities as precipitated by human disturbance even leading to extinction of species. Mills (1969) questioned whether Möbius stated a concept of community homeostasis, but Möbius wrote that in any territory, "all the organic material which is there ready to be assimilated will be entirely used up by the beings which are procreated in each such area." Möbius's conceptualization, or verbal model, of a community was criticized by Dean (1893) as erroneous in its assumption that the community was limited by food supply – "resource-limited," in current parlance (Hedgpeth 1977). Thus, shortly after a formal name was devised for community, the questions of the community as open or closed, in equilibrium or nonequilibrium, surfaced. These questions permeated the beginnings of ecology and persist as the crux of disputes about current theory of community ecology (Wiens 1977; Caswell 1982a; Schoener 1982).

Interactions between plants and animals, and the consequences for communities, were not unfamiliar to naturalists or to late 19th-century biologists who were not yet self-conscious ecologists. One of these was the zoologist Semper (1881) whose book *Animal Life as Affected by the Natural Conditions of Existence* was, as later ecologists recognized, an early treatise on animal ecology, although Semper did not mention ecology. He did explicitly state concepts, later to be formalized and named *food chain* and *pyramid of numbers* (Shelford 1913; Elton 1927). He also provided a quantitative statement of a much later hypothesis of a 10 percent transfer between trophic levels, although attempts to formalize, much less test, this hypothesis did not eventuate until the 1960s and 1970s. Semper anticipated the need for hypothesis testing. He commented on the extensive influence of Darwinian theory on biology, but said that there had already been enough philosophizing by Darwinists and that it was "time to apply the test of exact investigation to the hypothesis we had laid down." Semper wrote of the earth and of food relations among the organisms of an area:

> We know that its surface – dry land as well as land covered with water – is capable of producing only a certain limited number of plants depending on the conditions of the locality. Assuming then that a given number of plants – the maximum number being present at the time – offered, let us say, a thousand units of food to these two classes of animals, the carnivorous and herbivorous species would not be able to have an equal share of the space or the food it would afford. The flesh-eaters would only obtain food from the soil indirectly through the plant eaters. Now the transmutation of the nutriment derived from the plants into the flesh of the plant-eaters is inseparable from a certain loss in the whole mass, since the oxidation of a certain amount of the organic constituents is necessary for the production of animal heat and for the movement and due use of all the functions of the body. Now we will

assume – arbitrarily – that the proportion of the whole mass of plants produced by the soil is to the animals which can subsist on them – converting them into animal tissue as ten to one; then, in the area we have assumed, only 100 units of feeders – individual herbivous animals – can live on 1,000 units of plant food. The maximum of nourishment, then, which exists for monophagous carnivorous animals, can amount only to 100 units. In the transmutation of these 100 units of food in the organs of the Carnivora a considerable loss will be incurred; organic matter will be consumed, the indigestible portions, as hairs, hoofs, and horns, will be ejected, and if the proportions were such that ten units of animal food could suffice only for one unit of the animal body, the maximum of food as supplied by 100 herbivorous animals would enable 10 carnivora at most to exist. Thus the same area can never produce and maintain so large a number of carnivorous as of herbivorous animals, an inference which is perfectly confirmed by the facts. It is well known that the number of Herbivora is much greater than that of Carnivora. (Semper 1881:33)

Semper's trophic conception of the community, and his own philosophical bias, were explicit in what he described as "universal physiology." Semper shared the organismic view of the community with most of his contemporaries, and he anticipated Clements's famous organismic analogy by comparing species to the organs of individual animals in forming "a vast organism" which has its own "embryology" and "functions." According to Semper (1881:33), the organismic community was characterized by different species which "are interdependent by the most various physiological relations, like the organs of a healthy living organism." Semper's speculative arithmetic model of the trophic organization or structure of a community was not seized on by contemporary zoologists. The basic ecological concepts of food chain and pyramids of number, biomass, or energy were not more explicitly developed until Shelford (1913), Lotka (1925), and Elton (1927) made them the essence of animal ecology. The detailed concepts of trophic structure, or "trophic aspect" as Lindeman (1942) called it, and particularly efforts to quantify it, were largely the work of marine and freshwater biologists. Semper's crude 10 percent guess came to be called much later, and equally crudely, the 10 percent hypothesis or even 10 percent law, only to fail when put, as he had suggested, to the test because the actual figures diverged greatly from 10 percent (Slobodkin 1972; McIntosh 1980a).

The genius of S. A. Forbes was evident in his article "On Some Interactions of Organisms" (Forbes 1880a). In it, he distinguished between structural and functional relations of living organisms and, like Semper, extended this analogy to the relationships among species. Forbes explicitly reiterated the long tradition of balance of nature, and he joined most contemporary biologists, notably George Perkins Marsh, in attributing disturbance of the balance of nature to the activities of humans. Forbes wrote:

> There is a general consent that primeval nature, as in the uninhabited forest or the untilled plain, presents a settled harmony of interaction among organic groups which is in strong contrast with the many serious maladjustments of plants and animals found in countries occupied by man.

Forbes saw, even in the turmoil and struggle evident in nature, beneficent laws and forces at work tending toward a "healthful" and "just equilibrium." He described, in perceptive detail, an effective system of checks and balances restricting oscillations in populations. Herbivores and predators, he said, exercised prudent self-interest in maintaining populations of the organisms they exploited. The ideal balance was maintaind by food-producing species furnishing just the "required amount of food" and predatory species using only enough to avoid depleting the resource. This adjustment, he acknowledged, is not perfect, but the inevitable oscillations are kept within bounds by natural forces. In Forbes's nature, predator and prey had identical interests promoted by Darwinian natural selection. Natural selection, he said, also operated to enforce diversification of food or habitat use to assist species in maintaining stable populations, a concept anticipating a major theoretical dispute nearly a century later (Goodman 1975). Forbes (1887) wrote:

> While small fishes of all sorts are evidently competitors for food, this competition is relieved to some extent by differences in the breeding season, the species dropping in successively to the banquet.

Unlike most of his contemporaries, zoologist or botanist, Forbes was prone to seek quantitative evidence concerning his ideas. He examined feeding habits of insects, birds, and fishes in respect to their effect on regulation of populations. Forbes (1883a) examined the regulative action of birds on insect populations, posing three specific questions: (1) Does feeding of birds originate oscillation of insect populations? (2)

Does feeding of birds prevent or restrain oscillation of insect populations? (3) Do birds switch to superabundant insects and reduce their excessive numbers? He addressed the last question, noting that many species of birds congregated and fed on cankerworms when they were superabundant while reducing their use of all other insects. Forbes was an early proponent of the importance of predation in controlling population growth, and he recognized the distinction between opportunist and generalist feeders. He was aware of two forces, competition and predation, which subsequent schools of ecologists urged as operating, singly or together, to regulate populations.

Long before he wrote his widely cited "Lake as a Microcosm" (Forbes 1887), Forbes described a lake as functioning as an organic unit and urged biologists not to stop with lists and descriptions but to "direct principal attention to the laws of its activity." Like most 19th-century biologists, Forbes accepted the precepts of organismic biology variously advocated by philosophers, sociologists, and biologists (Haraway 1976). He joined Semper (1881) and his younger botanical contemporary Clements (1905) in applying the analogy of organism to community:

> A group or association of animals or plants is like a single organism in the fact that it brings to bear upon the outer world only the surplus of forces remaining after all conflicts interior to itself have been adjusted. (Forbes 1883b)

He anticipated later usage by specifying energy relations of the community as a critical concern. The emphasis on the "economical balance of supply and demand, of income and expenditure . . . among the inhabitants" (Forbes 1883a) permeated Forbes's writing well before he summarized these ideas in "The Lake as a Microcosm." Forbes's holistic, organismic, and equilibrium concept of nature was evident as he described a lake:

> One finds in a single body of water a far more complete and independent equilibrium of organic life and activity than in any equal body of land. It forms a little world within itself – a microcosm within which all the elemental forces are at work. (Forbes 1880b)

Hutchinson (1944) recognized two contrasting themes in early ecology: the "holological," which was the omnipresent organismic conception of the community of the late 19th century, and the "merological," which was the tendency to examine the parts and build the community from these, basically a reductionist approach. He described Forbes as expounding the latter, although, as the above suggests, Forbes was firmly in the hological camp. Whatever his philosophical bias, Forbes did attend to the inner details and workings of both terrestrial and aquatic communities. In an era when most field naturalists were innumerate, Forbes was among those actively sampling and counting the numbers of organisms of diverse types and examining in detail what they ate (Forbes 1880b, 1883a,b). Forbes emphasized population regulation and the dynamic nature of community in his diverse studies; and he wrote that studies of individual species "are merely preliminary to a general study of the dynamic system of organic life as exhibited in its larger and more complex units" (Forbes 1909).

## Dynamic plant ecology

Although plant ecologists have sometimes been stereotyped as being concerned only with static descriptions of plant communities, early plant ecologists were, in fact, much concerned with function, process, change, and dynamics of vegetation. Warming (1895), a major stimulus to plant ecology in Britain and America, wrote that plant communities were not static or in equilibrium but that an unceasing struggle was going on within and between them; any equilibrium was disturbed by changes in physical conditions, changes induced by animals or fungi, and struggles among the plant species. He wrote rhetorically, "Situation wanted is the cry in all communities," and he credited Darwin and, before him, A. P. DeCandolle for directing attention to this struggle and competition.

Nowhere in the formative years of self-conscious ecology was the emphasis on dynamic ecology more explicit than in the writings of F. E. Clements – it became his trademark. Clements (1905) deplored the "chaotic and unsystematized" state of ecology and set about remedying it. In his earliest work with Pound (Pound and Clements 1898a,b) they had followed the largely phytogeographical model of Oscar Drude. Drude (1906) asserted that the communal life of species was an "everpresent dynamical factor" in the changing appearance of the earth. Clements (1904, 1905, 1920) seized on Drude's view of vegetation and became the major exponent of the dynamic view of the plant community. Tobey (1976, 1981) described Clements's dynamic ecology as a profound shift from static biogeography and attributed it to the technological demands of developing agriculture in the American grassland. Clements (1905) formalized much of his influential thought in *Research Methods in Ecology,* which was as much an exposition of general theory or world view of ecology as it was of methods. He emphasized the need to merge ecology and physiology methodologically and stressed the importance of function. He also enlarged on what he described as "a new concept of vegetation," "a complex organism," with structures and functions susceptible of exact methods of study just as physiology studied individual organisms, their parts and functions. Although Clements's organismic concept of community was a metaphor he shared with many predecessors and contemporary biologists, such as K. Semper and S. A. Forbes, he and some of his supporters (Phillips 1934–5) applied it to ecology in such extreme and explicit detail that some later ecologists believed that the organismic concept of communities originated with Clements – as he himself apparently believed. Clements's ideas achieved considerable currency in Britain and America but were not accepted on the Continent. Nevertheless, his concepts of community, formation, and association were inextricably linked with his concepts of succession as a process of progressive change and constituted what he called "dynamic ecology" (Clements 1916, 1935). Clements's ideas are notably resilient and persist, often under different names.

Clements and other ecologists in the early 20th century decried what they called "descriptive" ecology, meaning the verbal descriptions of vegetation, often accompanied only by species lists. Clements wrote of such descriptive ecology that no method can "yield results farther from the truth." Dynamic ecology was, in Clements's conception, quantitative, concerned with changes in time of communities, the populations of which they were composed, and the sites they occupied. The handful of plant ecologists then working were overwhelmed by the magnitude of even the straightforward description of the earth's vegetation. It should be noted that this task is still going on apace, both verbally and quantitatively, in spite of the fact that the zoologist Orlando Park (1941) had said it was "largely accomplished." Ironically, later critics of descriptive plant community ecology derogated the extensive quantitative studies of plant communities which proliferated in the early decades of the 20th century, following Clements's quantitative precepts. These quantitative studies, in their turn, were often criticized as static, as mere descriptions, and for their presumed failure to develop proper scientific hypotheses or theories about what communities were, how they came to be, or how they changed. The failure of plant ecologists to deal adequately with populations and the inadequacy of some plant community studies to treat effectively the dynamic aspects, which were urged by Clements and many others, were often pointed out by animal ecologists, who had turned largely to studies of populations, leaving terrestrial community problems largely to plant ecologists (McIntosh 1976, 1980a). Animal ecologists returned to consideration of community, especially the theory thereof, with much fanfare in the 1950s and with much the same emphasis on quantitative sampling and description which characterized early plant community studies. The necessity of effective, especially quantitative, description of the distribution and change of population and communities was correctly seen by Clements, Raunkaier, and other early ecologists. That they and their immediate successors failed to resolve these problems is not grounds for the sniffy criticisms of mere description sometimes encountered. Simple solutions are commonly frustrated by continuing failure to adequately describe ecological phenomena as they occur in nature.

Clements (1905), in his concept of dynamic ecology, urged not solely description of vegetation, its distribution, and classification, but studies of changes in vegetation and explanations of these as a result of a dynamic process. To Clements, vegetation and habitat have "precisely the relation that exists between cause and effect"; but he added that "neither plant nor formation is altogether the effect of its present habitat." A third element, he said, must always be considered, namely the "historical fact." He shared the belief in the significance of history with most ecologists. Clements was the most explicitly philosophical and historical thinker of the early plant ecologists. He urged an "inductive procedure" based on facts but using these to test and reject hypotheses in the method of "multiple working hypotheses." He perhaps had read T. C. Chamberlain's (1890) article on multiple working hypotheses, and he anticipated latter-day ecologists who became devotees of Karl Popper in recommending "elimination of those that prove inadequate." Clements's grand theory of vegetation and its cause was predicated on a concept of vegetation which required effective measure of the cause, which he regarded as the climate and its effect on the vegetational formation. He sought effective means of describing the latter to accompany the better-established means of describing habitat.

Tobey (1981) described the adoption of the quadrat to sample vegetation by Pound and Clements (1898a) as the basis of "the leap to numerical quantification in ecology." The major transition between

Pound and Clements's *Phytogeography of Nebraska* (1898b) and Clements's *Research Methods* (1905) was, Tobey argued, the recognition that description based on direct sensory impressions of vegetation or simple floristic lists was inadequate; counting numbers of individuals was essential to distinguishing plant formations and the boundaries between them. With the introduction of sampling methods, plant ecology became inextricably involved with the populations comprising a community, changes in populations, and the reasons for the observed changes. Clements's interest in dynamic ecology is apparent in that of several uses of the quadrat method the most important, he said, were the "chart" quadrat, on which positions of individuals were marked, the "permanent" quadrat, which could be examined repeatedly, and the "denuded" quadrat, from which all vegetation was removed and subsequent regrowth followed. The crux of all of these was that they were designed to examine and follow change in vegetation, not only to report the status quo.

The key to Clements's concept of vegetation was *change*, which included coincident developmental changes of both vegetational formation and habitat. Clements (1905) distinguished three functions of a formation – association, invasion, and succession. Unfortunately, he used *association* both as a verb and as a noun, specifying the former as the process of grouping or aggregating, the latter as the resultant state or community. *Association* in Clements's lexicon was *climax. Invasion,* he said, was any movement of plants into a different area and their successful "colonization" of the area. *Succession* was a series of invasions of sufficient magnitude and persistence to bring about the "decrease or disappearance of the original occupants." Clements had a facility for covering all eventualities. For example, in 1905 he wrote, "Complete and permanent invasion . . . regularly produces successions, except in the rare cases where a stable formation entirely replaces a less stable one without the intervention of other stages" (Clements 1905). In his magum opus *Succession* (Clements 1916) he described a "universal law" that "all bare places give rise to new communities except those which present the most extreme conditions of water, temperature, light, or soil." In either case, "except" could be followed by the phrase "where it does not" with equal validity. Cain (1939) observed that Clementsian philosophy, principles, and terminology "meet nearly every exigency," and careful reading of the Clementsian corpus bears this out. Clements's voluminous writings, labyrinthine logic, and proliferation of terminology, characterized as "chronic logorrhea" (Cox 1979), produced, nevertheless, the major synthesis of most early 20th-century ecology. Tansley (1935), Clements's peer in British plant ecology, wrote: "Dr. Clements has given us a theory of vegetation which has formed an indispensable foundation for the most fruitful modern work." Although few, if any, ecologists today would admit to being Clementsian, and one historian (Tobey 1981) described Clements's theory as being in "disarray," Clements retains the dubious merit of being the "fall guy" of many current ecologists (Allen 1981). Clements's ideas and terminology changed during his long professional career as an ecologist (ca. 1895-1945) and underwent even more change in the hands of his interpreters and critics. Some of his suspect ideas persist in the new ecology under new rubrics (McIntosh 1980a,b).

The essence of Clementsian theory of vegetation was that the plant formation was a "complex organism" and, like an individual organism, it changed not in haphazard ways but by progressive development (Tansley 1920, 1929). Vegetation was, he said, "essentially dynamic"; *static* was an unusual term in Clements's lexicon, since "development" was the essence of vegetation. Clements and some other plant ecologists used the term *development* as inclusive of, or synonymous with, *succession.* Later ecologists sometimes seized on *development* as an out to avoid the presumably rigid deterministic connotations of *succession,* especially in its Clementsian sense, but etymologically *development* is an unfortunate choice, particularly for biologists. It would be folly to venture into the subtleties of meaning attached to many terms widely used in ecology. A traditional problem of ecology has been that ecologists, like Lewis Carroll's Humpty Dumpty, often used a word to mean just what they chose it to mean with little regard for what others said it meant. This tendency has not disappeared.

The dynamic process of progressive development of the formation, was, according to Clements, "succession." This included evolution of the component species which, in Clements's Lamarckian views, were directly molded by the environment. Later plant ecologists generally excluded evolutionary changes as beyond the time scale of succession; but more recent plant ecologists have shortened the time scale of evolutionary change so that the distinction is no longer clear (Bradshaw 1972). Plant succession in Clements's theory was initiated by invasion and successful colonization of bare areas and by "reaction," the effect of the developing formation on the habitat, and "coaction," the interactions of the colonizing species among themselves, particularly competition (Clements 1916). Later critics of Clements and of other early plant ecologists commonly failed to recognize that much of the early explication of succession was based on primary succession, in which the formation was developing on newly formed bare areas unaffected by previous occupants (McIntosh 1980b). Reoccupation of disturbed sites, secondary succession, was acknowledgedly different, in many respects, depending on the nature, intensity, area, and frequency of the disturbance. Secondary succession started at different stages, and the resultant sere was, as Clements stated, shorter and different from primary succession. Clements assumed that the earliest occupants, or pioneer stages, of a sere reacted on the habitat in such a way as to make it less favorable for themselves and more favorable for successive invaders of later seral stages. The universal tendency of the vegetation in a uniform climatic area was to converge from diverse bare areas, rock, sand, mud, or open water to a "climax" stage which was controlled or "caused" by the climate. The climax "association" (*climax* being redundant in Clements's usage) was, barring external disturbance, a stable and self-reproducing collection of populations which, in Clements's scheme, was the culmination of the developmental sequence and formed a superorganism inclusive of the developmental sequences, or seres, from which it came. Some early critics of Clements's superorganismic community as being homologous with an individual organism pointed out the anomaly of an adult organism which had multiple embryonic stages from different starting points and lacked a genetic basis, but superorganisms are not easily killed by mere logic.

Although Clements and other plant ecologists concentrated on the plant community, they explicitly noted changes in the habitat associated with succession, such as accumulation of organic matter, changes in water supply, light, and availability of nutrients, and regarded these as induced by organisms and, in turn, affecting organisms. They also recognized the effect of animals in initiating or inhibiting plant succession or in maintaining stable, but not climax, communities. To this extent they were concerned with the larger system transcending plants, or even living organisms, anticipating ecosystem ecology. Clements, Tansley, and other early plant ecologists distinguished between "open" and "closed" communities to describe not only the availability of space in the former but also closure or resistance to invasion by additional species due to limited resources. According to Clements (1936), "A plant community cannot be regarded as completely closed until all levels for abstracting water, minerals, light and air are filled with sets of species of dissimilar habitats and requirements." Open communities were incomplete, unstable, and heterogeneous, closed communities more uniform and stable. Tansley (1923) described "open" communities restricted by an environmental factor such as "available water" as being in "stable equilibrium," even though open space was available. If water were added, more plants could enter.

The entire premise of Clements's dynamic ecology was that the "seral stages" of a series of populations or groups of populations followed in sequence. In his earlier expositions, at least, stabilization was described as unusual. Pound and Clements (1898b, cf. 1900:313) wrote, "In nature both formations and subordinate groups are in stable equilibrium only rarely and usually for a comparatively short time." Later, in Weaver and Clements (1938), the impression was given that extensive areas of the landscape were in a climax state in the absence of human disturbance. This was in the tradition of 19th-century ideas about the balance of nature. The degree to which the vegetation of an area reaches a relatively stable or equilibrium state, Clements's "climax," was and is a subject of dispute among ecologists (Cairns 1980; West, Shugart, and Botkin 1981).

Although some recent commentators on community ecology and succession unwarrantedly impute homogeneity to early plant ecologists, many early plant ecologists did not believe what came to be called the Clementsian dogmas which are still attacked as if they represent all plant ecology. H. C. Cowles, Cowles's student W. S. Cooper, H. A. Gleason, and Forrest Shreve, among American plant ecologists, and Arthur Tansley, the leading British plant ecologist, and practically all Continental European plant ecologists rejected much of Clements's thought. Tobey (1981) traced the rise and presumed fall of Clementsian ecology in grassland ecology. In the United States, however, Clementsian ideas came to dominate the major textbooks of plant ecology prior to 1950 (Egler 1951). The Clementsian emphasis on succession and organismic community also permeated major animal ecology textbooks, such as Allee et al. (1949) and Odum (1953), and even, much later, the "green version" of a textbook for high school designed to upgrade science education following *Sputnik* (Biological Science Curriculum Study 1963). Ghiselin (1981) commented that the organismic concept persists in ecology because it has aspects of romanticism, even of mysticism, and that ecologists possessing these "share an unwillingness to see natural occurrences, and especially biotic communities, as they are rather than as the observer wishes." Clementsian, organismic, holistic ecology has an orderly neatness which makes it pedagogically useful, even though much of it was widely criticized at the research level. Whatever the explanation, 19th-century organismic concepts of community, whether derived from Clements or others, persist in current ecology (McIntosh 1976, 1980a,b; Simberloff 1980).

The Clementsian doctrine of a progressive trend toward a climax and stable state under the control of the climate was specifically denied by some early ecologists. Clements's contemporary at the Desert Laboratory of the Carnegie Institution, Forrest Shreve, had little use for Clements's ideas on organismic community or succession. He emphasized the individualistic behavior of species and the variability of association with other species, anticipating the similar view of Gleason (McIntosh 1975a, 1983a). Shreve (1914) denied Clements's concept of climax, writing:

> No one of the types can emerge from its own habitat and under no possible physiographic change of the region can any one of these habitats come to occupy all or even a preponderant part, of the region.

H. C. Cowles, the founder of "physiographic ecology" at the University of Chicago, agreed with Clements on the significance of physiology for ecology and that it must be dynamic. Cowles (1901) commented that ecology is the study of the origins and development of vegetation as well as classification and description—"a classification to be true must be genetic and dynamic," that is, based on succession. He recognized an analogy between the dynamic changes of topography and climate and change in vegetation which was equally dynamic, although he noted that change in vegetation was more rapid than either climatic or topographic changes, which could be regarded as relatively static. Cowles, like Clements, rested his conception of vegetation upon succession. He differed in saying that "a condition of equilibrium is never reached." Cowles (1901) wrote, "Succession is not a straight-line process. Its stages may be slow or rapid, direct or tortuous and often they are retrogressive." Cowles described succession as a "variable approaching a variable rather than a constant." However, he agreed with Clements that change must be strongly emphasized and that not only is a plant community the product of present conditions but that the past was also involved. Tansley (1920, 1929, 1935), although he recognized Clements's contribution to succession, did not accept Clements's organismic concept of the community. He went only as far as "quasi-organism" and became impatient with extreme Clementsian views, notably as expressed by J. F. V. Phillips (1934–5). W. S. Cooper, a student of Cowles and notably influential in American ecology as the mentor of H. J. Oosting and R. Daubenmire, the authors of major American textbooks of plant ecology, was also an advocate of dynamic ecology. In his famous study of the forests of Isle Royale, Cooper described an equilibrium which, he said, was based on a thorough investigation of the dynamics of the forest (Cooper 1913). He departed from Clements's concept of a linear succession and provided a more complex metaphor of a "braided stream." Cooper described a climax of a very different sort from that of Clements. Cooper had sampled stands, mapped the trees on them, and aged them by means of ring counts. Contrary to the common image of the community as essentially homogeneous, Cooper's forest was, he said, a "mosaic," or patchwork, of different ages which was in a state of continuous change. As Cooper (1913) put it, "The forest as a whole remains the same, the changes in various parts balancing each other." Cooper's "mosaic" was a complex of small areal disturbances, largely windfalls, of different ages, and his explicit exposition of this phenomenon is widely unrecognized by later entrants into the lists of plant community succession.

In Britain, A. S. Watt early in his long and distinguished career recognized the same phenomena in British beech forests. He mapped the distribution of beech, ash, and other seedlings in openings in the forest canopy and followed the growth and success of the individuals which came to fill the gap (Watt 1924). Watt, happily, exemplifies the longevity of many distinguished ecologists, including Cooper, Gleason, Elton, and Sears, and he continues his productive work in ecology examining, as he said, the community as "working mechanism." He is famous as the founder of the descriptor *gap-phase* for the pattern of reproduction in a community, recognized clearly in his early work and that of Cooper, as due to small-scale disturbance in the community (Watt 1947).

Ecologists early in the 20th century recognized that most areas were in a state of flux. Some agreed with Clements that change or succession was progressive, barring interruption, and led to a large-scale regional "climax." Others argued it could be retrogressive and could terminate on specific sites for diverse local reasons. Many ecologists believed that disturbance was omnipresent and equilibrium an unlikely and ephemeral event. Diagrams of chronological sequences of species populations representing seres abounded in the literature, and some authors showed, diagramatically or numerically, changes in numbers of individuals from pioneer to climax stages (Cooper 1923). Although it was commonly asserted that "reaction" changed the habitat and competitors resulted in the replacement of earlier occupants, demonstration of actual population change was rare. A few farsighted ecologists, such as Cooper, established specific permanent quadrats which could be resurveyed at a later date; some settled for resurveying the same general area. Most ecologists selected sites representing a putative chronological sequence and inferred that the differences observed between sites were a consequence of the successional process. The nature of the process itself was much in dispute, some holding that it was substantially influenced by forces outside the vegetation (allogenic, *sensu* Tansley 1920), others that the vegetation itself produced the changes (autogenic, *sensu* Tansley). Lest one think too badly of these early ecologists, it should be noted that the exact mechanism of succession, or the direction and end of succession, are still far from settled (Connell and Slatyer 1977; Cairns 1980; West, Shugart, and Botkin 1981).

Classical descriptions of succession commonly envisioned groups of species populations arriving in sequence and rising or falling synchronously in seral stages as succession proceeded, presumably depending on arrival of appropriate species. This came to be called "relay floristics" in contrast to a concept of groups of species developing sequentially from sources already present on the site–"initial floristics" (Egler 1952–54). Neither of these concepts, as described by Egler, represents another view of succession developed early in the 20th century which held that it was, in large part, a product of variable conditions of the site and the arrival and development of individuals of a species, a process in which chance played a substantial part (Gleason 1926, 1939; McIntosh 1976, 1980a,b).

## Animal community dynamics

Although plant ecology developed essentially synchronously in Britain and America, animal ecology followed plant ecology more closely in America than in Britain. C. B. Davenport, a better-known figure in genetics and eugenics at the laboratory established by the Carnegie Institution at Cold Spring Harbor, applied himself briefly to ecology by conducting a study of the Cold Spring Sand Spit (Davenport 1903). Although a conventional description of animals at different points on the beach, it lead Davenport to some interesting generalizations:

1. The world contains numberless kinds of habitats.
2. Each organism has its own habitat consonant with its own structure.
3. Dispersal distributes organisms to better and worse habitats.
4. Those reaching a habitat for which they are better fitted will thrive and multiply – and the converse.
5. This process goes on until the organism is found primarily in suitable environments.

Davenport saw this process as a complement to natural selection in that unadaptive mutations became adaptive only if the organisms possessing them can find the proper habitat. Charles Elton later described this as "selection of the environment by the animal" (Hardy 1968). Quite independent of his evolutionary inferences, Davenport was stating some of the ideas later outlined by Gleason in developing his famous individualistic concept of the community (McIntosh 1975a). Davenport's ecological ideas had little influence on his contemporaries.

Terrestrial animal ecologists in America adopted the dynamic and successional emphasis of plant ecology although, as it developed, they gave it a different twist. Adams (1913:82) wrote in one of the earliest books explicitly devoted to animal ecology:

> The most striking advance in scientific methods of thinking during the present century will be in the direction of interpretation from the standpoint of processes – dynamically.

Adams lamented that "ecology is a science with its facts out of all proportion to their organization or integration," and he noted an "immediate need of integration." Adams acknowledged the influence of S. A. Forbes and, like Forbes, emphasized the balance-of-nature concept. He noted the need for recognizing a "biotic base" or balance toward which relations tend and at which equilibrium will be established. His ideal, as for Forbes, was the primeval condition before humans intervened and which would return if humans were removed. Adams's (1917) "new natural history," as he described ecology, was the study of "causal" relations of the animal, with emphasis on their activity and response. He extended the concept of succession from plants to birds, fish, and insects, and his pages are heavy with allusions to "change," "sequence," "development," "process," and "dynamic" processes. According to Adams, it was necessary to study an area to determine if it was in a condition of "stress," "adjustment," or "relative equilibrium," in order to determine the rate and direction it may tend to move and the conditions in which an equilibrium will become established.

Victor Shelford was a product of the early University of Chicago school of ecology and, like Adams, had later associations with S. A. Forbes at the Illinois Laboratory of Natural History. The task of organizing the data of ecology "seemed hopeless" to him (Shelford 1913). He resolved the dilemma by adopting a threefold approach, taking into account (1) the physiology of the whole organism, (2) animal behavior, and (3) comparable data of plant ecology – essentially communities. He omitted, as he said, the attendant problems of evolution and heredity; indeed, it was many years before the merger of ecology, evolution, and genetics was seriously pursued. He neatly circumvented the problem of organization by defining *ecology* "as those phases of natural history and physiology which are organized or are organizable into a science, but [it] does not include all the unorganizable data of natural history."

Shelford noted that zoologists had typically concentrated on individual organisms, a point also made by Adams; and, in his early ecological work, he took a different approach of concentrating on many species, their dependencies on one another, and their relation to the environment – in a word, communities. Like Forbes and Adams, Shelford envisioned a primeval balance of nature subject to disturbance and subsequent equilibration. Equilibrium was a balance between supply and demand, and Shelford provided some of the earliest diagrams of food chains. Balance or equilibrium, he said, was largely a matter of food supply and reciprocal fluctuations of predators and prey. For Shelford, succession was a primary aspect of change in the animal community, as in the plant community. He described communities as "systems of correlated working parts" which grew by addition of species, declined, and disappeared as the environment changed. He distinguished "geological succession," as equivalent to evolutionary change, and "seasonal succession," as *periodicity* due to seasonal changes in life cycles, from ecological succession, which he described as a succession of "mores." *Mores* were the general ecological attributes of organisms, or groups of animals, having particular ecological attributes. In spite of his early emphasis on the animal community, Shelford spent much effort on studying the physiological attributes of organisms, asserting, "If we knew the physiological life histories of a majority of animals most other ecological problems would be easy of solution" (Shelford 1913). In this he anticipated a major thrust of ecology in the 1970s which similarly sought a basis for community and succession in the life history "strategies" of species. Early plant ecologists, such as Warming and Schimper, stressed the primary significance of water. Most ecologists, however, recognized that the environment acts on organisms as a complex of factors, and Shelford emphasized that several factors can operate to control the distribution of organisms. Shelford formulated a "law of toleration," which stated that the success of a species was determined by the deviation of a factor or factors from the optimum toward either a minimum or a maximum limit of tolerance. He specified that the crucial factor or factors would differ accordingly as the conditions deviated from the optimum habitat in different directions and that organisms would change accordingly.

At this time, plant ecology and animal ecology were substantially discrete, a condition which was to persist for many decades and still does to a considerable degree. Shelford, however, wrote that ecology could not be logically divided into plant and animal ecology but that it may be divided into ecology of sessile and motile organisms. This criterion has been used by many marine ecologists studying littoral habitats and coral reefs to consider problems of community succession and pattern which were traditionally the domain of plant ecologists. Shelford adopted much of the successional concept of Clements, including convergence toward a regional climax, and was later to collaborate with Clements in an effort to integrate plant and animal ecology into "bio-ecology" (Clements and Shelford 1939). This effort failed to achieve notable success, for reasons detailed by Hutchinson (1940).

The capstone of the search for organization or integration of the myriad facts of natural history and physiology which had been assimilated into animal ecology was Elton's *Animal Ecology* (1927). Elton was a product of the great British natural history tradition. Hutchinson, another product of this tradition, wrote that he was brought up in a family with no professional botanists but in which Bentham and Hooker's *Handbook of the British Flora* was second only to the Bible as an essential household book (Hardy 1968; Cox 1979). He added that this was true of many academic families in Britain in the early part of this century. Elton described ecology as "scientific" natural history. He was confirmed in his interests in natural history by association with Julian Huxley and by studies and travels in the Arctic. He was also influenced by Shelford's *Animal Communities in Temperate America,* particularly Shelford's physiological emphasis (Cox 1979). Elton did not find Shelford's view of animal and plant communities as coextensive useful, however, because his Arctic experience indicated that an animal species might be found in different plant communities, only a few being exclusive to one plant community. Elton's famous book, *Animal Ecology,* was in effect commissioned, for, as a young man at Oxford, he had been designated by Julian Huxley to write it, which he did in 85 days in addition to other duties (Cox 1979). At the time of writing there were no courses in animal ecology at Oxford, yet Elton's small volume was described by G. E. Hutchinson as one of the greatest biological books of the century (Cox 1979). The remainder of Hutchinson's accolade is hyperbole: "It provided one half of the foundation for modern ecology, the other half coming from Volterra, Lotka, Nicholson, Gause, and Thomas Park." This list is, of course, a *Who's Who* of contributors to mathematical and experimental animal population ecology. It illustrates the tendency of ecologists, even the best of them, to use the generic term *ecology* when they should specify some part of it – for example, animal ecology.

Elton commented in the introduction to his book that most ecological work had been concerned with adaptation and evolution, subjects which Shelford had eschewed. Elton described his book as chiefly concerned with "the sociology and economics of animals" rather than structural and other adaptations, which may account for a socioeconomic influence on his ideas ascribed by his scientific biographer (Cox 1979) to his long association with the Hudson's Bay Company. In the years prior to writing *Animal Ecology,* Elton had participated in several expeditions to Spitsbergen (1921–4) which surveyed both plant and animal communities. These were unusual cooperative efforts involving numerous specialists and substantial technical support, and they marked the beginning of a dichotomy in Elton's work. On these expeditions, Elton was concerned with the nature and distribution of plant and animal communities and their coexistence. Elton and his associates emphasized food or trophic relations of communities and, anticipating later emphasis, provided a qualitative diagram of the nitrogen cycle illustrating the food relations. However, much of Elton's subsequent work was directed at population dynamics of species. Elton's later masterwork *Voles, Mice, and Lemmings* (1942) was subtitled *Problems in Population Dynamics.* Out of his Arctic experience he secured a position as "biological consultant" to the Hudson's Bay Company (1925–31), which gave him access to its records of fur sales and drew his attention to the problem of animal numbers, specifically, the long-term periodic oscillations of those numbers evident from the fur returns. Cycles had also occupied the attention of plant ecologists and climatologists (Clements 1916). Later animal ecologists even went so far as to define *ecology* as the study of numbers and distribution of animals. Elton entered this aspect of ecology just as Raymond Pearl was resurrecting Verhulst's mathematical equations for human populations and Lotka and Volterra were applying them to animal populations (Scudo 1971; Kingsland 1981,1982). He paralleled other early animal ecologists, such as Hensen and S. A. Forbes, by conducting empirical studies of animal populations in the field and of animals as members of communities. Elton's interest in animal populations, their fluctuations, and the regulation thereof led him to the idea of "optimum density." Significant among the factors in achieving and maintaining it were (1) food–"the manner in which animals are organized into communities with food-cycles and food-chains"; (2) disease and parasites; (3) environmental variation–"the chief cause of fluctuations in animal numbers [being] the instability of the environment"; and (4) hereditary and intrinsic means of control of population.

Elton was faced with the dramatic and apparently cyclic fluctuations of populations of Arctic animals, the most famous being the lemming. He was, according to Cox (1979), somewhat ambivalent in dealing with the widespread contemporary concepts of balance of nature or equilibrium. The early chapters of *Animal Ecology* read "as if the numbers of animals remained fairly constant," and Elton described "the general mechanisms which assist in bringing about the optimum density of numbers for each species" (Elton 1927). In his chapter 9, Elton dealt with populations more realistically, writing, "practically no animal population remains the same for any great length of time," and "the numbers of most species are subject to violent fluctuations." Elton's attention, like Darwin's and S. A. Forbes's, turned to what controlled the numbers of a population. He stressed (1) epidemics caused by parasites, (2) migration and (3) "the switch arrangement" in feeding by which an animal changed its food depending upon availability and quality.

Cox (1979) contrasted Elton's stress on "functionally dynamic properties" of communities with a "descriptive, static, species-list notion of community" that Cox attributed to plant ecologists. This accusation is common enough, but not entirely warranted. Certainly the leading contemporary plant ecologists were as emphatic as Elton in advocating a dynamic approach to ecology, and, like Elton, they stressed change as of the essence. Some publications on plant communities were descriptive, or species lists, but plant ecologists concentrated on community succession and changes in species populations, often on inferential evidence, although they did not adopt the emphasis on populations which became standard in animal ecology. However, many of these inferred a dynamic process, competition, from species lists or composition data. Elton differed from some plant ecologists who stressed the importance of physiology, or even its identity with ecology (McIntosh 1983a), and from some animal ecologists like Adams and Shelford, who stressed the significance of physiology. Elton (1927) wrote:

> When studying limiting factors, it is really more important to have a nodding acquaintance with some of the things which are going on in the environment, than to know very much about the physiology of the animals themselves.

Elton's book certainly deserved Hutchinson's praise, for it codified the organizing ideas which Adams and Shelford had sought, and more effectively than either, although he admittedly built on their efforts. Elton provided four "principles" which served as a basis for integrating population and community ecology. These were (1) food chains and the food cycle, (2) food size, (3) niche, and (4) the pyramid of numbers. Elton focused attention on what the animals were doing in the community – specifically, what ate what and how. Studies of food habits were hardly novel, and Elton acknowledged borrowing from Shelford, but he stressed the idea of *food chain* or *food cycle*. Food chain was subsequently replaced by *food web,* which was in fact what Elton illustrated. *Food cycle* improved on *food chain* in providing the essence of what was to be called the biogeochemical cycle because it integrated the organic food chains with the nonliving environment, an essential attribute of much early ecological thought that was later christened the "ecosystem" (Tansley 1935) or the more euphonious "biogeocœnose" (Sukachev 1945). Corollary to the food chain or what came to be called the "trophic structure" of a community, Elton generalized that body size increased at higher levels in the food chain in the carnivorous line and decreased in the parasite line.

The *pyramid of numbers* was not a new idea, but Elton's apt phraseology provided an all-too-readily-grasped and diagramed concept which expressed his belief that populations of smaller animals increased more rapidly than those of larger animals and that more small animals were required to sustain fewer of the larger animals. Elton recognized that all animals were dependent on plants for energy but did not stress the importance of energy, which was already being seized on by limnologists and was later to be the substrate of Raymond Lindeman's (1942) classic, "The Trophic-Dynamic Aspect of Ecology." In this and much subsequent ecology the pyramid of numbers was transformed into the pyramid of energy as a necessary consequence of the second law of thermodynamics, as anticipated by Semper (1881). A consequence of this widely hailed "revolution" in ecology was that energy was made the currency of trophic structure, although Elton was one of the ecologists who later questioned the appropriateness of regarding energy as the only important measure of ecosystem function (Elton and Miller 1954).

The concept of niche is a descendant of the earlier concept of place, which described either the geographical location of a species or its position in an order in nature. *Niche* is commonly attributed to the American zoologist Joseph Grinnell, but the term had been used earlier (Cox 1980). It has become one of the more disputatious terms in ecology, and a plethora of meanings have been ascribed to it. Grinnell (1908) asserted that competition between species led to their adoption of similar but not identical habitats or methods of food getting. Grinnell described species as fitting together "like soap bubbles, crowding and jostling," a description which is aptly reflected in Shelford's (1913) diagrams showing life history relationships of the species in a community. Elton (1927) defined the *niche* of an animal as its "status in the community, . . . what it is doing, most specifically, *its relations to food and enemies.*" *Niche* continued as a general term, principally in animal ecology, until it was reassessed by E. P. Odum (1953) in the first edition of his famous textbook and finally "revolutionized" by Hutchinson's (1957a) mathematical definition of *niche* as an *n*-dimensional hyperspace. Hutchinson's definition opened a semantic war which paralleled that following Clements's definition of *climax*. Elton's *niche* was more ambiguous than Hutchinson's and was, in addition to the function of a species, an abstract function in a community which could be filled by any of a variety of species which served the same general purpose. The Hutchinsonian niche is peculiar to a species and led to a one species-one niche concept.

It is somewhat anomalous that Elton incorporated niche as a major component of his early concepts of ecology without the emphasis on competition given by Grinnell and by later ecologists who made it the cornerstone of "niche theory." Elton (1927) was not impressed by the concept of competition and did not discuss it in the context of niche. Unlike plant ecologists such as Clements and Tansley, who ascribed major importance to competition as the major organizing force in community organization, Elton (at this date) and other early animal ecologists did not. Adams, Shelford, and Elton allude to it only obliquely, and Elton asked, "What precisely do we mean by competition?" This question was shortly to exercise animal ecologists in the 1930s when competition moved to center stage (Nicholson 1933; Gause 1934, 1936), and it continues as a focus of dispute in both empirical and theoretical ecology (McIntosh 1970; Schoener 1982). In later work, Elton came to accept the concept that competition was a fundamental clue to community organization (Elton and Miller 1954; Lack 1973).

Elton's principles provided the organization and integration for animal ecology which Adams, Shelford, and others had seen lacking. Elton reoriented animal ecology by developing a coherent verbal model linking several concepts of a functional animal community and its component populations. It is fashionable in current ecological discourse to deplore the construction of concepts in place of falsifiable theories, but in science, as elsewhere, it is necessary to walk before you can run. Cox (1979) noted the parallel between Elton and Darwin in their choice of metaphors. He quoted Manier (1978) as describing Darwin's careful selection of *struggle* as intermediate between *war* and *equilibrium*. Elton's *Animal Ecology* introduced many terms which were appropriate to the state of ecology in its first decades as a self-conscious discipline. Later critics commonly called for more rigorous and exact, preferably mathematical, definitions and spoke of mathematical metaphors, ignoring the fact that the beauty of a mathematical symbol ($X$) is that it has no metaphorical overtones. It means just what it is said to mean – no more, no less. Elton's language was, as Cox noted, dynamic, functionally oriented, and elastic. He avoided the format of a glossary, formal definitions, and premature formalisms. While his principles were not original with him, and their individual essence is seen in earlier work, which he commonly cites, the relationship of ideas, as of populations, is what makes for an integrated system.

## Aquatic communities

Conceptions of "dynamical equilibrium" were evident in early books on marine biology (Johnstone 1908). Marine biologists, such as Edward Forbes and Victor Hensen, had pioneered in developing quantitative sampling of benthic and planktonic communities and in treating the population and community as statistical entities. Johnstone noted that quantitative methods were necessary to provide approximations to actual "density," using a word which defined the number of individuals of any kind of organism in a given area. Johnstone devoted a large portion of his book to "quantitative marine biology," analyzing in one chapter methods of quantitative sampling and in a second spatial distribution, and in a third offering "a census of the sea." Terrestrial animal ecologists were, for the most part, at this time still talking of presence and absence or in qualitative estimates of abundance or variety. Elton used the long-term fur records of the Hudson's Bay Company in his earliest population work but not density data. Johnstone introduced the traditional concept of uniformity versus heterogeneity of distribution, commenting that if distribution is not uniform, "the investigation of marine microscopic life, apart, of course, from the collection of material for geographic or morphological study, is futile, a proceeding without rhyme or reason." Many ecologists, especially plant ecologists, avoided a sense of futility for many years by basing their quantitative studies on the assumption that they were dealing with a homogeneous area, at least in respect to the phenomena of interest. The realization that this was rarely so came shortly, but because of the enormous difficulties introduced by recognizing the heterogeneity, variability, and stochastic aspect of nature, recognition of these was suppressed, notably by theoreticians. Early marine biologists were aware of sampling error and were even estimating it in the 1880s, but as Johnstone (1908) reasonably wrote, "It is no service to science only to urge counsels of perfection, one should rather make use of what data are available," and he advised his readers to "trust that the provisional results thus attained may assist in the further elaboration of methods of investigation."

Marine biologists arrived early at estimates of productivity, making the now familiar distinction between the number of individuals (density) and the amount of organic material (biomass) per unit area at one time (standing crop) and the number of individuals or living material produced in a unit area per unit time (production, productivity, or yield). Such estimates were attempted by Hensen for plankton and various fisheries commissions for fish and shellfish. Johnstone was able to compare productivity in a variety of sites on the basis of kilograms per hectare per year, citing data as early as 1878. The only comparable terrestrial data he cited were for the long-familiar measures of agricultural production of grains, hay, and beef. Comparative production data were, of course, of great commercial interest, and marine biology and agriculture both had the benefit of substantial government support in an era when there was much concern about impoverishment of the sea. Johnstone (1908) also considered the "metabolism" of the sea, using the now standard phraseology "producers" and "consumers." Marine biologists were largely zoologists, and for the most part they dealt with the organisms in the marine habitat without the distinction of plant ecology and animal ecology which permeated terrestrial ecology. According to Johnstone, the metabolic distinctions were not as clear in the sea as on land, and he wrote, "We can only draw a rather indefinite line of distinction between plants and animals." However, Martin (1922) provided an early version of a compartment diagram showing the trophic distribution of the sea.

Although Elster (1974) and Rigler (1975a) agreed that much early limnology was in a descriptive phase, largely attempting to classify lakes, some early limnologists were explicitly concerned with the dynamics of lakes as interacting physical and biological systems. One of the major concepts permeating early limnology was the widespread holistic organismic conception as evidenced in S. A. Forbes's (1887) "Lake as a Microcosm":

> A lake is an old and relatively primitive system, isolated from its surroundings. Within it matter circulates, and controls operate to produce an equilibrium comparable with that in a similar area of land. In this microcosm, nothing can be fully understood until its relationship to the whole can be clearly seen. . . . The lake appears as an organic system, a balance between building up and breaking down in which the struggle for existence and natural selection have produced an equilibrium, a community of interest between predator and prey.

Elster (1974) observed that Forbes was in advance of his time and that ecology would have developed more quickly if more biologists had been familiar with his work. Many later limnologists, however, believed that the lake was not a self-contained microcosm but that consideration of the watershed was necessary to understand a lake. Forbes (1880a) recognized that exact adjustment was never achieved and that all species populations oscillated, but he suggested that the oscillations were kept within bounds, tending toward equilibrium. Since the biotic interactions are self-correcting – in modern parlance, have a "negative feedback" – Forbes argued that the ultimate limits to a population are the inorganic factors of the environment.

Limnology paralleled oceanography in many respects; indeed, Forel

wrote that "la limnologie est donc l'oceanographie des lacs" (quoted in
Berg 1951). Among its early concerns were studies of plankton populations, including their diurnal movement in the water column. Early
studies of plankton in streams (Kofoid 1903) and lakes (Birge 1898;
Birge and Juday 1911) provided estimates of plankton numbers. Birge
was concerned with Crustacea, followed seasonal changes in populations and their vertical movement in the water column, and considered
several factors which contributed to both observations. Birge commented that maximum numbers of Crustacea in the plankton remained
"singularly constant," and he assumed that these numbers were limited
by competition. Like some early plant ecologists, Birge recognized that
an organism in possession of a territory and its resources was difficult
to oust. Birge addressed the question of uniformity of distribution
which had been debated by Hensen and Haeckel and found some
nonuniform distributions or "swarms," but cautioned that his data did
not support either theory. He included, among limiting factors, food
quantity and quality, temperature, and competition. Vertical distribution, he said, was influenced by food, several physical factors, age, and
specific peculiarities of any species. Birge commented on the well-
known phenomenon of seasonal development of algal populations and
compared it to the seasonal progression of species appearing in a
forest. This periodic sequence was later to be confounded with terrestrial succession.

Kofoid (1903) determined the quantity of plankton volumetrically.
He used these data to compare quantitative "mean annual production"
on the basis of 235 observations over five years, having found few
similar studies for comparison. He commented that such figures contain "a large element of conjecture" and suggested requirements to
"solve adequately the problem of productivity of water." Nevertheless,
Kofoid was examining, as he noted, both "amplitude" and "direction"
of change and found them to be "correlated with differences in the
environment." Birge and Juday (1922) undertook a study to determine
the "food value" of plankton. This clearly distinguished between
"standing crop," "turnover," and production and provided an analogy:

> The plankton of a lake may be regarded as analogous to a pool
> in a stream, with a current of water constantly flowing in on
> one side and a regular outflow on the other. The pool itself
> represents the standing crop of plankton, while to the process
> of plankton production and the outflowing one typifies the
> losses of this material from various causes. The stream of

water that is continually passing through the pool closely resembles the constant stream of plankton like [that] which exists in a body of water. (Birge and Juday 1922)

"Pool," "inflow" or "input," "outflow" or "output," and "current"
were among the metaphors used when a variation of the dynamic view
of ecology was energized by systems analysis some decades later.
Birge, like S. A. Forbes and some other ecologists, compared studies
of lakes to studies of agricultural production measuring the amount of
organic material (biomass) present at various times during the season
("standing crop") and its chemical composition, and recognized the
problem of determining annual production. Birge and Juday considered the determination of annual production of a lake more complex than determining the productivity of land, but measurement of
productivity of lakes was to develop more rapidly than that of terrestrial productivity, as it turned out. While they were busy determining
numbers, biomass, and chemical compositon of plankton, Birge and
Juday considered the essential data needed to measure annual production: (1) rate of production of plankton under natural conditions, (2)
their length of life, and (3) average weight of each kind.

Although Birge and Juday clearly realized that the problem of production was not static biomass (standing crop), but rate of turnover,
this concept did not permeate ecology for some decades. In the first
major textbook of limnology, *limnology* was defined as "that branch of
science which deals with biological productivity of inland waters and
with all of the causal influences which determine it" (Welch 1935).
Welch's student D. C. Chandler (1963), however, commented that
Welch thought of productivity in terms of standing crop. Since Welch's
text dominated the field for many years, the conception of flow as
advanced by Birge and Juday lagged. Juday pursued studies of productivity and, with the plant ecologist John T. Curtis in an unaccustomed
role as limnologist, conducted early studies of biomass productivity
using oxygen production in light and dark bottles (Curtis and Juday
1937). This method had been developed earlier in studies of production of marine plankton (Gaardner and Gran 1927).

Limnologists and oceanographers, because of the nature of the places
they studied, were forced to consider physical conditions more than
were plant and animal ecologists working in terrestrial environments,
where organisms were physically more conspicuous. Tansley (1935) exemplified this characteristic of terrestrial ecologists when he wrote,
"The organisms may claim our primary interest." However, he contin-

ued, "When we are trying to think fundamentally we cannot separate them [organisms] from their special environment, with which they form one physical system"; and to the combination of and interchanges between the organic and inorganic he gave the name *ecosystem*. "Ecosystem" was to become the rallying cry of the "new" ecology in the 1950s and etymologically, at least, to link ecology with the rising philosophy of systems analysis. In Tansley's conception, ecosystems were of diverse kinds and sizes intermediate in scale between the atom and the universe and were included as parts of larger systems and interacted with each other. He stated that among ecosystems there is a kind of natural selection of incipient systems and those which can attain the most stable equilibrium survive the longest. The "universal tendency" toward "dynamic equilibria" was evident, he said, in ecosystems:

> In an ecosystem the organisms and the inorganic factors alike are *components* which are in relatively stable dynamic equilibrium. Succession and development are instances of the universal processes tending toward the creation of such equilibrated systems. (Tansley 1935)

Tansley recognized that physical factors, such as fire, or biotic factors, such as grazing, could create and maintain a dynamic equilibrium if they were persistent or recurrent. Tansley distinguished succession as a general process of change but specified, contrary to Clements, that the change could be retrogressive as well as progressive. He specified that the term *development* was better applied to "autogenic successions leading to climaxes," while acknowledging that these were somewhat analogous to the situation with individual organisms, which justified describing communities as *quasi-organisms*. The term *ecosystem* lay fallow for several years until it was integrated with the trophic-dynamic concept stimulated by progress in the study of food cycles in lakes by Raymond Lindeman (1942). Lindeman traced a chronological sequence from "static-species distributional viewpoint" through a "dynamic species-distributional viewpoint" to his own extension of the ecosystem, which he defined formally as "the system composed of physical-chemical-biological processes active within a space-time unit of any magnitude."

## Paleoecology

One of the dominant themes of dynamic ecology was the significance attached to the long-term historical perspective of change in populations, communities, and environment. Ecology developed shortly after widespread acceptance of Continental glaciation and associated climatic change had added a new perspective to the already dynamic view of the earth's surface developed by 19th-century geologists. Among the prominent protoecologists of the 19th century was the major founder of marine "dredging" studies of benthic organisms, Edward Forbes (Rehbock 1983). Forbes was described as the "founder of paleoecology," a term devised to describe historical changes of organisms and environment. Forbes linked his biological observations of sea bottom invertebrates with geological thought about the fossil record of such organisms and environmental changes associated with it (Ladd 1959). The link between geology and ecology was evident in the overlapping interests of such eminent geologists as T. C. Chamberlain and the geologist-turned-ecologist H. C. Cowles. In the sense that Lyell, the geologist ally of Charles Darwin, is said to have provided the latter with "the gift of time" essential for his idea of natural selection, paleoecology enriched ecology by providing it with a long-term perspective.

The study of fossils, paleontology, long antedated self-conscious ecology, and the logic of stratigraphy and paleontology was established in the 18th century. Traditional studies of fossils stressed morphology, systematics, and, after Darwin, evolution. That fossil assemblages differed from place to place and were associated with, and indicated, general environmental conditions in which the fossil had lived was the basis of much geological inference. That fossils of particular organisms were commonly found in areas with a current environment very different from the inferred environment of the fossil organism, implying environmental change, was a manifest link with ecology. Interpretation of fossils and their environment is predicated upon knowledge of the habits and environments of their living relatives. There was, prior to approximately 1900, no recognizable ecology to contribute to such knowledge, although familiar natural history lore served in its stead. As ecology established clearer recognition of the relation of living organisms, particularly as populations and communities, to the environment, the symbiotic relation with paleontology produced paleoecology. Ladd (1959) observed that marine paleontologists had paid some attention to ecological considerations for 25 years and that this interest was growing. This suggests that marine paleontologists discovered ecology in the 1930s. Ager (1963), however, noted a continuing dichotomy between systematic paleontology and ecologically minded paleontologists. Imbrie and Newell (1964) perpetuated the dichotomy in describing ecology as a branch of biology and paleoecology as a branch of geology. There are divisions between terrestrial animal and plant paleontology and marine paleontology which make it as difficult to unify paleoecology as to unify ecology. Ager described ecology as but a tiny aspect of paleoecology, which somewhat misstates the relationship. The insights of paleoecology derive from understanding of ecology of living organisms, and ecology derives insight concerning the present from the past via paleoecology. West (1964) observed that "the historical development of Quaternary palaeobotany closely parallels that of ecology." In the late 19th century qualitative studies of macrofossils and microfossils had clearly established general sequences of change of organisms and, by inference, of environment. Marine areas had changed to freshwater and freshwater to marine or either to dry land. In the larger perspective of geological time, areas once dominated by fernlike plants come to be dominated by conifer plants and in turn by flowering plants, each with different associates. Most of these studies considered fossils inert specimens. Ager (1963) wrote, "We must consider fossils as living organisms." This hope to revivify paleontology was essentially the merit of paleoecology.

The most important link of early ecology to geology was the adoption by ecologists of a rigorous uniformitarianism, following in the footsteps of Lyell and Darwin, although this, like Darwinism, came to be questioned in the early 20th century (Ladd 1959). Cowles (1901) developed physiographic ecology linking long-term landscape changes with vegetational change, and Adams (1901, 1905) considered the faunal significance of base-leveling and of postglacial dispersal of vegetation and animals. Clements (1904) affirmed that "succession was essentially the same during the geological past that it is today." The early studies of sunspot cycles by A. E. Douglass, an astronomer, led him to propose in 1901 that the annual growth rings of trees may be influenced by climatic changes induced by sunspots. Whatever the cause, the correlation of growth rings and climate produced a thriving discipline of dendrochronology (Fritts 1966). Appropriately enough, the pioneer work was funded by the Carnegie Institution of Washington (Douglass 1928). This institutional connection and the geographical proximity of the University of Arizona to the Desert Laboratory near Tucson ensured that early plant ecologists associated with the Desert Laboratory, including Clements, would seize on tree ring analysis for reconstructing the history of past vegetation and attempting to predict future changes. Clements (1916) proposed the name "paleo-ecology" for the study of past vegetation, although the term properly became inclusive of the ecology of all past organisms.

Clements's concept of dynamic ecology emphasized succession as the cause and explanation of all existing climax formations. More ambitiously, he turned from the sere, the ontogeny of the climax, to the "clisere," the sequential change in climax or the phylogeny of climaxes, which was associated with long-term changes in climate. Clements adopted a uniformitarian view of present succession as a clue to past succession and viewed fossil floras as climaxes. He even adapted the then widespread view of Haeckel concerning embryology and evolution and suggested that the ontogeny or seral development of a community recapitulated its phylogeny. According to Clements, the climaxes were the static units of today, each having its own seral development and its own phylogenetic development from previous climaxes evident in fossil sequences or as geographic zones of vegetation. Paleoecology, as Clements noted, was complicated by adding to the consideration of fossil biota and environment the subsequent effects of postdepositional change (diagenesis) (Ager 1963). Paleoecology incorporated all time scales of geological change, although ecologists mostly became concerned with the relatively short geological time scale of Pleistocene or Recent events. Clements's confidence in the older fossil record was strengthened by his belief that even though fossils were in some cases brought to a deposit from many sources, they would represent the climax because most of the area from which the fossils came would be in climax in the absence of human disturbance. However, among the earliest studies recognized as paleoecological were studies of peat bogs where the deposits were found in place as they accumulated in a vertical sequence. Inferences of succession as evident in zones, presumed sequences of vegetation in horizontal space, and peat deposits as vertical sequences in a time series began in the early studies reviewed by Clements (1916). The earliest dated from the 17th century, but most were from the late 19th and early 20th centuries. He placed these studies in his own dynamic ecological framework.

Clements's definition of *paleoecology* antedated the major development which would revolutionize paleoecological studies of vegetation, pollen analysis or palynology. The studies he cited up to 1913 were based on macrofossils in peat deposits. Gleason (1953) lamented his own efforts, many years earlier, to study vegetational history in peat deposits by using macrofossils and throwing away, unknowingly, the detailed evidence of microfossils in the form of pollen grains and spores. By 1920, however, Von Post, Erdtman, and others in Europe had discovered the presence of myriads of well-preserved pollen grains in peat and sediment deposits and began the detailed and eventually quantitative analysis of post-Pleistocene vegetational and associated climatic change (West 1964). Clements (1924) was on hand again with an appropriate volume, *Methods and Principles of Paleo-ecology*. Early pollen studies were primarily developed in the Scandinavian countries but were introduced into Britain and America in the 1930s, notably by Godwin (1934) and Sears (1935a,b), respectively. These studies led to more detailed knowledge of the changes and particularly the chronology of change in postglacial vegetation. They also provided a commonality of interest between terrestrial ecologists and limnologists, although they did not break down the barriers which separated them (Tutin 1941).

Early recognition of succession of lakes as a dynamic process dates to the 17th century. According to Walker (1970), however, "The general theory of the hydrosere as we know it was formulated in modern terms by Clements [1916]." Clements described the process as one in which water fortuitously "permits the development of one seral stage at the same time that it is accomplishing the preservation of another." Thus the hydrosere in filling in lakes provided the crucial material for paleoecology and is at the same time the central theme of limnology. Studies in the seral development of lakes began in Britain in the work of Pearsall (1917) and Godwin (1931), which provided the details of sediment and peat stratigraphy, later amplified by pollen profiles (Godwin 1934; Tutin 1941; Walker 1970; Worthington 1983). During the 1920s limnologists long concerned with productivity of lakes formulated it, under the term *eutrophication,* as a major basis for lake development and classification (Lindeman 1942; Elster 1974). Lindeman's (1942) famous article "The Trophic-Dynamic Aspect of Ecology" asserted that "the descriptive dynamics of hydraulic succession is well known." Lindeman, however, turned to productivity, the "organogenic" aspects of the succession process. Specifically, he argued that succession of lakes involved increased productivity accompanying a change from oligotrophy to a "prolonged eutrophic-stage equilibrium" followed by lake senescence as it became filled with the results of its productivity. The confounding of allogenic (siltation) and autogenic (organic production) processes and their relation to eutrophication provided material for extended disputation about the nature and sequence of lake succession. Hutchinson (1969), for example, in the introductory paper to a symposium on eutrophication, started tentatively, saying, "It would be well, at the beginning of this symposium, to try to find out exactly what we are about to discuss." Careful reading of the papers that followed suggested that the desired exactness was not achieved even at that late date (National Academy of Sciences 1969).

Studies of hydroseres by terrestrial, or at best amphibious, ecologists were a primary source of information concerning the history of organisms from diatoms to mastadons. Both micro- and macrofossils provided terrestrial ecologists with the means of interpreting long-term changes in flora 'and fauna (West 1964; Walker 1970). The discovery that fossil pollen sequences provided a general chronology of change, particularly for the Pleistocene and post-Pleistocene periods, was a major contribution to the reconstruction of vegetation and climatic history. Paleoecology provided significant insights concerning biogeography, the process of succession, and the nature of community. The Prairie Peninsula in America, for example, was first identified floristically by H. A. Gleason in the 1920s and named and further defined by E. N. Transeau in the 1930s. The detailed history of the Prairie Peninsula and associated climatic changes were based on the then newly available pollen studies in lakes and bogs (Sears 1935a; King 1981). The general consistency and correlation of the pollen strata in Britain and America, as well as on the Continent, showed remarkably similar climatic shifts and provided a general sequence and a rough chronology of vegetational change. This clearly established the long-term succession characterized by Clements, but it generally overestimated the age and duration of the changes. Greater precision in both was not achieved until the advent of radiocarbon dating after World War II, which, however, required no fundamental revisions of the earlier sequences (Libby 1952; Deevey 1964). Then it became apparent that the recession of the last (Wisconsinan) glaciation was both more recent and more rapid than previously believed. Combining the older tree-ring analyses and radiocarbon-dating methods showed that the carbon-14 level of atmospheric carbon dioxide varied and that radiocarbon dates required correction to correspond with calendar years (Suess 1973). Such refinements added to the accuracy of the paleoecological record. The general trends and pace of vegetational and climatic change were well established by inferences based on the presence and relative frequency of pollen grains of species found in lake sediments and peat deposits. A significant development was the modification of pollen analytic techniques by M. B. Davis (1969) to provide estimates of annual pollen influxes. Techniques of extracting pollens from soils extended the use of pollen studies into relatively modern periods, allowing extensive cooperation with archeologists (Dimbleby 1952). More recently, pollen studies, which had been largely confined to northern, humid, largely glaciated regions, have been extended to non-glaciated arid regions (Martin 1963) and tropical regions (Vuillemeer 1971), modifying earlier interpretations of vegetational history of these areas.

Clearly, climatic change and glaciation had profound effects on the distribution of vegetation. Recent studies of paleoecology require substantial modification of Clementsian concepts of paleoecology as the record of climaxes. Moreover, the entire concept of the community unit and coevolution in ecology must be reviewed in the context of paleoecological findings. West (1964) wrote:

> We may conclude that our present plant communities have no long history in the Quaternary, but are merely temporary aggregations under given conditions of climate, other environmental factors, and historical factors.

He suggested that the changing series of climaxes predicated on a slowly changing climate required reassessment in that the time available for development of a putative climax is only "on the order of a few hundred years." West also posed the reciprocal relation. Interpretations of historical ecology require more knowledge of modern distribution of species also found as fossils and of the ecological factors which control the distribution of such species. In West's words, "the development of Quaternary palaeobotany waits on ecological advances."

## Equilibrium

It is clear that major ecological figures in Britain and America were concerned with the basic problem of stability or equilibrium of populations and of the newer entity with which ecology was concerned, the community. They lived, somewhat uneasily, with the natural history tradition of balance of nature as studies, particularly quantitative studies, of populations and communities increased. They addressed the questions which exercise ecologists to the present: (1) Are species populations in an equilibrium state in which the population size is constant or oscillating within limits around an "ideal density?" (2) Are communities assemblages of populations at or near stable equilibrium so that community properties are similarly stable? and (3) If disturbed by changing conditions, do populations or communities return to, or at least tend toward, the equilibrium state? Clements's concept of the climax posited the development of a stable self-perpetuating association in which the dominants, at least, were in equilibrium. If the climax was not actually present, all sites in an area were tending toward it, and if disturbed, succession started the trend toward the climax again. Smaller areas than Clements's regional climaxes were seen by some ecologists as tending to stabilize under the control of a local factor. Clements's general theme of climax was widely evident. Adams (1908), although considering bird communities, wrote:

> the primary characteristic of the climax is its *relative stability* due to a dominance or relative equilibrium produced by the severe environmental and biotic selection and adjustments throughout the process of succession.

Such ideas persisted among animal ecologists. W. C. Allee (1931) wrote about oxbow lakes:

> Year after year in such lakes and in other animal communities there is a fairly steady balance of organic life. The community remains in dynamic equilibrium. The rate of reproduction about equals the death rate.

One of the more harried concerns of ecology and the environmental movement is the relation of stability and diversity in a community (Goodman 1975). This question surfaced in earlier natural history, and Darwin took as a principle that the greatest amount of life can be supported by great diversification of structure and function (Coleman 1977). A major concern among ecologists has always been the number of species in an area or community. Early exponents of the idea of a climax or stable plant community did not, however, see stability as associated with species number. Clements wrote of succession:

> The number of species is small in the initial stages, it attains a maximum in intermediate stages and then decreases in the ultimate formation, on account of the dominance of a few species. (Clements 1905:266)

Tansley agreed:

> The later stages of development are often marked by an actual decrease in the number of species, since many of those existing in the middle stages of development . . . are unable to subsist

> under the ultimate more extreme and more uniform conditions. (Tansley 1923:127)

Later ecologists who were to seek the cause of stability in number of species or diversity (or vice versa) with relatively little success often ascribed the concept to "classical ecology" and even described it as "a central dogma" but it is not clear who they had in mind as its proponents.

In spite of the recognition by early ecologists of the dynamic nature of ecology and their emphasis on change and development of communities, the underlying mechanism of population regulation and community development remained elusive. A. S. Watt (1947), who had explored some of the aspects of reproduction and replacement of populations of beech and heath communities, perhaps, overstated the case in the light of his own efforts:

> It is now half a century since the study of ecology was injected with the dynamic concept, yet in the vast output of literature stimulated by it there is no record of an attempt to apply dynamic principles to the elucidation of the plant community itself and to formulate laws according to which it maintains and regenerates itself.

The search for the laws and principles and theories to explain the regulation of populations and the maintenance of communities has indeed proved frustrating (McIntosh 1980a). Nevertheless, during the period of which Watt was writing the effort was under way.

# 4

## Quantitative community ecology

Among the more startling assertions in the contemporary ecological literature are "Community ecology is in its infancy" (Pianka 1980) and "Recently ecologists have expanded their scope from studies of single species populations to include analysis of broader assemblages of several co-occurring species loosely defined as communities" (Peterson 1975). In fact, the study of communities or assemblages of co-occurring species is one of the oldest of concerns that may be reasonably identified as ecological. The clearest way to distinguish self-conscious ecology from the other elements of natural history, genetics, physiology, or evolution with which it overlaps is its concern with organisms as members of multispecies aggregates, under a variety of pseudonyms: *census, formations, cœnoses, associations, societies, guilds,* or more generally, *communities*. The long tradition of natural history, the ordinary experience of farmers, seamen, woodsmen, hunters, anglers, and herbalists, indeed, of the earliest of food gatherers, and the plethora of words in many languages describing particular kinds of aggregates of organisms, and often their associated habitats, testifies that the earth is covered with a complex pattern of "more or less" recognizable plant and animal communities.

### Biogeographical origins

Although references to communities studded the classic literature of natural history, it is usual to attribute to Humboldt the earliest formal recognition of "association" based on the growth forms of the plants which gave the association the distinctive appearance or physiognomy by which it was recognized (Humboldt and Bonpland 1807). Humboldt described the latitudinal and vertical distribution of zones of vegetation and gave major impetus to the tradition of concern with geographic distribution of plants and animals. This tradition was vital to the founding of ecology and remains a significant concern of present-day ecology. Under the rubric of "biogeography," a host of 19th-century

107

naturalists, biologists, and, as professionalism developed, zoologists and botanists pursued the characterization and distribution of communities of plants or animals and, less commonly, plants *and* animals. Most traditional biogeographers examined the distribution of various taxonomic units – for example, the flora or the fauna, plants, birds, or mammals of an area – and some were primarily concerned with collection of new or rare species. Extremes of this gave rise to criticism of such natural history as a "vulgar mania" and produced Wordsworth's description of a naturalist as "one that would peep and botanize upon his mother's grave" (quoted in Lowe 1976). According to Lowe, one Professor Kendall, in 1903, described such biologists as "on much the same level as the collector of postage stamps." Lewontin (1968) resurrected this analogy in describing some population biologists concerned with objective description of nature as "the stamp collectors of biology," with the same pejorative implication. It is unfair to attribute so limited a perspective to many of the great collector naturalists who, often at the risk of life, limb, and purse, established the taxonomic, biogeographic, and natural history phenomena on which later biologists built. Many such observations are still essential to a full understanding of significant biological phenomena (Beebe 1945; Doncaster 1961; Liebetrau 1973; Worster 1977; Browne 1983; Rehbock 1983).

Some 19th-century biogeographers followed Humboldt's lead in using what he called in 1815 "botanical arithmetic" (Browne 1980; Tobey 1981; Rehbock 1983). This technique mapped a grid of areas in a landscape and recorded the species present in each. To compare any two areas, the species lists were compared and the number of species in common was counted, or recorded as a ratio of the number of species (or families) in common to the total number. A significant distinction between a description of the standard "flora" which listed the species of a region and one which attempted to "show their relations to the earth, as local productions of the ground and climate" was made by the first British phytogeographer H. C. Watson (Egerton 1979a) in distinguishing his book as *Cybele Britannica*. Watson might have irritated 19th-century feminists by his footnote:

> It may not be amiss to observe for the benefit of lady readers, or others who are not familiar with Greek and Latin names, that the one adopted for the present work, is to be pronounced in three syllables, thus, "cy-be-le." (Watson 1847:69)

Watson, like many of his contemporaries in natural science, was opposed to simple collecting and cataloging. He quoted Sir John Herschel, the arbiter of science of the day, concerning the nature of science. Specifically, he argued that simple location or even number of individuals of a species comprised only the necessary data:

It is in the digestion and arrangement of facts which, when so arranged, will tend to show causes and their effects and the laws of nature, that we find a close approach to natural science. (Watson 1847:21)

Watson, like some 19th-century oceanographers, was alert to the problem of "census" and the effect of sample area on numerical differences in testing the incidence of a species within its overall range. He wrote of sample areas or "spaces" as a measure of plant distribution, "The nearer we can reduce the 'spaces' into 'places' by increasing their number, and diminishing their extent, the more exact will the test become" (Watson 1847:12). His stated object was to take the first steps toward forming a "census" with a "numerical scale." Almost exactly 50 years later, Pound and Clements (1898a,b) moved to reduce Watson's large spaces (1 square mile each) to smaller spaces (1 square meter each) and to increase their number in a major step in quantitative community ecology (Tobey 1981; White in press). Watson's early venture into the problem of sample area and species-area relations was promptly criticized and "corrected" by W. H. Coleman (1848). Coleman decried Watson's use of arbitrary political or geometrical sample areas and turned to natural areas – river drainage basins, anticipating a later preference of ecosystem ecologists and limnologists. He cataloged an area by listing and sampling a "pinch" of each species encountered while walking through the area. The length of the "walk" was determined by the size of his vasculum, for he stopped when it was filled, recorded its contents, and started another walk. He used data thus gathered to correct "the statement of Mr. Watson . . . that a single square mile will be found to contain half the species of a county." Coleman provided an equation:

$$f = \frac{aF' - nF}{a - n}$$

where $f$ is the number of species common to every square mile of a county; $F$ is the number of species in the flora of the whole county having $a$ square miles; and $F'$ is the number of species in any portion of $n$ square miles. This equation, he said, produced a figure of 502 species common to each square mile of a total of 900 species, which, he allowed, appeared to confirm Watson's estimate. Coleman, however, then turned to the assumptions of the equation, which, he said, "vitiate the above calculation." The assumptions were that all but the most common species were equally rare and all square miles are alike in their proportionate distribution of habitat. Both assumptions, he said, were untrue, and the estimate of the number of species common in each square mile was unrealistically high. Coleman's questioning of the validity of the assumptions anticipated much later discussion concerning quantitative analysis of community and, particularly, mathematical theory. Even this early forerunner of quantitative method in community ecology was a portent of things to come.

Biogeography developed as, and remains, a very loosely organized branch of natural history and biology. Part of its concern was to distinguish and explain the natural divisions of the earth's surface (Nelson 1978). In the words of one of its mid-19th-century practitioners, its purpose

> is that of ascertaining the most natural primary divisions of the earth's surface, taking the amount and similarities of organized life as our guide. (Sclater 1858)

The explicit assumption developed by biogeographers that the earth had "natural" divisions, and that similarity of organisms should be used as the criterion for recognition, anticipated and underlies the tangled history of community ecology. Use of species lists and quantitative measures of species distribution to describe and compare areas and communities and to map their distribution is a vital part of this history.

### Marine biology

Early marine biologists developed concepts of regional and local natural communities in assessing the distribution of communities of the ocean bottom similar to those of terrestrial biogeographers (Allee 1934a; Rehbock 1983). Edward Forbes (1844), the premier British "dredger," wrote of marine bottom (benthic) organisms as forming "zones," each with species "peculiar" to it:

> Living beings are not distributed indifferently on the bed of the sea, but certain species live in certain parts, according to the depth, so that the sea-bed presents a series of zones or regions each peopled by its peculiar inhabitants.

Forbes, like Humboldt said that zones "are distinguished from each other by the associations of the species they severally include," and he stated that some species were peculiar to a zone. He noted that the number of species diminished with depth, giving credence to a conception of an "azoic zone" below 300 meters in which no organisms could exist. Forbes was instrumental in establishing the Dredging Committee which provided a quantitative survey form on which to record locations, environmental measurements, and the number of living and dead individuals of each species (Rehbock 1979; Rice and Wilson 1980). Forbes (1859) summarized the results of extensive dredging studies, recognizing marine provinces as areas "of the special manifestations of the Creative Power." More mundanely, he described a *province* as an area having some fraction of species "peculiar" to it and speculated whether the fraction of such species should be as much as one-half. Forbes also conceived a "law of representation," which held that similar species are found everywhere in the world in similar environmental conditions, firmly linking environment and biota in the tradition of subsequent ecology (Mills 1969). Forbes's early work and much subsequent dredging paralleled terrestrial biogeographic studies in recognizing biotic zones or provinces, variously defined on the basis of their organisms and related to environment, especially temperature, soils or sediments, nutrients, or salinity. A major limitation of the early dredge was that it scooped up organisms from an indeterminate area of bottom sediments and could not be used to examine quantitatively local or small-scale distributions.

The concept of benthic communities as "statistical" units is attributed to C. G. J. Petersen, a Danish biologist who in 1896 developed a bottom sampler with two jaws like a clam shovel which was not, as later critics noted, a fully successful effort to secure a measured sample volume of the sea floor and the organisms thereof (Petersen and Jensen 1911; Petersen 1913; Baker 1918; Thorson 1957). Baker (1918) described Petersen as the first to count the actual number of animals in a limited area of ocean bottom. Petersen's sampler covered a surface area of $\frac{1}{10}$ square meter and under ideal circumstances enclosed a unit volume of bottom sediments. Like most sampling devices, the ideal was not always met. Brinkhurst (1974) dedicated a volume on benthic studies of lakes to all those who have pulled such a sampler up 50 meters on a cold winter day only to find a stone caught between the jaws and the sampler empty. With all its technical faults, particularly in hard or stony bottom sediments, users of the Petersen dredge and subsequently the Ekman sampler faced the same problem then being addressed by terrestrial botanists and by limnologists—how to secure a measured area, or volume, of sample and an accurate appraisal of its biological content.

Marine biologists raised basic questions about animal communities similar to those plaguing contemporary terrestrial plant ecologists. Terrestrial animal ecologists were not yet involved in these disputes. Petersen's surveys of bottom-dwelling animals of the Skagerrak and the Baltic Sea suggested to him a regular recurrence of groups of a few species, and he recognized and mapped eight community types based on the presence of a few large, conspicuous animals, a method similar to the use of "dominant" plants by some terrestrial plant ecologists. Petersen and Jensen (1911) had their sights on more than counting individuals. They wrote:

> When the percentage of dry matter has been determined for the different years, the number of individuals, as also the total rough weight of the species for 100 stations or more, will give good information regarding the mass of animal life per square meter. (Quoted in Baker 1918)

In their view, such measurement of benthic biomass would lead, more effectively than plankton determinations, to an estimate of fish food. Petersen warned that it would "scarcely be an easy matter" to determine even from such quantitative investigations of food animals "the quantity of food available yearly, annual food production, for the consumption of fishes." He, like Hensen and other early quantitative marine ecologists, was aware of the limitation of quantitative measures of communities taken at one time.

Marked parallels in concepts and problems concerning community and methodology arose in studies of benthic communities and terrestrial plant communities. Many marine biologists accepted the reality in space and persistence in time of benthic animal communities and regarded a classification of such as "imperative for future work" (Thorson 1957). Thorson wrote that Petersen's map of level bottom communities remained "essentially true" after 40 years of research. Marine biologists focused, in varying degrees, on two concerns crucial to quantitative study of communities: (1) the relation of organisms to, and the limits imposed by, the physical environment; and (2) the interrelations among organisms affecting their distribution and activities. Quantitative community ecologists, whether working in aquatic or terrestrial habitats, faced the dual problem of measuring the physical environment and measuring the biological components of the community and their response to environmental change. It proved relatively easy to measure physical conditions; and as instruments became available they were seized on to measure with increasing, and often unwarranted, precision the recognized environmental variables or "factors." Physical phenomena dominated oceanography. The biological component was measured with greater difficulty and much less accuracy, a problem which remains today a concern of ecologists. Even determining the presence and quantity of organisms in an area posed difficulties. Estimating the response of organisms to environmental conditions (and its reciprocal, the effect of organisms on the environment) and the nature and degree of the effects of organisms upon each other (their interactions) has confounded generations of ecologists. Nevertheless, introduction, late in the 19th century, of quantitative methods for study of aquatic organisms helped to differentiate ecology from natural history (Chapman 1931). Tobey (1981) described the introduction of the quadrat and counting the plants therein as "revolutionizing" terrestrial plant ecology in the same era.

Quantitative approaches to marine and freshwater communities were also used in studies of organisms in the water column. Associations of microscopic, free-floating organisms (plankton) were differentiated in biogeographic studies of diatoms in the last quarter of the 19th century when Arctic and tropical forms were recognized (Patrick 1977). Plankton communities, like benthic communities, were known only as statistical entities in samples collected by drawing nets of fine silk cloth through the water. The first systematic quantitative studies were those of Hensen (Johnstone 1908; Lussenhop 1974; Taylor 1980). Hensen, on various voyages, notably the famous Plankton Expedition of 1889 (Damkaer and Mrozek-Dahl 1980), elaborated the equipment and rationale of sampling methods in developing quantitative plankton studies and using these to assess and compare plankton communities both regionally and locally. Hensen assumed that if the environment was uniform, the plankton was uniformly distributed and collections of a limited number of samples could be extrapolated to much larger areas. This assumption and Hensen's counterintuitive finding that Arctic seas produced more plankton than tropical seas were vigorously attacked by Haeckel (Lussenhop 1974). Haeckel deplored Hensen's technique of counting individual organisms and argued that the only useful method was to determine the mass, weight, and chemical constituents of the collective plankton. Haeckel's dispute with Hensen revolved around a basic problem which plagues ecology to the present – uniformity, homogeneity of distribution, or what has come to be called pattern. Johnstone (1908:143) aptly stated the question:

> But should we be justified in stating that the Irish Sea 10 miles from Llandudno over an area of ten square miles contained these numbers of organisms underneath each square metre of surface over this whole area, and that the aggregate number of organisms could be calculated by simply multiplying the numbers of each species contained in the sample catch by the number of times that one square metre was contained in the entire area? If we say that we can do so then we assume that the plankton is uniformly distributed over the whole area referred to and that it is generally evenly spread over the sea throughout wide areas. Now is this the case?

In answer, he described Hensen's use of paired, identical sampling nets drawn up together and said of the resulting samples that "no two were exactly alike," a finding all too familiar to generations of later quantitative ecologists. Hensen addressed the eternal ecological problem of similarity of samples and made what was perhaps the first effort to assess it quantitatively by comparing the divergence of individual samples from the mean of the samples. If all samples were similar, then the area was uniform. Johnstone (1908) concurred with Haeckel's criticism of Hensen's assumption that plankton was uniformly distributed; but he was not as adamantly opposed to quantitative methods as was Haeckel, who wrote, "Mathematical treatment . . . does more harm than good, because it gives a deceptive semblance of accuracy, which is in fact not attainable" (Lussenhop 1974). It is interesting that Haeckel excused Hensen's "error" partly because, he said, 19th-century physiology, "in its one-sided pursuit of exact research, has lost sight of many general problems which are not suited for exact special investigation." Haeckel notwithstanding, Hensen and contemporary marine biologists avidly pursued the problems of "census" and "productivity" of the sea, initiating a tradition of quantitative studies of marine organisms, their abundance, and their distribution. Johnstone (1908:157) noted that the validity of their conclusions depended on the truth of the "postulate" of uniform distribution and that, if this was not true, general statements about abundance are futile and quantitative investigation of marine life is "without rhyme or reason." However, he said that students of marine biology will not readily come to this conclusion; and they did not, but struggled valiantly on. They sometimes recognized the imperfections of their results but sometimes basked in comfortable, if unwarranted, assumptions of the accuracy of their quantitative studies, which often foundered on the rock of non-uniform spatial distributions in nature, which some ecologists still, oddly enough, choose to ignore.

The late 19th-century concern of kings, princes, and governments with fish and fisheries, which produced large-scale funding of oceanographic research, was in large part due to concern about declining fish production and resultant economic problems. Thus measurement of productivity was an important element of early oceanographic studies, as it was for forestry and agriculture. Assessments of marine productivity were based on data of commercial fisheries, much as Elton's famous later studies of terrestrial animal population cycles were based on the commercial fur trade records of the Hudson's Bay Company. Fisheries studies, however, allowed calculation of productivity, at least of catchable fish, given as weight per area per year. Practical limitations to achieving a true measure of total productivity were clearly recognized by Johnstone (1908), who commented, "Fishing boats do not go to sea to make scientific deductions but to earn money for their owners." Nevertheless, the substance of the idea of productivity, rough ideas of its measurement, and the problems inherent in these efforts were clearly evident in these early efforts. The concern of early marine biologists with productivity was exemplified by Johnstone, who provided a list of what was needed:

1. Rate of reproduction of each species under different conditions;
2. Rate of growth of each species under different conditions;
3. Average duration of life of each species;
4. Duration of reproductive activity in the life history of each species; and
5. Amount of natural destruction due to enemies.

As in terrestrial biogeography, census was a major concern of marine biologists, who, being much better funded, produced (or collated from commerical landings) extended data on fish production. It was this that drew attention to both benthic and plankton communities in efforts to determine the food relations of the fish populations. The link with commerical fisheries and the attendant institutionalization of marine studies in government-supported organizations separated them from the nascent science of ecology.

In subsequent decades marine biologists learned the hard facts of variation and of sampling problems, although some preferred to over-

look them. Allee (1934a) commented, "Many studies in modern oceanography lack the community approach." MacGinitie (1939) wrote:

> There seems to be a tendency for those who write papers
> about marine animals or, for that matter, animal communities
> in general, to give the impression that the picture presented of
> the animal community is one which will be the same at any
> time in the future, and that practically all of the necessary or
> important work on the animal community has been completed.

MacGinitie stressed the importance of variation even in a short time or a
limited space and even when the environment was relatively constant.
He posed the uncomfortable choice of using locality or habitat for recognizing a community rather than generic or specific composition of the
organisms. In the former case he suggested that the resultant community resembles "a patch work quilt, a Joseph's coat." Dividing the quilt
would produce many communities with definite boundaries but would
be "very confusing from an environmental point of view." The problem
of boundaries or limits of the community were, he said, best left to the
"good judgement of the investigator." It was better if it was the good
judgment of a good investigator, but the eternal problem of subjective
choice and the qualifications of the chooser are manifest. MacGinitie
addressed the perennial problem of "homogeneity." Many marine biologists, like most terrestrial ecologists, believed that a community had
to be homogeneous–at least, as Petersen suggested, with respect to its
dominants. One way of achieving homogeneity was to split an area, or
set of samples, into progressively smaller units until homogeneity, by
some criterion, was achieved. MacGinitie despaired–"there are no two
environments exactly alike" and "no two communities alike." This lit-
any reappears frequently in quantitative community studies, whether
aquatic or terrestrial. The comfortable assumption of homogeneity or
uniformity was not readily sustained by quantitative analyses. In spite of
these manifest difficulties, MacGinitie expressed the optimistic view
that "it is from the marine animal communities that we should be able to
get many of our fundamental concepts of animal communities."

MacGinitie's (1939) article appeared in a symposium described "as
the first ambitious stock taking of ecology" (Allee 1939). This "stock
taking" is of particular interest in that it is the earliest effort to bring
together terrestrial plant and animal community ecologists, marine biologists, limnologists, experimental population zoologists, and animal
behaviorists to assess the state of work on ecological communities (Just
1939). The discussion following MacGinitie's paper is redolent of re-

peated and continuing concerns of community ecologists. Mottley remarked on the "inability of the human mind to grasp the whole picture," Lippma commented that "the chief problem of both animal and plant communities is the problem of the delimitation of particular communities," and Carpenter doubted "the possibility to predict the general structural emergence of a community from the autecology of its constituent species." MacGinitie, to the contrary, asserted that knowing the natural history of the individual species would allow prediction "to a very great extent."

Reviewers, at least animal ecologists, were not impressed with the stock taking. Allee (1939) wrote that the concept of the plant *and* animal community, the biome, received only "lip service," although J. R. Carpenter's (1939) famous paper "The Biome" was included. Elton (1940), under the heading "Scholasticism in Ecology," deplored the absence of quantitative data about communities and populations, their dynamics, natural rates of increase, and mortality in nature of plant species. His assessment of the conference was of an

> unreal atmosphere because of terminology, . . . a firework display of grand sounding terms descriptive of the community and its constituents and their interactions which might mislead the reader into thinking that something really solid was already known about these subjects.

Thomas Park (1939), one of the participants, was more temperate, even positive, in providing a thumbnail sketch of the history of ecology. He suggested that the simple fact of the symposium having occurred contributed to a recognition of the need for coordination and formalization of several disparate aspects of biology which were intrinsically ecological. He shared Elton's disappointment that few of the papers presented had a statistical approach. Thus some 40 years after quantitative studies of communities had begun, leading British and American animal ecologists were still concerned about the inadequacies of quantitative and statistical work in community ecology.

The other contemporary attempt to integrate the several approaches to community was an ambitious effort to "correlate the fields of plant and animal ecology" in the book *Bio-Ecology* (Clements and Shelford 1939). The authors attempted to bring together, in the Clementsian framework of organismal successional ecology, plant and animal, terrestrial and aquatic communities. They even attempted to improve upon Petersen's concepts of marine bottom communities by linking the more mobile fishes to the bottom community in a manner analogous to land birds and grassland associations. The major interest in this volume is in its effort to develop community ecology in the context of the biome concept. That concept presumes that biotic communities exist and that the biome is the primary community unit consisting of both plants and animals "inseparably united in the structure of any community" (Carpenter 1939). *Biome* was an "exact synonym of formation and climax" (Clements and Shelford 1939), a connotation tacitly ignored in the widespread choice of *biome* as the basis for big ecosystem ecology in the 1960s. Clements and Shelford asserted that the concept of the organismic community was an "open sesame to a whole new vista of scientific thought, a veritable *magna carta* for future progress." Elton (1940) at least thought no better of *Bio-Ecology* than he did of the symposium *Plant and Animal Communities*. According to Elton:

> From this book on ecology it is easier to find out what the authors believe than what is the evidence for these beliefs.

Elton's own early experience in his Arctic studies had persuaded him that animal and plant communities were only loosely linked, the animals occurring in more than one plant community. Hutchinson (1940) criticized the emphasis of *Bio-Ecology* on classification and terminology. He particularly deplored its failure to use statistics and mathematics in dealing with ecological problems. It is striking that both of these efforts to examine plant and animal communities in a general sense failed effectively to use any of the promising approaches to quantitative community ecology evident by 1939. It is anomalous in the case of *Bio-Ecology* because Clements had been the pioneer in developing the quadrat as the basis of quantitative community ecology.

Segregation of ecologists and their evolving concepts by habitat or taxon is evident in the long tradition of studies of marine bottom communities. Jones (1950) and Thorson (1957) reviewed the concept of animal communities based on marine bottom studies. Mills (1969) surveyed the community concept in more general terms, comparing the problems encountered by terrestrial botanists and marine benthic biologists. Stephenson (1973) examined the quantitative methods used by plant ecologists and their relevance to marine benthic communities. Among the concerns marine biologists shared with terrestrial plant ecologists was the nature of the community unit – indeed, its very existence as an entity. The traditional assumption that communities existed as entities in space and could be defined, surveyed, and mapped was widely accepted by most marine biologists (Thorson 1957). However, as detailed and, particularly, quantitative studies continued to follow in the wake of the pioneer efforts of Hensen and Petersen, the utility and reality of a community unit concept was questioned. Stephen (1933) noted, in phraseology strikingly similar to Gleason's (1939) famous comments on forest transition in the valley of the Mississippi River:

> The fauna of the coastal zone in the North Sea is shown to have a slightly different composition in its northern and southern parts, the transition taking place gradually. Still greater differences are provided by the offshore zone, where a definite change takes place on passing from the southern to the northern limits. Species are gradually eliminated, but there are no sharp transitions which would justify separation into communities.

The alternative to comments of this type has a familiar ring to students of terrestrial plant communities. Jones (1950) wrote:

> However, it is not possible to divorce entirely a classification of the fauna into communities from the faunal evidence. Even though the classification is based on external factors, it must in the first place be derived from a study of the distribution of the animals concerned. It seems that at present the only consistent way to divide the fauna into communities is to survey it, as far as it is known in relation to the environment and to erect communities based on more-or-less definite limits to the physical condition.

Few phrases are as ubiquitous in community ecology as "more or less," usually introduced in defense of one or another system for defining and classifying communities and in providing sufficient elasticity, not to say lubricity, to make it difficult to grasp and attack assertions about communities. Jones (1950) wrote that there is little ground to support the idea that "any large assemblage of animal species reacts as a unit or is bound together by purely biological factors." He explicitly stated that competition, while it may limit some organisms, is of secondary importance, thus contradicting the then rising tide of competitive exclusion as a basis for limiting organisms. Some marine biologists continued to assert that well-defined communities exist (Hedgpeth 1957a). Sanders (1960), however, discovered, as had many terrestrial plant ecologists, that

> in fact, the species of components of the benthic fauna in Buzzard's Bay constitute a continuum varying with the gradual change in sediment composition.

Sanders and Hessler (1969), using improved methods of sampling deep-sea benthos, found gradual change with depth up to a point on the continental shelf where they found a faunal discontinuity.

Convergence of questions, methods, and theories concerning communities of marine ecologists and terrestrial plant ecologists became increasingly evident in the 1960s and 1970s. Sanders's work on marine benthic communities paralleled findings based on terrestrial plant communities. Students of marine littoral communities discovered succession and gap-phase phenomena. Connell (1978), for example, expanded his early interests on marine communities and coral reefs and examined parallels in these and tropical rainforests.

## Limnology

The analogy between marine biology and limnology drawn by Forel is evident in parallels of method, concepts, and empirical studies of community. *Limnology* has been variously defined to include lakes, or all freshwaters, including running water, or, more inclusively still, all inland waters (Welch 1935). Most early limnology was the study of lakes. Hutchinson's (1957b) *Treatise on Limnology* is exclusively concerned with lakes. Their ubiquity and relative discreteness drew the attention of 19th-century geologists and geographers who were concerned with their formation and classification, based largely on morphometric and physical attributes. Substantial concern with the purely biological attributes, the communities, of lakes, did not begin until the last third of the 19th century. The "father of limnology," Forel, started studies of the bottom fauna of Lac Léman in 1869, and his monographic work on Lac Léman began to appear in 1892 (Berg 1951; Egerton 1962; Elster 1974). Forel exemplified, in this earliest systematic work in limnology, the tendency of limnologists, like oceanographers, to emphasize the physical conditions of the lake more than its biological attributes. The familiar observation that aquatic bodies are more evidently physical systems than are terrestrial systems was thrust on Forel and subsequent limnologists by their experience. It persists symbolically in that the first volume of Hutchinson's monumental work on limnology treats physical conditions. Berg (1951) refers to limnology as "universal, comprehensive, and comparative" as evident in the research program of Forel and as explicitly stated by S. A. Forbes (1887). Forel, in fact, adopted Forbes's term *microcosm* in treating the lake as an entity, essentially adopting explicitly the ecosystem concept well before the term was coined by the terrestrial botanist Tansley (1935).

The concept of the lake as a microcosm fitted firmly the organismal holistic view of most early limnologists, including Forel, Birge, and Forbes. As Forbes put it, no component of a lake can be fully understood until its relationship to the whole is clear. He asserted that the laws of natural selection have produced a community of interest among the component organisms which produce an equilibrium. In this view, lakes were seen as more or less closed systems. Appreciation of their real complexity as open systems was yet to come. Much of limnology early in its history was an effort to cope with the embarrassment of factual richness provided by studies of lakes around the world. Numerous lake laboratories were established in Europe and America in the 1890s and early 1900s, and surveys of lakes, their physical attributes, their plankton, benthos, nekton, neuston, and a host of other subcategories of the flora and fauna proliferated (Worthington 1983). Murray and Pullar (1910) reported on a survey of 562 Scottish lakes between 1897 and 1909, including all lakes on which a boat could be found (Maitland 1983). Statistics proliferated from over 60,000 soundings and biological collections from 400 lakes. Murray's interest in lakes was a logical extension of his marine studies, notably in connection with the *Challenger* expedition, and Murray himself reported on the biology of the Scottish lakes. Usually, only one collection of plankton was made from each lake, providing, as he noted, limited ground for generalization. Murray nevertheless assumed that freshwater plankton is uniform over vast areas, the very assumption questioned by Haeckel and Johnstone in discussions of marine plankton. Yet Murray foresaw the necessity of "vast accumulations" of facts before it would be possible to tackle the problems of animal and plant distribuion. Even at this early date the bibliography of the volume ran to 93 pages of small print, references to Forel alone taking up nearly four pages. That even this bibliography was far from complete is evident in the limited references to E. A. Birge, by then a preeminent American limnologist.

Early quantitative studies of lakes produced surprises. Birge (1898) adopted a variant of Hensen's vertical net tow which allowed him to sample plankton at different depths as well as an entire vertical column of water. He found, as had European limnologists, that the plankton was not uniformly distributed vertically, any more than it was horizontally, and moreover that its composition changed seasonally. In these early studies, Birge's data shifted from percentages to absolute numbers of organisms per square meter of lake surface or cubic meter of water volume as sampling techniques improved, compounding the problem of quantitative analysis (Frey 1963b). These studies led Birge to study temperature distribution in lakes, and he introduced the term *thermocline* to describe the vertical layering or stratification characteristic of temperate-zone lakes. Subsequent studies examined the effect of dissolved gases, notably oxygen. Birge and Juday (1911:xvi) expressed a feeling which became commonplace among limnologists and persists to the present among ecologists seeking a unifying theoretical framework:

> As our work has progressed we have been increasingly impressed by the complexity of the questions involved. This has become more and more manifest as our experience has extended to numerous lakes and to many seasons. . . . The extension of our acquaintance with the lakes has been fatal to many interesting and at one time promising theories.

Relatively unheralded among earlier quantitative limnological studies were the benthic studies of Oneida Lake, New York (Baker 1916, 1918). It is of some note that these studies were done under the direction of C. C. Adams, who described them as the "1st important quantitative study of fish food of the bottom ever made in America" and "one of two known to have been made in the fresh-waters of the world." Baker meticulously recorded distance, from shore, the water depth and bottom type for each sample. He sampled areas of multiples of 16 square inches and provided detailed calculations. Ordinarily he used 80 samples, determined the mean number of organisms per sample unit to the third decimal, and then boldly extrapolated his sample area to the total area of bottom type. In one case he reported 51,341,558 mollusks and 73,758,405 associated animals. Such naive precision is perhaps not to be derogated in a true pioneer of quantitative study when presumably more sophisticated ecologists a half-century later calculated secondary estimates, such as the Shannon-Weaver index of diversity, to three and even four decimal places. Baker compared his findings with other studies and related the distributions of species of mollusks to water depth and bottom type. He provided an early contribution to trophic organization of the benthic community in one area where he calculated that 7,743 million individual animals were herbivores or detritivores and only 23 million were carnivores. Baker noted, as had Johnstone (1908) for marine habitats, that determining numbers was not enough. It was also necessary, he said, to "find out what mass of living substance is periodically generated." He also used the now familiar economic analogy in which the mass of life at the beginning of a study is the capital and the additional amount generated during the year's growth and production is interest, raising the question, What is the rate of interest?

Complexity and variability became increasingly apparent as lake studies proliferated. Needham and Lloyd (1916) commented on the changes in plankton: "The coming and going of plankton organisms has been compared to the succession of flowers on a woodland slope." They did not approve of this analogy to woodland periodicity, but confounding of annual changes of plankton and terrestrial plant succession persisted. They also noted that plankton populations come and go, with species reappearing in different proportions. Studies of this inherent variation and complexity made it evident that single observations, such as Murray's in Scottish lakes, were of limited use, and even a season's or a year's observations were of marginal value. A triumvirate of problems plaguing quantitative community study from its earliest era involved sampling methodology, taxonomic base for effective identification, and duration of sampling to deal with the recognized variation in environmental conditions and biotic composition. That these problems persist in current ecology is evident in Brinkhurst's (1974:vii) lament that

> there has never been a study of the benthos of a lake in which . . . the sampling methodology and schedule have been properly evaluated, most of the major species identified, and which extended over all seasons for a consecutive number of years.

To this triumvirate must be added problems of data analysis which are imposed by collection of substantial amounts of quantitative data. These are complicated by the omnipresent heterogeneity or pattern which characterizes the distributions of organisms in all habitats.

To bring order into the vast accumulation of facts which Murray had seen as necessary and which poured from the newly established lake laboratories, early 20th century limnologists, like their contemporary plant ecologists, turned to classification. Lake typology dominated the early decades of 20th-century limnology (Mortimer 1941–2; Brinkhurst 1974; Elster 1974) and persists in a "new typology" (Rigler 1975a). The necessity of classification was clearly stated by one of the major figures of European limnology, A. Thienemann (1925):

> If one investigates a lake typologically, one cannot expect the impossible from nature, who, if she is ever to be scientifically comprehended to any degree in all her peculiarities, pattern and processes, must be categorized. (Quoted in Brinkhurst 1974:9)

Lakes were classified on diverse bases. Kolkwitz and Marson (1908) developed a "Saprobien" classification for detection of pollution based on organic content and depletion of oxygen thereby. Naumann (1919) defined lake types largely in terms of phytoplankton, dissolved nutrients, metabolic processes, and consequent biological production (Rodhe 1975). He elaborated the now standard concepts of "oligotrophy" and "eutrophy," thereby opening a Pandora's box of definitions and interpretations which remain problematic to the present. Thienemann (1925) based a classification on benthic organisms. Variants on these came thick and fast. Rodhe (1975) quoted Elster as saying in 1958:

> The challenge of lake types is the great catalyst of limnological research. It has amalgamated the various branches of lake studies into limnology. There is hardly any truly limnological problem that lacks connection with the Seetypenlehre ["lake-type-knowledge"].

Thienemann and Naumann collaborated in ecological studies and in the founding of the International Association of Limnology in 1922, even before limnology had its own regional societies in America or Britain. The British Freshwater Biological Association was not established until 1929 (LeCren 1979), and the American Society of Limnology and Oceanography until 1936 (Lauff 1963). Thienemann in a draft recommendation to establish an international association avoided the term *limnologie,* preferring *hydrobiologie* (Rodhe 1975). This was possibly related to his suggestion that the independent science of limnology was not recognized until 1922, an assertion with which Berg (1951) strongly disagreed, crediting Forel with founding limnology and asserting that "Forel was an ecologist." Limnology shares with ecology some differences of opinion about its nature and origins.

Many limnologists, including Thienemann, shared the holistic organismic tradition forcefully expressed earlier by S. A. Forbes (1887) in "The Lake as a Microcosm" and by the terrestrial botanist Clements (1905). Bodenheimer (1957:84) translated Thienemann as stating:

> Every life community forms together with the environment which it fills, a unity and often a unity so closed in itself, that it must be called an organism of higher order.

In Thienemann's view, as in Forbes's, the lake was a unit, and the aim of quantitative limnology was to arrange lakes, with all their myriad variations, into an orderly system.

Limnologists, like biological oceanographers, also turned their attention to production. Birge and Juday (1922) stated the now familiar distinction between the actual quantity of organic matter at any one time (standing crop) and the necessity of determining the rate of "turnover" to estimate the annual "production" of plankton. Juday followed this recognition with studies of productivity, attempting to measure primary productivity and rates of productivity and turnover (Frey 1963b). Welch (1935) went so far as to define limnology as "that branch of science which deals with biological productivity of inland waters and with all of the causal influences which determine it." The plant and animal communities of the lake were, in Welch's view, "the direct result of biological productivity of waters which they occupy." Out of these and comparable studies came the trophic level concept. In its earlier manifestations it was predominantly based on standing crops of the various biotic components and the pyramid structure of community organization as suggested by Charles Elton's food pyramids. The transition from the static pyramid to the trophic-dynamic concept was not easy. Chandler (1963) commented that even Paul S. Welch, author in 1935 of the first major American textbook of limnology, thought of productivity in terms of standing crop. This may be the reason that Welch was opposed to publication of Lindeman's classic paper on trophic-dynamic aspects of lakes (Cook 1977). Lindeman's (1942) much-acclaimed article was a watershed in ecology. Lindeman reviewed the traditions of community in limnology. He recognized three stages: (1) early surveys of lakes and their biotas as static, concerned with the distribution of species; (2) the dynamic concept, with emphasis on succession; and (3) the trophic-dynamic view, which emphasized the "energy availing relationships within the community to this process of succession." The emphasis on succession linked this trophic-dynamic aspect with the dynamic ecology of Clements and the terrestrial plant ecologists. Lindeman's article is basically a study of succession, addressing the then presumed relation of lake development from oligotrophy to eutrophy and beyond, as related to productivity.

Lindeman considered the lake as an ecological unit in its own right "since all the lesser communities . . . are dependent upon other components of the lacustrine food cycle," and he endorsed the then relatively unknown term *ecosystem*. Lindeman attributed the idea of the lake as a superorganismic entity to Thienemann in 1918. Patrick (1977) attributed the first use of the analogy of the functions of a lake to those of an organism to Hutchinson in 1941. However, the long tradition of a community or a lake as analogous to, or even homologous with, an individual organism in the functioning of its individual components long antedates these sources. The concept of the community as a highly integrated, even evolving, superorganismic entity was carried into limnology and ecology from its natural history origins and made a strange bedfellow with the mechanistic reductionist mate from 19th-century physiology. Bodenheimer (1957) criticized the organismic tradition and denied its foundations as inadequately based on any evidence, but recognized it as the most widespread conception of the community in all aspects of ecology. Elster (1974) suggested that the ideas of the unity of a lake and of nature as indivisible attracted biologists to limnology rather than to special botanical or zoological works. He raised the question, "Is the view of limnology as a whole still tenable and what tasks and duties does it lay upon its practitioners?" He answered the first part affirmatively and celebrated the "holological" approach to the study of lakes. However, achievement of the holistic ideal in community study does not come easily, not is it universally recognized among limnologists or community ecologists as the ideal. Quantitative community studies commonly deal with some subset of the total attributes of a lake, and the search for macrovariables which integrate or synthesize the whole has proven frustrating.

The diverse traditions of limnology take on a bewildering diversity. Rigler (1975a) commented, "The first impression one receives is of a lot of sub-groups, each of which is going its own way." He divided these subgroups into two major groups: holists, who chose to deal with properties of the entire and intact system (i.e., the lake as microcosm), and reductionists, who prefer to study individual parts of the system. Rodhe (1979) identified these same groups but expressed the hope that limnology would progress "through a sound combination" of them. The ideal of both groups was advanced by the widespread adoption of the experimental approach, which enhanced the study of the functioning of lakes. Hasler's (Hasler et al. 1951) studies of whole lakes as affected by changing the pH, Hutchinson and Bowen's (1947) pioneer studies of the phosphorus metabolism of lakes using radioactive tracers, and a host of other studies of lake chemistry, the biotic processses of plankton, benthos, primary and secondary producers, consumers, and decomposers continued the exponential expansion of quantitative studies of lakes. The period 1937 to 1975 saw a tenfold increase in the scientific staff of the Freshwater Biological Association Laboratory at Wray Castle on Lake Windemere. The chemistry of aquatic environments was advanced there by the notable studies of C. H. Mortimer, who subsequently linked British and American limnology by moving to Wisconsin and continuing his studies in the territory of Birge and Juday (Worthington 1983).

Brinkhurst (1974) acknowledged that a holistic approach to lakes derived from early limnologists. In his view, however, the concept of the lake bottom as uniform and unchanging "still persists as a dangerous tradition" and is "not justified by what we now know." What Brinkhurst suggests of the lake bottom may be applied to the lake at large. The "dangerous tradition" of the holistic view of the unitary lake provided a satisfying basis for organizing limnology, which underwent a series of metamorphoses, although not all limnologists would concur on the stages. Brinkhurst echoed the concern, long expressed by terrestrial community ecologists, that

> any attempt to create unified classification soon falls down over the problem of lack of correspondence of the schemata based on different sets of criteria. (Brinkhurst 1974:159)

His commentary about transitions, multivariate interactions, and sampling problems all have a familiar ring for contemporary terrestrial ecologists. Brinkhurst posed the problem which is endemic in ecology: Lakes are not, he said, units, they are composites – "We must be prepared to subdivide lakes into their functional units if we are to have any sort of working classification." He goes on (1974:159) to pose another perennial problem of community ecology both aquatic and terrestrial: "To have a useful classification we must have real discontinuities between groups of equal status made up of recognizable discrete units." In a world in which almost all classifications have the phrase "more or less" liberally sprinkled in statements about discontinuities and discreteness, such classifications are difficult to achieve. Brinkhurst (1974:164) goes so far as to say, "No rational man would chose to become an ecologist or limnologist." This is no doubt hyperbole, but many ecologists or limnologists have wondered, as had Birge and Juday in 1911, if the complexities evident in quantitative studies would elude the rational man.

## Terrestrial plant ecology

Probably no aspect of the crystallization of terrestrial plant ecology as a distinctive science was as confused as the terminological morass, which is not entirely clarified even today and which has extended even to the name of the science itself. Whittaker (1962) reviewed the problems and theory of classification of natural communities of vegetation and recognized seven major traditions, simply as a means of conveniently classifying the myriad "schools" or "invisible colleges" which had formed in response to the problems of describing and classifying vegetation. Mueller-Dombois and Ellenberg (1974), McIntosh (1978), and Trass (1976) review the many terms which, with various nuances, have been applied to the study of vegetation. Trass traced the development of geobotany (broadly, plant ecology) in America and England and on the Continent. He noted the general similarity of plant ecology in the English-speaking countries and the Balkanization of plant ecology on the Continent. Westhoff (1970) identified four categories of vegetation study: "the practical, the logical, the usual Anglo-American and the negative." He recognized that "this division implies that the usual Anglo-American terminology regarding the science of vegetation research is neither practical nor logical" and stated that this is the opinion of the majority of European students of vegetation. Since the present work examines in large part Anglo-American ecology, the challenge to make it logical, if not practical, must be met.

There is widespread consensus that the largely "floristic plant geography" of the 18th century and early 19th century was transformed into the geography of vegetation. The crucial change in plant geography of the 19th century from the floristic emphasis of the traditional systematically oriented naturalist is the recognition of an entity based on properties of plants in the aggregate. What later came to be called "ecological plant geography" is commonly credited to Humboldt's recognition, shortly after 1800, of zones of vegetation on Teneriffe and his concept of groups of associated plants. The significant point is that 19th-century plant geographers developed the concept of a different entity, or a new ontological view, of vegetation, as contrasted with the flora (list of species); and much of the history and subsequent problems of plant ecology, and of ecology generally, are a consequence of this. One notable distinction between terrestrial plant and animal ecology is that there was in animal ecology no generally recognized term bearing the same relation to *terrestrial fauna* that *vegetation* does to *flora* (Udvardy 1969) or comparable to the aggregate terms *plankton* or *benthos* in aquatic ecology. The study of vegetation, as against plant individuals or species (flora), required recognition of supraindividual and supraspecific levels. These levels had to be made the object of study, to be described, and, in the minds of most early ecologists, classified and named.

The belief in the existence in nature of recognizable, describable, classifiable, and mappable natural entites, or communities, which came to be called "associations," "cœnoses," "formations," or "societies," among a host of other names, has a long and polemic history. It revolved around the basis of distinguishing such units, developing a system for naming and classifying them, or determining whether such units exist at all or are merely figments of the biologist's imagination or, more temperately, a useful artifact of his methods. The origin of this concept may be traced from Humboldt, who recognized that certain plants commonly grew together in areas or zones, through Schouw, a Danish botanist who in 1822 provided a nomenclature for such units, should they exist, by attaching the suffix *-etum* to the generic name of a plant which dominated (i.e., was most conspicuous or numerous, e.g., Quercetum for an oak [*Quercus*] forest). Later botanists, such as Kerner von Marilaun and August Grisebach, emphasized the importance of the community as a functional entity (Whittaker 1962; Mueller-Dombois and Ellenberg 1974; McIntosh 1978). The traditional natural history expectation of order in nature was exemplified in Kerner's well-known statement, which was typical of the views of most 19th-century biogeographers and turn-of-the-century ecologists:

> The horizontal and vertical assorting of large plant communities is by no means accidental in spite of its apparent lack of order. It follows certain immutable laws. Every plant has its place, its time, its function and its meaning. . . . In every zone the plants are gathered into definite groups which appear either as developing or as finished communities, but never transgress the orderly and correct composition of their kind. Science has given to such groups the name Plant Formations. With the comparative study of landscapes botanists found it necessary to define and characterize these ever-recurring elements which are so conspicuous in the physiognomy of landscape. (Quoted in Conard 1951:41)

The concept of groups of species as recurring elements or arrays in vegetation pervaded 19th-century plant geography. The plant formation was described by Grisebach (1872) as the "fundamental unit of vegetation," expressing precisely what Whittaker (1962) later called the "community-unit theory" of ecology which dominated much of the history of plant ecology. The last decade of the 19th century in Europe was rife with incipient geobotanical, phytosociological, and phytogeo-graphical schools, which were often restricted to particular countries or regions (Moss 1910; Gleason 1936; Whittaker 1962; Shimwell 1971; Trass 1976; McIntosh 1978). The multiplicity of systems later produced the idea of "an ecology of ecologists," a phrase of Sears (1956) sug-gesting that plant ecologists' ideas were conditioned by the vegetation in which they found themselves. As early as 1910 Moss reviewed the complex problems of terminology and methodology which had already developed around the concept of the plant community and proliferated in the early decades of the 20th century, causing Du Rietz (1930) to again attempt to bring order out of the terminological "chaos." The one common ground in the chaos was that vegetation was believed to be composed of "more or less" discrete communities. Whittaker (1962) recognized two interpretations of this concept: (1) the plant community was a basic natural unit as a product of evolution, or (2) it was a practical consequence of the method of analysis. In the first instance, communities existed in nature to be discovered; in the second they were devised according to some scheme of the investigator. There were essentially three basic ways of recognizing and categorizing plant communities: according to (1) the habitat; (2) the general appearance or "physiognomy" of the vegetation derived from the "life form" of the most conspicuous plants (trees, shrubs, herbs, etc.); and (3) the taxonomic composition of the vegetation, in its simplest and earliest form a species list, later supplemented by some estimate or measure of quantity of the species.

Most traditional schools of plant ecology adopted "the community-unit theory," although they differed drastically as to the nature of the community unit. However, many early plant ecologists qualified their recognition of the unit of community. Thus, Warming (1895) could write, in the modified English version (1909:12) of his influential *Pflanzamfund* of 1895, "An association is a community of definite floristic composition." Yet in the same volume he wrote:

> The different communities, it need hardly be stated, are scarcely ever sharply marked off from one another. Just as soil, moisture, and other external conditions are connected by the most gradual transitions so likewise are the plant commu-nities, especially in cultivated lands. (Warming 1909:13)

Nevertheless, plant ecologists proceeded to describe and name plant communities in diverse ways. Gause (1936) in the process of a later "revolution" of animal population ecology described this period:

The turning point in the history of biocoenology has been the publication of numerous botanical investigations at the close of the last and the beginning of the present century, which demonstrated that the vegetable covering of the earth is divided into natural units of structure or associations. The establishment of a definable unit has automatically led to a greater precision of observation and of thought.

The pioneer of American plant ecology, Clements (1905:202), believed that homogeneous groups occur due to environmental variation and the tendency of plants to associate or group together:

This fundamental peculiarity has given us the concept of the formation, an area of vegetation or a particular association, which is homogeneous within itself, and at the same time essentially different from contiguous areas.

The attributes of being "homogeneous" and "essentially different" became increasingly elusive as quantitative methods of describing and comparing communities became more widely used. The classical publications of MacMillan, Ganong, Harshberger, Pound and Clements, and Cowles in America, R. and W. Smith, Moss, Praeger, and Tansley in the British Isles, and a host of Continental plant ecologists, including the young J. Braun, later to become J. Braun-Blanquet by marriage, all dealt with the problems of the community unit. Although they differed substantially in their conceptions of the community unit, they uniformly provided verbal descriptions of the vegetation, its habitat, and often species lists.

Ganong (1903), among other plant ecologists, suggested the desirability of finding ways to estimate, quantitatively, the biological factors in a community – the precise effects of competition and cooperation among organisms in determining the makeup of a plant association. A first, less ambitious step in that direction had already been taken by his contemporaries from Nebraska, Pound and Clements (1898a,b). Pound and Clements in the first edition of their landmark *Phytogeography of Nebraska* (1898b; see also 2nd ed. 1900) started out by describing occurrence of species in the American township of 36 square miles as *frequence*, and this number divided by total number of quadrats and multiplied by 100 gave a *frequence index* or *percentage frequence*. *Abundance*, in Pound and Clements's usage, referred to the dual aspects of the number of individuals and their distribution, that is, whether as single individuals or large masses or clumps. Pound and Clements (1898b) used a series of descriptive terms (e.g., *copius, gre-*

*garious*) which incorporated number and distribution of individuals and size. They in effect calibrated these terms by actual counts of the number of individuals in plots 5 meters square (25 square meters), using a mean of several plots to assign a name to a numerical range. They also provided an abundance index by the formula

$$A^I = \frac{t \times e \times a}{T}$$

where $T$ is the number of units in the quadrat ($=36$), $t$ is the number of these in which a species occurs, $e$ is the mean extent covered by the species (estimated), and $a$ is the number of individuals per 25-square-meter plot. Pound and Clements optimistically stated that the only source of error in this equation was in determining $e$. Their index was not extensively used, even by themselves, but in the course of their considerations of abundance, Pound and Clements arrived at a momentous conclusion (Tobey 1981). After some 10 years of observation of prairie and of forming mental pictures of the vegetation, they decided that conclusions formed from experience and observation "without actual enumeration of individual plants" were invalid. Pound and Clements noted that transitions between communities were better shown by figures obtained from such enumerations than in any other way. They were explicit in stating that the enumerations themselves had nothing to do with the "mode of disposition" of the individuals, recognizing that plants were not uniformly distributed.

The failings of direct sensory observation and the advantages of counts which "furnish results which amply reward the time and work required" (Pound and Clements 1898b) have been the subject of extended discussion. A major result was the effort to develop the best and quickest way to secure accurate counts or other estimates of quantity of species in a community. Marine biologists, limnologists, and terrestrial animal ecologists worked largely, or only, with the "statistical community." That is, the counts of benthic organisms, plankton, and so forth were often the only information about the community they had. Terrestrial plant ecologists had to contend not only with the long tradition of natural history which held that what was significant could be directly sensed but also with the problem of whether the results obtained from counting corresponded with what was discernible to the senses. Many agreed with Haeckel in expressing doubt that there was anything to be gained by counting and by applying mathematics to the study of distribution of organisms or their aggregation in communities. Even Clements (1905:104), who actively pushed the merits of the quadrat method and quantitative measures, wrote, "In its present development biometry contains too much mathematics and too little biology." Doubts concerning the utility of quantitative methods persist throughout the history of ecology. Ecologists disagreed on the best way of quantifying the biological attributes of the community (quantification) or of distinguishing the community in the first place (entitation). Most traditional plant ecologists, even those advocating quantitative methods, chose the communities or stands to be studied on the basis of subjective judgments of the essential characters.

Tobey (1981) denied that the quadrat method used by Pound and Clements was an extension of biogeographic statistics as used by Humboldt. He distinguished these earlier statistics as "qualitative quantification," meaning the use of presence, rather than actual counts or weights, as a basis of determining quantities. This distinction introduces a mix of concept and terminology which has permeated quantitative plant ecology in particular and quantitative community ecology generally. Marine biologists, limnologists, terrestrial plant and animal ecologists, whether self-conscious ecologists or not, all faced much the same problems in transforming floristic biogeography into a quantitative science of communities. In spite of notable efforts in this direction, ecologists would be criticized for being inadequately quantitative and mathematical (McIntosh 1974b, 1976, 1980a). Early 20th-century plant ecologists nevertheless addressed the problems of developing a quantitative community ecology. Pound and Clements (1898b) adapted the statistics of vegetation from the statistics of flora as practiced by plant geographers. They specifically acknowledged Drude whose statistics were based on large areas (square kilometers) and calculation of "frequence" of species in such areas, a floristic distinction. Frequence was based on a qualitative distinction between areas – a species was present or absent in the area. Pound and Clements, and later Weaver and Clements (1938), found frequence an undesirable basis for quantifying vegetation, although ecologists still find it a useful characteristic and some find it preferable to counts of individuals for some purposes. Pound and Clements turned to small-scale areas (25 square meters) and a measure they called "abundance," which incorporated three aspects of individual plants, their number, distribution, and size. In their "index of abundance," described above, they combined the statistics of flora and the statistics of vegetation. Pound and Clements recognized that individuals of different species varied greatly in distribution, so they adopted Drude's terminology in establishing classes of abundance described as copious or gregarious. Here they used a technique which was characteristic of most Continental plant ecology, notably the burgeoning school of J. Braun-Blanquet located at Montpellier. Various scales were developed, with five to ten grades weighting estimates of number and size of individuals as a basis for quantifying vegetation. These numerical scales, with appropriate descriptive terms (scarce to crowd), were and still are widely used on the Continent (Greig-Smith 1957; Whittaker 1962; Mueller-Dombois and Ellenberg 1974).

It is something of an anomaly that Clements, who with his early associate Pound hailed the quadrat method and numerical counts as essential to distinguishing communities and changes in communities, subsequently in his own work seldom used quantitative approaches to ecology (White in press). Pound and Clements (1898b) refer to numbers of individuals and changes thereof in the text but do not provide tables of quadrat counts to buttress their statements about vegetation. Although Tobey (1981) asserted that with Pound and Clements "ecology took leave of its senses" and hitched its intellect to mathematics in a "revolution" in ecology, a revolution he compared to that associated with Galileo, Clements did not get beyond simple counting, and more sophisticated statistical considerations were left to others. Nevertheless, Clements was an earnest cheerleader for quantitative plant ecology and was the notable American developer and advocate of the quadrat method. Tobey (1981) noted the difficulty of following the genesis of Clements's thought concerning the quadrat method. By 1905, when he published the earliest how-to book in ecology, *Research Methods in Ecology,* Clements had reduced the size of the basic quadrat to 1 square meter and the "major" quadrat to 16 square meters down from 25 in 1900. He had redefined *abundance* to equal "the total number of individuals in an area," a meaning which it usually retains to the present, although sharing that definition with *density* used by some early limnologists and marine biologists and preferred by most later plant ecologists, whereas animal ecologists commonly used *abundance.* Clements, in 1905, did not allude further to *frequence,* although he did recognize the problem of size of quadrat, which is most commonly a problem in quantifying frequence.

Clements (1905) shared with other ecologists a recognition of the perennial problem of quantitative community ecology. He wrote that it is fruitless to seek accuracy in measuring the environment if a corresponding accuracy of measurement of vegetation was not possible. A continuing problem of quantitative community ecology and its hybrid descendent quantitative ecosystem ecology is the relative ease of obtaining precise measurements of physical attributes and the difficulty of getting precise measurements of biological characteristics of communities or ecosystems and of interpreting the response of organisms to the physical environment. This difficulty was explicit in the writing of the Danish plant ecologist Raunkaier (1908), who, with Clements, was among the early proponents of the quadrat method and was also an early explorer of sampling statistics. Raunkaier noted the ease of measuring the physical environment, but wrote that "the numbers obtained tell us nothing about the biological values which result from a harmonious co-operation of these factors." He also stated the commonplace of the complex environment, later to be called the multivariate environment, which plagues ecologists to the present:

1. "Identical values of one factor may in different combinations with others have different biological effects."
2. "Different combinations of factors may have the same biological value."

In the face of widespread recognition of these concepts as truisms, ecologists and physiologists pursued studies of single factors (for which they were often criticized) as a necessary preamble for the ideal study of the holistic environment.

Raunkaier was a pioneer in quantitative community ecology in his attempts to divorce it from the taxonomic units, usually the species. Raunkaier used "life form" as a basic biological unit, whereas Clements and most other quantitative community ecologists used the species. *Life form*, by Raunkaier's definition, was basically the position of the plant part which survived the most severe season in any area. In his earliest use of biological statistics, Raunkaier used life form statistics as a basis of "biological plant geography," but later he examined plant formations of an area in respect to proportionate distribution of life form. Raunkaier's use of life form as a means of a biological measurement to integrate the effect of environment (indicator value) assumed that a given environment will produce convergence of life forms in different taxa. In this way, quantitative community comparisons would be possible between areas of different taxonomy.

When Raunkaier (1910) turned to the statistics of plant formations, he concurred with Pound and Clements that it was a necessary move

"to improve upon the uncertain picture we obtain by subjective estimates of plant communities." He noted also the distinction between
qualitative floristic comparison, in which all species count equally, and
comparisons of vegetation, where quantity by some measure weights
individual species as components of the vegetation. Raunkaier anticipated later terrestrial ecologists in assessing the problems of measuring
size or bulk (biomass) of species. He noted that it was necessary to do
this when a species had reached its maximum size, and since the several species of a formation do this at diferent times, he decided that
weighing was not feasible. He recognized, as had Clements, that
counts of individuals did not measure bulk, but unlike Clements, he
turned to occurrence in quadrats as an estimate of bulk.

Raunkaier's approach was to determine what he called species'
"frequency" or "valency" (the number of quadrats in which a species
occurs) in a number of quadrats (usually 50) of a given size. He thus
went beyond Clements in his systematic exploration of the effect of
quadrat size upon frequency. He investigated the effect of quadrat size
on the number or "richness" of species in different formations and
explored the effect of quadrat size on the ratio of frequency of the
dominant to that of all other species. He determined that this ratio
stabilized depending on the size of quadrat, and this served his avowed
purpose of finding a method which would give a measure related to the
true mass relationships within the community.

Raunkaier's most notable contribution to community statistics came
to be called "Raunkaier's law." He observed that if the numbers of
species in each of five frequency classes (20 percent interval) were
plotted in sequence, the resulting distribution was a reversed J-shaped
curve. That is, the frequencies declined in the first four classes but
increased in the highest (80–100 percent) class. This idea was widely
advanced as a basic quantitative property of a community until it was
shown that the shape of the curve was largely a function of the size of
the quadrat (Gleason 1922; Goodall 1952; Greig-Smith 1957). However, Raunkaier's law proved to be relatively immune to refutation
and persisted in the literature in the face of repeated attacks (McIntosh
1962; Hanski 1982). Although Raunkaier concentrated on frequency as
the basic quantity, whereas Clements preferred counts or, at least,
estimates of individuals, they agreed that it was possible and necessary
for plant ecology to get beyond the uncertainties of subjective estimation by using "actual figures," as Raunkaier (1910) had it. They faced,

along with other ecologists, the difficulties of determining which figure was most repesentative of "reality" and how such figures were best determined.

Among the notable early explorers of quantitative plant ecology were H. A. Gleason of the United States and L. G. Ramensky in Russia. Both were largely ignored as heretics in the context of more conventional views of community ecology in their respective countries (Ponyatovskaya 1961; McIntosh 1967, 1975a). Both, however, made notable contributions to quantitative plant community ecology. Ramensky (1924), in an article summarizing work he had begun in 1911, saw the future of ecology "in deeper analysis of relations, acting factors and equilibrium mechanisms" (quoted in McIntosh 1983b). To this end he asserted that plant ecology would "need quantitative and methodologically substantiated registration of facts." Ramensky used yet another definition of the familiar word *abundance,* which he measured as "a specific area of horizontal projection of ground shoots" or what came to be called "cover." Ramensky used this measure as a percentage of the total area of samples using squares (quadrats) having a diagonal of 2 meters. Ramensky, more than any of his contemporaries, documented his assertions about plant communities by detailed tables, comparing the percentage cover within and between communities. Well in advance of most other quantitative community ecologists, he used the standard deviation as a means of expressing the variation among samples. He noted the decrease in standard deviation as the area of sample increased. Another perceptive distinction Ramensky made was total absence of a species ($-$) from absence (0) in which it was possible that a species might appear. This breakdown between an absolute qualitative distinction and a probabilistic quantitative one, both indicated by absence, reappears in subsequent quantitative ecology. Ramensky joined his American contemporary Gleason in emphasizing that vegetation was, to a large extent, a phenomenon influenced by chance arrivals and worked out by struggle among the available species by community ("biocœnotic") interactions which did not produce distinct unit communities but a continuous gradient of change of vegetation with change in environment. In America, H. A. Gleason, the self-described "good man gone wrong" of plant ecology, arrived at conclusions similar to those of Ramensky, although lacking in Ramensky's extensive backing of quantitative data (McIntosh 1975a, 1983b).

**Problems of quantitative community ecology**

During the early decades of the 20th century, plant ecologists, like contemporary marine biologists and limnologists, were much involved in developing methods of describing, in quantitative terms, communities whose existence and extent in nature were largely assumed. A distinction arose between descriptive or analytic statistics and qualitative or synthetic statistics (Oosting 1948). The former were estimates or measurements of individual sites or stands, the concrete community in the usual ecological phrase; the latter were estimates or measurements based on a number of individual sites or stands, the abstract community. Concrete stands were assessed in terms of presence or absence of species in the entire area, presence of species in a number of samples (frequency), by estimates or measurements of quantity as number of individuals (density), amount of ground covered (cover), or weight of living material (biomass). These quantities were expressed in scale units or numbers – the latter in absolute or relative (percent) terms. The means of assessing these quantities was commonly based on a sample area, or quadrat, which varied in size, shape, and number. Methods were also devised to eliminate the need for a sample area by restricting the sample to contacts with or projections on a line or, later, to contacts with or distances from points in space (Cottam and Curtis 1949; Greig-Smith 1957). Most community sampling in the early decades was based on the assumption that the concrete stand was homogeneous. Indeed, a common practice on the Continent was to sample a single quadrat large enough to encompass the characteristics of the community which was described as the "minimal area." The area which the data were supposed to represent was chosen subjectively, either by recognition of some habitat characteristic or on the basis of some attributes of the organisms. In terrestrial vegetation studies this was usually the physiognomy (life form) or the taxon of the dominant species or of species considered "characteristic" of the community. A conundrum which appeared early in ecology was the meaning of *dominant*. To most it was simply the largest or most conspicuous component of a community; to others dominance was a measure of function of a species in or of its effect on the total community rather than number or size of its individuals. Whatever the criteria used, subjective recognition of homogeneity, commonly achieved by studying very small areas, was typical. It persisted in quantitative studies of areas commonly described as "more or less" similar.

One of the earliest disputes in aquatic ecology, as we have noted, was between Haeckel and Hensen about whether plankton organisms were uniformly distributed in space, which was largely determined by their subjective experiences. Goodall (1952) commented that Gleason appeared to be "the first man to study, quantitatively, the distribution of individual plants." H. A. Gleason, after extensive unpublished work with quadrats, was among the earliest to use the quadrat to examine distribution of individuals of terrestrial plant species. Gleason (1920) used probability theory to test whether plants were dispersed at random and found that they were more often distributed in patches as Haeckel had contended for plankton. Peculiarly, the astute Gleason contradicted his own experience by later treating plant distribution as random. This work continued the long contention concerning random versus nonrandom distribution of organisms (pattern) which pervades all aspects of empirical and theoretical ecology. Questions of pattern, and its determination, as noted by Hutchinson (1953), Greig-Smith (1957), and Pielou (1969), among a host of later ecologists, are fundamental. More recently, Schaffer and Leigh (1976) asserted that the old-fashioned problem of pattern is still of paramount concern. They suggested that mathematical models proposed for animal populations are not applicable to plants because they are clumped (as are many animals). A limit to the usefulness of these models, they suggested, is imposed by the difficulty of adequately describing clumping or pattern.

Study of distribution of individuals of a species always comes up against the basic question of what constitutes an individual. The question is relatively easily answered by terrestrial animal ecologists or students of vertebrates generally. It is more difficult or even impossible to answer with respect to some terrestrial plants and various kinds of aquatic invertebrates. Statements about species distribution and quantity are commonly influenced by the confidence with which an investigator can determine the individual. Criteria such as presence and absence, cover or size, may not be affected by this problem. Number of individuals (per area or volume) and any relation involving it are largely contingent upon determination of what constitutes an individual. The traditional expression of number of individuals is the total or mean number of individuals per area or, less frequently, the mean area per individual. Some ecologists noted that the relationship of most concern is not the mean density (number per area or mean distance) but the distance to its neighbor or neighbors, which is influenced primarily by the pattern of distribution of an organism. Since most organisms tend to be aggregated or clumped (a condition also described by a variety of less meaningful synonyms), the actual distance between individuals of the same species is apt to be less than the mean distance. Later students of competition, pollination, and other phenomena asserted that effective ecological study requires measurements of pattern or of actual spacing between organisms.

One quantitative property long attributed to a community, however defined, was a characteristic number of species. Gilbert White, an 18th-century "arcadian" ecologist, in Worster's (1977) phraseology, had commented that the more an area is examined, the more species are found. A corollary to this item of naturalist lore is evident in statements of 19th-century biogeographers and protoecologists that the larger the area examined, the greater the number of species encountered. Quantitative interest among biogeographers is also evident in the relationships between number of species per genus in an area. An early contributor to quantitative ecology was P. Jaccard, whose name appears routinely as an early, if not the first, contributor to many aspects of quantitative ecology in the first decade of the 20th century (Goodall 1952; Greig-Smith 1957; Connor and McCoy 1979). Goodall wrote that Jaccard was the earliest to express clearly that there was an increase in the number of species with area. The relationship between species and area was formulated mathematically by Arrhenius (1921). Gleason (1922) criticized Arrhenius's formulation as giving unreasonably large numbers of species for large areas and offered an alternative formula. Neither model was immediately pursued by ecologists. Nevertheless, number of species of an area or community was widely regarded by terrestrial and aquatic ecologists as an extremely significant characteristic.

Baker (1918) recorded number of species per area of lake bottom type and said that sand bottoms were "richest" in species and boulder bottoms "poorest." By 1920, the premier limnologist in Europe, A. Thienemann, had identified two "ecological principles" (Hynes 1970):

1.  The greater the diversity of conditions in a locality, the larger is the number of species that make up the biotic community.
2.  The more the conditions in a locality deviate from normal, and hence from the normal optima of most species, the smaller is the number of species that occur there and the greater the number of individuals of each species that do occur.

According to Hynes, Thienemann later added a third principle, the stability-diversity hypothesis, which came to be regarded as dogma among some ecologists (Goodman 1975):

3.  The longer a locality has been in the same condition, the richer is its biotic community and the more stable it is.

Species number came to be regarded as an important attribute of plant or animal community. Elton (1927) wrote, "There is some important principle involved in the total number of species in an animal community" but commented that it was not clear what the principle was. Hynes commented that the first two of Thienemann's principles were ignored by English-speaking ecologists and "yet they [were] repeatedly rediscovered and put forward as new ideas" to the "shocked surprise" of German scientists. Hynes identified a parochialism all too common in ecology, which has impeded its progress. The species-area relation of Thienemann's first two principles was seized on as an attribute of a community by diverse ecologists. The curve describing the increase in number of species with area was used to determine the characteristic area of a plant community (Cain 1938). Cain and others soon found this was an artifact. Goodall (1952) commented that the intrinsic interest of species-area curves is limited, but the subsequent history of quantitative ecology has seen a dramatic increase in interest in species-area relationships. Preston (1948) explored species-area relations, culminating in assertions about the "canonical" distributions of species (Preston 1962). This was seized on by MacArthur and Wilson (1963) as a key to their *Theory of Island Biogeography*. Most recently, all of the mathematical formulations of species-area relationships were reviewed and questioned by Connor and McCoy (1979). Thienemann's third principle relating number of species and community stability was, perhaps, a legacy of the balance-of-nature and evolution concepts that limnology shared with terrestrial ecology. Although commonly attributed to "classical ecology," its genesis is not entirely clear. Some classical ecologists, among them Clements and Tansley, explicitly stated that number of species was highest in intermediate seral stages and decreased in the stable or climax community (Goodman 1975; McIntosh 1980a). The question was resurrected in the 1950s in the context of the new theoretical ecology (MacArthur 1955). MacArthur suggested that increased number of links among species in a food web increased community stability. Resurgent interest in communities and their properties perpetuated the familiar problem. The organizers of a famous symposium commented that "a major means for assuring the continuity of life appears to be the number of species per unit area, diversity" (Brookhaven Symposia in Biology 1969:v). By this time *diversity* had taken on expanded meaning. In addition to number of species, it involved the proportionate distribution of individuals (or other quantitative measures among species). The symposium wrestled unsatisfactorily with the dual problems of *diversity* and *stability* in amended and not entirely clear meanings. Besides the problem of definition, neither property of a community was measured to everyone's satisfaction, an all too familiar problem in quantitative community ecology.

Another major problem faced by quantitative community ecologists was how to use quantitative data, not only to describe stands as concrete individual representations of a community but to compare and analyze many concrete stands to form an abstract community. Unfortunately, the term *association* had been attributed to both the concrete and the abstract community, which created unwanted confusion among plant ecologists. The substance of such comparisons was that individual stands of a "homogeneous" community should be "similar" with respect to each other and different, with respect to their similar attributes, from stands of other homogeneous communities. One such characteristic used in several Continental schools of phytosociology was the concept of *constancy*, that is, species which occurred in some minimum percentage (usually 50 percent) of the stands of a community. Allied to this was *fidelity*, the degree to which a species was restricted to one community, which concept suffered because it was quantifiable only after the several communities of an area had been distinguished. Neither constancy or fidelity was ever effectively incorporated in quantitative ecology as practiced in Britain or America. Quantitative means of comparing similarity among stands or samples were introduced by early animal ecologists. Marine biologists, such as Hensen in the 1880s, used the percentage deviation from the mean as an estimate of the variation among samples. S. A. Forbes (1907a) developed an index for comparing co-occurrence of species in several stands.

However, animal ecologists, particularly terrestrial animal ecologists, did not follow the lead of plant ecologists, whom they recognized as the leaders in establishing community ecology. Dice (1952) wrote that correct recognition of communities depended on the competence, knowledge, and previous experience of the ecologist, thereby essentially following the tradition of European plant ecologists. Southwood (1966) commented that animal ecologists usually delimited communities by reference to plants or to a vegetational factor. In both of these standard references to animal community ecology most of the references to quantitative community studies are to the work of plant ecologists and almost all reference to studies of pattern, association, species number, and quantitative approaches to synthesis of samples into communities are either derivative from plant ecology or cite references in the late 1940s and after. Prior to about 1950, terrestrial animal ecologists devoted most of their effort to quantitative studies of populations of a single species or to the interaction between two species, such as competitors or predators. It may be, as Elton said, that the tendency of animals to hide or rush away at the approach of an ecologist made sampling of multispecies aggregations difficult. Whatever the case, in the early decades of self-conscious ecology, exploration of quantitative aspects of community and the idiosyncracies of sampling methods fell largely in the domain of plant ecologists, often paralleled by marine biologists and limnologists.

Goodall (1952) provided a useful outline of the quantitative aspects of plant distribution containing ideas which can be readily extrapolated to questions of distribution of organisms of any kind. These approaches were pursued intensively by plant ecologists in the first half of the 20th century in their efforts to develop a quantitative community ecology. Animal ecologists dealt variously with some of these relationships, although some of them looked askance at plant ecologists' devotion to quantitative "description" of community and the problems it uncovered. Allee (1934) reviewed the introduction of quantitative methods in ecology, citing Shelford's "quantitative estimate of physical and biotic factors" in succession of ponds in 1911 and quoting himself in the same year as noting the need for quantitative data. He made the point that he and Shelford were "alive to the needs of the time." Allee also made the point, often repeated by biologists since, that not all biological relations are revealed by quantitative studies. He cited the need for information furnished by what is "at times disdainfully dismissed, as naturalistic observations." Goodall provided a useful caveat to the devotee of quantitative community ecology:

> It is not claimed that the whole of . . . ecology can be expressed in quantitative terms. . . . quantitative methods can never be more than an adjunct to description – they can never provide interpretations. Interpretation is a process in the ecologist's mind when he has fully surveyed the descriptive data, whether qualitative or quantitative . . . quantitative de-

scriptions may greatly facilitate and even guide these mental processes, they cannot replace them.

It is ironic that Clements and other early proponents of quantitative ecology deplored as "description" their predecessors' and contemporaries' verbal accounts of vegetation, its appearance, species composition, and segregation into formations, and the relation of these to the environment or to each other in space or in time. Quantitative community ecology in its turn came to be described as "mere description," or even numerology, and deplored as static. Tobey's (1981) assertion that with the advent of the quadrat method and counts of individuals ecology had taken leave of its senses was just what Goodall's comment was all about. The continuing problem of quantitative ecology is the extent to which it facilitates description and understanding (explanation) of vegetation, its distribution, and its functions. The loss of direct sensory perception in using quantitative methods was the major reason in the minds of some early plant ecologists for not using quantitative methods, but it was not, as we have noted, a problem for many aquatic ecologists. Quantitative data were, to many ecologists, objective and more accurate means of describing vegetation. The early years of the 20th century produced volumes of tables of data of many different characteristics of vegetation using increasingly detailed methods of sampling (Gleason 1936). Until about 1950 the basic data were only one step removed from the ecologists' senses, and ecologists examined tables and graphs which numerically represented characteristics of vegetation only once removed from reality. In spite of many studies concerned with problems of quantitative analysis, many ecologists were hopeful, and some were assured, that quantitative community studies, if not a panacea, were at least a means of assessing objectively the attributes of organisms. Beginning in the early 1950s, quantitative community studies took a new turn with the introduction of multivariate analysis of communities. The "concrete" community became, instead of a relatively palpable entity on the ground, a nebulous cloud of points in multidimensional space. Numerical methods turned from description of communities to multivariate methods of classification and ordination of communities (McIntosh 1958b, 1967, 1974b, 1976; Whittaker 1967, 1973).

The merits of community recognition based on experience and intuition versus quantitative and objective analysis have long been debated among ecologists. For many it was assumed that recognition of communities was a necessary or at least useful preamble to experimental or physiological studies because organisms are always affected by the habitat in which they occur (Curtis and McIntosh 1951). The traditional concept of a unit community was shared by plant ecologists such as Braun-Blanquet and Clements (although their conceptions of the unit differed drastically), marine biologists such as C. G. J. Petersen and G. Thorson, and limnologists such as S. A. Forbes and A. Thienemann. The community unit concept was questioned on the basis of developments in quantitative studies in terrestrial and marine communities (Jones 1950; McIntosh 1967; Whittaker 1967; Stephenson 1973). The difference between animal ecologists and plant ecologists regarding the importance of communities disappeared with the rise of a new generation of theoretical animal ecologists in the 1950s who claimed community ecology as their own. Current ecologists continue to differ in how they view communities. Christiansen and Fenchel (1977) wrote that the problem of biological communities is "resolved or rather rendered a nonproblem when the results of theoretical ecology are considered." They asserted that community ecologists have not considered that simple experiments and observations are more fruitful than "complex statistical analyses of quantitative data" of communities. Tonn and Magnuson (1982), however, reverted to an older view in a study of fish communities:

> The identification of these assembly patterns describes what we feel are ecologically striking fish assemblage structures which appear to result from deterministic mechanisms of assemblage maintenance. Only now that these patterns have been described can meaningful, specific hypotheses be tested by intensive autecological or experimental studies.

# 5

## Population ecology

The early traditions of self-conscious ecology were marked by the tendency of ecologists to study either an individual species or aggregates of species. Proponents of the new biology of the 19th century concentrated on morphological and physiological properties of species, typically in the laboratory. As protoecologists returned to study of organisms in the field, they combined some of the interests and skills of physiologists and morphologists with the concerns of biogeographers and natural historians about distributions of and interrelations among species. One of the earliest terminological distinctions made in the emergence of "self-conscious" ecology was (in 1896) the addition of prefixes to create "autecology" and "synecology" (Chapman 1931). *Aut-* literally designates "self" or "individual," but in ecological practice it described studies of a small group of individuals of a species, which was regarded as a unit. Ambiguity was avoided, temporarily, by Adams (1913), who distinguished three classes of ecology: "individual," "aggregate," specifying the taxonomic unit, and "associational," citing Möbius's biocœnose as an example of the last. Adams's contemporary, Shelford (1929:608), had little use for autecology. To Shelford, at that date at least:

> Ecology is a science of communities. A study of the relations of a single species to the environment conceived without reference to communities and, in the end, unrelated to the natural phenomena of its habitat and community associates is not properly included in the field of ecology.

Plant ecologists at the Third International Botanical Congress in 1910 formally adopted the terms *autecology* and *synecology:*

> Ecology, the study of conditions of environment and of adaptation of plant species is if taken isolately "autecology," if taken in association "synecology." (Chapman 1931:5)

Chapman confirmed this meaning of *autecology* for animal ecologists, commenting that it was this aspect of ecology, bordering on physiology, which even raised the question of whether ecology was a distinct science. However, turning to the subject matter of synecology and the interactions of species and the complex of environmental factors, Chapman clearly recognized "a field no longer that of general physiology" but "more distinctly as that of ecology." Chapman's question about the distinctiveness of ecology at the autecological end persists particularly in a recent hope to merge it with population genetics. The overlapping interests of physiological ecologists in physiological attributes of populations, of population geneticists in genetic variability of populations and their evolution, and of population ecologists concerned with the dynamics of populations are currently included under the term *population biology*.

Self-conscious ecology emerged at the turn of the century, its founders claiming a relationship with natural history and evolution, especially in explaining adaptation, and also linking it to physiology (McIntosh 1980a, 1983a). Notwithstanding Haeckel's definition of *ecology* as the relation of organisms to their environment, explicitly including other organisms, much protoecology and early ecology concentrated on relations of organisms only with their physical environment. The zoologist Semper (1881), for example, considered the effects on animals of factors of the inanimate environment – light, temperature, and water relations. Merriam (1894) based his "law" of distribution of animals on temperature relations of animals. The botanists Warming (1895) and Schimper (1898) emphasized water relations of plants. Pound and Clements (1897), reviewing MacMillan's (1897) classic contribution to plant ecology, noted, with some disapproval, that he was solely concerned with the physical environment. The earliest physiological-ecological work in America funded in 1903 by a private foundation, the Carnegie Institution, stressed measurement of the physical environment, and physiological responses of plants at the Desert Laboratory and provided a microcosm of ecology emerging from physiology (McIntosh 1983a). Some ecologists expressed the hope that application of the rapidly developing methods of 19th-century physiology would provide the touchstone for ecology, or even make it unnecessary, so that it would merge with physiology. No merger occurred; physiology and ecology separated, but produced hybrids, or at least "hopeful monsters."

**Physiological ecology and population ecology**

Segregating ecology from physiology and, subsequently, distinguishing the several hybrids, physiological-ecology, ecological-physiology, and ecophysiology, is not easy (Allee et al. 1949; Andrewartha and Birch 1954; Billings 1957; Tracy and Turner 1982; McIntosh 1983a). Earlier terms were abandoned. "Response physiology" was concerned mainly with behavior of animals; "relations physiology" or "toleration physiology" was concerned with the distribution and responses of a population, normally of one species, to individual environmental factors (Allee et al. 1949). A problem of ecologists is deciding what is the appropriate relation of ecology to its parent science and what physiology contributes to ecology per se or to the several hyphenated combinations. Livingston (1909), one of the early staff of the Desert Laboratory, was straightforward:

> By physiological ecology is here meant merely the study of factors which determine the occurrence and behavior of plants growing under uncontrolled conditions.

Shelford described both controlled laboratory and field experiments, defining the response of animals to environmental factors as physiological ecology. Shelford was one of the early animal ecologists who studied the community and stressed its significance in ecology. However, he also voiced the hope of other contemporary and later ecologists:

> If we knew the physiological life histories of a majority of animals, most other ecological problems would be easy of solution. (Shelford 1913:33)

Shelford, perhaps anticipating later controlled environmental chambers, phytotrons, and biotrons, allowed that physiological life histories could be worked out in a laboratory "with elaborate facilities." However, he centered on the "mores" problem, that is, physiological life histories in natural environments together with other organisms in communities. In 1929 Shelford published *Laboratory and Field Ecology*, and his famous *vivarium* at the University of Illinois became the seat of a distinguished tradition of experimental and physiological ecology of animals.

Ecologists were, and are, ambivalent and inconsistent in their use of the terms *autecology, environment,* and *physiological ecology.* Chapman (1931) distinguished *physical autecology* and *biotic autecology.* Some ecologists seeking the historical beginning of physiological ecology found it in organisms as related to the physical environment in the work of Reaumur, Priestley, Lavoisier, and Van't Hoff (Kendeigh 1961; Andrewartha and Birch 1973). Although all ecologists recognize that *environment* includes other organisms, the tendency to concentrate on physical factors – in more up-to-date phraseology, "variables" or "parameters" – is difficult to resist. This may be because they are more easily measured. Physiological ecology is a diverse if not elusive subject. In one sense it is physical autecology and stresses the internal function of individual organisms or parts thereof (Briggs 1980). In its more typical sense it concentrates on the function of organisms in natural environments, stressing the entire organism (Billings 1957; Andrewartha and Birch 1973). A recent survey of physiological ecologists asking "What is physiological ecology?" yielded diverse answers. The great, if not unanimous, consensus was that it involved natural conditions and the whole organism (Tracy and Turner 1982).

Early studies of physiological responses of organisms concentrated largely on the response to a physical factor of the environment. Since these studies normally examined the response of a group or population of organisms to the factor, they constituted a facet of population ecology. The classical rationale of such studies was the so-called law of the minimum formulated by the famous 19th-century German agricultural chemist Justus Liebig. Liebig's "law" stated that the rate of any process is limited by the least, or slowest, factor affecting it. Shelford (1911, 1913) elaborated on the idea of "limiting factors" in his "law of toleration," which asserted that a population or species is limited in its distribution or function by a minimum *and* a maximum level of any factor, with an optimum (later preferendum) between these at which the organism grows and reproduces best. Various branches of early self-conscious ecology examined the effect of different physical factors on the distribution, growth, and reproduction of populations, particularly those of economic or public health concern. This emphasis on the response of organisms and populations to the physical environment was evident in the organization and emphasis of most first-generation reference works and textbooks in ecology. Chapman (1931), for example, devoted 146 pages of his pioneer textbook of animal ecology to physical autecology and 19 pages to biotic autecology, with 20 pages of nutrition in limbo between them. Oddly, he said that biotic autecology was more usual in ecological studies. Egler (1951) strongly criticized the pre-1950 textbooks of plant ecology for concentrating on single-factor autecology. Andrewartha and Birch (1973), in a history of insect population ecology, started with ecological physiology, an extended review of the physical environment, and the relation of insects to physical variables. In their view, "The concept of the environment is the very essence of the theory of population ecology." Theoretical population ecology, as it developed in the 1920s and 1930s, had strong

links with physiology and environment, and some of its earliest proponents were cognizant of these links. G. F. Gause (1932) wrote, "The
study of the correlation between the density of population and environment represents the leading problem of the ecology of populations." Gause expanded the qualitative concept of Shelford's "law" of
tolerance to provide a specific mathematical expression to describe the
relation, or degree of "ecological amplitude," between a population
and an environmental factor:

> The correlation between the density of population of very dif-
> ferent organisms and ecological factors in natural conditions
> can be expressed by means of a special type of curve, that of
> Gauss.

Gause joined his Russian compatriot Ramensky, among other early
ecologists, in using the mean and standard deviation of a normal Gaussian curve as a description of the conditions in which a species grows
(McIntosh 1983b), and Gause used the standard deviation to characterize the "ecological plasticity" of a species (Gause 1932). Physiological tolerance ranges of species populations, with respect to one or
more factors, were commonly measured in experimental contexts and
in nature where they anticipated "niche breadth" curves. A major
problem in experimental physiological studies lay in the assumption
that tolerance ranges and optima, determined in experimental contexts, are effective in explaining or predicting the distributions of
species in their normal habitat in relation to many variables and their
interactions with other species. Autecology, *sensu stricto*, has limits,
since it omits such interactions, although it may provide suggestive
evidence (Macfadyen 1957).

## Definition and antecedents of population ecology

A *population* is commonly defined as a collection of individuals of a
species. In human demography, and etymologically, it is clearly one
species, *Homo sapiens*. In general biology, ecology, and statistics,
*population* is less straightforward. *Population* was used by biologists
and early ecologists in a collective sense to describe all organisms of a
group or area, for example, a population of invertebrates, fishes, or
birds. Johnstone (1908), like many of his predecessors and contemporaries, defined *population* (in the case of mollusks) as the number of
individuals per square foot or referred to the total population of the
sea, but he also described a population as the numbers of individuals

of each kind of organism with its own birth rates and death rates. Thomas Park (1939), a notable experimental population ecologist, considered both "single-species" and "mixed-species" populations and saw no difficulty in using the word *population* for both. Park also provided the convenient terms *population biology* and *population ecology* (Park 1945, 1946) to add to population dynamics a term used earlier by Elton. The dual meaning of *population* persisted in the leading mid-20th-century reference of animal ecology (Allee et al. 1949). A glossary prepared by the Committee on Nomenclature of the Ecological Society of America (1947) defined *population* as "the sum total of the individuals in a given area; sometimes used with the implication that individuals are of the same species." The looser use of *population*, which characterized early ecology, gave way, with some qualifications, to the definition of *population* as the number of individuals of a species as the unit of choice. Aggregates of species populations had long been called communities (Dice 1952). Cole (1957) reviewed the history of the term and the study of populations and allowed that no one, not even students of classical languages, was offended any more by reference to nonhuman "populations." By this time, the autonomy of population ecology as an important – some believed *the* important – aspect of ecology was secure. Population ecology, as it became a more discrete discipline, usually included the study of dynamics of single-species populations, the interactions between two-species populations with very tentative excursions into three-species interactions, and sometimes promised to provide a theory and explanation of multispecies communities (Slobodkin 1961; May 1974a).

Comments on and interest in populations of given kinds of organism and attributes of populations date to antiquity. These have been reviewed by Cole (1957), Egerton (1967, 1968a,b,c, 1976) and Hutchinson (1978). As might be expected, populations of locusts or disease organisms such as plague attracted attention even when not recognized as populations. Specific concerns about population growth of humans and animals of economic interest are scattered through the literature up to the 18th century, without leading to formulation of any general concepts other than balance of nature. Similarly, interactions between populations were matters of practical and speculative concern to many, among them Benjamin Franklin, who considered the effect of predation by birds on insects (Otto 1979), and A. P. DeCandolle, who recognized that competition might influence geographical distribution of organisms (Clements 1916). The famous and much disputed exposition of human population growth by Malthus (1798) in his *Essay on the Principle of Population* posed the dire consequences of geometric increase of human populations and the tragic means of their limitation. Darwin and Alfred Russell Wallace both derived from Malthus the basic idea of struggle for existence which stimulated their concept of natural selection and the idea that environment limits populations. Formal mathematical formulations of population growth appeared with greater sophistication and led to intense activity in theoretical population ecology in the 1920s and 1930s and a grand upheaval in the 1950s and thereafter. Darwin, who anticipated many of the basic concepts of ecology, also presaged the attitude of some biologists who were less than enthralled by mathematical formulations of population growth implicit in Darwin's verbal model (Andrewartha and Birch 1973). He wrote:

> We have better evidence on this subject than mere theoretical calculations, namely the numerous recorded cases of the astonishingly rapid increase of various animals in a state of nature, when circumstances have been favorable to them during two or three following seasons. (Darwin 1859:117)

In fact, the forerunner of "mere theoretical calculations" of population growth antedated Darwin's work. In 1838, going beyond Malthus, P. F. Verhulst formulated the famous "logistic" equation of population growth which, like Mendel's similarly premature effort, went unnoticed until it was rediscovered in the 1920s (Hutchinson 1978). With perhaps some poetic justice the botanist Karl Nageli, who had failed to appreciate Mendel's work, produced a promising start in the quantitative study of plant populations, which was ignored, like the work of Mendel and Verhulst (Harper 1977c).

Park (1946) provided a useful outline of the history of "modern population ecology" stemming from four largely separate sources, "human demography" and "biometry" in one dyad and "early ecology" and "general and comparative physiology" in another. He illustrated each of these as having a laboratory population shunt and fusing in modern population ecology. Physiological ecology or autecology, as we have seen, is not readily dissociated from modern population ecology, and insofar as it focuses on elucidating processes that influence population growth (e.g., fecundity, mortality, and interactions with other populations), sharp definition may be unnecessary. Park's "early ecology" may be taken to include general natural history and biogeography. One of their concerns was the distribution of populations of various taxa, including species, and that most important population phenomenon the distinction between absence, or zero, and some, at least enough to be encountered and to record, as present. This distinction was not as dichotomous as it seemed, since zero may be a function of sampling intensity. The problems of spatial limits, range boundaries in biogeography, or local habitat limits in the ecological scale, and the factor(s) accounting for these, were among the earliest and most specific concerns regarding populations and still persist (Shelford 1913; Slobodkin 1961). The distinction of boundaries in time in which a population entered a locality by migration or introduction, or ceased to exist there by migration, extirpation, or, with greater finality, extinction, was another aspect of population studies (Lack 1954; Green 1959).

## Population census and survey

Park (1946) included, in his history of population ecology, quantitative "census" of natural populations as a link between "early ecology" and "modern population ecology." Most early census studies were of many species based on the habitat or the collecting technique and in the modern sense would be community studies. Park recognized that quantitative knowledge of populations was required for community analysis. He also noted that Möbius's community definition "focussed attention on the ineluctable interdependence between the natural populations comprising the community instead of on particular habitat relations exhibited by species." The problems and interest of population ecology may, in fact, be seen as beginning and ending in community ecology. Slobodkin (1962:8) began his book on population ecology as follows:

> If you were to make a fence around any region of the earth's surface and list the kinds and numbers of organisms found within that fence, you would be starting to define the problem of population ecology.

Ecologists started in just this way, and the population as a group of organisms, of one or several species, with particular properties, and in a specific area (or volume), was of paramount interest. Clearly a population had:

1. Spatial extent, areal and habitat boundaries, and physiological tolerances.
2. Number, variously known as abundance or density.
3. Distribution or dispersion within the area, commonly and conveniently described as uniform or homogeneous but subse-

quently recognized, with much frustration by empiricist and theorist, as heterogeneous or patterned.

4. Individual or collective size, such as area covered or volume or weight (biomass) per unit area.
5. Less readily quantifiable attributes, such as vigor or success in completing a population's growth and life cycle, and chronological or seasonal attributes, known as phenology or periodicity.
6. "Aggregation" or social properties among its members, which were extensively studied in animals by Allee (1927, 1931). Allee demonstrated what came to be called the "Allee effect," in which reproductive rate decreased when the population dropped below a certain critical density, contrary to the assumption of the classical logistic model of population growth (Christiansen and Fenchel 1977).
7. "Associational" properties shown by tendencies to co-occur and, presumably, to interact with other populations. These, of course, can only be discerned by examining mutual distributions of populations and their interactions in nature, and such studies range from examining two-species relationships, such as pollination, predation, or competition, to multispecies communities.
8. "Dynamic" properties, those that changed as a consequence of reproduction, mortality, and dispersal in the form of immigration and emigration.

Empirical population ecologists were concerned with all of these; theoretical population ecologists preferred to ignore questions of *dispersal* or migration, and *dispersion* or pattern of distribution in space. Population ecologists sought understanding of numerical change, population growth, fluctuations or oscillations, stability or equilibrium, and decline or extinction. A major and continuing concern, as Park (1946) noted, is "dynamics of production," the amount of biomass produced.

Under the rubric of "biological survey" or "census," late 19th-century and early 20th-century biologists charted the distribution of species or aggregates of species of an area, largely at first in qualitative terms, later quantitatively (White in press). *Census* was a misnomer, since it rarely involved a complete count or was not of a population of a single species, but was usually a sample, sometimes extrapolated to a very large total, of several species (Johnstone 1908; Baker 1918). Marine biologists and limnologists were well in advance of terrestrial animal ecologists in sampling populations. Hardy (1965:296), a distinguished British marine biologist, wrote:

> We have a better idea of the population density, per unit area of different molluscs on many parts of the sea floor than we have of the snails of our countryside; our knowledge of the numbers of small crustacea per cubic metre of water in many seas of the world is far in advance of such information regarding insect numbers on land.

Hardy, in fact, claimed that the new science of ecology was more advanced in the sea than on land because marine animals were nondomesticated and governments had supported fisheries research, "which is essentially ecological." An interesting dichotomy appeared among aquatic biologists which continues to the present. Students of benthic organisms and plankton emphasized communities and synecology, whereas those interested in fishes and aquatic mammals concentrated on autecology. Marine biologists and limnologists captured organisms in the aggregate by seine, dredge, trawl, and net. Hensen (1884) and Petersen (1913), for example, counted the numbers of plankton and benthic organisms, respectively, which sometimes were collectively referred to as *populations,* as well as being comprised of individual populations of taxa, depending on the current capabilities of identifying organisms. Haeckel (1891), in addition to questioning the applicability of mathematics to population studies, criticized Hensen because, he said, the enormous labor of counting plankton had potential for "ruin of mind and body." Haeckel advocated "mass and weight and chemical analysis" as the proper measure of a population. Hensen had, in fact, measured weight in addition to counts. Hensen even went beyond the usual collection and counting of adults. His plankton studies grew out of his efforts to determine the numbers of fish eggs and larvae, and he attempted to calculate from these the number of female fish that produced eggs. Such estimation of total numbers of adults required determination of sex ratios (Johnstone 1908). Quantitative surveys of aquatic animal communities and their included populations proliferated, and the variation of numbers of organisms from place to place and time to time became apparent from these surveys. In these studies, the distinction between studies of populations and quantitative description of communities was etymologically and empirically confounded. Johnstone (1908) calculated the density of the fish "population" of the North Sea based on an estimate of 9,000 million individuals of six fish species. In addition to the usual estimation of density as number per unit area, he calculated the reciprocal, or mean area per fish, as terrestrial botanists sometimes did for plants. Each fish inhabited an average area of bottom of 60 square meters. Johnstone wrote that accumulated observations pointed to the conclusion, now the conventional wisdom of marine ecologists, that the density of both vertebrates and invertebrates is greater closer to land than farther out to sea. He also said that quantitative methods were useful for investigating "dynamical equilibrium" in total sea life and the variability in one or more species. Gross changes in fish populations of the Great Lakes also became a matter of concern in the 1920s, paralleling the observations of population declines in marine fisheries (Smith 1968). Although population problems were increasingly recognized, ecologists had not made substantial progress toward understanding population phenomena in the early decades of the 20th century. Some marine biologists risked ruining mind and body and adopted Hensen's counting techniques, but like him, they sometimes weighed and chemically analyzed their collections. Some objected to counts because of the errors due to "excessive fatigue" and suggested the time was better spent on estimations of more samples (Lloyd 1925).

Early limnologists were also concerned with populations, their numbers, and their distribution. Birge (1898) followed swarms of *Daphnia hyalina* in surface waters, with between 800,000 and 1,492,000 individuals per cubic meter, which, he said, attracted immense numbers of perch. Birge also counted numbers of plankton and applied the term *population* to individual species and more inclusive taxa up to the total crustacean population. He followed the increase in numbers of species in the samples and the vertical distribution of several species, finding that all but one species conformed to a "general law" that numbers became maximum and uniformly distributed simultaneously, anticipating a later search for a principle of numbers of species in a community. Birge and Juday (1922) subordinated numerical counts to biomass measurements of plankton, and terms such as *standing crop* and *productivity* were added to *population* and *community*. Continuing surveys of plankton and benthos included studies of emergence and populations of insects and even population growth of higher plants (Pearsall 1932; Frey 1963a).

Studies of commercial fish and shellfish populations proliferated because of concern about declining populations in the late 19th and early 20th centuries (Ricker 1977). Age class determination of fishes by "scale ring" counts and, less familiarly, by ear stones, or otoliths, began in

1898 and 1899, respectively. This led to estimations of rates of growth and age composition of populations and a long tradition of population studies of fish. Ring counts of fish scales, although not annual, paralleled the problem of tree rings in being less useful in the tropics than in temperate or Arctic waters. Perhaps because of emphasis on commercial species, institutional constraints, and limitations of technique, fish stocks were mostly considered as single species. Population data of many fish and invertebrates were derived from commercial catches, but there were efforts to address basic population attributes. In the last decade of the 19th century, C. G. J. Petersen, in an early mark-recapture study of movement, marked plaice with bone buttons. Shortly after the turn of the century, J. Hjort, using the new technique of aging by scale counts, followed the age distributions of fish populations, notably herring, and illustrated the effect of year classes on fluctuation in abundance of fish (Schlee 1973). Hjort urged study of birth rate, age class, and migration of fish (Hardy 1965). Herrick (1911), in his monograph *Natural History of the American Lobster,* concentrated on morphology, habits, and growth but turned briefly to the need to restore and maintain population equilibrium. The traditional mechanisms, closed seasons, size limits, protection of females, and release of young or adults were all cited; and Herrick estimated number of eggs per female, probability of survival, and mean number of eggs laid by a female in its entire life span. He also made the logical point that, if the sex ratio were 1:1, each female would have to produce two young which survived to adulthood if the population were to remain in equilibrium. Much of the early study of aquatic populations and the emphasis on the benthic and plankton communities was based on the idea of the "chain of biological relations" (i.e., trophic structure), which was assumed to limit fish populations (Baker 1916). The rationale for studying all the species which was evident in much early census and survey ecology derived, according to Baker, from the balance-of-nature concept as stated by Forbes (1880b):

> Nowhere can one see more clearly illustrated what may be called the *sensibility* of such an organic complex – impressed by the fact that whatever affects any species belonging to it, must speedily have its influence of some sort upon the whole assemblage. He will thus be made to see the impossibility of studying any form successfully out of relation to the other forms – the necessity for taking a comprehensive survey of the whole as a condition to a satisfactory understanding of any part.

Forbes fell back on the familiar simile of clockwork, likening a missing species to leaving out one wheel of a watch. This mechanistic model is sometimes applied in ecology to illustrate the necessity of a holistic or hierarchical approach (Allen and Starr 1982). Population surveys of many sorts of aquatic organisms proliferated.

Somewhere in the development of fisheries biology the traditional holistic concept, so eloquently stated by Forbes, was lost. Fisheries biologists turned to an autecological emphasis on stock and production of single species, thereby divorcing themselves from major developments of ecology. This is most concisely evidenced in a recent dispute concerning the relevance of ecological theory to fisheries biologists (Werner 1977, 1980; Kerr 1980; Rigler 1982). Werner, in a number of book reviews, noted the largely independent development of fisheries biology and ecology and urged the necessity of basic ecological, particularly community, theory for fishery studies. Kerr rebutted, distinguishing between the synecological and evolutionary perspective of "academic ecologists," as stated by Hutchinson (1957a), and the "basic fisheries approach," or the "autecological perspective," set out by F. E. J. Fry (1947). Fry's "perspective" was essentially similar to Shelford's "tolerance" concept, extending the "zone of tolerance" into a surrounding "zone of resistance." As its defender, Kerr, and its critic, Werner, agreed, Fry's concept stressed autecological response to physicochemical factors of the environment. Hutchinson's theoretical niche was also related to Shelford's "tolerance" concept, but incorporated biotic interactions or a synecological approach.

The above exchange is useful in a number of ways. Kerr (1980) sharply criticized "academic ecology" and "academic theory" for its "parochial" perspective and failure to understand fisheries ecology. His distinction suggested the institutionalization of fisheries ecology in nonacademic, commonly governmental research organizations with different funding and purposes not shared by most academic ecologists. The American Fisheries Society, organized in 1870, long antedated ecological societies, and later fisheries biologists were largely trained as specialists in fisheries departments or as systematists with little general ecological concern, according to Werner. Werner argued that fisheries biologists should be trained as ecologists and that ecological theory, emphasizing interspecies interactions and community, is essential for effective management of fisheries populations. Fisheries ecologists had, however, developed theoretical population constructs of their own (Ricker 1954, 1977). Rigler (1982), like Werner, took note of the minimal interaction between limnologists and fisheries biologists, ascribing it to their having quite different "paradigms." Rigler described the fisheries biologist's paradigm as stating that "the reproduction, survival and production of any fish population is virtually independent of changes in abundance of other biotic components." Limnologists, he said, continued the Forbesian view, and even went beyond it, in believing that "the appropriate system to study comprises the whole lake or stream and, more recently, even the entire drainage basin." Rigler urged convergence of these ideas in a return to empiricism, which, he argued, has been misunderstood and unfairly maligned. Actually, all the participants in this discussion deplored the independence of these different aspects of fisheries ecology and saw mutual advantage in improved communication. None, however, held out much hope for any proximate rapprochement, because of the long institutional and intellectual traditions which separate the two. It is unfortunate for ecology that most of its concepts and theories developed largely in academic contexts, commonly divorced from the facilities, funding, and data available in government agencies concerned with natural resources. Although individuals employed by government fisheries agencies, forestry departments, biological surveys, and game departments made notable research contributions to ecology, ecological science was largely peripheral to the major concerns of most such agencies. A striking demonstration of the lack of recognition of professional ecology is that until 1977 there was no classification of ecologist in the U.S. Civil Service (McCormick 1978), although one had been proposed to Congress in 1920.

Early terrestrial plant ecologists, having the luxury of sessile and visible organisms, commonly estimated the abundance of species populations but, after 1898, also turned to counting. They were, at the turn of the century, favored in that taxonomy of plants was relatively complete and, then and since, by the fact that plants, unlike Elton's terrestrial animals, did not run away or hide at the approach of an ecologist. Early in the 20th century, counts of individual plants were supplemented by estimates or measures of area of cover, or basal area, which provided an index of size or quantity. Foresters had long since measured timber quantity or volume and growth, but such "mensuration" was usually restricted to commercial species and to usable timber rather than total production. Clements (1905) advocated "clip quadrats" to measure production of herbage; and the pioneers of grassland ecology, such as Pound, Clements, and Weaver, and of its offspring range management, such as A. W. Sampson, measured production of aboveground herbage in relation to the environment and the effect of grazing (Weaver 1924; Tobey 1981). This is one of the few instances where there was effective interaction between agriculture and academic ecology. In most ways agricultural biologists, like fisheries biologists, did not develop close connections with ecology. As John Harper complained many years later, population studies of crop and pasture plants and weeds done by agricultural scientists and range managers were largely ignored by later ecologists (White in press). The division was again largely in terms of autecology versus synecology. Agricultural biologists concentrated on growth and production of populations, whereas most ecologists sampled populations as members of communities.

Terrestrial animal ecologists, by all accounts, including their own, were laggard in population and community studies, although a limited number of bird populations were censused in the 19th century (Lack 1954). As usual, S. A. Forbes (1907b) was out in front with a survey of birds in a cross section of the center of the state of Illinois, showing their distribution in relation to various habitat types. W. L. McAtee, (1907) did an intensive census of 4 square feet in which all "plant and animal objects of classes known to be used as food by birds were counted." Forbes had stated that applied entomology was ecology long before *ecology* became a familiar term; but few applied entomologists seized on this observation to label themselves ecologists. Nevertheless, members of the long-established American Association of Economic Entomologists were among the 307 charter members of the Ecological Society of America (Burgess 1977), and entomologists were prominent among the leading pioneers of population ecology. Among the earliest animal population studies of theoretical and empirical interest to ecology were those of the economic entomologist-parasitologists Ronald Ross, (1911) and L. O. Howard, then chief of the Bureau of Entomology of the United States Department of Agriculture, and his associate W. F. Fiske (Howard and Fiske 1911). Ross developed mathematical equations showing the relation between the incidence of malaria in humans and the population of anopheline mosquitoes. From manipulation of these equations he stated as "laws" that the maintenance of the disease required a given number of mosquitoes and that beyond this maintainance level small increases in mosquito populations caused large increases in incidence of malaria. Howard and Fiske, though less formally mathematical than Ross in their treatment of parasites in controlling pest insect populations, addressed a key aspect of population regulation. They distinguished between factors such as storms, which destroyed a fixed percentage of a species whether it was rare or common – that is, independently of its abundance – and "facultative" factors, such as predators or parasites, which, they said, were radically different. They wrote that

> a natural balance can only be maintained through the opera-
> tion of facultative agencies which effect the destruction of a
> greater proportionate number of individuals as the insect in
> question increases in abundance. (Howard and Fiske 1911:169)

The substance of their "proposition" was that a parasite could control a pest organism only if the numerical increase of the parasite were directly affected by the numerical increase of the host. Howard and Fiske's proposition is an early, if not the first, statement of what came to be called the theory of density-dependent population regulation, which was to occupy the attention of animal ecologists for decades. Its longevity and contentiousness is suggested in Krebs's (1979) lament that "the density-dependent regulation model is the ecologist's phlogis-ton theory, useful years ago but now an obstruction to progress."

Oddly, although these significant developments in ecology were based on work with parasites, parasitology generally did not mix with ecology. Parasitologists were few (three) among the charter members of the Ecological Society of America. A continuing anomaly is that parasitologists generally remained aloof from ecology in its formative years and did not expressly couch their discipline in ecological terms, although it is the most ecological of biological disciplines. Ecologists reciprocated by marked disinterest in parasites, preferring to concen-trate on predation and competition as the significant two-species eco-logical processes.

Ecologists per se were still a handful in the 1920s and 1930s. Mem-bership in the American Ecological Society had, by 1925, nearly 10 years after its founding, approached an asymptote, as the then newly rediscovered concept of the logistic curve said it should, of about 600 members, which lasted until 1950 (Burgess 1977). The British Ecologi-cal Society around 1930 had about 450 members, largely botanists. It is a matter of some interest that animal ecologists in America were rela-tively numerous and active in the earliest years of ecology and in the formation of the Ecological Society of America. The society's first president was a zoologist, and its first journal, *Ecology,* included plant and animal papers. The British Ecological Society was initiated primar-ily by botanists. Its nine presidents in the first two decades of its existence (1914–33) were botanists; and its first publication, the *Journal of Ecology,* was largely botanical. In 1917 the abstracts of a meeting of the newly formed Ecological Society of America were published in the *Journal of Ecology* with the remark that "it will be noticed that animal ecology occupies a prominent place in the programme." O. W. Richards (1926) also commented on the neglect of animal ecology in Britain, as did Elton (Elton 1933; Worthington 1983). Although plant ecologists were active in Britain, there were no academic or government posts for plant ecologists as such, and growth of plant ecology was inhibited until the 1940s. Animal ecology and limnology were, however, gathering interest and support, as evidenced by the establishment of the Freshwater Biological Association in 1930 and the Bureau of Animal Populations in 1932 (Le Cren 1979; Duff and Lowe 1981; Worthington 1983). The *Journal of Animal Ecology* was also established in 1932, by Elton. Prior to about 1925, relatively few ecological studies of terrestrial animal populations had been published. Lack (1954), in one of the first volumes dealing with regulation of numbers in natural populations of animals, referred to the "despair of some ecologists of the population problem being capable of solution." He reviewed the early long-term censuses of animal populations, largely of birds, relatively few of mammals and invertebrate animals. The earliest, of a moth, started in 1880, and that of a bird, the great crested grebe, in 1860 (Harrisson and Hollom 1932). Most early animal population records were made by amateur ornithologists, economic entomologists, or fisheries personnel for economic reasons, not primarily to resolve ecological questions, which were not very explicitly phrased in any event.

The first decades of the 20th century marked the rise of statistics and its introduction into biology, including ecology. As early as 1907, Hjort urged the use of actuarial statistics in fisheries (Hardy 1965). Pearl (1914) noted the important contributions of statistical science to biology, namely (1) describing a group in terms of its own attributes, (2) estimation of probable error, and (3) measuring association or correlation between variations in a series of characters or events. Ecologists of various persuasions had established the utility of describing a population in terms of its numbers of individuals, frequency of occurrence in samples, and productivity or biomass in both absolute and relative (percentage) terms. Marine ecologists, such as Hensen, had used percentage deviation of a sample from the mean, although not with an estimate of probability, as a measure of variation among samples.

Ramensky (1924) and Gause (1934) used standard deviation in describing population variation. Measures of association between species had been proposed by Forbes (1907a) and were elaborated by Shelford (1915) and Michael (1921). Michael reexamined Forbes's index and found it wanting as a useful coefficient. His article voiced the dilemma, later to become endemic in ecology: Shall quantitative methods in biology be worked out by mathematicians, biologists, or both in cooperation? His solution was to require "proficiency" in mathematics of biologists. As he put it (in italics), "*This means reform.*" The editor (Tansley) questioned whether the time was right to insist on proficiency in mathematics for biologists, although he allowed the need for adequate training in calculus and statistics. The full impact of mathematical and statistical ecology was in the wings in 1921, although many ecologists managed to evade it for some decades; and the perennial debate about the use of and need for mathematics begun by Haeckel was to flourish in the 1920s and 1930s and be rekindled in the 1950s. Studies of what Park (1946) described as "quantitative census of natural populations," although made at various levels of accuracy and with limited check on the validity of the sample as a representation of the populations, indicate the interest of early ecologists in numbers of organisms. This interest was ubiquitous in all areas of ecology and gave rise to what Elton (1933) called the "statistics" of populations. By this he meant the descriptive statistics of the population, which he equated with numbers of individuals at one time. He contrasted it with "population dynamics" or change of populations in time. His analogy was with morphology, and he compared statistics to a still photograph, and dynamics and development to moving pictures. This is a conveniently logical distinction, but not all population censuses were purely descriptive, although only a few concentrated on the elements of natality, survival, mortality, and dispersal or migration of populations, which were to become the essence of a new era of dynamic population ecology. Repeated and (particularly) long-term studies of populations to follow changes were few, except in studies of commercially valuable species.

Early plant ecologists have commonly been criticized for their undue attention to description, qualitative or quantitative, of vegetation and their presumed lack of interest in dynamics of populations. Tansley (1923) wrote, "It is the fashion in some quarters to deride descriptive science as not science at all." Tansley commented that plant ecology should go beyond description to causation, a hope repeated nearly six decades later in an article entitled "After Description" by John Harper, the leading contemporary student of plant population ecology. Harper (1982) exemplified the view that the causation urged by Tansley required

> concentration of effort on the lives and deaths of individual plants – a reductionist approach – as the most likely to reveal those forces at present operating to determine the distribution and abundance of plants.

It is somewhat ironical that the onus attached to description in Tansley's era was directed at verbal or natural history descriptions. By Harper's time, the pejorative phrase "mere description" was largely intended for statistical descriptions of populations and communities, even when these were concerned with succession or change of the populations of the community.

Plant ecologists had anticipated Slobodkin's dictum that making fences around areas of the earth's surface and listing the kinds and numbers of organisms present constituted the beginning of population ecology. Sometimes the fences were literal (exclosures) for the purpose of excluding grazing animals. More often the fence was abstract, enclosing an area of ostensibly homogeneous vegetation, and sampling smaller areas therein was taken to be representative of the whole (Clements 1905; Goodall 1952; Greig-Smith 1957; Mueller-Dombois and Ellenberg 1974). Although these ecologists usually failed to address questions of reproduction and survival of individuals, which became the crux of population ecology, they did address significant problems about populations. Not the least of these was how to determine, reasonably accurately, the presence of "how many" or "how much." The distinction of dominant and subordinate species and the propensity of a species to become dominant or relatively very numerous were major concerns. Thus studies of the distribution and abundance of plants served as a necessary preamble to or concomitant of the studies of lives and deaths of individual plants, as advocated by Harper. To explain how a population got that way, it was necessary to ascertain how it was.

In spite of the preoccupation of most terrestrial plant ecologists with the community, for example, with vegetation, they necessarily were concerned with the plant species and the populations thereof. Like their aquatic ecologist counterparts, they counted numbers of individuals in areas (abundance or density) and estimated quantity in a variety of ways, usually by projecting the plant area onto the ground (cover or basal area). Terrestrial plant ecologists and early range managers at several experimental ranges in the western United States initiated extensive quantitative studies of plant populations. Unfortunately, little of this was ever published (White in press).

Terrestrial plant ecologists, like marine ecologists, commonly assumed homogeneity as an attribute of the community and its populations, often while paying little attention to whether this was true. Goodall (1952) wrote that H. A. Gleason, in 1920, was the first to study quantitatively the spatial distribution of individual plants. Gleason was aware of the effects of quadrat size and number on estimates of population. He was among the first to apply probability to the examination of field populations and to devise an estimate of aggregation or clumping of a population using the mathematics of probability (McIntosh 1975a). The issue of population distribution, whether homogeneous, heterogeneous, random, or patterned, arose in ecology in the 1890s with Haeckel's criticism of Hensen's plankton theory. It continued and remains a stumbling block for population, community, and theoretical ecology. Using the attributes of spacing, such as the mean area per individual or, more significantly, direct measurement of interorganism distance, was advocated in the early decades of the 19th century but rarely used until recently (Goodall 1952; Greig-Smith 1957). If, as Gleason thought, plant species were randomly distributed, "frequency," the number of sample areas in which a species occurred, would have solved many problems of sampling. Because of the ubiquity of clumping in species distribution and the effect of size of sample area on frequency, it was inappropriate to use frequency as a refined estimator of populations. However, in conjunction with density counts, it did serve as a rough indicator for indicating homogeneity of distribution (Curtis and McIntosh 1951a; Goodall 1952; Greig-Smith 1957). The other use of frequency in quadrats was to determine co-occurrence of two species as a means of expressing association between them, a technique used earlier by S. A. Forbes (1907a). Gleason (1925) recorded joint occurrences of pairs of species and compared them with the number expected on the basis of their individual frequencies, although he did not use tests of significance. Tests of interspecies association were slowly incorporated into quantitative plant ecology in the 1930s and 1940s and adopted by animal ecologists in the late 1940s (Cole 1949). Association between species is itself an indication of departure from randomness and suggests either biological interaction between the species or similar, or inverse, relation to the environment, depending on whether the association is negative or positive. Quantitative measures of populations were also used to test correlation between vegetation and environment to examine the tolerance of plant species to environmental variables, particularly soil attributes. Many such studies suffered the usual problems of correlation without grounds for inferring cause and were often criticized as a descriptive-correlative approach to ecology.

The literature of animal ecology in the 1930s included numerous studies denoting numbers of individuals of one or more species populations with very little consideration of how they reached the observed number or if, or how, they might be changing. When the *Journal of Animal Ecology* was founded in 1932, nearly 70 percent of the articles published in it used quantitative methods; by 1970 this increased to 100 percent (Taylor and Elliot 1981). Many studies which provided statistics of populations also suggested something of the factors involved in the dynamics of the population. Elton, like Shelford before him, joined plant ecologists in placing major emphasis on the community. Andrewartha (1961:5) claimed that Elton predicted that "the laws governing the distribution and numbers of animals in nature would emerge from the study of communities." According to Andrewartha, the converse is more nearly true: "We must first discover the laws governing the distribution and abundance of animals before we can advance very far in our understanding of the relationships between the populations that make up a community." In fact both Shelford and Elton turned their attention to populations, albeit in different ways.

Charles Elton is clearly a preeminent figure in animal ecology (Hardy 1968; Cox 1979). Elton diverged from the laboratory emphasis of early 19th-century zoology and was a pioneer in establishing ecology as "the quantitative and experimental study of living organisms in relation to their environment" (Cox 1979). In Elton's well-known phrase, this was "scientific natural history." Elton's early work involved survey of communities, an emphasis apparent in his famous book *Animal Ecology* (Elton 1927). A major contribution of this book was that it brought together in a coherent verbal model many concepts previously scattered in the literature of ecology. These concepts included food chain, pyramid of numbers, and niche. Elton also emphasized the dynamic tradition of ecology in succession, periodic change and rhythms in communities, variation in populations, and dispersal of populations. According to Cox (1979), Elton wanted to "create a sociology and economics of animal communities," a process, Cox believed, that was furthered by

Elton's association with the Hudson's Bay Company. In spite of his early emphasis on community, Elton devoted a major portion of his attention to populations. In 1925, he was engaged as biology consultant to the Hudson's Bay Company and, using its data of fur returns, began extended studies of fluctuations of fur-bearing animals and long-term cycles of populations. In 1932 Elton formed the Bureau of Animal Populations (BAP), which had as its goal "knowledge of fluctuations in numbers of wild populations," and he began studies of vole populations, leading to his famous *Voles, Mice, and Lemmings* (Elton 1942). Even before his extended studies of animal populations, Elton developed ideas contrary to those previously established in ecology. He came out flatly opposed to the balance-of-nature concept:

> The balance of nature does not exist, and, perhaps, never has existed. The numbers of wild animals are constantly varying to a greater or less extent, and the variations are usually irregular in period and always irregular in amplitude. (Elton 1930:17)

In the process he attacked the ubiquitous clockwork simile, which had been used by Forbes (1880b) and other ecologists, on the grounds that the animal "wheels" each have their own mainspring and retain the right to move to another clock (Elton 1930). Elton emphasized the capacity of animals to migrate and described what he termed selection of the environment by the animal rather than the more usual selection of the animal by the environment. This had been emphasized many years before by Davenport (1903).

Aldo Leopold, among American animal ecologists, shows some interesting parallels and contrasts with Elton. Leopold was trained as a forester at the Yale Forestry School. He graduated in 1909 and was employed by the then young U.S. Forest Service (Flader 1974). In 1915 he turned his attention primarily to fish and game protection, sharing a widespread concern about depleted populations. In these years he was, according to Flader, more attracted by conservation than the still undeveloped science of ecology. Following a tour at the United States Forest Products Laboratory, he returned to his interest in game. In 1928 he began a series of game surveys funded by the Sporting, Arms, and Ammunition Manufacturers Institute and turned his attention irrevocably to the scientific, practical, and political aspects of wildlife populations. In this era, a burgeoning interest in game and pest populations in various state and federal agencies, notably the U.S. Biological Survey, spurred the production of surveys of game populations of varying scientific merit. Some, like H. L. Stoddard's

(1932) on the bobwhite quail and A. Murie's (1944) on the wolves of Mount McKinley, were classic life history and management studies of wild populations. Leopold wrote *Game Management,* the premier book on wildlife management, at that time only beginning as a profession (Leopold 1933). Flader observed that Leopold's book contains only one indexed reference to ecology ("ecologic niche") and commented that it was not until the mid-1930s that Leopold began thinking in more formal ecological terms. Leopold had met Elton at the Matamek Conference on biological cycles in 1931, and they had a common interest in population cycles. In 1933 Leopold was appointed to a newly established chair of game management in the College of Agriculture at the University of Wisconsin. In the mid-1930s Leopold and his students found that ecological research was necessary for management of populations, although he would have to contend with the life-long problem of applying scientific management in the face of political and public opposition to policies dictated by scientific knowledge. In 1939 the university established a Department of Wildlife Management, and Leopold started a course in wildlife ecology. Leopold had, as early as 1914, begun deer censuses in the areas under his charge. He pursued his interest in deer populations, including the Kaibab Plateau population, which became a famous case history of the eruption and crash of a wildlife population, although the traditional interpretation of these events has since been disputed (Caughley 1970; Burk 1973; Miller 1973). Leopold did not incorporate theoretical population ecology into his thinking about populations. Unlike Elton, he was a firm adherent of the widespread ideas of balance of nature or equilibrium and of land as an organism sometimes disturbed from a state of "aboriginal health." He viewed populations as approaching a state of dynamic equilibrium which was maintained by environmental resistance inhibiting biotic potential, apparently influenced by Chapman's (1931) electrical metaphor. Although he recognized a number of factors affecting productivity of a population, hunting and predation topped his list. Leopold inferred that natural predators might control deer populations. With his gift for expressing ecology and population problems in ethical terms, he referred to his own "sin against the wolves." Leopold was much less involved than Elton in scientific ecology and more concerned with management than theory of populations. He transformed ecological concerns into problems of ethics, morality, and aesthetics as well as science, resource management, and public policy (Leopold 1949).

Studies of natural populations and of the problems of securing adequate samplings during the 1930s and '40s followed in the tradition of ecologists such as Elton and Leopold (Allee et al. 1949; Lack 1954, 1966; Bodenheimer 1958). Bodenheimer noted "the two greatest steps in ecological progress": The first puts numeric changes of populations in the center of all research; the second is the principle of compensation. *Compensation* is the tendency of a population to react to stress to maintain its numbers. Bodenheimer identified A. J. Nicholson and P. A. Errington as two figures connected with these steps. Nicholson worked primarily with insects and stressed density-dependent control of populations. Errington worked with mammals and was an outstanding authority on predation but allowed that diverse mechanisms controlled populations. Bodenheimer illustrated the gap in animal population studies. He recommended, as an introduction to such concerns, studies of the mackerel by Rachel Carson, of the bobwhite quail by H. L. Stoddard, of the robin by D. Lack, and of the fulmar by J. Fisher. These, he said, have the advantage of being "disrobed of all tables, ciphers, and formulas."

It has become commonplace to say that plant ecologists studied communities and animal ecologists studied populations (Cox 1979). It is certainly true that terrestrial plant ecologists of the first half of the 20th century spent much effort in describing, classifying, and mapping communities by the credos of different schools (Whittaker 1962). Their interest in community was supported by extended samples of the populations thereof and by various, often unsupported, inferences of the reasons why the populations changed. It is true that theoretical population ecology and some of the experimental work associated with it were done largely by animal ecologists or by nonecologists. Terrestrial animal ecologists were preoccupied with numbers of organisms of individual populations and the changes therein, and they even went so far as to define *ecology* as the study of numbers of animals. It is a matter of some interest to inquire why this distinction should be so commonly asserted and to what extent it is true. Certainly some plant ecologists as early as 1919, notably A. S. Watt in his studies of woodland, were concerned with population phenomena. Watt's later studies of gap-phase replacement and grazing by rabbits were also concerned with population phenomena. Both Clements and Tansley conducted experimental studies of competition, a favorite concern of animal population ecologists. Clements, Weaver, and Hanson (1929) produced the first major reference work on competition and offered an explicit definition of the term, while some animal ecologists, such as A. J. Nicholson (1933), still confounded its meaning. Terrestrial animal ecologists may have turned to their traditional emphasis on single-species populations because of the difficulty of sampling animal populations, as noted by Elton. Plant ecologists found it efficient to sample several species at once. Some plant ecologists believed it was necessary to establish the community and environmental context of species so that autecological studies could be accomplished most efficiently (Curtis and McIntosh 1951). The conspicuous variation of vegetation in form and composition, evident to the casual observer, challenged plant ecologists to seek, or to provide, an orderly arrangement. The relative ease of collecting data on multiple species perpetuated the emphasis on plant communities, in part because there was so much variation. During the 1940s and 1950s, new methods of sampling and data analysis focused attention on problems of sampling, pattern, and association of species in communities, largely attended to by plant ecologists (Greig-Smith 1957). The details of demography of individual populations or limited two-species interactions, which intrigued animal ecologists, were largely ignored by plant ecologists, although Salisbury's (1942) work on plant reproduction pointed in that direction. Whatever the reasons, studies of plant population dynamics lagged. Harper (1967) wrote about a demography which has never "gained a momentum in plant ecology" and later said that plant ecologists "largely ignored population phenomena" (Harper and White 1974). E. O. Wilson (1969) even wrote of Harper that he was "the first plant ecologist to talk to the animal ecologist in his own language – of population ecology." Plant population biology was described in the 1970s as yet another "revolution" and one of the paradigm changes which were epidemic in ecology. In fact, this revolution was described as "the most important event in the field of ecology" in the 1970s (Antonovics 1980).

This particular revolution included the hope of merging evolutionary biology, physiological ecology, and population ecology in the 1980s. The essence of this hope was that detailed studies of population phenomena would provide generalizations which could be extended to encompass the phenomena of communities which had long engaged plant ecologists and which intrigued animal ecologists of the new theoretical ecology which had emerged in the 1950s. It is not now clear that this merger will bring together plant and animal population ecologists. Schaffer and Leigh (1976) questioned the relevance to plants of population theory primarily based on animals. Harper (1980) also noted idiosyncracies of plants which suggest that observations and theories based on plant populations may not be readily miscible with those of mobile animals. Another concern of current plant population ecologists, which they share with turn-of-the-century ecologists, is the meaning and identification of *adaptation* (Antonovics 1980; Harper 1982). Harper suggested the word has lost its value. With all these difficulties, some plant population ecologists share with many animal population ecologists the belief that "ultimate ecological explanation" must derive from studies of populations on the "lives and deaths of individual plants" – a "reductionist approach" (Harper 1982).

## Theoretical population ecology

The 1920s can be seen as a watershed in animal ecology because the decade produced a significant codification of what ecology was all about in Elton's (1927) *Animal Ecology*. Essentially simultaneously, mathematical population theory was formulated and served, according to later mathematical ecologists, to add insight to most of the ideas Elton had outlined as the essence of ecology (Christiansen and Fenchel 1977). The dichotomy between those who saw the community, or later the ecosystem, as the ecological theater in which the play of populations took place and as the key to understanding the functions of the parts, or species, and those who claimed that it was necessary to comprehend the working of the species populations, as a preamble to understanding of community, really began in the 1920s with the formalization of theoretical mathematical population ecology. Theoretical mathematical ecology was accompanied by increased study of experimental populations in the laboratory, thus completing the triad of "modern population studies" – "natural populations," "experimental populations," and "theoretical populations" – described by Park (1946). This set the stage of the ecological theater for extended discussion about the relative merits of each part of the triad and the relevance of each to each which continues to the present. The tradition of census or enumeration of aggregates of natural populations of organisms, which had been one of the forerunners of self-conscious ecology, persisted particularly in benthic and plankton studies and to a lesser extent in terrestrial animal population studies. An interesting view of the continuance of the link between community and population studies is found in Elton and Miller (1954:463) in a review of survey of animal communities:

As [the majority] of the main classes of biotic relations . . . are between different species, it follows that some reconnaissance of species associations in nature is needed in order to understand the population ecology of any one of them.

The 1920s marked the beginning of theoretical mathematical population ecology – its "Golden Age," according to Scudo and Ziegler (1978). Nowhere in ecology is the contrast between the inductive/empirical and deductive/theoretical approaches more marked than in the traditions of census of natural populations and of models of abstract populations or experiments with markedly constrained populations designed to test mathematical models and theories. Fortunately, several recent considerations of the history of ecology are concerned with theoretical population ecology and its earliest and omnipresent model, the logistic curve (Scudo 1971, 1982 pers. commun.; Scudo and Ziegler 1978; Hutchinson 1978; Ohta 1981; Kingsland 1981, 1982, 1983, 1985). The potential of populations to grow geometrically had been recognized by Thomas Malthus at the end of the 18th century. Interest in the mathematics of population growth was evident early in the 19th century, notably in the form of the logistic curve formulated by Verhulst in 1838, which went largely unnoticed. Early in the 20th century, mathematical models of growth of individuals intrigued a number of biologists, among them the zoologist-geneticist Raymond Pearl. Pearl's interest in human populations was stimulated by working for Herbert Hoover in the Malthusian context of Europe at the end of World War I. Two concerns manifest at that time were population pressure on the limited means of subsistence and population statistics. In 1920 Pearl and L. J. Reed rediscovered Verhulst's unheralded logistic equation with quite different results due to Pearl's effective public relations campaign supporting it as a "law" of population growth (Kingsland 1981). Pearl arrived at a conception of the population as a whole. He made the point explicitly in 1927 that "populations of whatever organisms are, in their very nature, aggregate wholes, and behave in growth and other ways as such" (quoted in Kingsland 1981:48). The holistic concept which traditionally permeated community ecology was thus explicitly introduced into theoretical population ecology. Pearl and Reed recognized two key assumptions of the logistic equation: (1) the rate of growth of a population is proportional to the number of individuals at any time, and (2) there are still unutilized potentialities of support existing in any given area (Kingsland 1981). The logistic curve describes the growth of a population over time. Graphically, it takes the form of an S-shaped or sigmoid curve. It is variously represented mathematically, most commonly and understandably in the form of a differential equation:

$$\frac{dN}{dt} = rN\left(\frac{K - N}{K}\right)$$

The equation includes $r$ and $K$ as constants, $r$ being the maximum rate of population increase in an unlimited environment and $K$ the limiting population or asymptote; $r$ came to mean other things, and the original meaning is sometimes specified as $r_{max}$ in later usage. The number of individuals is $N$. The crux of the logistic equation is that the realized rate of growth decreases as $N$ increases and approaches $K$. Pearl provoked considerable animus in human demographic circles because he described the logistic equation as a law, comparable to Boyle's and Kepler's laws, and useful in predicting population growth as well as describing it. The result was a long and sometimes vitriolic exchange between Pearl and his critics (Kingsland 1981). Numerous curves of growth of animal populations were published, ostensibly as good fits to the logistic curve, but others did not fit. Allee et al. (1949) suggested the possibility of a bias of publications in its favor "since an author would be loath to present one not adequate," although they didn't take this objection "too seriously."

In 1921 Pearl invited A. J. Lotka, who had been trained in physics, to work in his laboratory. Lotka had for some years been concerned with evolution, population growth, and mathematical formulation of these, but he did not become interested in the logistic equation until around 1923. Lotka incorporated a less dogmatic view than Pearl's of the logistic equation into his book *Elements of Physical Biology* (1925), one of the landmarks of population theory. In it he drew attention to Ronald Ross's malaria equations, noting the similarity of Ross's curve to the logistic. He also reviewed W. R. Thompson's efforts to analyze mathematically the effect of a parasite on its host. Finding Thompson's formula inadequate, he developed paired differential equations, showing the effect of a parasite (or predator) on its host (or prey). These equations produced cyclic fluctuations of both populations. Lotka proposed studies in "general demology" and reviewed some field studies, particularly of aquatic organisms, which, he said, were facilitated by the three-dimensional aquatic system and their connection with practical fisheries problems, which furnished "financial support on an extended scale," an unusual characteristic of ecological studies until very recently. His own work concentrated on the abstract one- or two-species cases.

Independently of Pearl and Lotka, Vito Volterra, a mathematician, arrived at equations for two-species interactions (Scudo 1971; Kingsland 1981, 1982). Volterra had early interests in mathematical biology, but his ecological interest came by marriage of his daughter to a zoologist (Umberto D'Ancona), who was interested in fish populations. Volterra's attempts to explain mathematically the balance of nature started with the logistic equation, arrived at by methods different from those of Lotka, and equations of two-species interactions. Hutchinson and Deevey (1949) wrote of these:

> Perhaps the most important theoretical development in general ecology has been the application of the logistic by Volterra, Gause and Lotka to 2 species cases.

Somewhat overlooked in the subsequent widespread application of the logistic equation and its extension to the two-species interactions – competition, predation, and parasitism – was Volterra's claim that he had treated as "new" the application of the "fundamental laws" of population ecology to the "cohabitation of *n* species," that is, to the community (Chapman 1931). Volterra's *n*-species models were largely ignored, only to be rediscovered in the 1950s (Scudo 1971, 1982 pers. commun.). Also lost in the general isolation of population from community ecology was the fact that Lotka and Volterra were after bigger game than populations. As Leigh (1968) emphasized, both Lotka and Volterra focused on the community, characterizing it as a state vector with as many components as there were species in the community. Lotka was far more ambitious than Volterra, aiming at a kinetics of life, consciousness, and human social organization, a reach not seen again until H. T. Odum's (1971) extensions of aspects of Lotka's work. Volterra's work was given unprecedented visibility to ecologists when a key article was translated and reprinted as an appendix in an early textbook, *Animal Ecology* (Chapman 1931).

The community focus of theoretical and experimental population ecology was explicit in the work of G. F. Gause, a young Russian zoologist and a student of V. W. Alpatov, a privatdocent at the University of Moscow. Alpatov had spent nearly two years in Raymond Pearl's laboratory and absorbed some of Pearl's interest in experimental and theoretical population ecology. He transmitted this to Gause, who had been working on natural populations of insects and relating their density to environmental variables such as temperature, humidity, and evaporation. These studies were in the mold of physiological ecology, and Gause (1934) in a book entitled *The Struggle for Existence* urged physiology as the model for ecology to follow. He wrote, "The complicated relationships between organisms have as their foundation definite elementary processes of the struggle for existence" (Gause 1936). The way to study the "elementary processes" of nature, he said, is to extract them from the complications of natural communities and reduce the number of variables. Gause showed the use of the logistic and related equations for experimental ecology. Kingsland (1982) described the logistic curve as one of the more fruitful and at the same time more unsatisfactory models of population growth. She noted that

> the people responsible for legitimizing the logistic curve . . . all had different degrees of direct contact with Pearl in the early years of its use, and these personal contacts facilitated the acceptance of the logistic curve despite the heavy criticisms.

Whatever the criticism of the logistic equation, mathematical population ecology, initiated by it, became and continues as one of the most active areas of ecology. According to Hutchinson and Deevey (1949),

> Population biology is the only part of biology other than genetics to have developed an autonomous quantitative theory independent of the physical sciences.

It may be questioned how autonomous or independent of the physical sciences mathematical population theory is. Some of its major proponents, from Lotka and Volterra to Robert May, have been mathematicians or physicists, and much of its rationale is explicitly derived from physical science. This is a virtue in the eyes of those seeking to turn ecology into a "hard" science and a vice to those who deplore "physics envy." Kingsland (1981) traced the explicitly physical sources of the logistic equation and the mathematical theory of populations. Pearl derived his concepts, in part, from a physical-chemical analogy to individual growth, and he compared density effects to kinetics of gases. Lotka treated the organic and inorganic as a single system and analyzed the population as a chemical system with exchanges of energy and matter as the criteria. He drew largely on the second law of thermodynamics and treated organisms as engaged in competition for energy. His grand thesis was that evolution would increase the flow of energy and matter through the system. Kingsland noted that the audience which Lotka hoped to reach consisted of physicists, and it was C. C. Adams who pointed out to him the connection of his work with ecology. Volterra used the same physical analogies as Lotka, if less literally, but was really concerned with a mathematical problem. The entomologist A. J. Nicholson developed a verbal model of two-species population interaction and induced a physicist colleague, V. A. Bailey, to provide a mathematical formulation (Nicholson and Bailey 1935). Nicholson assumed a machine-like balance in nature, and Bailey's proof treated the organisms as gas molecules. Nicholson (1933) provided "a simple analogy" of a population in balance with its environment like a balloon as the environment fluctuated, rising and falling in accord with the gas laws. The original mathematical formulations generally assumed all individuals were identical and the environment was homogeneous and constant.

Criticism of mathematical population theory began early and continues to the present. Charles Elton, in a review of Lotka's book, wrote a common complaint of many later ecologists:

> Like most mathematicians he takes the hopeful biologist to the edge of a pond, points out that a good swim will help his work, and then pushes him in and leaves him to drown. (Quoted in Kingsland 1981:249)

Allee (1932), reviewing Chapman's text, with its appendix of Volterra's work, called for simpler mathematics. However, many criticisms were directed not at the mathematics but at the simplifying assumptions of the equations, stated or otherwise. Criticisms of the mathematical models were commonly based on the ecologist's observation that organisms do not behave like gas molecules, a common assumption of population theory. Stanley (1932) commented:

> criticism may be leveled against Volterra's work on the grounds that so many assumptions have been made in order to simplify the mathematical treatment that the entities considered can nowhere be found in the roster of living organisms.

Margaret M. Nice (1937:207), the author of one of the classic studies of a natural population, wrote:

> I have one chief criticism of theories on population questions. . . . they all present too much theory based on too few facts. Their authors generalize too much, simplify too much.

Nice expressed the concern, common to many ecologists working with natural, or even experimental, populations that the diversity and complexity of natural populations could not be effectively expressed in simple mathematical formulations. She allowed that the fault had to be shared by naturalists in not giving theorists the data on which to work. She joined other ecologists in emphasizing the need for "a great body of facts intelligently and conscientiously collected before we can safely launch into elaborate theories." Ironically, Thomas Park (1939), in a discussion following his review of theoretical and experimental population studies, commented that even Nice's unusually long (seven-year) study was not long enough to indicate stability of populations, and thus posed a familiar problem of natural populations as applied to theory. Theoretical mathematical ecology of the Golden Age made headway in spite of the reservations expressed by many ecologists. In 1949 Park joined his distinguished associates in commenting that "theoretical population ecology has not advanced to a great degree in terms of its impact on ecological thinking." Nevertheless they saw "bright promise" in experiments "based on theory" (quoted in Allee et al. 1949:271). F. E. Smith (1952) commented on theoretical population ecology's "profound effects on applied fields," but he described the several mathematical formulations widespread in the field as hypotheses. In Smith's view, "With the possible exception of the concept of exponential growth, it is a misuse of terms to refer to any of the interpretations as 'theories.'" At the threshold of the resurgence of theoretical mathematical ecology in the 1950s Smith wrote, "The degree of acceptance of such concepts as, for examples, the Verhulst-Pearl logistic and the Lotka-Volterra equations, is astonishing."

Clearly, in current ecological jargon, these mathematical formulations, and the assumptions about science on which they rest, are "resistant," "resilient," and "persistent." Efforts by ecologists to make them conform more closely with biological reality began with G. E. Hutchinson's (1947) addition of a time-lag term to the logistic equation. Watt (1962) reviewed population theory and noted that the conclusions of Volterra, Lotka, and Nicholson and Bailey are valid deductions from their assumptions but that "the assumptions are not drawn from biological reality." Current volumes of theoretical ecology still begin with these workhorse equations, as amended and expanded, and review progress in their use often with little reference to early and continuing doubts concerning their utility in providing explanations or predictions (May 1976; Christiansen and Fenchel 1977). May (1981a), however, reviewed the conundrum of the classic deterministic logistic equation producing random dynamics rather than a smooth approach to the asymptote. In May's words, "To see mathematical ecology informing theoretical physics is a pleasing inversion of the usual order of things."

The real issue is, of course, how well it informs ecology. Slobodkin (1975) provided a list of dos and don'ts for mathematicians in population biology. One which is germane is the tendency he noted of mathematical theorists to dodge criticism. Slobodkin suggested that mathematicians learn biology and then create new and appropriate mathematics rather than fitting poorly understood biology into mathematical molds which were created for hydrodynamics, thermodynamics, economics, or other concerns.

### Theoretical ecology, competition, and equilibrium

Modern population ecologists conventionally interpret the history of theoretical population ecology as if theory led to the idea of competition and its use as a basis for community organization and niche theory. G. E. Hutchinson (1978) said that Volterra's mathematics stimulated Gause and that from Gause's experimental studies the concext of competitive exclusion really entered the minds of biologists, henceforward to be known as Gause's law. Diamond (1978) asked a related question in an article entitled "Niche Shifts and the Rediscovery of Interspecific Competition: Why Did Field Biologists So Long Overlook the Widespread Evidence for Interspecific Competition That Had Already Impressed Darwin?" The correct answer was that they had not overlooked it, and Diamond's several reasons for his assertion that they had were effectively refuted by Jackson (1981). Jackson made the point that ecologists, particularly plant ecologists, "did not need a mathematical formulation of the niche . . . to have the same idea"; and they had, he asserted, "a well developed theoretical framework, namely succession" before formal population theory existed. Jackson reviewed the history of the concept of competitive exclusion and niche theory in American and British ecological journals and concluded that much work on interspecific competition antedated or developed independently of the mathematical theories of Lotka, Volterra, Gause, and their successors. He observed that mathematical population theorists ignored the accomplishments of earlier ecologists:

> Much of what is considered original to modern niche theory of competition, except the mathematics, was well formulated and understood by many plant ecologists, especially in England, as early as 1914.

Since many recent proponents of theoretical ecology see "modern" ecology as primarily stimulated and led by theoretical ecology both in the 1920s–1930s and the 1950s–1960s, Jackson's evaluation of the way ecology progressed in respect to competition is a useful and timely caveat which warrants examination (cf. Schoener 1982).

F. E. Clements and his associates J. E. Weaver and H. C. Hanson, in the earliest treatise on competition (Clements, Weaver, and Hanson 1929), reviewed early ideas about competition in the work of Malthus, DeCandolle, Darwin, and Nageli. Warming (1895) reported the restriction of plant species from certain habitats by competition, forcing the species to grow in another habitat, which gave it the appearance of preferring that soil. He anticipated the interest in competition of later generations of ecologists: "There is scarcely any biological task more attractive than that of determining the nature of the weapons by which plants oust each other from habitats." Experimental studies of plant competition began, according to Clements, with his own work in 1903, which included both field and greenhouse experiments (Clements 1905; Clements, Weaver, and Hanson 1929). He noted the consequences as numerical reduction or disappearance. He also cited Tansley's inference about the difference in habitat of species of plants (*Galium*) when grown together and alone. This is one of the earliest experimental examples of what came to be called *niche separation.* Plant ecologists studied the relation of competition to succession, and a great deal was made of the "complementary" status of species in occupying different soil depths, seasonal periods, or aerial strata as a consequence of evasion of competition. Some of these studies were guilty of inferring competition from the fact of segregation, a guilt which they shared with a very large number of subsequent studies of niche segregation of animals which also assumed competition was the cause of spatial, habitat, and morphological separation of species (Connell 1980). The significance of competition was clearly stated by early ecologists: "Competition exerts a controlling influence on succession" (Weaver and Clements 1938:164). Although terrestrial plant ecologists had the advantage that plants stood still, they also had the difficulty that the different parts, root and shoot, existed and interacted in different media, creating the problem of differentiating root from shoot competition (Jackson 1981). Among the other observations of early plant experimentation was that competition between species might be masked by grazing of the dominant species. Much of the work of plant ecologists on competition was concerned with invasion or replacement of species through generations in the process of succession. Given this interest, it is striking that the experimental demography of plant populations was not pursued in the 1920s and 1930s, when animal demography came to the fore. Although plant ecologists and foresters were concerned with age structure, commonly (and dubiously) inferring it from size classes, the first actuarial analysis of a plant population in the sense of a life table was a study of *Plantago lanceolata* in 1959 (Sarukhan and Harper 1973). One important legacy of Clements and his associates was a clear-cut definition of competition:

> When the immediate supply of a single necessary factor falls
> below the combined demands of the plants, competition be-
> gins. (Clements, Weaver, and Hanson 1929:317)

Experimental studies of the dynamics of single-species populations and two-species populations of animals did develop in substantial part in association with mathematical theory. Pearl began studies of *Drosophila* to study the effect of density on fecundity and population increase. Pearl and several associates studied mortality and survival and urged careful study of cohorts and the use of life tables, but, as Deevey (1947) put it, ecologists were "busy elsewhere." Nevertheless, a tradition of experimental population ecology was established. An important sequence of this tradition began (ca. 1928) with studies by Chapman using flour beetles (*Tribolium*) and continued in the notable experimental studies of Thomas Park (Park 1946; Allee et al. 1949; Watt 1962; Park 1962; Kingsland 1981, 1982). The earlier hope faded that experimental studies or studies of growth of natural populations would validate the logistic equation as a "law," but the "heuristic" merit of mathematical theory was established as it stimulated much discussion of populations and life history phenomena.

Gause (1934) called for experimental studies of the "elementary processes" of the struggle for life, concentrating on competition to such a degree that the theoretical effect of competition, the exclusion or death of one of the competitors, came to be known as Gause's principle or law or more descriptively as the "competitive exclusion principle" (Hardin 1960). Gause noted the early experimental studies of Tansley and those reviewed by Clements, Weaver, and Hanson (1929), but asserted, inaccurately, that they were concerned with ontogenetic development of individuals rather than with studies of replacement of one species by another over a number of generations. He also noted that there were few studies of animal competition to provide exact data on competitive exclusion or replacement of one species by another. Gause clearly defined the elementary process of "competition for a common place between a small number of species in a limited microcosm." In his experimental work, Gause elaborated on such elementary processes as population growth, competition, and predation; but he joined Lotka and Volterra in emphasizing that his eventual goal was the study of the entire community. In spite of his emphasis on populations, he was a proponent of the holistic ecology which dominated ecology. Gause even adopted some of the criteria of organicism as identified by Haraway (1976). Gause wrote:

> It would be incorrect to fall into an extreme and to consider the complicated phenomena of the struggle for life in nature as simply a sum of such elementary processes. . . . The elementary processes of the struggle for life take place (in nature) amid a totality of most diverse living beings. This totality presents a *whole,* and the separate elementary processes taking place in it are still insufficient to explain all its properties. It is also probable that changes of the totality as a whole put an impress on those processes of the struggle for existence which are going on within it. (Gause 1934:2) [Italics his]

Gause invoked the whole-and-parts relationship which has pervaded ecology from F. E. Clements to E. P. Odum. He allowed that there was a difference between the whole and the sum of its parts, which is often and variously stated but never effectively quantified (McIntosh 1981). However, he likened community ecology in his day to 19th-century biophysics, which, he said, made progress by fruitful studies of the parts or "elementary processes . . . and thereupon only did the question arise of studying the organism as a system constituting a whole." Gause's analogy was questionable, for natural historians, protoecologists, and "self-conscious" ecologists had been trying to study the community, with the assurance that it was a whole and had to be studied as such for some decades; and formal theoretical study of the parts (populations) and their elementary processes was only beginning in the 1920s and 1930s.

Gause's hope for the utility of the study of simple experimental populations to extrapolate their lessons to complex natural communities was the basis of extensive studies of diverse taxa in the following decades, and many assert that such studies are the best or even the only way to real understanding of communities. Leigh (1968), perhaps prematurely, described this program as a failure, "for the curious reason that simple experimental communities are too unstable and erratic to exhibit lawful behavior." May (1976), the leading modern expositor of theoretical population ecology, wrote:

For communities with many species, any description of the population dynamics of individual species in terms of the interactions within and between them usually is very difficult.

The substance of the difficulty is that the mathematical models of single populations and two-species mixtures are not readily extended to more complex mixtures and to situations in which the biologically unrealistic assumption of the logistic equation and its derivatives are not valid. May's alternative was to abandon the analysis of populations and to focus on collective or aggregate attributes of communities such as energy flow, trophic organization, species-area relations, and diversity.

Gause (1936), in his article "The Principles of Biocoenology," stated that botanical investigations of communities and "the establishment of a definable unit" of structure, including plants and animals, had "automatically led to greater precision of observation and of thought." Like some later animal ecologists, he confidently regarded the structure of communities as consisting of "definite elements in a fixed numerical relation with each other." He quoted Elton's remark that the total number of species in an association is fixed and determined by some important principle. Gause's assurance that the organized community was an entity led to his statement of the one-species–one-niche concept decades before its reappearance in the heyday of niche theory in the 1970s. Gause also addressed the question of the association as a distinct combination of species sharply separated from other associations, and he noted that most botanists treated associations as relatively distinct. He was one, however, of the very few ecologists who cited Gleason's individualistic concept, which was an almost lone voice of dissent from the conventional organismic community-unit concept in the 1920s (McIntosh 1975a). Interestingly enough, Gause did not cite his own countryman, L. G. Ramensky, who was enunciating the same criticism as Gleason of the then conventional wisdom about communities.

Gause's review of the principles of biocenology is useful in that it addresses most of the key questions which were and are intriguing ecologists such as pattern, the relation of density and frequency, the relation of number of species and numbers of individuals, and the stability or equilibrium of the community as related to these elements of structure. Gause recognized two types of community, unstable and stable or mature. According to Gause, in the early stages of development of the biocenosis (succession) all of the principal species grew rapidly, but later a few species exercised dominance due to "biocœnotic relations," suppressing most other species. Gause, more confidently than later ecologists, wrote of lakes, as biocenoses, "It can be said with perfect confidence that the biocoenosis is subject to regular development and attains a certain stability," although he allowed that in temperate fresh waters a final stabilization of the system is never attained. Gause summarized his review by noting two fundamental problems raised by field studies: (1) the regulation of stable combinations of species, and (2) the separation of the biocenosis into individualized natural units, or types, in spite of an uninterrupted change in the external conditions. Gause (1934:11) noted the gap between mathematicians and ecologists and wrote:

> Mathematical investigations independent of experiment are of but small importance due to the complexity of biological systems, narrowing the possibilities of theoretical work here as compared with what can be admitted in physics and chemistry.

Nevertheless, his assurance to ecologists was that elementary processes can be successfully analyzed with the experimental method and "accounted for theoretically with the aid of a differential equation."

Thomas Park (1939) reviewed the development of analytical population studies and their relation to general ecology. Park, then well established on his distinguished career in experimental studies of animal populations, endorsed the logistic equation with reservations as a "valuable demographic tool," but noted conflicting experimental results. He remarked on the interaction of mathematical equations and experimental populations but said of population mathematicians that, contrary to their avowed intention of elucidating the community:

> To date they have not added much material of tangible value to community analysis. This is attributable to the fact that their concern has been of necessity with over-simplified situations.

Kingsland (1982) commented that Park, although he had spent four years in Raymond Pearl's laboratory, was not convinced that the logistic equation was either a law or predictor of growth. However, she noted, his section on population growth in Allee et al. (1949) stressing the advantage of the logistic as a demographic tool was important in the definition of population ecology as a discipline.

The idea of competitive exclusion, long familiar in ecology, formalized in mathematical population ecology, examined in minute detail in experiment, and commonly inferred from distributions of natural populations, became and continues as a cornerstone of population and community ecology. Clements (1909) quoted Darwin's "law of competition" as fundamental:

> As species of the same genus usually have, though by no means invariably, much similarity in habits and constitution, and always in structure, the struggle will generally be more severe between them if they come into competition with each other, than between the species of distinct genera.

A widespread assumption, derived from this type of reasoning, was that closely related species would not likely be found in the same area. This was a concept with a long history. J. B. Steere (1894), studying bird distribution in the Philippines, observed, "Every genus is represented by only a single species in any one place." Plant biogeographers and ecologists, notably Paul Jaccard, studied the ratio of genera to species, which approached one, and concluded that like elements were eliminated (Spalding 1903). David Starr Jordan (1905), the most prominent icthyologist of the era, asserted what some came to call "Jordan's law":

> Given any species in any region the nearest related species is not likely to be found in the same region nor in a remote region, but in a neighboring district separated by a barrier of some sort.

In 1944 the British Ecological Society addressed this question in a symposium "The Ecology of Closely Allied Species," centering on Gause's contention that "two species with similar ecology cannot live together in the same place" ("The Ecology of Closely Allied Species" 1944; Hardin 1960; Caswell 1982a pers. commun.; Jackson 1981). The brief report of that meeting noted that "a distinct cleavage of opinion revealed itself," which can only produce a feeling of déjà vu in an ecologist active in the 1970s. At the symposium, Elton, although he had expressed doubt about the significance of competition in *Animal Ecology* (Elton 1927), joined David Lack and G. C. Varley in supporting Gause's principle. Lack (1973), in his autobiography, wrote that this was "almost the only time in our lives . . . Charles Elton and I were on the same side." Lack based his defense on observations of niche differentiation and ecological release or expansion of habitat, when the competing species was absent or removed. Varley emphasized the evolutionary impact of mortality associated with competition and argued that a consequence of competition would be adaptive radiation, producing, for example, differences in feeding habits and, presumably, structures. Elton argued from community composition that a high proportion of genera are each represented by a single species. Unfortunately, none of the papers opposing Gause's principle were subsequently published, nor was the the "lively discussion" in which "arguments pro and contra were fairly evenly balanced" ever published. Dr. Blackman argued that exclusion did not always occur. Captain Diver and Mrs. Spooner asserted that the mathematical and experimental approaches were "dangerously oversimplified." Diver raised the difficult problem of defining "similar" ecology and asserted that direct evidence of competition between species was lacking because other factors kept populations below the level at which competition would occur. Caswell (1982a pers. commun.) noted that all of the arguments at the symposium have been elaborated continuously during the next 30 years. He also commented that Diver raised the issue, which has again been raised by critics of more recent expositions of competition as a basis of community theory, that other factors precluded the equilibrium conditions required by competitive exclusion theories (Wiens 1977, 1984; Diamond 1978; Schoener 1982).

Hardin (1960) commented that Gause's principle was born at that meeting rather than conceived, because it had been gestating in the ecological literature for an extended period whose length depended on the moment of conception. Jackson (1981) traced its conception to an earlier era of plant ecology. According to Jackson, Hutchinson and Lack, in their respective considerations of competition and niche in the 1940s misinterpreted the literature by ignoring terrestrial plant ecology. Competition in ecology, Jackson said, was biased by its equation with the formal mathematical theories of Volterra, Lotka, and Gause, and all questions about competition "were defined for the equilibrium case."

Oddly, although Hutchinson (1940) had described plant ecology as "arthritic," he did link the logistic curve with the growth of a biocenosis or "the development of a sere" – in a word, succession. He emphasized that the components of a sere do not have genetic continuity but endorsed the then conventional view that pioneer plants "play an essential part in preparing the ground for qualitatively different successors" and modify the substrate to support a "quantitatively greater flora." Hutchinson also commented that lakes developed rapidly from oligotrophy to eutrophy and a long period of equilibrium in a trophic state. Moreover, he said the growth curve of the lake resembled that of a single individual of a homogeneous population and was characteristic of a biocenosis, in general coinciding with Gause's view.

Although Gause made his major contributions to ecology in the 1930s, the principle attributed to him, according to Hardin (1960), remains a potent part of modern ecology. K. E. F. Watt made it into two principles (McIntosh 1980a). The principle became the subject of continuing dispute, as Hardin (1960) noted, because of an inherent problem of circularity. When Ayala (1969) reported an experiment demonstrating that competing species could exist in a stable equilibrium, Gause (1970) came out of ecological retirement to deny the inference on the ground that the two presumably competing species actually were occupying different niches. Ayala (1970) responded, defending his invalidation of the principle of competitive exclusion but noting the perennial problem of inadequate definitions of *competition* and *niche*. In effect, this exchange indicated the circularity problem noted by Hardin. Nevertheless, Hardin had asserted confidently, concerning the history of ecology and the study of population genetics:

> We stand at the threshold of a renaissance of understanding, a renaissance made possible by the explicit acceptance of the competitive exclusion principle.

Much of theoretical ecology from the 1950s to the 1970s rested on the competitive exclusion principle, but whether it constituted a renaissance of understanding is still in dispute. The ubiquitous attribute of balance, stability, or equilibrium arose and persisted in population ecology, as it had in community ecology. Biologists and ecologists involved in general survey or census of plant and animal populations had shared the belief that they were in, or would tend toward, a stable or equilibrium number, in the absence of human disturbance. Möbius (1877) described a "biocœnotic equilibrium" of a mean number of individuals of a biocenosis. S. A. Forbes (1887) described a benign result of the struggle for survival as an equilibrium of the interacting populations. In Forbes's dynamic view, populations oscillated, but the oscillations were kept within bounds and tended toward equilibrium. Adams (1913) recognized a "biotic base, optimum, or balance toward which relations under given conditions tend, at a time which an equilibrium will be established." Shelford (1913) described the community as a balance in the numbers of contending organisms. Chapman (1931) characterized the concept of equilibrium as "one of the most fertile in the field of ecology." He extolled the theory of biotic equilibrium being developed by Volterra but noted that, in addition to disturbance of the physical environment as a cause of population fluctuations, the biotic system may generate its own fluctuations.

Elton (1933) considered mechanisms which would bring about the "optimum density of numbers for each species" but noted that no population stayed the same for any "great length of time." H. S. Smith (1939) described population equilibrium in the context of the new population theory in terms of the rate of change being approximately zero. Allee et al. (1949) accommodated Elton's assessment of constantly varying populations by suggesting a "comparative balance in nature based upon long-term population relations." How their "long term" related to Elton's "great length of time" was not clear. Slobodkin (1955) commented that a "sufficient length of time" was a necessary condition for population equilibrium because the population had to be in an "equilibrium age-structure." Diverse views on population equilibrium and the relevant terminology persisted. Bodenheimer (1958) attempted to clarify the concept of balance or equilibrium in his turn, noting that the meaning differed from that of a physical equilibrium. Ehrlich and Birch (1967) described the idea of a balance in respect to population size as "demonstrably false." The 1960s and 1970s produced extended discourse about the meanings of stability (Brookhaven Symposia in Biology 1969) and heated discussions of equilibrium and nonequilibrium theory (Lewin 1983). Connell and Sousa (1983) returned to square one with an article "On the Evidence Needed to Judge Ecological Stability or Persistence" and the advice that "one should determine if a population was stable before applying a theory based on a premise of equilibrium."

The tradition of balance or equilibrium, so strongly imbedded in natural history and early ecology, led to varying assumptions about the factors responsible for maintaining equilibrium or for controlling populations in the absence of equilibrium. Clements (1905) assumed that populations were replaced until a relatively stable "climax" was reached in which the populations were self-perpetuating and stable. Among the earliest explanations was that offered by Howard and Fiske (1911) in a study of the introduction of parasites to control pest insects. They recognized natural balance of a population as maintained by "the operation of facultative agencies which effect the destruction of a greater proportionate number of individuals as the insect in question increases in abundance." This classic statement of density-dependent biological controls, they said, led to considering parasitism as "the most subtle in its action" in controlling a population. The theory of populations as being in or tending toward equilibrium was questioned by Uvarov (1931) as "directly contrary to the facts." He joined Elton in questioning the balance-of-nature concept and denied that a relatively stable "normal number," or uniform fluctuations around it, characterized populations. He also questioned the primacy of biotic factors in maintaining balance. The key to population control, he believed, was in the influence of climatic factors. It is fitting that this dichotomy was expressed in studies of insects, because entomologists have been prominent in the development and polarization of concepts of equilibrium and factors controlling populations. The entomologist Chapman, oddly enough, even offered reasons for "considering insect ecology apart from animal ecology" (Milne 1957).

The experimental studies of Chapman, Pearl, and Gause were taken by the entomologist A. J. Nicholson (Nicholson 1933; Nicholson and Bailey 1935) as evidence for the existence of balance or equilibrium of animal populations in nature. Nicholson joined forces with Bailey, a physicist, to investigate the problem of competition and the relation between animals and their environment and considered that observations and experiment supported the concept of balance. Nicholson (1933) asserted that it was "usual at present to deny . . . the existence of the balance of nature." In fact, it was widely assumed that balance was characteristic, and Nicholson cited only Uvarov and Bodenheimer to the contrary. Nicholson believed that animal populations are normally in equilibrium and fluctuated only within restricted limits. He used a gas-law analogy of a balloon to illustrate how a population would change if its environment changed but would rapidly come into equilibrium with the new environment, presumably as it stabilized. Moreover, he argued that the balance of populations is maintained by a factor which is "governed by the density of the population controlled," and he asserted that "competition seems to be the only factor that can be governed in this way." Although competition had long been assumed to be a major factor in limiting populations and in organizing community structure, Nicholson's assertion of the so-called density-dependent population regulation exacerbated a dispute which persisted for decades. Nicholson's somewhat dogmatic assertion of the primacy of "competition" and his extensive experiments attracted much attention. Although his definition of *competition* was unclear, his position was that "balance is produced and maintained by competition." In fact, his idea was somewhat circular. He said that competition is "capable of producing balance" and that "any factor that produced balance is almost necessarily some form of competition." Among these factors he included limitations of things required for existence and ease of being found by natural enemies. Nicholson's emphasis on mathematics was not acceptable to some population ecologists. W. R. Thompson, who had been much taken by mathematical ecology in the 1920s, became much opposed to Nicholson's ideas in the 1930s (Kingsland 1983). Thompson pressed the familiar argument that population biology was comprised largely of unique and complex events so that a general theoretical mathematical model was not possible.

Two landmarks of population biology and of the dispute concerning density-dependent control of populations appeared in 1954. Lack (1954) attempted a general assessment in a book *The Natural Regulation of Animal Numbers*. Lack supported Nicholson's idea of density-dependence, although he attributed it to a complex of interactions of food shortage, predation, and disease. Lack was explicit in his recognition of competition (Gause's principle). He inferred it from differentiation of species in food habits, habitat use, and morphological displacement. Andrewartha and Birch (1954) flatly disagreed with the concept of density-dependent control. They held that species fluctuated irregularly and were controlled, but not in any sense of balance or regulation, by factors, largely weather, which acted independently of the density of the population. As late as 1958, in the face of the substantial dispute, Nicholson asserted:

> Logical argument based on certain irrefutable facts shows not merely that populations may regulate themselves by density-induced resistance to multiplication but that this mechanism is essential. (Quoted in Andrewartha and Birch 1973)

The problem in the 1930s, in the 1950s, and revived again in the 1980s was not simply that individual populations were to be understood as in or near a stable equilibrium, but whether a community "was best understood as assemblages of populations at or near a stable competitive equilibrium" (Caswell 1982a,b).

Caswell (1982a) noted that Nicholson, who was much influenced by the theoretical mathematical work of Volterra and Lotka, and David Lack, who was not, were among the supporters of density dependence. They commonly argued, as had Darwin, that populations had the capacity for exponential growth or for extinction. To maintain a population somewhere between these levels the controlling factor must limit growth at high densities and enhance it at low densities. The perennial question of density-dependent and density-independent control of populations persisted, often confounded by misinterpretations of what these terms mean. Milne (1957), for example, commented that his definition of population control was factual and "not confounded with theory as to how it comes about," citing Nicholson's density-dependent control by competition as culpable in this respect. Nicholson's theory was widely accepted but was also attacked, particularly by the entomologists Andrewartha and Birch (1954). Andrewartha and Birch (1973), in a history of insect ecology, reviewed this dispute and argued that the probability of a population reaching a ceiling ($K$) which provokes a "density-induced resistance to multiplication" was low, and so was unimportant to population control. This argument turns on the assumption of equilibrium, and Andrewartha and Birch commented that "the controversy awaits a philosophical resolution." As with many other philosophical discussions, the resolution was a long time coming. The discussion persists in current disputes concerning the equilibrium status of populations and communities (Wiens 1977, 1984; Caswell 1982a,b; Schoener 1982; Willson 1981; Strong et al. 1984).

Population ecology was considered at a symposium in 1957 bringing together human demographers and animal ecologists, with little consensus on theory evident. A notable product of this symposium was Hutchinson's (1957a) "Concluding Remarks," which is certainly one of the least explicit titles in the history of population ecology, masking as it does one of the most highly touted and disputed productions of that discipline – a formalization of niche theory. Hutchinson's description of the symposium as "a Heterogeneous Unstable Population" is, however, particularly apt. He contrasted the comment of one participant about the uselessness of the logistic equation with

> the almost universal practice of animal demographers to start thinking by making some suitable, if almost unconscious, modification of this much abused function.

The extension of this tradition to the present is noted by Sale (1977), who commented:

> A fair statement of the current consensus is that the tropical community is a mature equilibrium community of numerous species whose coexistence is satisfactorily explained by the theory based on the Lotka-Volterra competition and predation equations.

Hutchinson also asserted, concerning populations, that "a difference in interest may underlie some of the arguments that have enlivened, or at times disgraced, discussions of this subject." He noted that laboratory workers in their experiments tended to keep all but a few factors constant and to vary these few systematically, whereas field workers tended to emphasize the changing environment. Not specified was that theoreticians ignored any variation in the environment, assuming that it was constant and homogeneous. Hutchinson's salient comment was:

> The initial differences of point of view are not the only diffi- culty. . . . It is also very likely that the differences in initial point of view are often responsible for the differences in the interpretation of the data.

Thus, Hutchinson summarized a perennial and continuing problem in population ecology.

The burden of Hutchinson's "Concluding Remarks" is a suitable place at which to terminate this chapter. He provided a formalization of the niche based on the competitive exclusion principle. *Niche* was the expression of the response of a population in an *n*-dimensional hyperspace in which "all $X_n$ variables, both physical and biological," were to be considered. The introduction of the concept of the multidi- mensional niche of a species parallels the concurrent introduction of the use of multivariate methods in plant community ecology by Good- all (1954) and Bray and Curtis (1957). Ecologists, of course, had long since thought of the entities which they studied as excessively compli- cated, perhaps too complicated for the human mind to grasp. Multidi- mensional analysis seemed admirably suited to treat the acknowledg- edly multiple factors affecting a species or the multiple species consti- tuting a community. The effort to bring them together in a unified theory of population and community by means of multivariate analysis essentially begins in the mid-1950s (Whittaker 1973).

The problem of how best to study the attributes of populations in relation to communities persisted in ecology. Slobodkin (1961), like many earlier students of population ecology, such as Gause (1936), assumed that complex communities are "assemblies of simpler sys- tems" and that "the same ecological laws operate in the simpler system as in a more complex one." Slobodkin described a difficult middle ground between very small and very large systems, such as the visible landscape, which is just where ecological problems are located, as Allen and Starr (1982) noted. Slobodkin also stated the belief, en- demic among field ecologists, that "all the conclusions of the experi- mentalists and theoreticians must eventually be formulated in such a way as to permit a field test." This is widely accepted among ecologists as the basic justification for mathematical theory, manipulations of models, and laboratory experiments on populations. There were and are, however, ecologists who believe that neither theoretical model nor experimental microcosm ever effectively addresses the complexities of nature, and the tension between these groups permeates the history of self-conscious ecology from its earliest days. Adequate measurement of field populations, whether static or dynamic, for empirical or theoretical purposes is a continuing concern of ecologists. Developing a theoretical basis for population ecology and extending it to community or ecosystems has proven difficult and frustrating to generations of ecologists (May 1976, 1981a; Brinck 1980; Gordon 1981).

# 6

## Ecosystem ecology, systems ecology, and big biology

Like the word *ecology*, *ecosystem* was applied to a concept with a long history. It also had a number of competing synonyms when it was coined, suggesting that the time was ripe for its appearance, and there was a lag period between its coinage and its widespread incorporation into ecological science. The British plant ecologist Tansley (1935) introduced *ecosystem* in the context of a discussion of the superorganism concept of the plant community and succession which was developed around 1905 by F. E. Clements and was still being strongly advocated in the 1930s by the South African botanist John Phillips. Tansley commented that Phillips's articles "remind one irresistably of the exposition of a creed – of a closed system of religious or philosophical dogma," a flavor not entirely missing from some later expositions of "systems ecology," facetiously called "theological ecology" (Van Dyne 1980).

Godwin (1977) noted that Tansley, like many biologists of his era, was "remarkably unspecialized" and a man "of wide culture and familiarity with many sciences," just what the ecosystem concept called for. Tansley was also well read in philosophy and psychology, having studied with Freud, which, perhaps, influenced his ecological thought. He defined *ecosystem* as

> the whole *system* (in the sense of physics) including not only the organism-complex, but also the whole complex of physical factors forming what we call the environment of the biome – the habitat factors in the widest sense. (Tansley 1935)

Tansley recognized a hierarchy of systems and specified that an ecosystem was one category of the range of systems between atom and universe; and although he identified the biome as an ecosystem, he allowed that ecosystems "are of the most various kinds and sizes." This convenient generality persists in current use of the term, although just what an ecosystem is, and what are its attributes and boundaries, may sometimes be obscure. According to Tansley, ecosystems "are the basic units of nature on the face of the earth." That the ecosystem is a

193

legitimate unit of study was described as the one element of consensus with "essentially no dissenters" in a workshop convened in 1975 to consider ecological theory and ecosystem models (Levin 1976).

The holistic tradition in natural history and early ecology of the unity of nature, the chain of being, or balance of nature is seen as antecedent to the ecosystem concept and persists in the holistic emphasis in some ecology as well as in modern nature writing and the ideals of the environmental movement (McIntosh 1960, 1963; Bakuzis 1969; Major 1969; E. P. Odum 1972, 1977). However, the familiar, if tenuous, distinction between the nonliving and living attributes of nature, the recognition of the historical development of the earth sans life, and the basic ecological concept of primary succession as a purely physical system modified by a superimposed living system lent itself to the separation of the animate, or biotic, and inanimate, or abiotic in early ecological thought. In Clements's concept of the climax formation or its later synonym the biome (Clements and Shelford 1939), the formation consisting of organisms was the result, the climate the cause. Environment *acted* on the populations, whereas the populations *reacted* on the environment, which was commonly defined as the *physical-chemical environment* (Allee et al. 1949). Although most ecologists clearly understood that organisms and physical environment were interrelated, much early ecological study was an effort to determine the effects (or even the cause) of the environment on organisms as populations or aggregates of populations, vegetation, or community, and less frequently the reciprocal effects of organism(s) on environment. Tansley (1920) had also coined the terms *autogenic* and *allogenic*. Although Tansley did not define them so, these came to mean, respectively, biotic effects and physical effects on succession, reinforcing the distinction between living and nonliving. However, that the environment of an organism included both the inanimate physical environment and other organisms was explicit in Haeckel's original definition of *ecology*. That a plant community had animals in its environment and vice versa was familiar to ecologists. If, however, one spoke of the total biota of an area, the residual environment was the inanimate physical surroundings. Ecological definitions of *environment* were not always consistent nor crystal-clear; and efforts to clarify them by "mathematical systematization" (Haskell 1940), "language analysis" (Mason and Langenheim 1957), or "semantics" (Maelzer 1965) were not notably helpful, nor has the difficulty of defining environment entirely disappeared from current ecology (Billings 1974; Niven 1982).

The history of the ecosystem concept was reviewed by Lindeman (1942), Sjors (1955), Major (1969), Odum (1972), Shugart and O'Neill (1979), Van Dyne (1980), and Golley (1984). Tansley's term fell on well-prepared ground. Aquatic ecology, which was heavily dominated by considerations of the physical environment, was particularly amenable to the ecosystem concept, which continued this emphasis on physical attributes. S. A. Forbes (1887) had described a lake as a *microcosm*, explicitly incorporating *all* biotic and physical attributes in a single entity. Möbius's biocœnose – a community of organism which had relations with the environment – was expanded to *geobiocœnose* as an independently derived synonym for *ecosystem* by the Russian plant ecologist Sukachev (1945). The limnologist Thienemann (1918) had suggested *biosystem*. The entomologist Friederichs provided *holocœn* or *holocœnosis*, which, like geobiocœnose, was used largely in Europe (Evans 1956). Other ecologists used the concept without applying a name. Olson (1958) described the early linking of organisms and environment in Cowles's (1901) "physiographic ecology": "Cowles . . . wove the physical and biological threads into a fabric showing orderly design." Olson commented that the idea of succession as "the transformation of the biological community and its habitat" – what Tansley later called the ecosystem – was what made succession "catch fire so rapidly" in early ecology. Jenny (1941) approached soil formation as an open system which could be treated as a dynamic system – with properties as functions of all the factors affecting it, including biotic and abiotic. This formulation was later adapted for vegetation by Major (1951), who noted that the several factors represented could determine an ecosystem. In the 1920s and 1930s, many ecologists were deploring the piecemeal approach which characterized most of ecology. Many urged plant and animal ecologists to get together with limited success. Taylor (1927) urged the need for "bioecology," on the premise that ecology had been appropriated by botanists. Allee (1934a) recognized a "sort of superorganismic unity not alone between plants and animals to form biotic communities, but also between the biota and the environment." He suggested the "superredundancy" "geo-bio-ecology" for this relation and commented, "Failure to recognize the essential unity of this animal-plant-environmental relationship retards progress in oceanic studies." Taylor (1935), by this time president of the Ecological Society of America, wrote, "The emphasis placed by bio-ecology on organism and environment as a great unitary problem is an inspiring one." Clements and Shelford's (1939) volume

*Bio-Ecology* did not, however, meet the ideal of a unitary approach to organisms and physical environment which ecologists were seeking and which *ecosystem* described. The several terms that were proposed, and the explicit recognition of the inherent integration of the organic and inorganic components suggested a favorable climate for the ecosystem concept. *Ecosystem* finally came to be the favored term, conceived to encompass the whole complex of biotic community and physical environment, and studies of this complex are commonly designated *ecosystem ecology*.

This promising gestation was a prelude to an extremely difficult birth if, like many ecologists, one sees the birth of ecosystem ecology in Raymond Lindeman's famous (and, sadly, posthumous) paper "The Trophic-Dynamic Aspect of Ecology" (1942). Lindeman's article is now widely acclaimed as one of the landmarks of ecology generally and of limnology and ecosystem ecology in particular. It was initially rejected by the journal *Ecology* but finally published by it, in the face of strong negative recommendations from two distinguished limnologists, only after the intervention of a third distinguished limnologist and a courageous editorial decision by Thomas Park (Cook 1977). Lindeman was trained in quantitative ecology and, appropriately enough, came from one of its sources, the University of Minnesota, where he was substantially influenced by W. S. Cooper (Cook 1977). In fact, Lindeman's "trophic-dynamic aspect" of ecology followed a consideration of the classic community concept and led to an interpretation of succession, much as had Tansley's (1935) article in which he coined *ecosystem*. Lindeman adopted Tansley's ecosystem concept as of "fundamental importance in interpreting the data of dynamic ecology," linking it to traditional successional views of ecology, but he added a new dimension to dynamics in ecology. He described the basic process of trophic dynamics as the transfer of energy in the ecosystem, adopting the terminology, by then familiar among limnologists, of production and the major trophic categories of producer (autotrophs), consumer (heterotrophs), and decomposer (saprophage) organisms. Lindeman's rationale for adopting the ecosystem concept, he said, was that it simply was not possible to distinguish the living from the non-living parts of the ecosystem. He recognized – but did not "introduce," as Colinvaux and Barnett (1979) suggested – the progressive depletion of energy in successive food levels of the "Eltonian" pyramid, which had been spelled out previously by Semper (1881) and Petersen (1918) on the grounds of basic thermodynamics. He attempted to produce realistic quantitative estimates of this depletion. Lindeman expressed (1) the concept of efficiency of production of a single level of a food chain by relating its respiration to growth, and (2) the productivity of one level of a food chain relative to (as a ratio of) the productivity of a previous level, particularly the immediate preceding level. The latter was called "Lindeman ratio" by Allee et al. (1949) but was soon immersed in a flurry of other efficiencies, which indicated the level of interest in ecological energetics (Kozlovsky 1968).

Lindeman's contributions to ecosystem ecology were to (1) "to stress the major role of trophic function, particularly quantitative relations, in the determination of community patterns through succession"; (2) "establish the validity of a theoretical orientation in ecology"; and (3) "identify a fundamental dynamic process, energy flow, with which the seasonal trophic relations of organisms could be integrated into the long-term process of community change" (Cook 1977). In an addendum to Lindeman's paper, G. E. Hutchinson stressed that Lindeman had presented the dynamics of a lake in a "form that is amenable to a productive abstract analysis." Hutchinson, who had earlier criticized a contemporary landmark of ecology, *Bio-Ecology,* for its lack of mathematics, wrote that the significance of Lindeman's article was that its reduction of the complexity of ecosystems to

> pairs of numbers, one an integer determining the level, one a fraction determining the efficiency, may even give some hint of an undiscovered type of mathematical treatment of biological communities.

Hutchinson was instrumental, then and since, in encouraging abstract mathematical analysis in ecology both by precept and example. The controversy attending publication of Lindeman's paper suggests that it was a watershed in the history of ecology. Senior limnologists of the day disapproved (Cook 1977). Chancey Juday asserted that lakes were "stubborn about fitting into mathematical formulae," a comment reminiscent of Haeckel's criticism of Hensen's mathematics of plankton counts. Paul Welch objected to the absence of data and suggested the manuscript be put away for 10 years to see what limnology produced in the interim. G. E. Hutchinson urged, successfully, that it be published. Hutchinson's contributions to the manuscript, acknowledged by Lindeman, were also revealed in a letter to the editor of the journal *Ecology,* Thomas Park, commenting that most of the specific points challenged by the reviewers "are matters for which I, rather than Lindeman, am responsible." Hutchinson had been thinking along the successional and energetic lines of Lindeman's trophic aspect of ecology. He provided a suggestion of the organismic emphasis which appeared in ecosystem ecology. Hutchinson and Wollack (1940) noted that the growth curve of a lake qualitatively resembled that of an individual organism. They also identified a dichotomy in ecology which was to become increasingly evident as ecosystem ecology developed. One method of ecology, they said, concentrated on the "bio-sociological," based on individual species and their relations. The other isolated a space and studied the transference of matter and/or energy across the boundaries of the space. In this approach, biomass is more important than taxa, and the "biogeochemical" approach advocated by Vernadsky (1944) and recognized in aquatic ecology since the early studies of Birge and Juday is of paramount significance.

Assigning credit or responsibility for a scientific contribution is usually difficult. In ecology, the "experimentum crucis" or the more current "breakthrough," frequently used to extract funds from granting agencies, is not usually identifiable. Many of the major figures of ecology are recognized primarily for bringing together and ordering disparate aspects of the work of others. Charles Elton did not, for example, discover food chains, pyramids of numbers, or niche, but he did integrate them into a useful framework for ecology (Elton 1927). Lindeman brought together data on trophic levels from his graduate studies of Cedar Creek Bog in Minnesota, a thorough understanding of old-style "dynamic ecology" and its major tenet of succession, derived from his association with W. S. Cooper, and G. E. Hutchinson's views on lake dynamics as "primarily a problem of energy transfer." This integration is evident in Lindeman's linking of the processes of production and eutrophication of lakes, developed by limnologists, and succession, largely the province of terrestrial ecologists. Lindeman's headings and subheadings anticipated E. P. Odum's (1968) review of ideas contributing to ecological energetics – community concept, trophic dynamics, qualitative food cycles, primary production of plants, secondary production of animals, efficiency, Eltonian pyramids, and trophic dynamics in succession. The idea of trophic dynamics, particularly the quantification thereof, was largely a product of limnology. When Kozlovsky (1968) reviewed the subject of trophic efficiencies, all of the quantitative examples he was able to marshal were of aquatic systems. Engelmann (1966) speculated on the late arrival of terrestrial ecologists in energetic ecology, citing Golley (1960) as the first to produce a terrestrial model in the Lindeman tradition. He ascribed the delay to the relatively clear bounding of aquatic systems, the ease of measurement and relative constancy of the physical components, and, less convincingly, the relative simplicity of the aquatic biota.

The ecosystem concept was clearly in the air in the 1940s, and many references retrospectively recognized the importance of Lindeman's contribution to the understanding of ecosystem function based on trophic dynamics, but the response was not immediate. Contemporary plant ecology texts paid little attention. The major midcentury compendium of animal ecology (Allee et al. 1949) included all of the subjects brought together by Lindeman but used the ecosystem primarily in the context of evolution. The major contributor to bringing the ecosystem to the fore in ecology was E. P. Odum, who organized his influential textbook (E. P. Odum 1953) around the concept of ecosystems and their structure and function (Burgess 1981a). When Odum defined *ecosystem,* he gave as an example a lake. The lag in general acceptance of the ecosystem concept and differences in interpretation are evident in Evans (1956), who still urged that the ecosystem, as Tansley had said, be recognized as "the basic unit in ecology." Evans succinctly stated that ecology "is primarily concerned with the quantities of matter and energy that pass through a given ecosystem and the rates at which they do so." Ecosystem ecologists seized on this idea in the 1960s and turned to the problems of measuring flows of energy or matter in ecosystems and developing a theoretical framework to integrate the resultant mass of data. However, Evans also identified the dichotomy in ecology, noted earlier by Hutchinson and Wollack (1940), which continues to the present. Evans wrote:

> Of almost equal importance, however, are the kinds of organisms that are present in any particular ecosystem and the roles that they occupy in its structure and organization.

The distinction Evans suggested between ecologists concerned with "functional" attributes of the ecosystem as a whole, or its input-output relations based on matter or energy, and those concerned with specific populations, their dynamics, genetics, life histories, and evolution, is evident in what is commonly described as a revolution in ecology or the "new ecology," which came into being in the 1950s and 1960s and is a major characteristic of subsequent ecology (E. P. Odum 1971, 1977; Levin 1976; McIntosh 1976; Burgess 1981a).

The "new" or "revolutionary" ecology actually came in two forms. One was acclaimed as the new approach to ecosystems in the mode of ecosystem ecology, the other was the rejuvenation of theoretical,

mathematical population ecology, notably in the work of Robert Mac-
Arthur (Cody and Diamond 1975; Fretwell 1975; McIntosh 1976,
1980a). Ecosystem ecology had its own divisions which create problems in tracing its development and content (Watt 1966; Van Dyne
1969; Patten 1971, 1972, 1975b; Levin 1975, 1976; Likens et al. 1979;
Shugart and O'Neill 1979; Horn, Stairs, and Mitchell 1979; Van Dyne
1980; Kitching 1983). George Van Dyne (1980), in a speech at the
dedication of one of the bastions of ecosystem ecology, the Environmental Sciences Laboratory at Oak Ridge National Laboratory, asserted, "In 1964 Gene Odum really put the term 'systems ecology' on
the board." Odum (1964) had stated:

> The new ecology is thus a systems ecology – or to put it in
> other words, the new ecology deals with the structure and
> function of levels of organization beyond that of the individual
> and species.

In part, the switch of "systems ecology" was to "ecoenergetics," and
Chapman's (1931) early electrical metaphors for population growth,
*potential* and *resistance,* were expanded to energy flows in the ecosystem and, even more shocking, to H. T. Odum's increasingly complicated energy-circuit diagrams (E. P. Odum 1968; H. T. Odum 1971,
1983). E. P. Odum (1968) stated, "Ecoenergetics is the core of ecosystem analysis." Strikingly, this core had its origin in the ideas of A. J.
Lotka (1925), who is more widely recognized as one of the founders of
the other "new" ecology, theoretical population ecology. Lotka had
asserted that evolution maximized energy uptake and increased the
metabolic rate of organisms. He wrote, "The net effect is to maxi-
mize . . . the energy flux through the system of organic nature." Allee
et al. (1949:598) commented, "The cosmic meaning of these manifestations of life eludes the scientific mind." Nevertheless, Lotka's "law of
maximum energy" provided a stimulus for a still elusive energetic approach to ecosystem analysis, succession, and civilization (H. T. Odum
and Pinkerton 1955).

E. P. Odum's assertion that the new ecology is "systems ecology"
was not the first intimation that a revolution in ecosystem ecology was
in the making but, as Van Dyne said, he put it "on the board." Odum
also focused attention on the descriptor *systems ecology* as a distinctive
approach to ecosystem ecology. He drew an analogy between the ecosystem as a basic unit of ecologists and the cell as the basic unit of
molecular biologists. Apart from hailing the arrival of the new ecology,
Odum identified two camps reacting to its arrival. One, he said,

wondered what was new, since "all of this is obvious, quite axiomatic in fact; any school child knows that the whole is not the sum of its parts." The other was a group "unconvinced that there is anything really new or different at ecological levels that cannot be ultimately explained . . . by the reduction of the whole into even smaller parts or by expanding knowledge gleaned from parts directly to the whole" (E. P. Odum 1964). Odum's recognition of a distinction between holist and reductionist approaches to ecology is not the first, but it marked a division which is still evident. Moreover, Odum associated the new "systems ecology" with holism and described the ecosystem as "the basic unit of structure and function" around which "ecologists can rally." Hutchinson (1964) identified different approaches to lake systems with a similarly contrasting approach. One approach was an extension of the holism of S. A. Forbes, Clements, Birge, Thienemann, and Allee, which had always permeated ecology. The other was an extension of the reductionist mathematical population ecology of the Golden Age of Lotka and Volterra represented by the rejuvenating effect of Hutchinson and Robert MacArthur. Odum clearly delineated these two camps and placed himself in the forefront of the holists, referring the reader to "the shortcomings of the reductionist philosophy." Many aspects of ecology in the last two decades must be seen as a split between these two camps, not purely on scientific or technical grounds but on philosophical grounds – on a fundamental difference about how to do science, sometimes rather dogmatically asserted. It would be neater if there was only one dichotomy in the advent of a functional approach to ecosystems. Ecologists could then be divided into those with white hats and black hats, as in movie Westerns. However, Odum's two camps each has its own subdivisions or positions along a continuum (Levin 1976; McIntosh 1976, 1980a; Burgess 1981a).

Ecologists who concerned themselves with ecosystems in the post-Lindeman era divided themselves into subcamps. One criterion by which these may be recognized is the degree to which they subscribed to the view that "systems analysis" was the "wave of the future" of "systems ecology" (E. P. Odum 1971). This was complicated because there were different approaches to ecosystem ecology, aggravated by the fact that systems ecology comes in a variety of forms, various of which were advocated by the new breed of "systems ecologist." The first course, billed as systems ecology, was explicitly based on the ecosystem concept (Patten 1966). However, the ecosystem concept was deemed inadequately implemented until the several disciplines (cybernetics, operations research, general systems theory) lumped as the "systems" disciplines became involved in ecosytems analysis. The linkage of "ecosystems, systems ecology, and systems ecologists" was explored by Van Dyne (1966). Van Dyne succinctly defined *systems ecology* "as the study of the development, dynamics and disruption of ecosystems." Thus systems ecology was put on the board, and ecologists were subjected to a flurry of books about systems analysis and ecology (Watt 1966; Patten 1971, 1972, 1975a; Jeffers 1978). The variety of new descriptions – "ecosystem ecology," "ecosystem analysis," "analysis of ecosystems," "systems analysis" – left some ecologists wondering if they were considering a horse chestnut or a chestnut horse. One basis of this division was stated, after its lineaments had become evident, by F. E. Smith (1975b), who had occupied a strategic position as director of the analysis of ecosystems (1967–9) of the International Biological Program in a critical era in the development of large-scale ecosystem studies. Smith distinguished between *ecosystem ecology* and *ecosystems systems science:*

> The former is a division of ecology, which in turn is a branch of biology. The latter is a division of systems science, which has its origin in various areas of mathematics and engineering.

Shugart and O'Neill (1979:vii) stated, "Systems ecology is a new and exciting subdiscipline of ecology. The field is characterized by its application of mathematical models to ecosystem dynamics." The tendency to equate systems analysis or systems ecology with ecosystem ecology is unfortunate and may be largely due to an etymological connection (Kitching 1983). Spurr (1964) had commented on *ecosytem,* "How should such a system be studied, if not by systems analysis and the computer?" R. L. Kitching provided a logic by which all ecology was system ecology. Systems ecology was even seen by some as transcending ecology. E. P. Odum (in press) wrote:

> Until recently ecology was generally considered to be a subdivision of biology dealing with the relationships of organisms with the environment. Then, during the environmental awareness decade, 1968 to 1981, a school of ecosystem ecology emerged that considers ecology to be not just a subdivision of biology, but a new discipline that integrates biological, physical and social science aspects of man-in-nature interdependence.

## Ecosystem ecology

In two decades ecologists had been faced with a "revolution" (E. P. Odum 1971) or "shotgun marriage" (Patten 1971) which produced either a "new discipline" transcending its biological heritage or a hybrid, depending on one's choice of metaphor. Sometimes lost in the confusion which is expected to follow revolutions, shotgun marriages, or other forms of hyperbole was that ecosystem ecology was not coextensive with systems ecology or systems analysis (Kitching 1983). Ecosystem ecology, or the study of ecosystems, took several forms, some of which eschewed both the revolution and the hybridization connected with systems analysis. The approach to ecology broadly called *ecosystem ecology* created difficulties for ecologists primarily trained as biologists, since it introduced components of other disciplines relatively foreign to most ecologists yet deemed vital to understanding the "structure and function of ecosystems," which became a new definition of *ecology*. The assertion, familiar from the earliest days of ecology, that ecologists needed to supplement their knowledge of organisms with knowledge of other sciences was being put to the test in the effort to examine physical attributes of ecosystems and the pattern and rate of flow of energy and materials in ecosystems, which constituted their structure and function in the context of ecosystem ecology. One of the attributes of much of ecosystem ecology was that it emphasized or even concentrated on the inanimate processes of the ecosystem and called for a level of knowledge of physics, chemistry, geology, geochemistry, meteorology, and hydrology beyond that of traditional ecologists. It also required new skills in methods of instrumentation, technique, and computation, which became available in the post-World War II era, to measure ecosystem parameters at increasingly sophisticated levels and to analyze large data bases.

One of the difficulties of following the development of ecosystem ecology is to match practice with the rhetoric accompanying the new ecosystem ecology in its several variants. As ecosystem became the basic unit "around which ecologists can rally," it was often used rather loosely. Certainly, traditional ecology had significant elements of the ecosystems concept. Early ecologists had clearly recognized that terrestrial and lake succession was accompanied by reciprocal changes in the physical environment which were, in part, induced by the organisms and which, in part, influenced the organisms. Accumulation of organic material, change in nutrient supply, and moderation of the physical environment by organisms, as well as changes in populations, were the essence of succession. Indeed, some ecosystem ecologists implicitly adopted Clementsian concepts in their versions of ecosystem ecology, as I have argued elsewhere (McIntosh 1980a, 1981). The stable entity which Clements recognized was the climax, which included all of the seral stages. Ecosystems ecologists, of whatever stripe, identified the ecosystem as a, or the, functional unit of nature, consisting of components such as species populations (or aggregates of these) linked together by multiple interrelations, notably food webs, organic debris, inorganic minerals, atmospheric gases and of water, and flows of these and of energy between the organic and inorganic components. The ecosystem was variously bounded, usually by the investigator, and measurements were made of inputs and outputs of the ecosystem and its holistic, "aggregate," or "macroscopic" properties. Various ecologists concentrated on particular aspects of the ecosystem, for example, energy flow, production, species diversity, or nutrient flows (MacFadyen 1964; Engelmann 1966; Phillipson 1966). The ideal was to consider the ecosystem holistically, the aim being to integrate the component parts and to consider the ecosystem as a unit. One early approach to the lake as "microcosm," in the sense of S. A. Forbes, was the addition of lime to an entire lake to note the change in physical and biological properties of the lake (Hasler, Brynildson, and Helm 1951). Among foresters who viewed the forest with an ecological perspective, some, like Joseph Kittredge, considered the interaction of the forest and environment (Kittredge 1948). Other forest ecologists were concerned with the problems of description and classification of ecosystems as landscape units, comprising community and habitat/site characteristics, with the aim of providing a classification of ecosystems (Rowe 1961).

One major development of ecosystem ecology was its response to the familiar assertion that the ecosystem was indeed very complex. Ecologists exploring ecosystems realized that such studies required a departure from the tradition of small-scale, low-budget research. By the early 1950s, most of the concepts were in place, but recognition that large-scale, complex research problems required a large-scale, multidisciplinary, and well-funded research organization was slow in being implemented. Perhaps the first effort to develop a detailed and integrated study of the structure and function of a particular ecosystem and to develop a model of "the ever mind boggling complexity of natural ecosystems," or at least one such ecosystem, was the Hubbard Brook Ecosystem Study (Bormann and Likens 1979a,b). Beginning in 1963 with a modest (in current terms) grant from the National Science Foundation, F. H. Bormann, a terrestrial plant ecologist, G. E. Likens, a limnologist, N. M. Johnson, a geochemist, and R. S. Pierce, a forest ecologist, instituted a long-term, multidisciplinary ecosystem study. Bormann and Likens, in common with other ecologists who became imbued with the ecosystem idea, turned their attention to developing "an ecosystem model that heavily involves inanimate as well as animate processes." Building on the background data of meteorology and hydrology already collected by the U.S. Forest Service on the Hubbard Brook Experimental Forest, they began exploring streamwater chemistry and the details of the input-output relations of a small watershed which had originally been selected because its geological substrate was impervious to percolation of water. The synergistic ecological skills and backgrounds brought to the studies by Bormann and Likens lent themselves to the long-term investigations of the interactions between the terrestrial and aquatic ecosystems in a limited area of northern hardwood forest which contained stream systems and a lake. The thesis of the Hubbard Brook Ecosystem Study was to focus on how the specific small-watershed ecosystem worked, to provide information on ecosystem parameters, and, emphatically, to include experimental manipulations of ecosystems. One of the salient advantages of the Hubbard Brook site was that it provided several similar watersheds, which allowed some to be used as controls for experiments conducted on adjacent watershed ecosystems. Whole ecosystem experiments were not entirely unprecedented, but they were certainly still unusual, and the availability of a control or reference ecosystem was even more unusual. The use of the watershed technique allowed measurement of input-output relations of key nutrients and calculation of nutrient budgets. The activities of the biotic components of ecosystems, especially their relation to the physical attributes of water and nutrient flow, were the primary concerns of the early Hubbard Brook studies.

The other landmark in ecosystem studies represented by the Hubbard Brook Ecosystem Study was a move toward "big biology." Traditionally an ecological study was conducted by a single investigator with one or two colleagues and, perhaps, a few students or technicians. The classical ecologist had once been described as working with some pieces of string and a pH meter in his back pocket. A major advantage at Hubbard Brook was continuity of work at a single site and a body of coordinated work on that site. The early research programs were largely concerned with biogeochemistry of the forest ecosystem. Later work concentrated on the structure, function, and, notably, the development (i.e., succession) of the forest and the response of the ecosystem to disturbance, such as clear-cutting. The multidisciplinary approach was achieved by incorporating visiting investigators and graduate students into the research program. During the first 18 years some 150 individuals, including 50 senior investigators, had participated in the research and produced over 450 articles. There was a steady increase in numbers of publications, from an average of 2.4 per year during 1962–6 to about 36 per year during 1978–80. During a recent interval of maximum research productivity, studies of diverse aspects of ecosystem processes and related concerns were published which illustrate the increased diversity of ecosystem work at Hubbard Brook. In the interval from 1978 to 1981 the work on biogeochemical cycles continued, particularly on interactions between cycles of individual nutrients and between different ecosystems. Associated with this were studies of processes which regulate nutrient flux and cycles in forest and stream ecosystems and the relation of air pollutants to ecosystem stress. Extensions of earlier studies of succession were explicit in the continued study of ecosystem development and of response to disturbance (i.e., perturbation) and work under the newer rubrics of "recovery" and "resilience." These studies specifically involved simulation modeling and so-called patch theory in the exploration of ecosystems responding to disturbances of various scales. Studies of energy flow and productivity took up another familiar aspect of ecosystem study. The broadened scope of the work was illustrated by studies of population dynamics, guilds, and niche as they relate to community structure in the forest and lake ecosystem. The traditional interest of ecologists in succession, which extended to longer time spans, was illustrated by studies of postglacial change in ecosystems of the Hubbard Brook region. The gross change in perception of ecological research was indicated by the inclusion of the Hubbard Brook Ecosystem Study in the category "little ecology" (Cantlon 1980).

Perhaps the crux of the Hubbard Brook study was its development of the "biomass accumulation model," which recognized four phases of ecosystem development based on changes in ecosystem biomass after a gross disturbance by clear-cutting. Bormann and Likens (1979b:3), however, disavowed the ideal of a holistic ecosystem model:

> We have no grand computerized model where all the animate and inanimate components of the dynamic system are ele-

gantly linked and where the details of the interactions can be spilled forth by a conversation with the computer.

Their ideas about the biomass accumulation model were, however, influenced by simulations of forest growth generated by the so-called JABOWA model (Botkin, Janak, and Wallis 1972). The JABOWA model calculated growth responses by mimicking the behavior of each species as defined by a limited number of characteristics influenced by a similarly limited number of abiotic attributes. The model predicted a stable or steady state achieved a few hundred years following clear-cutting. The biomass accumulation model suggested development of a steady state of biomass as an ecosystem parameter. A notable finding is that the stage with maximum biomass is not the steady state, but the stage which had preceded the steady state.

Data from this ecosystem study were used to test some of the "trends" associated with ecosystem development suggested by E. P. Odum (1969) in an important contribution to the concept of ecosystem development. The Hubbard Brook data produced some fundamental contradictions of the interpretation of ecosystem behavior postulated by Odum. Vitousek and Reiners (1975) and Bormann and Likens (1979b) contradicted E. P. Odum's (1969) interpretation of an overall ecosystem trend, nutrient loss. They argued that the Hubbard Brook data showed that the steady-state or "mature" (climax) stage of forest development has higher nutrient losses than earlier stages, contrary to the suggested trend that the later or stable stages should have minimum nutrient loss. Subsequent questions arose concerning this generalization as applied to the northern hardwood forests or other ecosystems. Woodmansee (1978) doubted the appropriateness of either nutrient flow model to grassland ecosystems. Such contradictions illustrate the familiar problem confronting the hope to "forge general models for all terrestrial ecosystems" (Gorham, Vitousek, and Reiners 1979).

The Hubbard Brook study is an example of ecosystem analysis which did not adopt its sometime synonym, systems analysis. Although it shared the search for ecosystem attributes with other studies of ecosystems and like them it "heavily [involved] inanimate processes," it concentrated on a single small area which it analyzed in great detail. It is more empirical and experimental and much less involved in abstract generalization and mathematical formulation than other approaches to ecosystems analysis. A list of some 80 cooperating scientists included only one systems analyst. Engineers, physicists, and mathematicians who "colonized" other aspects of ecosystem ecology were absent. One by-product of the long-term detailed studies at Hubbard Brook was its designation as a Biosphere Reserve as part of a program sponsored by UNESCO. It was also designated a site in a potential network of Long Term Ecological Research (Report for the National Science Foundation 1977; Lauff and Reichle 1979). The requirement for long-term environmental research and monitoring of ecosystems which are well understood is a critical need of a nation in which pollution problems increase with wealth and technological development.

Ecosystem ecology came in diverse guises. Although many ecosystem ecologists emphasized abiotic components and processes, a few turned to biotic attributes in the search for holistic or macroscopic "properties of ecosystems." The work of Lane, Lauff, and Levins (1975) in their "Feasibility of Using a Holistic Approach in Ecosystem Analysis" was based on the use of "holistic" parameters on the ecosystem level. They used measures of niche breadth, niche overlap, $K$ of the classical logistic equation, community diversity, and the ubiquitous Shannon-Weaver measure derived from information theory in various ratios to "describe macroscopic properties" of community structure. The basic data were standard population measurements. They asserted, "The belief that holistic approaches are not possible because ecosystems are too complex and dynamic should be dispelled as quickly as possible." These authors deplored the "ideological dichotomy of the reductionist versus the holistic approaches" and advocated delineating holistic properties of an ecosystem first, then using reductionist procedures to "clarify the underlying mechanisms of the community invariants." The major problem to be resolved was the determination of the "invariants."

Wiegert (1975, 1976) described another approach to developing theory at the ecosystem level. Unlike most ecosystem ecologists, he advocated starting with the component populations or trophic groups, modeling their interactions, and finally predicting ecosystem or "extensive" properties. Wiegert's assumptions were essentially those of the logistic equation, and he asserted that these can be applied to ecosystems modeling. Wiegert has used these techniques in experimental studies of thermal springs, an extremely simple ecosystem, and a salt marsh. He developed mathematical models "representing transfer of matter/energy into biotic components."

These and other authors contributed to a burgeoning literature dealing with ecosystems and representing extremely diverse approaches. Their efforts may fall short of a bona fide ecosystem study depending on the criteria which are applied by various ecosystem ecologists. They converged on a common concern with the ecosystem as the basic unit and determination of ecosystem properties and changes in them as dynamic processes (Levin 1976).

## Systems ecology

One of the difficulties faced by the ordinary ecologist in the decade from approximately 1968 to 1978, which E. P. Odum identified as the era of an emerging "systems ecology," was finding out what systems ecology was or even that it was there. The difficulty was compounded by a tendency in some quarters to equate systems ecology with ecosystem ecology or at least to intimate that it was indispensable to studies of the complexities of ecosystems. As systems ecology entered ecology, it came in different guises and from different sources and commonly appeared outside of the usual ecological publications. For example, Van Dyne (1980) reviewed the origin of systems ecology and cited 66 references, only 16 of which would have been encountered in ordinary ecological sources. Shugart and O'Neill (1979) commented on the difficulty of communicating the results of systems ecology in "the traditional journal format." Systems ecology entered ecology bringing with it new terms, new techniques, new types of training, and, most crucially in the view of some, a new philosophy. Van Dyne provided a useful chronology of events in the emergence of systems ecology which may be supplemented by reference to Shugart and O'Neill. The pioneers of systems ecology, like pioneers everywhere, were highly individualistic, so it is not possible to trace each of their contributions. There are clearly centers of origin, leaders, mutual interactions, and a network of reciprocal citations to be pursued by sociologists of science in delineating "invisible colleges" – a singularly appropriate name for the early systems ecology groups.

Ecologists in the early and middle 1950s began studies of energetics in field ecosystems in an effort to construct energy flow diagrams in the Lindeman format (H. T. Odum and E. P. Odum 1955; H. T. Odum 1957; Teal 1957). One of the notable findings was that the detritus or decomposer food chain, which had been largely ignored by Lindeman, was considerably larger than the grazing food chain, which was the primary one examined in traditional production studies because of its manifest economic importance to humans. The details of the transfer of energy in populations and between trophic levels were also being examined in laboratory ecosystems consisting of three species, including the experimenters as predators in the form of L. B. Slobodkin and his students (Richman 1958; Slobodkin 1959). These studies led Slobodkin to propose a hypothesis that there was an approximately 10 percent efficiency of transfer between trophic levels as a characteristic of ecosystems. The illustrative calculations of Semper (1881) and Petersen (1918) had used the 10 percent figure to show the reduction of biomass in successive trophic levels, no doubt because of its arithmetic convenience. Slobodkin later was at pains to show that his hypothesis was not justified and in fact that there were empirical and theoretical objections to it (Slobodkin 1972). Nevertheless, the arithmetic convenience of 10 percent still suggested to some the ideal of a "10 percent law" or "constant" (McIntosh 1980a).

H. T. Odum was a major force in reviving Lotka's "law of maximum energy" and introduced the input-output, energy-entropy interpretation of the climax community, thus grounding ecology, succession, and civilizations in the second law of thermodynamics (H. T. Odum and Pinkerton 1955). Margalef (1958) linked ecology and information theory by introducing the measurement of "order-information or negentropy" in communities. Margalef described information theory as allowing the ecosystem ideal of "the generalization of certain concepts on a higher plane which takes in, without any preference, both the living and the inanimate." He extended it to "the value of the message contained in Creation." Information theory introduced the Shannon-Weaver information equation into ecology to measure diverse things, often to unwarranted numbers of decimal places. Patten (1959) attempted to study the ecosystem from a cybernetic point of view, integrating order and information with complexity, diversity, productivity, and stability in succession and climax. This provided an entree for statistical mechanics in the form of the Boltzmann-Planck equation. Information theory was widely heralded as having promise for biology, but Johnson (1970) commented that the promise had not been fulfilled. Gallucci (1973) stated that the theory based on Shannon's work had not demonstrated its utility for ecology. However, Mulholland (1975) continued to see the prospect for ecosystem ecology of an index of stability "from the firm mathematical basis of information theory." Some ecologists considered ecosystems as cybernetic systems (Margalef 1968; E. P. Odum 1971). This later prompted a flat denial that an ecosystem was either an organism or a cybernetic system (Engelberg and Boyarsky 1979), precipitating a heated defense of the ecosystem as a cybernetic system and creating a certain amount of confusion among ecologists (Knight and Swaney 1981; McNaughton and Coughenour 1981). Jordan (1981) asked the question "Do Ecosystems Exist?" and, to the great relief of ecosystems ecologists, answered affirmatively. Since it seems indisputable that ecosystems follow the laws of thermodynamics, these were raised to the level of ecological principles (Watt 1968), and thermodynamics of both equilibrium and nonequilibrium systems was advanced as a basis of ecosystem theory. Hubbell (1971), in a unique linkage of "sowbugs and systems," asserted to the contrary, "It is unrealistic to expect the laws of thermodynamics ever to be sufficient to explain the organization and function of biological systems." Other ecologists questioned the emphasis on energy and thermodynamics, on the grounds that "animals are not bomb calorimeters" (Goldman 1966). Nevertheless, Johnson (1981) recently produced "a general theory of the origin of ecosystems in thermodynamic terms." Ecology seemed to be a tempting territory to try out various mathematical theories, for when information theory had proven of limited applicability, catastrophe theory was advanced, with less success, to fill the vacuum.

In spite of several earlier assays into analysis of ecosystems, Van Dyne (1980) nominated Jerry Olson, a plant ecologist at Oak Ridge National Laboratory, as the "father of systems ecology." His grounds were that Olson (Neel and Olson 1962) had modeled ecological systems using linear differential equations and done simulations of ecosystems on analog and digital computers. Shugart and O'Neill (1979) asserted that the "single most reliable fieldmark of the systems ecologist is . . . the use of mathematical models," and, using this criterion, they too ascribed to Olson the earliest report in systems ecology and the beginning of a new era of ecological models (Burgess 1981a). Given the early history of paternity in ecology, other claims may be expected. The focus on ecosystems, particularly on the movement of materials between the parts of a system, in what was then the Radiation Ecology Section at Oak Ridge National Laboratory and elsewhere was clearly due to earlier concern with the tracking of radioactive fallout from weapons tests (Auerbach 1965; Reichle and Auerbach 1972; Woodwell 1980). The paper cited by Van Dyne as the "real breakthrough" in systems ecology was an analog computer model simulating isotope movements in ecosystems. The atomic age had brought with it both the use of radioactive materials in studies of natural environments in the late 1940s (Hutchinson and Bowen 1947) and the threat of adverse effects of radiation on individual organisms and ecological systems (Woodwell and Whittaker 1968). Some ecologists claimed that radiation ecology had begun in the early 1940s, although these earlier examples apparently involved largely physiological and tissue responses of organisms to radiation (Whicker and Schultz 1982). This harks back to Chapman's (1931) comments about the difficulty of distinguishing physiology from autecology. John Wolfe (1969), one of the first ecologists on the Washington scene, described the early studies of radiation effects in 1955 as the beginning of the interest of the U.S. Atomic Energy Commission in ecology. He commented that much of the earliest ecological work on radiation effects using radioactive tracers was obscured under health physics and hoped that someday it would be incorporated into the history of ecology – a hope yet to be realized. Olson (1964, 1966) reviewed, in a nonecological journal, the scope of radiation ecology and the early experimental and modeling approaches to ecosystem structure using radioactive tracers. The major conclusions he stated persist in ecosystem studies, with or without radioactive materials:

> The complexity that is inherent in either terrestrial, freshwater or marine ecosystems does not necessarily preclude mathematical modeling for preliminary calculations to suggest whether or not environmental nuclide movement is likely to have major impact on man. However, ecological complexity does demand more careful analysis under locally applicable conditions, where such movement could be significant for human health, or for research on basic problems of ecological transfers or radiation effects. (Olson 1966)

Concern with radiological effects on the environment was transformed from the early emphasis on environmental health to concern with the health of the environment, to borrow John Cantlon's useful phraseology. This transformation turned the ecology group at Oak Ridge National Laboratory into the major center of systems ecology described by Van Dyne (1980).

Systems ecology was advanced as being particularly suitable for precisely the problems which had long concerned ecologists – those involving large-scale biological communities or ecosystems of very great complexity. Early ecologists had commonly asserted that mathematics gave an illusion of accuracy to assertions about such complexity. The resolution offered by systems ecology was a mathematical approach different from that of classic theoretical, mathematical population ecology of the

Golden Age of Lotka and Volterra. A major ingredient consisted of "techniques and approaches developed in systems analysis, operations research, and cybernetics" (Shugart and O'Neill 1979). According to Watt (1968:5), the complexity of ecosystems was such that

> even mathematical models based on oversimplified and hence unrealistic assumptions would be insoluble using traditional paper-and-pencil methods. Therefore the emphasis is shifted from ingenuity of mathematical manipulation to realism of description with computer simulation being substituted for paper-and-pencil solution.

This required, he noted, knowledge of the processes so that computer simulations of mathematical models could mimic nature and be used to complement experiments or, as some suggested, conduct experiments not possible in nature. Such models were often described by systems ecologists as attempts to develop ecological theory (Patten 1975a). Other ecologists were less sanguine about this prospect. May (1974b) at the pencil-and-paper end of the continuum of model makers for the new ecology said the systems analysis approach "does not seem conducive to yielding general ecological principles, nor does it claim to." The latter statement misrepresented the position of most proponents of systems analysis, who claimed to be developing ecological theory and principle as a basis for management. Nevertheless, the availability of the computer encouraged, as Watt suggested, the proliferation of large-scale systems models following Olson's initial effort. According to Shugart and O'Neill, "Literally hundreds of models have been produced." Since they were referring only to systems models, and these were added to the plethora of models produced by population ecologists, it was a trying time for ecologists (McIntosh 1980a). Some of the systems models, May (1973) commented, "could benefit most from the installation of an on-line incinerator." Systems ecology nevertheless burgeoned in the 1960s, claiming to take advantage of mathematics to advance ecological theory.

**The International Biological Program**

The early entrants into the new field of systems ecology were followed, in the 1960s, by a flood of scientific studies of ecosystems, grafting of systems analysis onto ecology, and, notably, by the introduction of ecology into "big biology," represented by the International Biological Program (IBP), which was crucial to the development of systems ecology (Smith 1967, 1968; Worthington 1975, 1983; Clapham, Lucas, and Pirie 1976; Blair 1977a; Burgess 1981a). F. E. Smith (1967), in the first annual report of the Analysis of Ecosystems Program of the IBP, pondered the causes for the overwhelming interest in ecosystems analysis and decided, "Whatever the causes, a revolution among ecologists is under way and the IBP is in the middle of it." It is more likely that the IBP, or at least its United States contingent, was out in front leading the pack and providing the opportunity for the emergence of a very different way to do ecology. Jerry Olson (1983 pers. commun.), in a eulogy of George Van Dyne, one of the pioneer managers of a large-scale ecosystem program, provided a cogent mixed military-ecological analogy. He compared systems ecology to a "beach head, or a moving dune, rather open for the colonization by those invading scientists who can endure the stress of an open, turbulent environment." This analogy, a mixture of classic Clementsian succession and seaborne warfare, fits appropriately the opportunistic or pioneer-type scientist ready to seize and colonize a new intellectual beachhead. The establishment of the IBP, providing new and unprecedented funding for ecological studies, suggests an analogy perhaps better stated in more current rhetoric of ecology which stresses the ability of opportunist species to seize on newly available resources, in this instance research funds. It is possible to see the beachhead as the standard landing place for buccaneers, Norse invaders, or perhaps the Francis Drakes of the new ecology, since colonization is a favorite metaphor for the entry into ecology of persons trained in other disciplines. In any event, the mid-1960s saw the juxtaposition of what many ecologists urged as a dramatic new approach to ecology – the study of functional ecosystems using the methods of systems analysis and the institutionalization of an international program of biological research fueled by large-scale funds, released by the then current "environmental revolution" (Worthington 1975). No history of ecosystem ecology, ecology at large, or systems ecology is complete without consideration of the IBP. Burgess (1981a) stated, "In all probability, the single most important event for U.S. ecology in the last thirty years was the participation in the International Biological Program."

The International Biological Program was stimulated by the earlier successes of the International Polar Year and the International Geophysical Year. Planning for it was initiated in 1959, primarily by European and British biologists. Following several years of preliminary discussions, its first formal presentation was in 1964, when the International .Council of Scientific Unions (ICSU) created a committee charged with planning research with the theme "Biological Basis for Productivity and Human Welfare." In the interim, the biological community in Britain and America, dominated as it was by physiology, biochemistry, and molecular biology, had displayed a notable lack of interest. According to C. H. Waddington, a distinguished geneticist, then president of the International Union of Biological Sciences (IUBS), and much involved in the early planning for the IBP, one response of the ruling class of molecular biologists to the prospect of studies of world productivity and ecosystems was "that any organism bigger than *E. coli* serves only to confuse the issue" (Worthington 1975). Waddington, however, sponsored the idea, then developing in ecology in the aftermath of Lindeman's work, that "ecology should be looked at as a matter of energy through-put and processing." This idea was communicated as a basis for the IBP to W. F. Blair, who was president of the Ecological Society of America. Blair was a member of an ad hoc committee for the IBP of the U.S. National Academy of Sciences. In his highly personal account of the IBP entitled *Big Biology*, he recorded the backroom aspect of U.S. participation in its early stages (Blair 1977a). It included a poll of the Ecological Society of America concerning the prospect of such a program, which produced 104 responses, one-fourth of which identified the respondent as an ecosystem specialist which, in 1964, was still largely a gleam in the eye of an ecologist. Most of these were strategically located at three centers, the University of Georgia and the Oak Ridge and Hanford national laboratories, the latter two principally funded by the U.S. Atomic Energy Commission. Georgia and Oak Ridge were to provide much of the impetus and key personnel for the IBP.

Blair (1977a) recorded numerous communications pro and con U.S. participation in the IBP. These are particularly interesting in indicating where ecology stood in national and international scientific circles in the 1960s. Although the worldwide biological problem which had been identified for IBP attention was fundamentally an ecological one, and F. E. Smith described the IBP as "lifting a minor subject to a position of major status," the status of ecology and ecologists at the inception of IBP was clearly "minor." La Mont Cole commented that the early planning of IBP, which had been in the hands of the U.S. National Academy of Sciences, had not involved the only two ecologist members of that august body. More telling still was the appointment of a nonecologist as chairman of the U.S. National Committee for the IBP.

Blair objected, saying he was "shocked" at the appointment of a non-biologist, let alone a nonecologist, to head a largely ecological program. President Seitz of the National Academy of Sciences responded that his advisory committee, no doubt sans ecologists, had recommended that the program should initially be "in the hands of a scientist who is widely conversant with the international scene and a diversity of international problems affecting science." Presumably no ecologist qualified. However, in January 1968, Blair was named chairman of the U.S. National Committee for the IBP (USNC/IBP). It is not feasible here to trace the intricacies of the IBP or of British and American involvement. Of particular interest to U.S. participation was a meeting of the U.S. National Committee at Williamstown, Massachusetts. The outcome of this meeting was the formation of an Integrated Research Program (IRP) on "Analysis of Ecosystems," with F. E. Smith as its director. Some ecologists protested this choice because Smith's own work had been largely in population ecology. However, in the 1960s Smith was doing computer models of three-species communities, and he was instrumental in establishing ecosystems studies as the theme of the U.S. IBP program. The Analysis of Ecosystems program was to form the major part of the U.S. IBP and to absorb the largest share of the funding. The First Annual Report of the Analysis of Ecosystems program noted that the role of systems analysis had been the subject of a working session which "had a profound effect upon the development of the program." One additional result the report noted was continued liaison with the professional field of systems analysis, involving a consulting firm. Thus early in the planning of the U.S. IBP program, systems analysis was formally introduced, although the contributions of the original consultants proved unsatisfactory.

The U.S. program did not develop without crisis. Some ecologists and legislators, including some in a position to control funding for the program, were not convinced of its merits. H. Curl, Jr. (1968) wrote in a letter to *Science,* "It is highly improbable that a group of individuals who cannot agree on what constitutes a community can agree to get together for international cooperative research on communities." Reports from the Analysis of Ecosystems program indicated that early "scientific support for the IBP was far stronger than the funding level suggests." In 1969, two years into the operational phase of the IBP, F. E. Smith resigned from the directorship of the Analysis of Ecosystems program, citing his frustration in the attempt to develop a research program in the IBP. His parting comment was: "We should not delude ourselves into believing that the national priority for research related to environmental management has risen above negligible" (Smith 1969). The initial hope had been that much of the U.S. contribution to the IBP would come from ongoing programs of several federal agencies with missions concerned with the environment or biological production. Few of these agencies evinced much interest in diverting any of their funds to the IBP, and eventually the major portion of the U.S. program was supported by the National Science Foundation and the Atomic Energy Commission, which by then had active groups in ecological research. Securing specific funding for the IBP required a major effort in gaining recognition at the presidential and congressional levels for environmental problems and the capacity of ecological science to attack them and to provide guidance for management policy. Blair (1977a) reviewed the difficulties of moving ecology from a science practiced by a few individuals, almost exclusively in academic institutions, into "big biology," with teams of many people working in diverse institutions and in large-scale programs involving several institutions. The lack of understanding of ecology and the absence of ecologists from strategic positions in the critical power base of Washington was a major difficulty. Only after World War II were ecologists such as John Wolfe and Stanley Cain present in Washington, and they were few. The Public Affairs Committee of the Ecological Society of America tried without success in 1968 to place an ecologist on the president's Science Advisory Committee. Ecologists were not substantially represented as members or part of the administrative structure of the National Academy of Science. Except for a term served by Paul B. Sears, pre-IBP ecologists were not represented on the National Science Board, which governs the policy of the National Science Foundation, then the major source of support for basic research in ecology. S. Dillon Ripley (1968), Secretary of the Smithsonian Institution and a significant figure in scientific circles in Washington, in his testimony before the Subcommittee on Science Research and Development of the U.S. Congress, correctly stated that ecologists had "certainly no large political voice within the scientific establishment." Then chairman of the U.S. National Committee for the IBP Roger Revelle, in his testimony, however, incorrectly stated the reasons for ecology not being well established:

> Ecology has been a science which inevitably tended to lag
> behind the laboratory biological sciences because it was neces-
> sary to get basic information at the molecular and the cellular

level and the organ level in many respects before it was possible to attack the whole organisms and their relationships to each other.

If it lagged, this was not the reason, since ecology had not waited on the laboratory sciences to study whole organisms and communities. It had, admittedly, lagged in the supply of research funds. Nevertheless, Revelle declared, "The time has come for ecology. This is a device for pushing ecology and for formalizing our support and our interest among all the scientists of the United States" (Subcommittee on Science Research and Development 1968).

The Public Affairs Committee of the Ecological Society of America, chaired by W. F. Blair, prepared a report, "The Importance of Ecology and the Study of Ecosystems," for a key congressional hearing in 1968 on a bill to provide funds for the IBP (Blair et al. 1968). Its major thrust was that great advances were expected in the field of ecosystem analysis, and it emphasized the prospects of such studies for resolution of environmental concerns, which were then belatedly becoming of paramount interest to the American public and, consequently, to the Congress. Perhaps the most dramatic change for ecology the committee envisioned was that "ecologists will have to learn to curb some of their traditional individuality, to learn how to work in large teams harmoniously and effectively." The tortuous process of securing funding wended its way through the Congress, not helped, as Blair noted, by less than enthusiastic support from Philip Handler, then president of the U.S. National Academy of Science. Fortunately, the enthusiasm of many ecologists and some other scientists, the active support of the Ecological Society of America, the interest of the Division of Biological and Medical Sciences (BMS) of the National Science Foundation (NSF) and of some congressmen attentive to environmental concerns alleviated the starvation budget of which F. E. Smith had complained. Congress voted funds for the IBP. Initial funding of IBP had been supplied largely from the budget of the BMS. The new funding established a line item in the budget of the National Science Foundation for the IBP. In 1969, a separate Ecosystem Studies Program was organized in the BMS to review and fund proposals for ecosystem studies. Funding for this program increased from F. E. Smith's "negligible" amount of $600,000 to about $3 million in 1970 and $6 million in 1971. In its peak operational year (1973) the Analysis of Ecosystems program of the IBP was funded at about $8.5 million, largely from the NSF, and during the life span of IBP, from 1968 to 1974, a total approximating

$27 million was expended on various aspects of ecosystem studies. The IBP included programs on insect pests, genetic material, conservation, and human adaptability, but nearly three-quarters of all funding was devoted to the ecosystem programs (National Academy of Sciences 1974). Although the formal IBP ended in 1974, funding of programs implemented under its umbrella continued in the subsequent ecosystems program. By the standards of traditional ecology these were very large sums and were instrumental in changing the way ecology was done and the way many ecologists thought about ecology. Ecosystem ecology, in Frank Blair's phrase, became "big biology." Not all ecologists rejoiced at the prospect. Some noted the trend to large-scale programs entailed by ecosystems studies and deplored the managerial emphasis. Others claimed this allowed funding of research which would not be funded on its own merits. By that time, however, it was clear that there would be a major U.S. contribution to the IBP, and that its major thrust would be large-scale, managed, and, it was hoped, integrated ecosystem analysis. The concept of the ecosystem, the effort to quantify it in terms of trophic aspects, and the introduction in the 1950s of flows of energy and matter and systems analysis as the way to understand ecosystems were institutionalized, computerized, and managed in the late 1960s and early 1970s. One IBP report commented, "Unfortunately, the administrative and funding obligations of 'big ecosystems science' have precluded any significant advances in our research program since last November" (Eastern Deciduous Forest Biome 1972). This is not to denigrate the program but to suggest the start-up problems of a new scale of ecosystem studies. Apart from routine activity, time was needed for memo reports, site progress reports, new research proposals, hiring of unprecedented numbers of staff, and endless meetings to implement all of these. Van Dyne (1972) described in detail the novel problems of organizing and managing the Grassland Biome, the earliest and largest of the integrated ecological research programs funded under the IBP.

British biologists such as C. H. Waddington and E. B. Worthington, although not all ecologists, made notable contributions to formulating the IBP and shepherding it through a decade of trials (Clapham, Lucas, and Pirie 1976). Waddington commented that there were few ecologists in the launching party, and John Kendrew was variously quoted as saying that at the outset of the IBP, ecology was "a word unknown to all but a select band of environmental specialists" or to a "few obscure specialists." Whatever the correct version, such comments suggested that as late as 1964 ecology was hardly a household word. It is therefore particularly interesting that the recognition in the 1950s of major problems of human needs and environmental degradation justified an international effort that was essentially a program of ecological studies. In Waddington's phraseology, its central theme was that

> ecology considered in terms of energy flow and production . . . and human biology, considered as something in which man is linked to the rest of the biosphere, should be recognized as major and substantial parts of biology. (Clapham, Lucas, and Pirie 1976:501)

Waddington agreed with F. E. Smith that the IBP "had converted ecology from an obscure and neglected branch of biology into a major branch." It is an appropriate example of scientific preadaptation that ecology was there with three-quarters of a century of basic work when the need for it became generally apparent. The ideas of production, trophic-structure, nutrient cycles, energy flow, and their relation to the environment had been established for a half-century and codified in Lindeman's trophic-aspects paper two decades prior to the IBP.

The United Kingdom approach to the IBP was quite different from that of the United States. Research funds were derived from usual channels, which had been the early hope of the planners for the U.S. IBP. There were no special funds earmarked for the U.K. IBP. The Royal Society was the national body responsible for the U.K. contribution, but there was little of the large-scale organization and management of research programs which characterized the American effort. The British National Committee might certify that a given research project was relevant to the IBP, but granting of funds was dependent upon independent evaluation of scientific merit by the usual research councils. For this reason it is not readily possible to determine the amount of funds devoted to the IBP by the British.

Certainly the British contribution to the IBP was not on the relatively monumental scale of the United States, and, perhaps characteristic of a British approach, it was not accompanied by the rhetoric manifest in the campaign to fund the U.S. IBP. An explanation for the rhetoric may be sought in the necessity to secure specific funds for the IBP from the U.S. Congress at a time when budget retrenchment was in vogue. Proponents of the IBP in hearings before the congressional committees promised much, and some of the presumed failings of ecology in the IBP were simply that it could not match the rhetorical promises made for it in order to secure funding. The IBP could not deliver on promises made in its name to produce "predictive power," "improve world-wide productivity," or provide "hope for solving the dangerous population explosion." Ecology suffered the problems of economics when more was claimed for it than it could deliver (McIntosh 1974a; McCloskey 1983). The solid achievements of ecology in the IBP ecosystem programs were sometimes masked by criticism of its failure to achieve the impossible.

## Systems analysis

Van Dyne (1980) had commented that E. P. Odum put "systems ecology" "on the board" in 1964. Systems ecology came as a surprise to most ecologists in 1964 and remained so to many ecologists for some years thereafter. Most ecologists were aware of ecosystems and the attributes of ecosystems incorporated in systems ecology. The rubric "systems ecology" appeared innocent enough and even etymologically natural for analysis of ecosystems or ecosystems ecology. In the middle and late 1960s and early 1970s descriptions of systems analysis started to appear, some in obscure places, some in what were to many ecologists obscure language or symbols. K. E. F. Watt (1966) produced the first book on systems analysis in ecology, describing the nature of systems analysis, defining a *system* as "an interlocking complex of processes characterized by many reciprocal, cause-effect pathways," and stating the axiom that a system must be studied as a whole. He added, however, "the operating maxim that extremely complex processes are best dissected into a large number of very simple unit components" to be fitted into the model at the end. Watt provided a vision of a prospective ecology in which the "drudgery" of systems measurement would be reduced from 80 percent of the effort of a research program to 63 percent and in which a compensatory increase in systems analysis from 0.9 percent to 27 percent would provide time for "a high level of thought." Although Watt extolled the ideal of holism, the articles in his book dealt with problems of populations, data acquisition, and analysis of data. Little is made of ecosystem analysis, nor is there mention of the emphasis on energetics, nutrient flow, or the physical attributes of ecosystems evident in other systems approaches. Van Dyne (1966) was more succinct in defining a system – "A system is an organization that functions in a particular way" – adding that it must be studied as a whole. He announced a new program in Systems Ecology at Oak Ridge National Laboratory and added an interesting comment:

> Neither is this area of work in ecology clearly defined nor do all ecologists view it equally. As with any new field, systems ecology is beset with vociferous skeptics (largely those who have done well under the old conditions) but supported primarily by lukewarm champions (largely those who may do well under the new conditions).

Van Dyne erred in one respect. Systems ecology indeed had (and has) "vociferous" and skeptical critics, but its champions were (and are) anything but "lukewarm," as we shall see.

Van Dyne, J. S. Olson, and B. C. Patten organized what was probably the first university course in systems ecology (Patten 1966). Its stated purposes as a guide to the "new ecology" were (1) appreciation for the natural affinities between ecology and mathematics, (2) familiarity with all principal techniques of systems analysis which are applicable, and (3) reasonable skill in the use of analog and digital computers. These were among the attributes which became the earmarks of systems ecology. Systems ecology was, in the view of Van Dyne and other systems ecologists, explicitly the study of ecosystems (Kitching 1983). Patten (1971) described the first of several books he edited on systems analysis as a book about "ecology in transition from a 'soft' science, synecology, to a 'hard' science, systems ecology." The link with synecology is misleading in that the book includes models of one-species populations as well as of ecosystems. Systems analysis is applicable to any system, ecological or not, but its utility for the analysis of ecosystems became paramount in the minds of many ecologists.

Efforts to enlighten ecologists about systems analysis and its merits for ecology proliferated. Dale (1970) explained systems analysis in ecology, defining a *system* as "a collection of parts together with statements of the relations, of some kind, between these parts." In addition, he defined *systems analysis,* unhelpfully, as "the application of scientific method to complex problems" and described its attributes as advanced mathematical and statistical techniques coupled with computers. It is of some interest that other aspects of ecology claiming novelty in the 1960s also stressed mathematics and statistics but deplored the extensive use of the computer and "number crunching" which characterized systems ecology, preferring "pencil-and-paper" mathematics. Dale (1970) stated:

Systems analysis has been presented as a desirable framework on which the investigation and comparison of ecosystems can be hung. . . . Examples of explicit use of systems methods in ecology are few, and it is by no means clear from these examples what a system is, what it does, what restrictions it imposes, nor how the variety of ecology . . . can be attached to this framework.

The versatility and, perhaps, the lack of clarity of systems analysis in ecology noted by several of these commentators may be seen by examining the books by Watt (1966), Van Dyne (1969), and Patten (1971, 1972, 1975a), which provide, respectively, chapters on the "Nature of," "Introduction to," and "Primer for" systems analysis.

Caswell et al. (1972) also commented on the results of various programs to enlighten ecologists about systems analysis:

There is so little agreement about what systems science really is that many ecologists return with a bewildering array of analytical and computational tools, and very little understanding of a scientific discipline as such.

Caswell et al. provided an *Introduction to Systems Science for Ecologists*, beginning somewhat in the form of metrical verse:

A system is a collection of objects. . . . An object is described by a set of behaviors. A behavior is a time series of acts. An act is an instantaneous tuplet of behavioral features.

The ecologist was introduced to the "free-body" description of an object as a major insight of systems science, which did little to alleviate his bewilderment; but, as the authors noted, "all however is not lost," the "concept of state arrives at this point," presumably to save the day. Discussions of systems ecology later appeared in general textbooks, sometimes with disarming simplicity:

The basic tools of systems ecology are few – a knowledge of a natural system, an understanding of its functional aspects, data on amounts of each important parameter and rate of change, and an awareness of the techniques available for constructing problem solving models. (Reid and Wood 1976:309)

Ecosystem maturation, based on the concept of energetics outlined by Odum and Pinkerton (1955) and on Margalef's (1958) use of information theory, was developed in a framework of twenty-four "trends to be expected" by E. P. Odum (1969). Odum confused succession and eutrophication (Carpenter 1981) and essentially reiterated some attributes of succession outlined by Clements many years previously. However, Odum's trends represented the attributes of the holistic ecosystem, which had become the central concern of systems analysis of ecosystems, and included the criteria of system maturation defined by maximum biomass, productivity, nutrient retention, and information content maintained per unit of energy flow. Some later formulators of systems models even took the "trends" to be established rules of nature rather than the hypothetical trends Odum intended (Gutierrez and Fey 1980). Odum commented, in this strategic period, how difficult it was to get scientists and granting agencies to develop and fund, respectively, functional studies of landscape units in the IBP. In spite of the reluctance of many scientists to adopt it, the systems approach to ecosystems flourished and became far too extensive to follow in detail here. Proponents of systems ecology were quite unlike the "lukewarm champions" described by Van Dyne (1966). Some, at least, were given to rhetoric, and the promise of systems analysis for ecology was widely hailed. E. P. Odum (1971) cited several pioneers of systems analysis in ecology (G. Van Dyne, J. Olson, B. Patten, C. Holling, and H. T. Odum) who were "revolutionizing" ecology. G. M. Van Dyne (1969) commented that the ecological revolution had only begun. B. C. Patten (1971), in the preface to an early volume on systems analysis in ecology, described it as an "enthusiastic and optimistic statement about the fundamental adaptability of the scientific mechanism to newly appreciated truths of existence" and as the "creation of young people at a time when youth in America is experimenting with if not revising and reorganizing the ethical and moral basis of contemporary civilized life."

E. P. Odum (1972) cited two approaches to ecology which were distinguished by Hutchinson (1964). Hutchinson had recognized a *hological* (holistic) approach, treating the ecosystem as a black box and considering only inputs and outputs, in contrast with a *merological* (reductionist) approach, which tried to build up the system from the parts. As an example of an exponent of the former, Hutchinson cited E. A. Birge, of the latter, S. A. Forbes. Both of these pioneer ecologists were avowed proponents of the lake as an organism but, according to Hutchinson, chose different approaches to understanding it. In Odum's view, the hological or holistic method as a "formalized model approach to populations, communities and ecosystems has come to be known as systems ecology," although many systems ecologists exhibit little interest in populations or even communities and many do not confine themselves to strictly input-output relationships. The distinction between the holistic and reductionist approaches to ecology was frequently a source of dispute during the 1960s and 1970s about how to do ecological research (MacFadyen 1975; Smith 1975a; Innis 1976; Woodwell 1976; Harper 1977b; E. P. Odum 1977; McIntosh 1980a, 1981; Allen and Starr 1982).

Smith (1975a) and MacFadyen (1975), former presidents of the American and British ecological societies, respectively, agreed in recognizing two approaches to ecology. One, systems analysis of ecosystems, was viewed as emphasizing the holistic, even organismic, properties of ecosystems. The other, population dynamics, described the ecosystem as best understood from reductionist studies of species populations, their life histories, and interrelations. E. P. Odum (1977) described the "new ecology as holistic" and as holding "that new systems properties emerge in the course of ecological development" not accounted for by species-level processes. Harper (1977b) vigorously criticized "the dangers of the systems approach" and urged ecologists to follow the lead of population theorists as represented by Robert MacArthur. Innis (1976) allowed room for both. Much of the discussion turned, ineffectually, around the concept of emergent properties of ecosystems and whether the whole was greater than the sum of its parts (Salt 1979; McIntosh 1980a, 1981). It is incorrect to see the distinction between ecosystem ecology and systems ecology as coextensive with the distinction between holism and reductionism in ecology. Some systems ecologists criticized other ecosystem compartment models as reductionist (Mann 1982) and urged "that we need new ecological theory to link cumulative properties of populations with 'emergent properties' of the whole" (Ebeling 1982). Levins and Lewontin (1980) argued that the computer models of systems ecology are not holism but merely a form of large-scale reductionism in which the wholes, ecosystems, are "naively" given parts. Allen and Starr (1982) also noted that most ecosystems models are large-scale reductionist approaches and suggested a "dual reductionist-holist strategy." There is no doubt that ecosystems can be studied either as aggregates of their component populations and the associated habitat or as areas of landscape in which particular processes occur. Whether the theory to link population properties with "emergent" ecosystems properties can be found, or at least agreed upon, remains for a new generation of ecologists to determine. It may be, as one theoretical ecologist commented, that ecology has not yet had its Galileo or Newton.

A notable difference between ecology in Britain and the United

States, and between the U.K. and U.S. IBP programs, was in the
visibility of systems ecology. Although the British programs focused on
ecosystems and some of the programs developed models, no one
hailed the "new" ecology in the form of systems ecology there with the
same fervor as some ecologists in the United States. In fact, Van
Dyne's (1980) description "lukewarm" may apply in Britain, generally.
Le Cren (1976) commented that in the 1960s ecologists became aware
of the potential of systems analysis but that this development came too
late for the British programs and was only used in "some of the late
starters" in the United States. Actually, as we have seen, the U.S. IBP
was permeated with systems analysis from its inception. Earlier proposals for the IBP had not aroused much enthusiasm in America, and
it was not until ecosystems analysis became its theme that it was enthu-
siastically adopted. Le Cren was also less sanguine about the general
use of mathematical models than most of the major figures in the U.S.
IBP. He commented on the limits of models, saying that they were not
effective in the explanation of the functioning of ecosystems. Le Cren's
low-key doubts about ecosystem models were more vigorously expressed by his limnologist colleague in Canada F. H. Rigler. Rigler
(1976) contrasted himself with the "new" ecologist as an "oldie." Rigler's review of one of the landmark volumes of systems analysis in
ecology raised the issue, which had struck many ecologists, that "a
branch of our own discipline is beyond some of us." Actually, Rigler
had missed the point made by several advocates of systems approaches
in ecology – systems ecology is *not* a branch of ecology, it is a *merger* of
a complex of things called systems analysis and ecology. Some of the
rhetoric even suggested that it was less a merger than a takeover and
that the resultant transcended not only ecology but biology as well. In
Rigler's somewhat acid commentary, systems ecology was more promise than performance.

The promise of systems analysis for ecology in Britain was considered
primarily in two volumes edited by Jeffers (1972, 1978). In the earlier
one it is considered only as one aspect of mathematical models. Jeffers
(1978) echoed his American counterparts in commenting, even at that
late date, on "the lack of knowledge of what is meant by systems analysis," and he provided the first introductory book to systems analysis in
ecology. Unlike some American ecologists, he described it as a "new
branch of ecology" rather than a "hybrid" or a "new discipline." Jeffers
stated that "little of the application of systems analysis has reached the
stage of publication, so that practical examples are not easy to quote." It

is not clear if Jeffers chose to ignore the large corpus of systems analysis that had amassed in American ecology by 1978, or if he did not regard it as including "practical examples." In any event, Jeffers was, in Britain, a voice crying in the wilderness of Rigler's "oldies," whereas he appeared very tame in the context of the revolutionizing of ecology by systems analysis in the U.S. IBP.

In spite of reservations on the part of some ecologists, the importance attached to systems analysis in ecology was commonly and fervently expressed – for example, in a symposium entitled *Systems Ecology: Where Do We Go from Here?* (Innis 1975). It might well have been subtitled *How Did We Get Here from There?* Innis saw ecology in a state of revolution – in a Kuhnian change of paradigm. He misrepresented the Kuhnian idea in stating that the old paradigm was lacking but the "new has yet to be accepted and may not have been enunciated." Kuhn's point was that a scientific community clings to an old paradigm in spite of manifest flaws until a new and better paradigm is available. The systems paradigm in 1975 was not yet accepted nor understood by many ecologists, and certainly not clearly enunciated, as even many of its proponents suggested. Innis lamented, "The efforts of scientists border on non-science and philosophy abounds." Another author in the symposium, B. C. Patten (1975c), made the point:

> The systems approach is a philosophy and a theory that comes with a formalism and a set of tools. . . . It is not the latter that are potentially important to ecology in the long run, but rather the philosophy and the formalism.

Many of the characteristic questions of ecology were seen as best addressed by systems analysis, which was described by some ecologists as a way of developing ecological theory: "Systems analysis has begun to synthesize disparate principles of growth, persistence and metabolism into a holistic theory of ecosystem function" (O'Neill and Reichle 1979). This prospective theory concentrated on general system properties (macroscopic or holistic properties) such as biomass, productivity, nutrient cycling, and "minimized consideration of taxa." The key theoretical construct of traditional ecology, succession, was rephrased in systems terms: "Succession is not a sequence of different systems, but a single system which exchanges transient species and populations through time." This statement is strangely redolent of Clements's climax, which included all seral stages and local environmental changes. In effect, it establishes the site or area as an ecosystem defined by whatever continuing property, such as productivity or a nutrient flow, can be measured through time to characterize the system.

Several ecosystem ecologists suggested this residue of Clementsian ecology as essentially the Clementsian approach cast in the context of ecosystem by E. P. Odum (MacMahon 1980). MacMahon, in fact, resurrected some of the discarded Clementsian terminology in the context of ecosystem studies. Marks and Bormann (1972) also described early successional species as part of the larger ecosystem, even though they were absent from the climax:

> Successional species especially adapted to exploit disturbed conditions ought to be considered integral components of the ecosystem, despite the fact that they are typically absent from the terminal climax community.

Woodwell and Botkin (1970) recognized the tendency in ecosystem ecology and wrote:

> There is something rejuvenating in the tacit but progressive acceptance of F. E. Clements' classical assertion that the community is an organism, . . . a concept that was hardly original with him but under his pen proved almost destructively provocative at least in America.

The link of ecosystem to protoecology and classical ecology was also recognized by O'Neill and Giddings (1979):

> Early students of ecology (*e.g.*, Marsh 1885; Clements 1916) already had an implicit concept of the ecosystem as a stable entity which persisted through time, even while populations were added or eliminated.

The most extensive compilation of systems analysis applied to ecological theory was *Theoretical Systems Ecology* edited by Halfon (1979), a volume notable for the dearth of ecologists among the several authors. This seems logical enough because Shugart and O'Neill (1979) described systems ecology as a "robust hybrid of engineering, mathematics, operations research, cybernetics and ecology," which leaves ecologists as a distinct minority. Other systems ecologists had described systems ecology as a hybrid of ecology and engineering, or even a shotgun marriage of these (Levins 1968b; H. T. Odum 1971; Patten 1971). Patten (1971) described a book he edited as "written in the language of systems scientists" to produce an "inevitable kinship between them and ecology by demonstrating multifariously how ecology can be cast in their terms." The literature of systems ecology is indeed replete with terms, and one of the major problems ecologists have had is to follow the ecology sometimes buried in the terms of systems analysis (Watt 1966; Dale 1970; Patten 1971, 1972, 1975a; Caswell et al. 1972; Levin 1976; Halfon 1979; Shugart and O'Neill 1979; Gutierrez and Fey 1980). Shugart and O'Neill provided a convenient summary of the "unique attributes" by which systems studies of ecosystems differ from other ecological studies:

1. Consideration of ecological phenomena at large spatial, temporal, or organizational scales;
2. Introduction of methodologies from other fields traditionally unallied with ecology;
3. An emphasis on mathematical models;
4. An orientation to computers both digital and analog; and
5. A willingness to formulate hypotheses about the nature of ecosystems.

It is difficult to identify any individual attribute of these as diagnostic, and they are certainly not "unique" to systems ecology. Traditional ecological studies encompassed large spatial or temporal scales. Indeed, the old-fashioned biome, the largest ecological entity short of the biosphere, was the favorite spatial scale in the IBP. Systems ecologists, like early ecologists, emphasized the significance to ecology of other disciplines, such as physics, chemistry, meteorology, and, notably, mathematics. Some systems ecologists returned to the emphasis on physical attributes of habitat of early ecologists. This had once been the butt of some academic humor. W. C. Allee (1934a) wrote, "One of the more intelligent of our university presidents once said that ecology seemed to be the study of the sty with the pig left out." Mathematical modeling was ubiquitous in ecology, although systems ecologists used large number-crunching models, which some mathematical ecologists deplored as inelegant. Computers and hypotheses were also widely advocated and used by ecologists who were not systems ecologists. Nevertheless, the sudden emergence of a new breed, hybrid and otherwise, of systems ecologists was a distinctive development of ecology in the 1960s.

Van Dyne (1980) and Shugart and O'Neill (1979) converged in identifying the origin of systems ecology with computer models of ecosystems using sets of differential equations. It may be that the scale and types of model used are the most distinctive attribute of systems ecology. Mathematical models were not new in ecology, and among the earlier publications of the IBP there were extended bibliographies of mathematical models in ecology (O'Neill, Hett, and Sollins 1970; Kadlec 1971). The broad sweep of the concept of mathematical models in ecology was evident in that, to my surprise, citations of my work appeared in both of the cited bibliographies, although I was innocent of knowledge of modeling. A. J. Rutter (1972) described the same reaction, comparing himself with Le Bourgeois Gentilhomme who found that he had been speaking prose for 40 years without knowing it. The justification for both bibliographies cited above was that the Analysis of Ecosystems program of the IBP was designed to make extensive use of mathematical modeling; indeed, it was to play a major role. Numerous symposia, workshops, articles, and volumes considered the newer style of modeling in ecology and its significance for ecology (Goodall 1972; Innis 1975a; Pielou 1981). Innis reviewed the controversy generated by the introduction of systems models, attributing it to mathematical models being presented as more than they were, to the view of mathematics as a threat by practicing biologists, and to the forcing of biological systems into available mathematical tools. Certainly some ecologists continued in the tradition of Haeckel, Juday, Nice, and others in arguing that the simplifying assumptions of most mathematical models vitiated their use with regard to the complexities of ecosystems. No doubt some ecologists were threatened by the flood of mathematical models in the 1960s and 1970s, but it is not clear that their concern was entirely due to Innis's assumption that "elderly people (past 20) have difficulty learning maths" (Innis 1975b). What was sometimes lacking was sufficient indication of the relevance of the mathematical model to justify learning the necessary mathematics (K. E. F. Watt 1975; Hedgpeth 1977; Pielou 1981). Doubt about the relevance of systems analysis was generated by the entry into ecology of substantial numbers of physicists, engineers, and mathematicians and, in some cases, application of their sophistication in mathematics to a discipline of which they had little grasp. Part of the approach of the IBP was to alleviate this problem by the use of the team approach to ecosystems studies, including mathematical modelers as members of the team along with ecologists. However, as Halfon (1979:11) wrote:

> There is a difference between mathematical model building and the systems approach. Modellers want to construct an adequate mathematical model of a given system. For the theoretician the analysis itself, rather than the real system, is the focus of interest.

The emphasis of some systems ecologists seemed to be on the model per se rather than on the system which it was supposed to elucidate or even predict. Smith (1975b) had made this point about ecosystems models:.

> I find this *ad hoc* kind of modeling satisfactory for *using* ecology in the sense that the models simulate the behavior of given ecosystems. But they are not useful for *doing* ecology in the sense of gaining new insights into ecosystem ecology.

Jameson (1970) had considered the appropriate relationship between mathematicians and ecologists, emphasizing that the biologist is best as the primary modeler with help from mathematicians. Many mathematical models have, however, been developed largely or entirely by nonecologists who are knowledgeable in mathematics. One of the common complaints heard in defense of some of the expensive models created is that the models are fine but the ecologists are remiss in not having the data to test the model. An obvious fact of life is that a mathematician or a biologist with a fertile imagination can create models far more rapidly than even a small army of ecologists can provide data to test them. Innis and O'Neill (1979) recognized this in the preface of their volume *Systems Analysis of Ecosystems:*

> Models are easy to build and becoming easier as more scientists enter the field with an affinity for this approach as model building becomes more common. Analysis and interpretation loom much larger as the challenges facing us.

This phenomenon was also recognized by Jeffers (1978:22), who wrote:

> Mathematical modelling is an intoxicating pursuit, so much so that it is relatively easy for the modeller to abandon the real world and to indulge himself (herself) in the use of mathematical languages for abstract art forms.

Not enough modelers have heeded these caveats, and one of the challenges facing ecologists is how to cope with multiple models. The ubiquitous problems of supplying adequate or appropriate systems measurements called for by the multiplicity of models produced for the ominivorous maw of the computer created substantial difficulties for the ecologist, whether inside or outside the IBP.

The literature of systems ecology contains many references to systems theory and systems analysis. The problem for the nonsystems ecologist is that systems theory and systems analysis come in a variety of forms, and various of these have been advanced in ecology. The classic figure in biology is Ludwig von Bertalanffy (1951, 1968), who applied systems theory in physiology and who sounds rather Clementsian in describing "principles of wholeness, of organization, of dynamic interaction" as appearing in biology in the form of organismic conceptions in contrast to the "analytical, summative, and machine theoretical of the the biology of yesterday" (Bertalanffy 1951). However, like most commentators on systems theory, he noted its origins are distinctly mixed. Lazlo (1972) considered a problem which often occurs to ecologists in his volume *The Relevance of General Systems Theory*. Many ecologists are not willing to pursue systems ecology to any of its several sources. A most useful review is Lilienfeld's (1978) *Rise of Systems Theory*, which identifies six sources which are commonly cited in the literature of systems ecology. Although Lilienfeld is among the numerous critics of systems ideas and philosophy, even one of those criticized acknowledged that he gave clear overviews of the ideas of systems thinkers (Lazlo 1980). The sources of systems ideas according to Lilienfeld which have been hybridized with ecology include:

1.  The *biological philosophy* of Ludwig von Bertalanffy;
2.  *Cybernetics,* associated with Norbert Weiner and the concepts of machines, feedback, and automation in the work of W. Ross Ashby;
3.  *Information theory,* based on the work of Shannon and Weaver;
4.  *Operations research,* which emerged during World War II;
5.  *Game theory* of Von Neuman and Morgenstern; and
6.  *Computer techniques for simulation* of complex systems as advocated by J. Forrester.

One of the principal theoreticians of systems theory wrote that a biologist must know physics, chemistry, and systems theory (Mesarovic 1968). Ecologists frequently are urged to add some aspect of systems thinking to their repertoire, and a not unreasonable question is: Which one? Although systems analysis is most commonly encountered in ecology as a method, principally the mathematical model, it has overtones of a philosophy, as Patten insisted, or even, as Lilienfeld has it, an ideology. It is not easy for the ecologist to identify which of these is being alluded to in much of the discussion of systems ecology. Nor is it easy to determine if it is a method, philosophy, or an ideology. It may be more than any of these. Rosen (1972) wrote:

> The developing family of ideas and concepts which fall roughly
> under the rubric of systems theory amounts to a profound revo-

lution in science – a revolution which will transform human thought as deeply as did the earlier ones of Galileo and Newton. Systems theory is, in its broadest sense, an attempt to develop a unified science based on principles of systems. Much terminology of systems theory is congruent with that of ecology, although the meanings are not always isomorphic (cf. *adaptation, boundaries* and *environment, change, dynamic, equilibrium, growth, stability* – Young 1956). It is commonly claimed that ecology has much to learn from one or the other aspects of systems thought. The ideas of one of the major theoreticians of systems, Nobert Weiner, the founder of cybernetics, are described as organismic and fundamentally ecological (Rider 1981). Allen and Starr (1982), however, consider the problems of ecology using ideas "from that part of general systems theory which is beyond the mechanistic cybernetic approach." In their approach, emphasizing hierarchy, systems theory "is a conceptual framework within which one might develop new ideas about biology." They described the problem of scale as being of crucial importance, and it seems clear that much dispute in ecology derives from ecologists viewing an object of ecological interest at different scales.

An uncompromisingly negative review of systems analysis was given by David Berlinski (1976), who addressed aspects of the several sources of systems ideas, primarily by examining their mathematical basis. Berlinski, as some reviewers have noted, is not the best organized of critics, but he leaves little doubt where he stands. The rhetoric of recent scientific discourse has seldom seen such an array of criticism, ranging from "confusion" or "trivial" to "quite without sense," "logical vulgarity," and "nonsensical philosophy of science." Berlinski's summary of general systems theory states that "it is a movement that is all craving without content. . . . Great ambitions without great theories are insufficient." It is difficult for an ecologist to evaluate the justice of Berlinski's criticisms of the basis of systems thinking on which much of systems ecology is predicated. One reviewer (Bailey 1978) found some of his statements so abstract as to be meaningless; another, Sussman (1977), admired his effort and his mathematics, but outlined the reasons why Berlinski will fail to convince supporters of systems analysis. These can be read as common defenses which have been raised against critics of systems ecology:

1. The critic does not understand what he is criticizing.
2. Systems analysis is only a first attempt at explaining complexity, and results should not be expected immediately.

3.  The critic is just too harsh.
4.  Even if the critic is correct to the present, systems will work in the future.

A spirited defense of systems theory using several of these is Lazlo's (1980). Lazlo's defense against Berlinski's criticism of the mathematics of several systems approaches is simply that systems theory is a philosophy, not a mathematical method. Lazlo welcomed criticism as having an educational function for young and "relatively virginal intellects" not yet exposed to systems thinking. He anticipated a sequence of criticisms of systems theory eventually arriving at those which will use the "conceptual universe" of systems and will, in effect, become a part of systems theory. This is, indeed, heady stuff for the ecologist who has taken seriously Patten's statement that systems ecology is a philosophy. It opens up a new and somewhat hazardous sideline to ecology, even more difficult than earlier urgings that the ecologist learn mathematics and computer programming.

### Recent ecosystem ecology

The formal end of the IBP in 1974 coincided with the First International Congress of Ecology, whose proceedings were published under the name *Unifying Concepts in Ecology* (van Dobben and Lowe-McConnell 1975). This congress took place 70 years after ecology first appeared on the program of a major scientific congress (Drude 1906). The "unifying concepts" in 1974 were substantially those which were the concern of the IBP – the structure, function, and management of ecosystems. Not all of the concepts considered were new or unifying. Stability and succession were evident concerns, with expanded horizons but little consensus regarding their meaning. The very title of the 1974 congress was attacked by one of the participants, who argued that a major problem of ecology was that it was still dealing with concepts rather than with theories and their presumed merit of prediction and falsifiability (Rigler 1975b). This criticism coincided with one directed at the hope of the IBP to develop large-scale predictive ecosystem models as "unrealistic in view of the lack of valid theory" (National Academy of Sciences 1974; Boffey 1976). The IBP had been subjected to critical review before its inception, during its lifetime, and after its formal termination in 1974. It endured searching scrutiny and criticism from the scientific community involved, from those competing for funds from the same sources, and from the government agencies which provided the funds. Rarely has a "revolution" or "paradigm change" been so glowingly touted. It was not easy to fulfill the outrageous promises which had been made in the name of ecology to gain understanding of

> the strategy of nature well enough to provide operations advice to managers of farms, forests, and fisheries – to municipalities sharing a common watershed or atmospheric region – to the design of new population centers and the rebuilding of the ones we have. . . . We need to be told what we can and cannot do, what we should and should not do – backed up by solid scientific fact. This is what the IBP proposes to do. (Blair 1977a:94)

And all this in five operational years!

One of the emphases of defenders of the work in systems ecology done under aegis of the IBP was that the IBP was itself an experiment, a truly pioneer effort to transcend the limits of small-scale, short-term ecological studies with marginal levels of funding (Auerbach, Burgess, and O'Neill 1977). Much traditional work in ecology was done with little or no funding, and it is probable that some of the much criticized descriptive ecology was done because it was cheap and necessary, not because of the lack of intellectual capacity of the investigators, as is sometimes intimated. The abrupt recognition in 1967 that gross environmental problems required better understanding of how natural and artificial ecosystems operated produced a crash program for which ecological science was ill prepared. Carpenter (1976) contrasted the lack of knowledge of description and function of ecosystems and the inability to predict ecosystem behavior with the high expectations of administrators and legislators in an era of political sensitivity to environmental problems. He also noted the long-term lack of investment in historical and current baseline information on ecosystems: "There is nothing for ecological data akin to the U.S. Geological Survey, or the Department of Agriculture's soil mapping."

Part of the difficulty in evaluating the IBP is that it was a formal effort to achieve a large-scale advance in a neglected science based on planned and managed programs of research. It was an integrated team approach in ecology designed to achieve levels of multidisciplinary integration hitherto unknown in ecology. It was a minor league Manhattan Project lacking the acid test of whether the bomb would go off or a "breakthrough" (e.g., a cure for cancer) would be achieved. As an unprecedented and ultimately successful effort in ecopolitics, its proponents claimed, justifiably, that it secured money and achieved goals which would have not been attained by ecology as usual. Perhaps the greatest limitation in evaluating it was that the formal reviews of the IBP prepared at its prescribed termination were premature. The evaluation of the IBP and its impact on ecology necessarily awaits the completion of publication of an anticipated 30 to 40 synthesis volumes and digestion of these by ecologists rather than by planning or funding agencies.

As might be expected, the report prepared by the U.S. National Committee for the IBP viewed the results favorably and asserted that "the U.S. IBP has played a major role in establishing ecosystem science in its own right" (*U.S. Participation in the International Biological Program* 1974). A second report, commissioned by the National Science Foundation (Battelle Columbus Laboratories 1975; Mitchell, Mayer, and Downhower 1976) was restricted to three of the large biome studies and compared these with nonbiome research published between 1969 and 1974. This generally negative report brought forth a number of rebuttals (Auerbach, Burgess, and O'Neill 1977; Gibson 1977; Blair 1977b) and counterrebuttals (Downhower and Mayer 1977). Perhaps the most pointed conclusion of Mitchell, Mayer and Downhower was that the IBP

> taught a painful and expensive lesson concerning the ability of systems analysis and modelling to contribute to a research program when that program's original goals and research plans are revised and developed during the course of the program.

A third evaluation of the U.S. IBP was done by a committee of the National Academy of Sciences (1975). It asserted that the IBP made major contributions to all its major objectives, falling short mostly of the rhetoric which was instrumental in bringing it into being. This report also noted the failure to produce large ecosystem models, and it expressed the thought that modeling was overemphasized in some cases and that communication between modeler and field scientists was inadequate. Its summary statement, however, was that "substantial scientific contributions were made." It seems clear that the hoped-for large-scale ecosystem models were not successful, but there is little doubt that smaller-scale process models and modeling as an approach to ecosystem studies will continue as a significant part of ecology.

Evaluation of the British IBP was much less contentious, since not so much had been promised or invested, financially or emotionally (Clapham, Lucas, and Pirie 1976). The consensus of opinion was favorable. M. W. Holdgate allowed that Britain had not needed the IBP but that the results were nevertheless beneficial. C. H. Waddington noted substantial improvements and standardization of methods. E. D. Le Cren emphasized the training of young ecologists in new ways and the greatly expanded horizons for limnology. E. B. Worthington commented on the continuing lack of integration between plant and animal and between terrestrial and aquatic ecology. Le Cren noted limited contact even between the freshwater and marine sections of the IBP. British ecology was much less affected by the IBP and ecosystem analysis than that of the United States (Duff and Lowe 1981). Some Continental programs were more clearly affected (Argen, Anderson, and Fagerstrom 1980). These are not, however, considered here. A more significant evaluation of the success of the IBP will appear in the development of ecology in the future. According to Blair (1977b), admittedly from the very beginning a proponent of the IBP, its main achievement was the advancement of the ecosystem as the unit of research for ecology. Blair also credited the IBP with providing a generation of ecosystem modelers "identified by their youth, haircuts (long) and attire (informal)" whose influence on ecology will be lasting. He quoted A. R. Clapham, chairman of the British IBP, as saying: "50 years hence people will point to important developments in biology and say these are a direct result of IBP."

Such semiofficial pronouncements necessarily mixed political, managerial, and fiscal components with the scientific judgment of ecologists, pro and con, particularly as the pressure of the IBP format was released and the deluge of IBP publication subsided. The evaluation was complicated by the fact that the IBP had had multiple effects on ecology. Some asserted that "systems ecology as a named discipline is developing a genuine importance, spurred by the integrated biome programs of the IBP" (Patten 1975a). Neuhold (1975) provided an overview of modeling in the several biomes of the U.S. IBP. He noted a beneficial effect of "forcing" a holistic mode of thinking on all participants. Neuhold added that ecosystem models generally included time but ignored spatial variation. It is striking that ecosystem studies and population studies have both run into the same phenomenon, pattern, which confounds easy generalization. It is fitting that K. E. F. Watt, one of E. P. Odum's revolutionist pioneers of systems ecology, should review the ecosystem models of the several biomes (Watt 1975). Watt commented that all of the biomes "focus attention on abiotic factors as being the ultimate drivers behind the systems," and he stressed the lack of consideration of variability of abiotic data. He offered a general stricture that

> 20 years of models of ecological phenomena do not describe the phenomena they purport to describe or contain internal mathematical problems or worse yet have both difficulties.

He questioned the use of linear systems theory in ecology, an approach more recently justified by Patten (1975b) on the grounds that complex nonlinear systems tend to become linearized. Watt raised the prospect that

> present ecological theory may be swept away by a tidal wave of linear systems theory simply because of the great body of standard methods available for linear systems.

Foin and Jain (1977) reviewed the post-IBP status of systems analysis and population biology and the several reports on the IBP described above and concluded:

> We may also have learned that large-scale funding, holistic approaches, and mathematical modeling do not inevitably overcome the traditional barriers to increasing scientific knowledge.

They asserted that the failure of the IBP to produce "a substantial and general ecosystem level theory" suggested the need for more research concentrating on population dynamics. Emphasis on population parameters of dominance, niche relations, and population processes such as mortality and survivorship, dispersal and colonization, was the prescription offered by Foin and Jain to provide a basis for mathematical modeling as a "logical outcome." Foin and Jain called for "developing a model relating patchiness to the life history phenomenon, which will ultimately serve as the principal tool for resynthesis of the population data within the community framework." They neglected to note that patchiness or pattern had been characteristically ignored in traditional population models from 1920 on and that recent efforts to measure and integrate patterns into population theory have been frustrating. Schaffer and Leigh (1976) went so far as to say that pattern precluded application of standard population theory to plant populations. In any event, it is unlikely that most systems ecologists will be swayed by the appeal to a population theoretical approach, which they had often asserted was not useful for ecosystem-level phenomena. Patten (1976), for example, wrote:

> I believe that Volterra-type systems are too narrow and confining to attempt to base a whole ecological paradigm on them.

Theoretical ecology – population, community and ecosystem –
should spring from the most general, comprehensive and modern models of the time development of systems available. For
this general systems theory is recommended.

Ecologists agree on the ecosystem as an important aspect of ecology.
Some treat it as *the* fundamental unit and concentrate on the patterns
and processes of the ecosystem as crucial to or controlling the component parts. Some traditional ecologists, such as Clements, and current
ecosystem ecologists regard the ecosystem as having an evolutionary
unity (McIntosh 1981). An explicit statement of this position is given
by Patten (1975c):

The ecosystem can be taken to consist of biotic and abiotic
components that change and evolve together, and the term
ecosystem implies a unit of co-evolution.

Other ecologists regard the ecosystem as the consequence of populations and the interactions among them as related to the available resources. Ecosystem structure is examined by these ecologists in terms
of competitive interactions among species, niche, and matrices of community coefficients, but communities or ecosystems per se are not
regarded as evolving entities:

There is in the community no center of control and organization, and no evolution toward a central control system. . . .
Community evolution is a result of species evolution and
species behavior. (Whittaker and Woodwell 1972)

Ecologists differ in their conception of the ecosystem and do not all
share the systems philosophy, which, Patten asserted, is more important to ecology than the methods and techniques associated with
it.

The continuing evaluation of ecosystems ecology, systems ecology,
and the IBP is a part of the problem of developing an effective empirical and theoretical approach to the complexities of ecosystems which
has long daunted ecologists. Ecosystems ecology continues to represent a substantial portion of the ecological programs funded by the
U.S. National Science Foundation. The extended efforts of the past
two decades, in and out of the IBP, have increased the understanding
of how ecosystems function. Great advances were achieved in the
knowledge of the amounts, storage, and flow of nutrients in ecosystems and the physiological and inorganic processes involved. The
knowledge of ecosystem function gained from ecosystem studies during
the past 20 years can be extended to the movement of pollutants and

toxic materials in ecosystems (Loucks 1972), although the promise of ecosystems theory in applied ecology is viewed variously (Carpenter 1976, Suter 1981). There seems little doubt that such knowledge will allow much more effective response by ecologists to questions posed about many specific ecosystems. What remains to be settled is whether ecologists have achieved, or have in prospect, particularly in the introduction of systems thinking in any of its nonecological forms, the capacity to understand and predict the responses of ecosystems and to provide general solutions to problems as they arise.

One of the most familiar justifications of systems analysis and mathematical models applied to ecosystems ecology is their heuristic merit. It must be said for systems analysis and its ecological models that they induced serious and concentrated thought in an effort to penetrate the verbal and mathematical complexity which was substituted for the inherent complexity of the ecosystem. These did enforce efforts to think clearly and specifically about the structure of ecosystems and transferred attention from the amounts of materials in any part of an ecosystem, the "pool" size, to the processes of change in the ecosystem. A common complaint of modelers and mathematical theorists concerned the lack of appropriate data to test their models, which focused attention of ecologists on different aspects of ecosystem function. One clear finding was the lack of long-term measurements of ecosystem parameters. In fact, methods of measurement of many variables judged to be significant for the understanding of ecosystem processes were rarely adequate until recent years, and the IBP manifestly advanced the development and standardization of methods. One response to the evident need for long-term monitoring of ecological data and of ecosystem parameters was the proposal to establish a network of Long-Term Ecological Research (LTER) strategically located in different regions (Lauff and Reichle 1979). Literally buried in the mass of ecosystems studies was the recognition that very significant things about which little was known went on underground and in the sediments of aquatic systems. The effect of these hidden and difficult-to-measure portions of ecosystems on the whole was dramatized by E. S. Deevey's (1970) comments "In Defense of Mud." More visible was a new generation of young ecologists who had experienced personally or vicariously a quantum jump in the scale of ecological activity and in the ways in which it was done. They were exposed to a revolution in method and technique for measuring ecosystem properties and a concomitant revolution in techniques for synthesizing the results via the computer. It remains to be seen if the time freed from the "drudgery" of both is turned into "a high level of thought" as anticipated by Watt (1968), who came in at the beginning.

# 7

## Theoretical approaches to ecology

Discussion of theoretical ecology, like discussion of ecology generally, is plagued by the problem of determining what it is in order to ascertain how it got that way or even what it should be. Consideration of theoretical ecology is difficult in that it requires conceptions of what is theory, what is ecology, and how they combine. Some recent writers on theoretical ecology resolved the problems I suggest with disarming simplicity. E. G. Leigh, Jr. (1968), for example, opened an article with a "historical sketch of ecologic theory," moving directly to the "pioneers of mathematical ecology, Lotka and Volterra," the founders in the 1920s of the "Golden Age of theoretical ecology" as it was described by Scudo and Ziegler (1978). Robert May (1974a), the editor of the first book, entitled simply *Theoretical Ecology* (May 1976) offered a similar history, but overlooked Lotka in writing, "Theoretical ecology got off to a good start in the 1920s with Vito Volterra's seminal and still central contributions." This view of the alliance of mathematical theory and ecology had been described earlier in the volume *Theoretical and Mathematical Biology* (Waterman and Morowitz 1965): "There are few areas of biology where theoretical mathematical studies have had as much impact as they have had in ecology" (Morowitz 1965). The author of a volume entitled *An Introduction to Mathematical Ecology* wrote, "Ecology is essentially a mathematical subject" (Pielou 1969:v). Mathematical theory was described as the big advance in ecology over Elton's conceptual contributions to ecology (Christiansen and Fenchel 1977). The effort of mathematical ecologists to express the complexities of ecological systems in the form of tractable equations had, according to Christiansen and Fenchel, the several advantages of resisting false conclusions, clarifying the problem at hand, and allowing, at least, order-of-magnitude prediction. All of the above authors agreed that mathematical ecology was an improvement on nonmathematical ecology.

242

## The revolution in theoretical ecology

Robert MacArthur, who according to Fretwell (1975) provided "leadership and protection" to a resurgent school of theoretical mathematical ecologists in the 1950s and 1960s, divided ecologists into two camps. One he described as "critical of simplifying theory"; the other, he said, because it is "primarily interested in making a science of ecology arranges ecological data as examples testing the proposed theories and spends most of its time patching up the theories to account for as many of the data as possible" (MacArthur 1962). The latter "camp" was clearly that later described as that of "Theoretical Ecology: Beginnings of a Predictive Science" (Kolata 1974). This camp was sometimes considered to have been pitched by MacArthur and his band in a "revolution" against entrenched antitheoretical ecologists (Cody and Diamond 1975; Fretwell 1975). Paul Dayton (1979), however, commented that ecology was "splintered" into numerous "camps" and deplored the lack of communication among them, suggesting schisms in the 1960s and 1970s which made the camps harder to locate. MacArthur's straightforward distinction between two camps, theoretical and antitheoretical, was made in his review of one of the landmarks of theoretical population ecology, *Growth and Regulation of Animal Populations* (Slobodkin 1962), which illustrates the widespread optimism in the 1960s concerning the prospect for theoretical ecology. L. B. Slobodkin attempted to state, both mathematically and verbally, the basis of an all-purpose theory for ecology, linking it to evolution and genetics. In his words:

> We may reasonably expect to have eventually a complete theory for ecology that will not only provide a guide for the practical solution of land utilization, pest eradication, and exploitation problems but will also permit us to start with an initial set of conditions on the earth's surface (derived from geological data) and construct a model that will incorporate genetics and ecology in such a way as to explain the past and also predict the future of evolution on earth. (Slobodkin 1962:172)

Slobodkin (1961) was one of the few ecologists (cf. Bray 1958; Margalef 1968) of the 1950s and 1960s who attempted to outline a program to produce a "predictive theory of ecology." He commented, "The operational procedures will almost certainly be amplifications of the existing theories of population dynamics, population genetics and inter-specific competition." His estimate was not far off the mark, for an important development in this period was an attempt to merge theo-retical population ecology and theoretical population genetics. Slobod-kin was not alone in his optimism. One of the collaborators with Slo-bodkin on a speculative and controversial paper (Hairston, Smith, and Slobodkin 1960), so well known in the 1960s that it achieved the status among ecologists of an acronym (HSS), wrote of that paper in retro-spect, "When we wrote the paper we were optimistic about the future of ecology, and we were convinced that a theory encompassing the field might soon be produced" (Hairston 1981).

MacArthur's assertion that critics of simplifying theory were op-posed to those trying to make ecology a science was in the mode of numerous commentators on ecology in the 1960s and 1970s who la-mented the absence of ecological theory and urged its importance if ecology was to develop as a science (McIntosh 1980a). Cragg (1966) asserted, "There is no theory of ecology. There has therefore been little sense of progression or timeliness about ecological research." Gates (1968) urged, "Ecology must have a strong theoretical base before it can advance significantly." K. E. F. Watt (1971) echoed a familiar concern of earlier ecologists about masses of data and few generalizations: "If we do not develop a strong theoretical core that will bring all parts of ecology back together we shall all be washed out to sea in an immense tide of unrelated information." The cause of theoretical ecology was seen by a few ecologists during this period as being heroically pressed against an antitheoretical establishment which resisted, or even censored, efforts to change the ways of doing ecology which were being developed by mathematical theoretical ecologists (Fretwell 1975). If there was such resistance, it failed, be-cause by 1974 the fear was expressed that "mathematical ecology has now entered the establishment and appears to be pursuing a policy of competitive exclusion" (Van Valen and Pitelka 1974). The biblio-graphical success of theoretical ecology was certainly most dramatic. During the 1970s the number of papers in theoretical ecology was described as expanding with an estimated doubling time of less than three years, suggesting an explosion in the numbers of papers and an infinite number of journals as a horrifying prospect (May and May 1976). Mathematical theoretical ecology, in the notation of its paren-tal logistic equation, was in the $r$ or exponential phase (Patil and Rosenzweig 1979). It was commonly described as a "revolution" or as providing intellectual hormones for the "maturation" of ecology into a "predictive" science:

> The science of ecology has matured dramatically in the last few years. From what was primarily a descriptive science has developed a new mathematically based evolutionary ecology. (Craig 1976)

Cody and Diamond (1975:vii) claimed:

> Within two decades new paradigms had transformed large areas of ecology into a structured predictive science that combined powerful quantitative theories with the recognition of widespread patterns in nature. This revolution in ecology has been due largely to the work of Robert MacArthur.

An alternative view of the revolution in ecological theory was that ecology had become bedeviled by untested or untestable theory and models, while empirical study languished. Dayton denied that his article, which was later listed as a "citation classic," had been inspired by theory, and wrote:

> Ecology often seems dominated by theoretical bandwagons driven by charismatic mathematicians, lost to the realization that good ecology rests on a foundation of natural history and progesses by use of proper scientific methods. (Dayton 1980)

It is not clear which charismatic mathematicians Dayton had in mind, but Hutchinson (1975) had previously noted the need to temper mathematical abstraction with sound knowledge of natural history, commenting, "MacArthur really knew his warblers."

"Proper scientific methods" were at the core of much discussion about theoretical ecology. MacArthur, frequently lauded as the doyen of theoretical ecologists (Hutchinson 1975; McIntosh 1980a), allowed that the "making of nontrivial theory" for ecology was best done by field naturalists, but added the proviso that these should be "naturalists who know what science is all about" (MacArthur 1962). Whether ecology was a proper science had been debated by its earliest critics and practitioners, but many viewed it as finally arriving as a science in the 1960s. Assertions that ecology was becoming science, "experimental" science, "modern" science, "mature" science, "predictive" science, "nomothetic" science, "hard" science, or "mathematical theoretical" science were added to Sears's (1964) description of ecology as a "subversive" subject, with the implication that there was a consensus among ecologists as to "proper scientific methods" or what "science was all about." All but the appellation "subversive" were commonly accompanied by the assertion, or intimation, that what had gone on before was descriptive, old-fashioned, immature, static, soft, atheoretical, and done by natural historians who did not "know what science was all about" or, at least, did not know what later generations of ecologists had come to believe science was all about. A major problem derived from the fact that conceptions of what science was all about and how ecology fit these conceptions were in a state of flux among scientists at large, ecologists in particular, and among philosophers, the usual arbiters of what was science. Moreover, some ecologists who urged particular conceptions of theoretical ecology were not notably consistent nor lucid in expressing their conceptions of science or their relevance to ecology. Nor did they agree what science was all about.

Ecology was, in the 1960s, thrust into the limelight by the widespread perception of environmental crises. It was not unprecedented that ecological ideas and ecologists should be involved in environmental concerns. Grassland ecology had emerged, in part, as a response to an earlier environmental crisis (Tobey 1981). Important aspects of aquatic ecology had developed as a consequence of declining fisheries; and terrestrial animal ecology, particularly insect population ecology, was a product of concerns about affects of insect populations on agriculture and human health. The essential difference in the 1960s was that the environmental crisis was dramatically brought home to the general public and government policymakers, and ecology was seized on as an established science with capabilities for dealing with environmental concerns. The popular and administrative convention of science is as an idealized, objective body of laws, theories, and models ready to be applied to solve problems. Although ecologists had extensive experience and some successes in addressing problems on an empirical basis, they faced, in the 1960s, a dual problem. Ecologists were caught up in a press to develop a theoretical ecology inherent to the discipline and faced with demands that they provide specific guidance, based on poorly developed theory, for many applied problems. To paraphrase Slobodkin, they were being asked to make empirical bricks without theoretical straw. In part, the split which is evident between "systems" ecologists and "theoretical" ecologists was a product of the desire of some of the former to develop a management-oriented ecological engineering and of the latter to produce a theoretical science based on evolutionary theory (Levins 1968b). Neither side of this dichotomy, which pervades current ecology, however, abdicated its reciprocal claim. Theoretical ecologists claimed that effective resource management and public policy required developing ecological theory based on mathematical population theory. Systems ecology, although it borrowed methods, models, and personnel from engineering, and although some systems ecologists saw it as a merger of engineering and ecology, was also lauded as an advanced theoretical ecology. Some even described systems ecology as transcending its humble origins as a branch of biology and becoming a metaecology (E. P. Odum 1977, in press).

## Ecologists as philosophers

Theoretical ecologists of various persuasions in the era of the "beginnings of a predictive science" offered explicit, if parochial, guidance as to what "science was all about." They often reached into various sections of the extensive literature on philosophy of science for support. Some visualized ecology as following in the mold of theoretical science as represented by physics. Complex and notably heterogeneous biological systems would be treated by a theoretical ecology based on a body of general laws, principles, constants, and mathematical models. Others raised the question whether ecology, or even biology at large, can or should be expected to develop like physics in producing general theories explaining and predicting order in nature. The practitioners of natural science that had developed in the 18th century and that differed from classical physics in emphasizing the qualitative, historical, and concrete and gave rise to ecology and evolutionary biology (Lyon and Sloan 1981) had descendants in 20th-century ecology. Commentators on the philosophy of biology offered little assurance that biology was simply an immature physics (Simon 1971; Ruse 1973; Hull 1974). Some evolutionary biologists declared that biology was, in fact, an autonomous science and that it should not be expected to conform to the mold of science formed from physics (Ayala 1974; Mayr 1982).

It is apparent that part of the difficulty of assessing theoretical ecology is due to not only the traditional diversity of ecologists and the intrinsic complexity of the natural organization with which ecology deals, but also to a number of philosophical differences about science generally and ecology as a science in particular (Morales 1975; Mac-Fadyen 1975; McMullin 1976; McIntosh 1980a, 1981a; May 1981a; Willson 1981; Niven 1982). These differences must be explicitly addressed and, if not resolved, at least clarified in order that ecological theory can be clearly formulated and effectively tested. Much dispute

about ecological theory has been commonly due to reciprocal ignorance among the several traditions of ecology from its beginnings. This
dispute has been aggravated in recent decades by assurances of rival
"camps" of theoretical ecologists that their respective grasp of what
science is all about is correct. Confidence in molding ecology to a
particular philosophy of science is not justified by recent books on the
philosophy of biology or by the expositions of philosophy of science
offered by some ecologists. Robert May (1981a), one of the arbiters of
recent theoretical ecology, decried "naively simple formulations of The
Way To Do Science," especially when advanced by "doctrinaire vigi-
lantes." He goes so far as to suggest that the extreme views of Paul
Feyerabend (cf. Broad 1979) that science is not entirely a rational
pursuit may be preferable to those of Bacon or Popper. Ideological
attributes of classical science commonly urged upon ecology if it is to
"mature" may not be entirely suitable. Some theoretical ecologists
questioned just this point (Slobodkin 1965). May (1981a) modified his
earlier emphasis on the mathematical theory of ecology and allowed
that ecological theory comes in many forms, including verbal models.

Among the favorite recipes pressed upon ecologists in the 1960s and
1970s as the proper way to do science was the "hypothetico-deductive
philosophy," familiarly known as "H-D," and its appropriateness for,
and putative neglect by, ecologists were common themes. Fretwell
(1975) claimed that during the two decades following 1955, articles
published in the journal *Ecology* based on the hypothetico-deductive
method had increased tenfold. Rosenzweig (1976) wrote, "Maturation
is now underway in ecology," attributing this to ecologists developing a
"hypothetico-deductive philosophy" based on "generating hypotheses
and disproving them in controlled experiments." The hypothetico-
deductive method comes from philosophical sources with a variety of
meanings. Ruse (1973) described hypothetico-deductive systems as axiomatic in the sense of the theories of physical science. Biology generally and ecology in particular are not yet stated in axiomatic form, so it
is not likely that Rosenzweig and Fretwell had this meaning in mind.
More likely they had in mind Karl Popper's falsificationist conception
of science. This philosophy of how science should operate is one of
several now in the field filling the void left by the apparent demise of
logical positivism, and it has been frequently urged upon ecologists
(Jaksic 1981). MacFadyen (1975), however, commented that some
ecologists "find it hard to see quite how our kind of science fits into
the Popper and Medawar hypothetico-deductive image." He noted

problems arising from "misuse of the deductive method." Dayton (1979) reviewed several of the current views of philosophers, observing that "the philosophers themselves seem to have little common ground." However, he summarized Popper's well-known position, quoting him as writing, "The method of science is bold conjectures and ingenious and severe attempts to refute them." Part of Dayton's article dealt with the difficulty of applying this doctrine in ecology and, perhaps, other sciences. Certainly ecology has had its share of "bold conjectures" or even rank speculation, which has been rife in the ecological literature. Slobodkin (1962) had frankly entitled the last chapter of his book on population ecology "Speculation." He conjectured that a theoretical community ecology would be based on valid generalizations which "will set narrow limits to the properties of acceptable ecological theories." Setting limits for acceptable theories for ecology has proven difficult. Even more difficult to achieve are the "severe attempts" required by Popper to refute hypotheses or theories, much less to refute conjecture or speculation. Dayton (1979) considered the problem of inherently untestable hypotheses and cited an even more intransigent problem which was recognized in pre-Popperian science by T. C. Chamberlain, in 1890, so cogently that the editors of *Science* thought it desirable to reprint the article 75 years later (Chamberlain 1890). Chamberlain, a geologist, anticipated plant ecologists in his description in the 1870s of the plant communities of Wisconsin and later influenced H. C. Cowles at the University of Chicago. Chamberlain described a dangerous tendency among scientists to grow attached to a hypothesis and therefore to overlook its faults or even to avoid seeking out evidence which would expose them. Such a tendency, he said, led to the conservation of a "ruling theory." Popper's idea of rigorous testing and falsification of hypotheses, thus eliminating the unfit, in effect poses a problem of intellectual abortion and flies in the face of the tendency eloquently described, whatever its philosophical merit, by Chamberlain. Dayton similarly described problems in examining a hypothesis which arose when "the loyalty of its believers overcame their critical acuity." Theoretically, this difficulty should be overcome by appropriate objectivity and willingness to set aside inadequate hypotheses and models. Unfortunately, a tendency to verify rather than falsify appears in ecological schools or invisible colleges, or some ideas are "reified," in more philosophical parlance (Caswell 1976; Dayton 1979). Most recently, the H-D method was urged on applied ecology in the form of wildlife science (Romesburg

1981). Romesburg compared wildlife science unfavorably to medical research because wildlife ecologists failed to use the H-D method to detect errors in wildlife science. However, a disagreement about applying "the scientific method" to ecology is evident in this paper. Romesburg, for example, wrote, "Modeling was never intended to function as a means to scientific knowledge." He based this statement on the presumed inability of models to predict usefully. Some of the new generation of modelers in ecology, to the contrary, suggested that models lead to, or are, hypotheses or theories, and that the main advantage of models is that they will produce a predictive science (McIntosh 1980a).

Another philosophical consideration commonly encountered in pursuit of ecological theory is the advantage of deductive over inductive approaches. Traditional ecologists have commonly been criticized for being unduly committed to inductive methods, yet some well-known early ecological theories were deductive in the extreme. S. A. Forbes's "microcosm" was described by Hutchinson (1963) as "the first important theoretical ecological construct to develop in American limnology." Forbes (1887) adopted an explicitly deductive approach in proposing this theory, and he specifically denied that induction was adequate – an assertion commonly encountered in philosophy:

> To determine the primitive order of nature by induction alone requires such a vast number of observations in all parts of the world, for so long a period of time, that more positive and satisfactory conclusions may perhaps be reached if we call in the aid of first principles, travelling to our end by the *a priori* road.

Clements (1904, 1905) developed his influential deductive theory of the climax formation as a superorganism certainly before there was any inductive basis for such a generalization. Other protoecologists and early ecologists, however, held firmly inductionist positions. Semper (1881) cautioned against the pernicious habit of theoretical explanation from general propositions under the ominous heading "A Final Warning." Semper, however, foresaw "the prospect of gradually bringing even Organic Being within reach of that method of inquiry which seeks to determine mechanical efficient causes," namely physiology. Spalding (1903) wrote:

> The accumulation and expression of facts as they really are should take . . . nine tenths, possibly ninety-nine one hundredths, of the time that is being given to ecological work.

Hypotheses are fascinating, but we have all erred, perhaps, in demanding that those who busy themselves with such observations shall show us promptly their bearing on a theory of the universe. At present it is really the main business of the ecological student to ascertain and record fully, definitely, perfectly and for all time the facts.

Adams (1913), however, quoted the geologist Charles Van Hise as a model for ecologists:

I have heard a man say I observe the facts and I find them unprejudiced by any theory. I regard this statement as not only condemning the work of the man, but the position is an impossible one.

In Van Hise's view, the selection of facts to collect implies theories of their importance and significance, a position endorsed by later philosophers of biology and ecologists. However, overt and covert inductionist approaches to ecology persisted. The subsequent work of H. M. Raup was firmly and proudly inductive, Baconian, and opposed to deductive theory, at least Clementsian theory. Raup's studies from the 1930s on were described as approaching "truth" and "reality" inductively, ignoring "the shrill cries from peddlers of instant deductive explanations" (Stout 1981). Inductionist approaches in ecology persist in current ecology, sometimes in unexpected places. John Harper, an avowed proponent of a theoretical predictive science of ecology, wrote:

I suggest that it is from the repeated studies by *individuals* like Watt of *individual* plants in particular local conditions that most ecological generalizations are likely to emerge. Many of these are likely to be concepts, not laws. (Harper 1982)

Adams (1913) again turned to the geologists, in the person of J. Playfair in 1802, for good advice: "The truth, indeed, is that in Physical inquiries, the work of theory and observation must go hand in hand." This "truth" was echoed nearly two centuries later:

It is critical, however, that the theory now develop in concert with empirical work . . . to avoid the danger of accumulating . . . large amounts of trivial theory unguided by attention to what animals are actually capable of doing and therefore what the important problems are. (Werner and Mittelbach 1981)

This excellent advice has yet to diffuse uniformly among ecologists, and criticisms of inductive ecology coupled with praise of deductive theory, and the converse, are all too frequent.

Perhaps the most involved, persistent, and least conclusive argument among ecological theorists is that between traditional holists, neoholists and knowing, or unknowing, reductionists, the latter sometimes describing themselves as holists (Levins 1968b; Allen and Starr 1982). Most traditional ecologists, from S. A. Forbes, E. A. Birge, F. E. Clements, and A. Tansley through Aldo Leopold, and W. C. Allee, were explicitly holists and regarded the community as at least *like* an organism (Bodenheimer 1957; McIntosh 1976, 1980a). Holism continues as a major theme in current theoretical ecology, although many holists regard themselves as an embattled minority struggling against a demon reductionism, at worst, or developing a symbiotic relationship with it, at best. An extreme statement of the former called for integrating subcomponents of a problem into larger functional wholes and lamented that such efforts are

> vigorously resisted by much of the academic community thus depriving both society and students of a holistic view. The shameful aspect of this resistance is not that individuals refuse to attempt a holistic view themselves, . . . but rather that they block attempts of others to do so. (Cairns 1979)

E. P. Odum (1977) allowed that science should be both reductionist and holist, but made clear that there has been enough of the former and too little of the latter. Odum wrote: "Among academic subjects, ecology stands out as one of the few dedicated to holism," although he suggested that "even economics" is striving in that direction. Some ecologists, such as C. H. Muller, "felt in the 1950s and still feel a general distaste for invasion of ecology by reductionism" (Muller 1982). Margalef (1968), however, thought that "the approach called reductionistic is very effective in ecology." The unhelpful polarity of reductionism and holism in ecology has been frequently noted (Rosen 1972; Lane, Lauff, and Levins 1975; MacFadyen 1975, 1978; Innis 1976; Lidicker 1978; Salt 1979; McIntosh 1980a, 1981; Cody 1981; Harper 1982), although Colinvaux (1982) wrote that ecologists since Tansley had abandoned holism. Lidiker contended that a largely reductionist approach to population dynamics in ecology had predominated for 35 years. Cody said that he was trying to preserve the holistic approach against reductionism:

> This it seems to me is what ecology is all about, only thus can one keep one's nose above water in the seas of experimental reductionism and secular pedantry that currently threaten to swamp the field. (Cody 1983)

The religious overtones sometimes associated with holism are suggested in his contrasting it with a reductionism associated with "secular pedantry." MacFadyen (1978) described attacks by ecologists "often made on reductionist science which I believe to be absolutely legitimate." His justification for this belief was that ecology deals with complex systems which have dynamic properties of their own.

Attacks on reductionism and holism are indeed frequent in the ecological literature and related work on evolutionary biology, and some have attacked both. Repeated attacks by holistic biologists on the body of reductionist biology might have been expected to lead to its demise and funeral. Lewontin (1983) wrote that he saw the corpse of reductionism going up in the elevator in his department last week (at Harvard University). Lewontin (1968) had once decried as "stamp collectors" biologists "who insist that the problems of ecology and evolution are so complex that they cannot be treated except by holistic statements." Lewontin is equally stringent in his criticism of "Cartesian reductionism" as applied to evolutionary biology (Levins and Lewontin 1980; Lewontin 1983). As a major advocate of the introduction of population genetics into ecology (Lewontin and Baker 1970) and a sometime commentator on philosophy for biologists, Lewontin's views merit attention. Lewontin firmly opposes Cartesian reductionism and what he terms "obscurantist" holism. It is possible, he suggests, to reject both conventional holism and reductionism and approach biological problems in the context of dialectical materialism:

> idealist holism which sees the whole as the embodiment of some ideal organizing principle, dialectical materialism views the whole as a contingent structure in reciprocal interaction with its own parts and with the greater whole of which it is a part. Whole and part do not completely determine each other.
> (Levins and Lewontin 1980)

R. Levins, Lewontin's collaborator in this article, is articulately holist (Lane, Lauff, and Levins 1975) but presumably does not advocate "idealist" or "obscurantist" holism.

The distinction between holists and reductionists appeared at various times in the development of ecology. Hutchinson (1964) wrote that E. A. Birge's concept, in 1915, of a heat budget of a lake was "holological," implying a single state variable, and that S. A. Forbes's "microcosm" concept of a lake was "merological," implying many state variables. Forbes and Birge shared the concept of the lake as an organism, and Forbes was explicit that the whole shaped the parts, although he studied the insect and fish components and Birge generally had concentrated on plankton before touching on heat budgets. However, Hutchinson's distinction foreshadowed the segregation of a brand of theoretical ecology which concentrated on the whole in terms of "macroscopic" variables (e.g., energy) from another brand which concentrated on numerous parts or "microscopic" variables (Orians 1980). The long dispute about the Clementsian concept of an organismic community and its long-submerged rival, the individualistic community concept of H. A. Gleason, was described by Richardson (1980) as due to their personal predispositions for holism and reductionism, respectively. It is unlikely, however, that their entire intellectual approach to ecology was influenced by the areas in which they worked, as Richardson suggested. Tobey (1981) wrote that Clements's holistic organismic views were influenced by reading Herbert Spencer and his association with social scientists of similar persuasion, which is more plausible than the effect of being raised on the prairie. The origin of Gleason's individualistic concept has not been thoroughly explored, but a substantially identical concept was proposed by a Russian ecologist, Ramensky, who, like Clements, worked in a grassland area (McIntosh 1975b, 1983b).

Richardson (1980) distinguished between holist and reductionist ecologists in terms of the insistence of many holistic ecologists that the whole has emergent properties distinctive to itself and that the whole is more than the sum of its parts. This assumption did not originate with ecologists but surfaced in the earliest "self-conscious" ecology and continues to the present in frequent and continuing references to sums of parts and wholes (McIntosh 1981). By 1935 Tansley questioned, somewhat wearily, if the sum of the parts had any meaning at all, but the distinction persisted. F. E. Smith (1975a), in his presidential address to the Ecological Society of America, said, "Two extreme views of ecosystems can be recognized." In one view, an ecosystem emerges as the sum of its parts: "Any understanding of the whole must derive from its parts." For the other group, he said, "ecosystems have uniqueness of their own that guides the evolution of species rather than emerging from the evolution of species." John Harper (1982) called for "faith" that "the complex is no more than sum of the activities of the parts plus their interactions." "Their interactions," however, are what make the whole more than the sum of the part, in the holist view. Harper saw the philosophy determining the ecology:

> There is an important sense in which our knowledge of terrestrial ecology has been determined by these contrasting philoso-

phies: an individualistic interpretation based on the history of
the community and a holistic interpretation that has seen a
community dominated by the constraining forces of limited
resource or driven toward some stable constrained state.
(Harper 1977b)

Harper's philosophical poles may not accurately describe all positions
of ecology because some proponents of the antiholist philosophy see
the community as controlled by resources in a stable or equilibrium
state. There may be some degree of independent segregation which
serves to complicate assigning ecologists to philosophies. Lewontin
(1983) characterized dialectical materialism as rejecting the polarized
argument about sum of parts and emergent properties of wholes:

It is not that a whole is more than the sum of its parts but that
the parts themselves are re-defined and re-created in the process of their interaction.

Prominent and articulate holists such as E. P. Odum, however, continued to propound the Clementsian idea that distinctive "macroscopic" properties emerge at higher levels of organization and that
these emergent properties control the components and are necessary to
explain the whole. E. P. Odum (in press) attributed this view to philosophers and ecologists at large:

The ecologist, and also philosophers, have for a long time
maintained that in levels of organization above the organism
the whole is more than the sum of the parts.

Not all philosophers agree (Macklin and Macklin 1969), and recently
the ecologist G. W. Salt (1979) joined Tansley in questioning the
meaning of emergence. Salt described emergence as a not very meaningful "pseudocognate" and argued that so-called emergent properties
are "collective" properties which are simply additive rather than
more than their sum. Salt noted the difficulty of identifying emergent
properties and said that their meaning in ecology is not clear. Other
ecologists turned to the literature of philosophy to examine Salt's
argument. Edson, Foin, and Knapp (1981) argued that the question
of emergence is irrelevant to ecology and impedes its progress. Ecologists have always worked with different "levels of organization," from
the individual organism and populations to communities of particular
taxa, biomes or aggregates of plants and animals, landscape units of
varying kind, and, most inclusively, the ecosystem. Each of these
requires a different method and conception, and empirically they are
quite different.

Much of the difference encountered among ecologists stems from their stance on the question of reductionism, holism, and emergence. Some reject the idea of emergence and the associated concept of levels of organization. The concept of organizational levels with their own properties and a special theory for such levels not based on the behavior of single-species populations was deemed an error. Harper (1982) rejected the "almost religious view" that communities have properties that are more than the sum of their parts. Others emphatically embraced the concept of organizational levels and insisted that such levels have distinctive rules or properties not discernible from those of the lower levels. Allen and Starr (1982), in a volume aptly entitled *Hierarchy,* wrote that emergent properties in ecology are due to the scale at which observations are made and recognized two types. One, they said, is simply due to the observer not knowing enough, so that the emergent property disappears on further study of the parts. Some ecologists attribute all emergent properties to such ignorance and argue that at least "in principle" all properties can be discerned by adequate knowledge of the parts. Allen and Starr, however, said that some properties of the whole are truly emergent and inherently not reducible to the parts and asserted that these properties must be examined at the appropriate hierarchical level and can be explained only by rules appropriate to that level.

## Ecological theory and evolution

In addition to the predilection of ecologists to adopt philosophical positions, another difficulty of assessing ecological theory is recognizing what is considered ecological theory or identifying redundant theories under different names. Traditional ecologists commonly referred to their ideas as concepts or principles and infrequently as theories (McIntosh 1980a). The need for theory to organize the growing body of ecological data was, however, stressed by several early ecologists, among them Elton (1927:188), who wrote that the methods of ecology

> require a wholesale overhauling in order that the rich harvest of isolated facts that has been gathered during the last thousand years may be welded into working theories which will enable us to understand something about the general mechanism of animal life in nature, and in particular to obtain some insight into the means by which animal numbers are controlled.

In spite of such urgings, the authors of the principal compendium of animal ecology of the mid-20th century noted, "Ecologists have not usually been concerned with biological theory" (Allee et al. 1949). Surprisingly, in view of the spate of ecological theory in recent decades, current textbooks and references of ecology rarely index "theory," even under descriptors usually associated with ecological theories – for example "competition," "equilibrium," "foraging," "niche," or "population." A recent *Dictionary of Theoretical Concepts in Biology* (Roe and Frederick 1981) cataloged numerous "theories" as belonging to ecology, but many of these are hardly theories and are dated, peculiarly named, or simply the idiosyncratic usages of one or a few individuals. Ecology, like biology, has commonly been criticized for its lack of an explicit and testable theoretical framework (Haskell 1940; Bray 1958; Slobodkin 1961; Orians 1962; Waterman and Morowitz 1965; Peters 1976). Lewis (1982) urged more effective use of formal theoretical postulates in teaching biology in order to aid students, and subsequent professional biologists, in comprehending biological theory. Although theoretical ecology is one of the more highly touted aspects of recent ecology, it is not easy to find consensus among ecologists about established theories, their basic postulates, sources, or even their names or pseudonyms. F. E. Smith (1976) wrote: "A present tendency in ecology to call a hypothesis a theory or to give credence to concepts through repetition has led to confusion between what has been verified and what has only been postulated."

Theoretical ecology is variously viewed by different beholders, and not all believe it began in the 1920s with mathematical ecology. Glacken (1967) and Egerton (1973) converged on the balance-of-nature concept, which Egerton described as the "oldest ecological theory." It may be argued that this conception is in the tradition of providential natural history and that the scientific writing of Linnaeus or Buffon is not ecological theory because it was written in a different intellectual context. Darwin's evolutionary version of the economy of nature was described by the historian of science Stauffer (1957) as a "fundamental ecological concept," falling short of Rigler's (1975b) desired falsifiable theory. However, Stauffer and many ecologists (Spalding 1903; Cowles 1904) attributed the founding of ecology to Darwin, although the historian Vorzimmer (1965) argued that Darwin ignored the significance of his contributions to ecology. Vorzimmer did, however, credit Darwin with recognizing that speciation depends "on the condition under which selection operates." He added, "This is that important juncture where ecology enters." The plant ecologist Harper (1967), using this rationale, claimed, "The theory of evolution by natural selection is an ecological theory – founded on ecological observation by perhaps the greatest of all ecologists." If this were accepted, then the frequent claims of early ecologists that the function of ecology was to elucidate adaptation apply properly to an ecological theory. In fact, Cowles (1908), anticipating Harper, wrote, "The interpretation of selection is a field problem, an ecological problem." Cowles (1909) described the "Lamarckian theory of direct adaptation" as "the most baneful of all *ecological* theories" (italics added). In an era when some ecologists such as Clements (1909) and biologists such as Lutz (1909) still believed that species were transformed by environmental influences, and Darwin was quoted by Lutz as regretting that he had not attached "sufficient weight to the direct influences of food, climate etc. independently of natural selection," the idea of natural selection, by whatever means, was seen as an ecological theory. Less heralded ecologists such as Charles Robertson (1906) described speciation as "only an ecological process." In Robertson's prescient view, "Species are characterized by non-competitive habits rather than by adaptive structures." New species were, he said, produced by natural selection through competition.

Early animal ecologists such as Shelford (1913) wondered if structural adaptations were a good basis for ecology and urged, as a working hypothesis, that animals arose one place and "by chance found places to which they were adapted." Adams (1913) distinguished between adaptation as "process" and "product" – the "process" being ecological and different from the evolutionary "product." He claimed that interpretations of evolution rest on the "ecology of living animals." Allee et al. (1949), however, commented on the "surprising reticence" of ecologists in developing evolutionary principles, suggesting, as John Harper had complained, that ecologists had largely abandoned "their" theory to geneticists and systematists. Nevertheless, the substance of the neo-Darwinian view of speciation became the conventional wisdom of ecologists. Hutchinson (1959) stated it explicitly and linked it to population theory:

> I subscribe to the view that the process of natural selection coupled with isolation and later mutual invasion of ranges leads to the evolution of sympatric species, which at equilibrium occupy distinct niches according to the Volterra-Gause principle.

In spite of the "surprising reticence" of ecologists to participate in developing evolutionary principles, ecology was seen by some as vital in the development of evolutionary thought. Ghiselin (1980) maintained that "the Darwinian revolution was basically a matter of ecology, not systematics." E. B. Ford (1980) wrote that one of six fundamental steps in the development of the evolutionary synthesis in the 1930s and 1940s was "the study of evolution in progress by a combination of ecology and laboratory genetics." This unnamed combination began early in the 20th century, and a considerable body of work addressed the hybrid questions of evolution, genetics, taxonomy, and ecology. The apparent reticence of ecologists is evident in that most of this work appeared in other than ecological journals and was usually classified in the academic framework as systematics or genetics rather than the less-well-established field of ecology. The classical, if incorrect, examination of environmental effects on speciation was done by a French botanist, Gaston Bonnier, who reported that when he transplanted lowland forms of a species to alpine sites and vice versa, each was reciprocally transformed into the other (Stebbins 1980). The American ecologist F. E. Clements, along with some prominent paleontologists, retained a belief in Lamarckian evolution, and he began similar experiments at his own alpine station. In 1928 he claimed that he had found it "possible to convert several Linnean species into each other, histologically as well as morphologically" (quoted in McIntosh 1983a). Clements had been working with Harvey M. Hall, a taxonomist, but when Hall visited the site of Clements's experiments, he found the methods of recordkeeping superficial and inadequate to support Clements's claims (W. M. Hiesey 1983 pers. commun.). Hall started his own transplant gardens in 1926, keeping meticulous records and photographs of clonal material and transplants. By the time of his death in 1932, he had joined the Swedish botanist G. Turesson (1922) in refuting the ideas of Bonnier and Clements. Hall and Turreson combined indirectly to establish a legacy of continued work in the relation of plant phenotypes and genotypes to the environment. Hall had hired an undergraduate student, W. M. Hiesey, as a "transplant assistant" in 1926, and Turreson recommended Jens Clausen, who joined the staff of the Carnegie Institution of Washington (Stebbins 1980). Hiesey and Clausen, along with D. D. Keck, expanded the research program outlined by Hall and in 1940 began publishing the notable series of monographs *Experimental Studies on the Nature of Species*, which clearly established genetic races of plant species adapted to the environment (Clausen, Keck, and Hiesey 1940).

Studies of genecology or ecological genetics of animals and plants antedated either name and were parallel in chronology and method. E. B. Ford (1980) described his famous studies beginning in the 1920s as "taking genetics into the field," which met the early criterion of ecology of returning biology to the field. Animal genecology used "artificial colonies" which were "transplants" of an animal from a parent area to an area where it was absent and introduced genes into an area by adding an organism with known genes to an extant population lacking them. Ford noted that, in the 1920s, experimental genetics was not regarded by zoologists as highly promising. However, he persisted and published a book on the genetic basis of populations (Ford 1931), after which work on ecological genetics slowly accumulated. Although Ford noted his association with R. A. Fisher, the mathematical theory of evolution developed by Fisher along with Sewall Wright and J. B. S. Haldane did not incorporate specifically ecological concerns, as later critics of theoretical population genetics noted. L. R. Dice (1947) examined coat color of deer mice and its relation to their background and to selection by predation. According to Arnold and Anderson (1983), the beginning of theoretical ecological genetics was marked by H. Levene's study (1953) of the relation of genetic equilibrium to multiple niches. Although Ford said he started to plan his book *Ecological Genetics* in 1928, it was not published until 1964, the same year in which J. Heslop-Harrison published his review "Forty Years of Genecology" (Ford 1964; Heslop-Harrison 1964). However, as late as 1969, E. O. Wilson described ecological genetics as still in a primitive stage because of the dominance of *Drosophila* studies (Wilson 1969).

Although ecological genetics dealt with adaptation as an ecological process, as suggested by Adams (1913), it was largely a product of geneticists and taxonomists. Ford's (1964) bibliography cited only four articles published in ecological journals. It was not until the 1950s that ecological genetics became more closely integrated with other aspects of ecology. A. D. Bradshaw (1952, 1972) began his studies of genetic ecotypes on mine tailings, initiating what Antonovics (1976) described as "the new ecological genetics." H. B. D. Kettlewell (1955) reported his famous studies of industrial melanism in Lepidoptera. C. McMillan (1959) studied the effect of plant ecotypes on grassland community organization on a gradient of habitat variation, and L. C. Birch (1960) studied the relation of genetics to population ecology. One difficulty faced by ecologists in dealing with ecological genetics, old or new, was fitting subspecific evolutionary categories, such as the ecotype, into an ecological framework or using species as ecological units. The traditional unit of study for ecologists was the species, and ecologists commonly assumed that species were the criteria by which communities were best defined or even that the species was a useful "indicator" of the environment. Some early plant ecologists avoided using species as their basic ecological unit by using growth form or life form of plants to describe an area. Raunkaier (1904) developed a widely used system of life forms and particularly used the statistics of life-form distribution as a basis for measuring "plant-climates" of an area. The use of these and other growth forms (e.g., evergreen) has been suggested to circumvent the problems posed by use of the taxonomic species as the unit of ecological description, but the species remains the unit of choice, and life history properties of species are currently pushed as a basis of theoretical ecology.

Ecological genetics dramatized genetic variability within the taxonomic species and the concomitant differences in the autecology of subspecific genotypes which were adapted to different environments. Turn-of-the-century taxonomists such as E. L. Greene (McIntosh 1983c) had often been accused of recognizing, as species, populations which differed only as a consequence of growing in different environments. Ecologists like H. C. Cowles believed that many named plant species would be eliminated by recognizing environmentally induced variants for what they were. Limnologists grappled with the problem of environmentally induced polymorphism in plankton. The problem of distinguishing genetically based variation from environmentally induced variation was exacerbated by the development of ecological genetics. Botanists generally recognized subspecific genotypes as "ecotypes," whereas zoologists did not adopt the ecotype concept. McMillan's efforts to incorporate the ecotype into ecology were not widely followed, and Curtis (1959) emphasized the difficulty of applying genotypic or ecotypic information in the field. Quinn (1978) reviewed the history of the plant ecotype and concluded that it was neither a good evolutionary nor a good ecological unit. Harper (1982) emphasized the problems of using the species as an ecological unit and the "failure of taxonomic categories to fit as ecological categories." Harper urged that explanations of distribution of species required detailed studies of autecology and genetics of species, and he properly described the distinguished contributions of A. S. Watt, throughout much of the history of plant ecology, as the model to follow. An alternative way to avoid the problem of variation of species is to minimize the interest in the biota and emphasize abiotic attributes, as urged by some systems ecologists. Harper, however, suggested that "only superficial generalities about ecosystems may be expected to emerge from systems studies of natural communities," and the problem persists. Clearly a species may include considerable genetic variation, and the combined problems of genetic variation and habitat pattern or grain are posing new difficulties only recently being faced by ecologists and evolutionary biologists.

Integrating field and theoretical aspects of ecology, ecological genetics, and genetics is a difficult problem. Some ecologists noted the division of ecology into two distinct categories, the functional and the evolutionary and argued that, in the absence of ecological theory, the only possible general theory was natural selection (Orians 1962). A continuing problem is the neglect of the ecological aspects of hybrid ecological genetics by some arbiters of population genetics and evolutionary theory. The effort in the 1960s to make ecology more genetical, which was hailed by Lewontin and Baker (1970), was not accompanied by effective efforts to make genetics more ecological. Ayala (1969) commented that important debates in genetics were largely deadlocked because of ecological complexities and that demographic realities were ignored. E. G. Leigh, Jr. (1970) wrote:

> As long as population geneticists refuse to visualize their populations in an ecological context, as long as they refuse to concern themselves with what makes one genotype more reproductive than another, they will have nothing meaningful to say about adaptation, and adaptation, after all, is what biology is all about.

According to another commentator, the extensive studies of ecological genetics omitted by Lewontin from his book *On the Genetic Basis of Evolutionary Change* "may discourage others from using the ecological methods that have proved to be the most successful in detecting natural selection" (Clarke 1974). Population geneticists did grasp the nettle by concerning themselves with environmental variation, spatial pattern, and demographic realities during the 1970s, but the satisfying prospect of a theory to incorporate life history and community phenomena has proven elusive. E. O. Wilson (1978), however, asserted optimistically that genetics and natural selection theory had "transformed ecology . . . by stark reduction." Much of the mathematical theory of population genetics is not, however, clearly applicable to population ecology, although Levin (1981) commented, "In recent years the mathematical models on which much of this theory is founded have become increasingly contaminated with the parameters of ecology." Peculiarly, the very criticisms which field ecologists have commonly directed at theoretical models of ecological genetics are described as "conclusions to be drawn from a theoretical model" (Lomnicki 1980). Lomnicki cautioned field ecologists not to look for the average individual or homogeneous conditions, and he commented, "Ecological theory is not a substitute for the knowledge of natural history." None of Lomnicki's counsel, derived from theory, comes as a surprise to nontheoretical ecologists long familiar with variation and heterogeneity and commonly abused for their attention to natural history. The problem of adaptation, which intrigued early ecologists, continued as a concern of evolutionary biologists (Williams 1966; Dobzhansky 1968). The concept of adaptation was continued in ecology, for example, in the adoption of the principle of optimum design to serve as a theoretical framework (Parkhurst and Loucks 1972). A new generation of evolutionary ecologists was again laying claim to natural selection: "The goal of ecology is to provide explanations for the occurrence of natural patterns as products of natural selection" (Cody 1974). However, interpretation of adaptation continues as a disputed topic in ecology and evolutionary biology (Gould and Lewontin 1979; Lewin 1982).

## Community theory

Apart from the linkage of ecology with natural selection and adaptation, the most significant general natural phenomenon recognized by early self-conscious ecologists and their predecessors was the concept of community – the "formation" of Drude and Clements or the "biocœnose" of Möbius and a myriad of other specifications. The most influential work of 19th-century plant ecology, Warming's (1895) *Plantesamfund,* addressed the question, "Why do these species unite into certain communities and why have they the physiognomy they possess?" Shelford (1913), writing of animal ecology, put it even more simply: "Ecology is the science of communities." The question *"Are* species united into communities with repeated attributes of composition and structure?" had not yet surfaced. Early community theory was largely developed by plant ecologists, notably Clements and Cowles, and explicated or amended by C. E. Moss, A. G. Tansley, and W. S.

Cooper. Clements's "dynamic ecology" was based on the plant formation and its presumed progressive development or succession to climax. It was recognized as the premier theory of plant ecology by his contemporaries and successors. Tansley (1935), although one of Clements's sharper critics, wrote, "Dr. Clements has given us a theory of vegetation which has formed an indispensable foundation for the most fruitful modern work." Robert Whittaker (1951, 1953) effectively criticized Clements's "climax theory," and Lewontin (1969a) commented on "Clements' theory of succession which is nothing if not an evolutionary theory of the community." In Whittaker's (1957) view, Clements's thought was influenced by an ideal deductive system exemplified by philosophy, mathematics, and physics. It represented a special case of the community-unit theory of vegetation which was almost universally accepted by ecologists (Whittaker 1957, 1962).

Clements's contemporary Cowles followed a different approach to community theory, according to Tobey (1981). Cowles (1901) developed what he called the "physiographic theory" of ecology, which related vegetation to physiography, as the "laws that govern changes in plant societies are mainly physiographic." Cowles (1909) reviewed the "wholesome influence of ecology" on physiology which, he said, had become a "mere" laboratory science prone to devising "bizarre" experiments on plants. He condemned vitalism as a hopeless theory because it "transcends the possibility of experimental test" and urged the mechanistic theory as "best as a working hypothesis." Cowles urged rigorous tests of the theory of succession, and he commented, "The importance of one's philosophy upon his research can scarcely be overestimated." His reasons were that philosophy dictated selection of problems and colored the results. He asserted, "It is not necessary that the working theory be true, indeed it is often better if it be most untrue." In Cowles's philosophy, "The fundamental test of a working theory is that it be the one which will stimulate the maximum of discriminative research." Cowles's thesis sounds advanced for the heyday of logical positivism and surprisingly modern in an era of Popperian philosophy, when the "fruitfulness" of a theory, as specified by Tansley, is pitted against falsification as a criterion of its worth (McMullin 1976).

Clements's organismic dynamic theory of communities was widely accepted by many plant ecologists and at least tacitly by animal ecologists until the 1950s. Orlando Park (1941), speaking for animal ecologists, wrote of the description and classification of community types by plant ecologists, "This necessary work has been largely accomplished." The major premises of Clements's climax were of the formation as an evolutionary unit evident in similarity of distribution of the dominant species and as a stable terminal stage toward which succession (seres) converged. Stability or equilibrium was in this era largely taken to mean persistence, with limited change, of species populations so that the overall formation retained its essential characteristics. This traditional belief was expressed more explicitly by Slobodkin (1955), who defined *equilibrium* as the total population size and relative number in each age class remaining constant. In recent years, diverse and sometimes irrelevant meanings of these terms have been injected into ecological discourse, and it is not safe to assume that authors using the terms mean the same thing (Connell and Sousa 1983). The premises of Clements's theory were questioned by contemporary ecologists such as A. G. Tansley, Forrest Shreve, W. S. Cooper, A. S. Watt, and, most familiarly, H. A. Gleason. All doubted the validity of much of Clements's theory of succession and climax. Cooper (1913) and Watt (1924) agreed that the climax was composed of a "mosaic" of areas of different stages of replacement following small-scale disturbance within the matrix of the species composition of the climax. This idea remained largely unnoticed in spite of Watt's exposition of his concept of gap phases (Watt 1947).

H. A. Gleason, in a series of three articles published over a span of two decades, formulated his "individualistic concept" of the community, later promoted to "individualistic hypothesis" (Gleason 1917, 1926, 1939; McIntosh 1975a, 1980a). The individualistic concept was based on Gleason's assertions that species had individualistic ecological characteristics and were assembled into local communities with a large stochastic component according to the vagaries of dispersal and the available environments. Gleason's ideas were ignored or even "pulverized" until they were dramatically reassessed in three separate articles in a single issue of *Ecological Monographs* in 1947. H. L. Mason, Stanley Cain, and Frank Egler all then endorsed Gleason's individualistic concept. Egler wrote that he "considered these all-but-forgotten papers as being of top importance in the entire development of American vegetational thought" (quoted in McIntosh 1967). In the 1950s an increasingly quantitative plant ecology tested the "association unit" theory and generally found it wanting, substituting continuum or gradient theory (Whittaker 1951; Greig-Smith 1957; McIntosh 1958b, 1967; Curtis 1959). It cannot be said, however, that such findings laid to rest the theory of a community of organisms as a closely integrated unit of interacting species, which had defined and repeated biotic composition and structure in areas of similar environment.

In the 1950s and 1960s, essentially contemporaneously with the effective contradiction of the plant community as having the attributes listed above, animal ecologists, primarily ornithologists, adopted the concept of the community as an entity composed of assemblages of species at equilibrium. These ideas were largely associated with the rise of theoretical ecology associated with Robert MacArthur (Simberloff 1974; Cody and Diamond 1975; Connell 1980; Wiens 1983, 1984). This theory of community derived largely from population theory, observations of patterns in natural populations, and the assumption that communities were organized as a consequence of competition among species to institute and enforce niche separation. Caswell (1982b) pointed out that "contemporary ideas of community structure arose from the earlier controversy among population theorists about density-dependent population regulation." Just as Nicholson (1933) long before had asserted that "competition" regulated "all" species populations, Diamond (1978) claimed that the idea that processes other than competition contribute to community patterns "strained one's credulity." Equilibrium theories of population and community flourished in the revolutionary era of theoretical ecology and were even said to develop "clear attributes of a Kuhnian paradigm" (Wiens 1983). If so, this is one of a "succession of paradigms in ecology" described by Simberloff (1980) in an era marked by "a confusion of paradigms" (Woodwell 1976) or "paradigms lost" (Woodwell 1978). The combination of population theory in the form of competitive exclusion, community theory (especially diversity and niche structure), evolutionary theory, and coevolution is a significant development. The crux of the dispute is that such theory presumes equilibrium conditions and sympatric evolution (Connell 1980; Caswell 1982a,b; Wiens 1983, 1984). Connell attacked the appeal of this theory to what he called "the ghost of competition past." Wiens (1983) provided an "iconoclastic view" of this theory of community reminiscent of Gleason's earlier attack on Clementsian climax theory. Strikingly, Wiens attacked the most explicit advocates of hypothetico-deductive approaches in ecology as lacking in scientific rigor and for failure to rigorously test hypotheses, thus illustrating the problem of the "ruling theory" described by T. C. Chamberlain nearly a century earlier.

A sensible piece of advice was recently offered to proponents of equilibrium theory as applied to communities: "We believe that, before one applies such theory to a natural population or community, one should first decide whether or not it is stable" (Connell and Sousa 1983). This has rarely been done, in part because of difficulties in defining stability and in part because of the difficulty of finding an appropriate measurement of stability. Wiens (1983) provided a list of six critical questions posed by the study of bird communities. The first questioned the merit of short-term studies unless the community was clearly in equilibrium. The second asked if observations of different observers using different methods are comparable, and Wiens answered, "probably not." Wiens responded to the urging of theoretical animal ecologists to adopt Popper's hypothetico-deductive approach by suggesting a philosophical blend of the formalist Popper and the nihilist Feyerabend (cf. May 1981a), if such a blend be possible. Wiens also raised the question, long debated by plant ecologists, "Are the bird communities that we have been studying real biological entities or artifacts that we have created for ease of study?" In fact, many of the problems Wiens identified as generating doubt about the knowledge of avian communities produce a déjà vu response in a plant community ecologist. Theories of community, approached from a holistic view in the sense of Clements's organism with no mathematical formulation, or a from a holistic view in the sense of Cody (1974, 1981), looking for patterns predicated on mathematical theories of populations, or a somewhat special holism described by Lane, Lauff, and Levins (1975), are still frustrating ecologists. The hopeful reductionist gleam in the eye of some theoretical population ecologists remains at best "a tiny element of a true understanding of the real world" (Christiansen and Fenchel 1977). At worst, it gets in the way of effective empirical studies.

## Ecological laws and principles

The commonly avowed functions of scientific theory are explaining or predicting observations, and if this is accomplished with simple, elegant equations, so much the better. A sufficiently bold and general theory will encompass many observations and consequently have a greater risk of falsification (McMullin 1976). Ecologists, like scientists generally, hoped to find order in the universe, and the tradition of balance of nature and economy of nature were predicated on such an order, divinely ordained or naturally engendered. Order is manifest in regularities or patterns, and classical traditions of science commonly involved identification of constants or laws. Usually *law* refers to observable events which are confirmed by observation. Hull (1974) asserted that a theory was described by philosophers of science as a deductively related set of laws but added that in biology the nature and relationship of theory and law are in dispute, and this is certainly true in ecology. One of the difficulties of ecologists has been to identify among the general untidyness, or "noise" as it has come to be called, of complex natural ecosystems the convenient regularity of structure or pattern which lends itself to explanation, prediction, or mathematization. Early ecologists sometimes seized on limited observations and described them as laws. The regularities, constants, or laws which were so convenient in the developing physical sciences, from the regular movements of heavenly bodies through Avogadro's number, valence, or the atomic table, have been difficult to identify in ecology. It is not surprising that some theoretical ecologists seized on the laws of thermodynamics in the search for ecological principles. Many ecologists have urged the merit of developing simple generalizations as a basis of ecological theory. Some have forgotten the second part of the biologist's aphorism, "Seek simplicity and distrust it," or ignored the old saw, "There are no straight lines in nature," in pursuit of linear models for ecology.

The earliest law commonly used in ecology was the "law of the minimum" or "Liebig's law," borrowed from the pre-Haeckelian agricultural chemist Justus Liebig. Liebig's law held that the growth of a plant or the rate of a process is limited by the availability or rate of the slowest factor, hence the minimum. The "law" went through a number of changes, gained new eponyms, and is still encountered in some textbooks. It may have favored the "single-factor" ecology which earned the derision of Egler (1951). Ecologists early recognized that some environmental factors were more influential than others, and they tended to concentrate on obvious ones such as water, temperature, or salient nutrients, particularly nitrogen. Later generations of ecologists latched onto pH, phosphorus, or energy, but the convenience of a nature controlled by single factors was not easily achieved.

Shelford (1913) introduced the "law of toleration" or "tolerance." This law added a maximum to Liebig's minimum, providing a range of a factor in which an organism could survive, grow, and reproduce and an intermediate area, or optimum, at which it grows and reproduces best. Many early and current physiological ecologists documented the familiar one-humped curve of distribution of physiological response and individual growth to environmental factors. It was left to Gause (1932) to assert that the curve of growth of a population could be formally described by a Gaussian curve. This general response became familiar among ecologists, and the strikingly distinct, or individualistic, distribution of overlapping and presumably Gaussian-shaped curves of species populations was represented for many taxa and habitats. In the 1950s these patterns of curves were taken as convincing evidence that the traditional community-unit theory of ecology must give way to the gradient or continuum concept of community (McIntosh 1958b, 1967; Curtis 1959; Whittaker 1967). Patterns of curves were a common product of the methods of ordination or gradient analysis which now pervade ecology, although their utility is disputed (Whittaker 1973). Such curves form the backbone of niche theory, which posits species as normal curves on a "response gradient" with assumptions about modes, standard deviations (i.e., niche width), and spacing (overlap) required by a doctrine of "limiting similarity" predicated on the basis of competition (Christiansen and Fenchel 1977).

Nineteenth-century biologists had looked for patterns of geographical distribution of organisms. C. Hart Merriam (1894) described a "fundamental law" that animal distribution was controlled by temperature, the northward extent limited by total quantity or sum of temperatures, the southern extent by the mean temperature of the hottest part of the year. A variant of this idea was "Hopkins's law" or the "bioclimatic law." This was similar to the "floral calendars" of the 18th and 19th centuries and recognized that biological events in the northern hemisphere went north with the spring. Hopkins's law stated that a biotic event lagged 4 days per degree of latitude northward, 5 degrees of longitude eastward, and 400 feet of altitude in spring and early summer (Hopkins 1920). Such general lore gave rise to the aspect of ecology known as phenology. One segment of the International Biological Program was intended to subject these ideas to rigorous tests but never really developed. A widespread premise among early ecologists was that distribution of populations and communities was largely controlled by factors of the physical environment, most easily measured singly. Livingston and Shreve (1921) wrote, "We can, in brief, put it down as a law of plant geography that the existence, limits and movements of plant communities are controlled by physical conditions." Much early autecological study involved measurement of environmental variables as instruments became available. One critic of this tendency commented that no ecologist was complete without a pH kit in his back pocket in an era when pH was the favorite and most easily measured factor. The danger of attributing a causal relation to coincidence of factor measurement and organism or community distribution, or later to formal correlation, was first ignored and later deplored as ecologists become more sophisticated.

Other ecologists recognized that the distribution of an organism was related to the distribution of other organisms. Early "dredgers" of marine bottoms and terrestrial plant ecologists noted that different species characterized adjacent zones. This recognition gave rise to a refinement sometimes called "Jordan's law" after the famous ichthyologist D. S. Jordan. It is not to be confused with Jordan's "rule" associated with number of vertebrae in fish related to temperature, also named after Jordan. "Jordan's Law" was stated by Cox (1980):

> As with zones and faunas, associations are often capable of subdivision; in fact such splitting may be carried logically to the point where but one species occupies each its own niche.

As early as 1913, there was a clear statement, attributed to Joseph Grinnell, of "niche," which was antecedent to the formalization of segregation of species known as, among a variety of eponyms, "Gause's law," the "Lotka-Volterra principle," or, more descriptively, the "competitive exclusion principle," which surfaced in the 1920s and 1930s (Grinnell 1917; Hardin 1960; McIntosh 1970; Vandermeer 1972; Cox 1980). This "law" or "principle" underlies much of traditional population theory and current theory of community. Following Hutchinson's (1957a) formalization of the multidimensional niche by simplifying Shelford's "law of tolerance" to a linear relation of organism response to environmental variables, competition became the cornerstone of a new theory of community structure. According to Vandermeer (1972), Hutchinson's reformulation of the traditional concept of niche as a hypervolume generated "perhaps the only specific principle or law of nature ever to be proposed in ecology." Vandermeer advanced Gause's principle or law to "Gause's axiom," an infrequent descriptor for an ecological phenomenon. The relationships among species in a community were later described by some theoretical ecologists as a product of competition and natural selection. Cody and Diamond (1975:5) wrote:

> It is natural selection, operating through competition, that makes the strategic decisions on how sets of species allocate their time and energy; the outcome of this process is the segregation of species along resource-utilization axes.

Clements (1905) wrote that insufficient work had been done to postulate definite "laws" but that a few "rules" were appropriate. Some of his headings and subheadings, however, identified "laws," and by 1916 he stated succession as a "universal law" that "all bare places give rise to new communities except those which present the most extreme conditions of water, temperature, light, or soil" (Clements 1916:33). Clements's "rules" or "laws" were basically old ecologist's tales, but like many such embodied a great deal of shrewd insight. Laws of succession proliferated in Cowles (1911) and Dansereau (1957), but few, if any, have been perpetuated in current ecology. Raunkaier (1918) proposed a "law of distribution of frequency." It held that if frequency numbers of a sample were grouped in five equal percentage classes, the resultant distribution followed a reverse J-shaped curve. This was because the frequencies decreased progressively from the lowest frequency class (0-20%) but rose again in the highest (80-100%) class. This law, which was largely an artifact of sample size, was perpetuated in textbooks and research papers until the 1960s (McIntosh 1962). The assurance of order in ecological phenomena is evident in Adams's (1913) *Guide to the Study of Animal Ecology,* which has chapters on the "laws of environmental change" and "laws" of orderly sequence of metabolism, growth, development, physiological conditions, and behavior. Few of the laws cited are to be encountered in current ecological references, not even a "universal law" of adjustment to strain (Bancroft 1911). A somewhat better fate was enjoyed by Lotka's (1925) "law of maximum energy," which was resurrected 30 years later by H. T. Odum and Pinkerton (1955) and built into an energetic concept of succession (E. P. Odum 1971). Vito Volterra provided three laws (Chapman 1931):

1. *Law of periodic cycles:* Fluctuations of two species populations are periodic and depend on the coefficients of increase and decrease and the initial conditions.
2. *Law of conservation of averages:* Populations remain stable unless the coefficients of the equations change.
3. *Law of disturbance of averages:* If an attempt is made to destroy two species in proportion to their numbers, the prey species increases and the predator diminishes.

Volterra's "laws" apply to the species of his theoretical model, but how well they apply to organisms was extensively debated in subsequent decades. Aldo Leopold, who according to a long-time associate never referred to the mathematical ecology that was engrossing so many of his contemporaries (R. McCabe 1983 pers. commun.), stated two laws of animal density relating their dispersion and interspersion (Leopold 1933).

Although the limitation of laws in early ecology was evident in their failure to persist as useful indications of order in ecological phenomena and suggested care in attributing the qualities of a law to ecological observations, new "laws" kept surfacing. Preston (1948) described the numbers of individuals of species as distributed according to a "log-normal law" and later (1962) as a "canonical" distribution. Along with other candidates to describe the relations of species and area, the log-normal was found wanting by Connor and McCoy (1979). Japanese ecologists produced a "law of constant final yield" and a "reciprocal yield law" relating biomass to density (Harper 1977c). Harper also cited as a general law that the number of cohabiting species is determined by the number of controlling factors, a version of the one-species–one-niche rule. Schoener (1972) commented, "The regular increase of species number with increasing area" is "one of community ecology's few general laws" and one of its "few precious regularities." Long-term naturalist lore held that the area most studied yields the most species and that the general ideas of increase in species with area or time of observation may be thought of as qualitative laws. It proved difficult, however, to transform such generalizations into the quantitative general laws familiar in the physical sciences, which gave rise to "physics envy" among ecologists. Ecologists persisted in their search for "realistic models of ecological communities" (Slobodkin 1961), "macroscopic variables that show consistent patterns in real communities" (Culver 1974), or examples of variables which are "constant and predictable at the level of community organization" (May 1976). May (1974b) hoped for the "perfect crystals" of ecology. Numerous ecologists converged on the size ratios of structures of competing organisms and the distribution of relative abundances of species, according to Robert MacArthur's famous "broken stick" model, as representative regularities. None of these suggested generalities rests securely among ecological laws or constants. Slobodkin suggested that food-chain efficiency had a maximum value of 15 percent, a prospect he subsequently demolished on empirical and theoretical grounds (Slobodkin 1972). As a consequence, Slobodkin warned of expecting global constants in ecology "in counter-distinction to most theories of physics." The search for ecological constants or laws has not been very satisfying to proponents of the new theoretical ecology any more than to the formulators of the old ecology. Richard Levins wrote, "It is now recognized that ecological systems are inherently complex" (Levins 1968b). This came as no surprise, for early ecologists were painfully aware of the inherent complexities of the phenomena they were attempting to define, analyze, explain, and predict.

A tendency of some ecologists is to extrapolate limited observations into law without careful specification of what *law* may mean or the domain in which it operates. Romesburg (1981) asserted that, although untested, Errington's threshold of security hypothesis was turned into a law. Roth (1981) wrote that G. E. Hutchinson's "tentative" ratio of difference necessary to allow two species to coexist had come to be recognized "as a biological constant." She offered the cautious advisory, "Before asserting that a biological law exists, one should establish that its empirical basis is statistically significant." The problem of what level of statistical significance is necessary to lend credibility to ecological generalizations is perennial (Simberloff and Boecklen 1981). Clearly one of the major difficulties of theoretical ecology is the dearth of regularities usually described as laws or constants, with little concern for statistical significance. Hence the tendency of some ecologists to seize enviously on the laws of thermodynamics and apply them to ecosystems. Apply they must, but they are hardly ecological laws. Van Valen and Pitelka (1974) stated flatly, "Unlike population genetics, ecology has no known regularities in its basic processes, the growth and regulation of populations." However, ecologists are ill advised to unduly envy population genetics, where regularities are achieved by ignoring most of the elements of ecology which are of concern to the process of natural selection, as ecologists have asserted from the earliest days of ecology. Pielou (1975) raised the question, "Are there any laws governing the composition and structure of many species communities? Maiorana (1978) stated unequivocally, if ill advisedly, that ecological constants "provide a firm base from which to investigate the nature of competitive interactions in natural communities." More pessimistic commentators said of ecology, "Its grand generalizations are hardly published before being embarrassed out of existence" (Patil and Rosenzweig 1979:preface). Such a comment may apply to some recent "grand generalizations" which should not have been published at all. Theorists, however, are a resilient lot, and the difficulty of identifying constants, laws, or rules has not inhibited them. If laws in the sense of universal generalizations are a necessary basis for theory, however, a satisfactory general or unifying theory of ecology will be difficult to achieve (Oster 1981). Okubo (1980), with a "glimmer of optimism," called for more time to reach the goal of "the establishment of laws and basic equations." He advanced, with undeniable logic, the proposition that if nothing is attempted, no results can be obtained. The problem for the ecologist is whether to adopt the attitude of hope that springs eternal. As Okubo said, "A mathematical treatment is indispensable if the dynamics of ecosystems are to be analyzed and predicted quantitatively" (Okubo 1980:3).

Ecologists of the early 20th century had found the search for generality frustrating. Cowles (1904) described ecology as "chaos," asserting that "ecologists are not agreed even as to general principles." His contemporary Ganong (1904) offered a start with five "cardinal principles of ecology," all concerned with adaptation. Ecologists began the search for unifying principles in response to early criticisms by ecologists like Ganong to the effect that ecology abounded with facts but lacked generalizations by which the facts could be organized. They followed in the footsteps of previous giants of science who had formulated aspects of 18th- and 19th-century science as general principles. Elton (1927) considered the animal community and surmised, "There is some important principle involved in the stability of the total number of species in an animal community." Elton's counterpart in America, Shelford (1932), provided basic principles for classification of communities, habitats, and terminology. Shelford's "first principle" was that terrestrial communities must involve "all the organisms of the earth's surface contained within an area." Gause (1936), similarly concerned with community, asked in an article entitled "The Principles of Biocœnology," "Do there exist any constant characters of constitution and of structure maintained by regulation?" His own answer was that "the solution of this problem can easily be reached with the aid of the analytical method." This brings to mind Dylan Thomas's lament, in *A Child's Christmas in Wales,* about easy solutions–"Oh, easy for Leonardo!" Allee and Park (1939) provided a summary list of "distinctly ecological principles" in an effort to help make ecological work more effective. This preliminary outline was fleshed out in the volume *Principles of Animal Ecology* (Allee et al. 1949). Unlike most ecologists before and since, these authors thought "a word is in order about principles," and proceeded to elucidate. Eschewing the intention of evaluating "laws," "concepts," and "principles," they discussed their ideas of how ecology proceeds. In their usage, principles "are simply those generalizations inductively derived from the data of ecology."

Such principles, they said, form the basis for deductive thinking and generation of hypotheses. This excellent advice was not always heeded in the search for more abstract and general but idealized theories. Allee et al. indexed some twenty-five principles. A traditional compendium of ecological principles consists of the several editions of E. P. Odum's textbook *Fundamentals of Ecology* (Odum 1953). Odum's third edition recorded 30-odd principles. In spite of these compilations, or perhaps because principles were difficult to identify, some later ecologists did not recognize them or came to doubt their existence. Margalef (1963) wrote, "Present day ecology is extremely poor in unifying and ordering principles." Mann (1969) commented that there was little sign of emerging general principles, in aquatic ecology at least. Other ecologists compiled new lists of ecological principles. K. E. F. Watt (1971) provided 15, which by 1973 had expanded to 38 (Watt 1973). Ecological principles not only became more numerous, but some were more specifically described as "grand principles," such as the principle of the Hutchinsonian niche (Mitchell and Williams 1979). Less frequently in ecology one encountered more formal statements such as the "postulate of the upper limit" (Hutchinson 1978). This postulate reasonably asserts that nothing can grow without limit, borrowing from Malthus and Darwin, but leaving a long way to go to demonstrate what sets the limit, which is what much of the discussion of ecology is all about. It is clear that ecologists are not unprincipled, but it is very difficult to find consensus among ecologists on what a principle is, or on specific principles. Part of this is semantic. Garrett Hardin (1960) followed the tangled web of eponyms such as Gause's law or the Lotka-Volterra principle applied to what he suggested was more descriptively called the competitive exclusion principle. Hardin noted that the principle of competitive exclusion was implicit in Darwinian theory and not properly credited to Lotka, Volterra, or Gause singly or even in triplicate. The competitive exclusion principle budded into at least two additional principles, the competitive displacement and coexistence principles, each of which spawned a substantial literature (DeBach 1966). Watt (1973) similarly turned it into two principles (McIntosh 1980a).

Principles may be introduced into ecology and then mutate. Haldane (1956) described the "Matthew-Kermack principle" as a trade-off whereby "increase in adaptation towards one factor is associated with a decrease in adaptation to another." This principle was subsequently described as the "principle of allocation," "trade-off principle," "Jackof-all-trades principle," or "principle of resource allocation," with attendant problems for catalogers and ecologists. One ecologist's principle may be another ecologist's poison. Odum (in press) cited an "emergent property principle" and advocated group selection as a mechanism for evolution of ecosystems. Both emergent properties and group selection are much disputed by many ecologists and make precarious principles. Mechanisms for arriving at principles are not agreed on. May (1973) commented that the systems approach "does not seem conducive to yielding general ecological principles nor does it claim to." Systems ecologists who regard the systems approach as a key to theoretical ecology, as the scientific method itself, and as a basis for management will dispute such an evaluation. It seems clear that principles come in a variety of guises, and a body of principles that would form the basis of deductive thought, as Allee et al. (1949) hoped, has not been developed in ecology, nor has much consensus been achieved. Levandowsky (1977) voiced a pessimistic view for ecology.

> It is unlikely there are general quantitative principles, comparable to Newton's laws, on which to base a general mathematical theory, and there seems little prospect of a physics of organisms.

There was, however, little room for pessimism in the several schools of ecology which brought a recrudescence of mathematical approaches to ecology in the post-World War II era.

### Theoretical mathematical ecology

Much of the rhetoric of the 1960s and 1970s referred to the "new" ecology exemplified by proponents of diverse theoretical approaches to ecology. The editors of a survey of worldwide ecology stated:

> This new ecology, while having its roots in the tangible plants, animals and microbes that constitute the biotic components of an ecosystem, has reached highly sophisticated levels of abstraction that would surely be baffling, if not overwhelming, to modern ecology's early and mid-twentieth century forebears. (Kormondy and McCormick 1981:xxiv)

It was indeed baffling *and* overwhelming to some ecologists living through the era of the "new" ecology and simply irritating to others. A metaphor favored by some "new" ecologists was "colonization." A chronology of the colonization was given by Patil and Rosenzweig (1979:preface), who had in mind theoretical population ecologists:

Spearheaded by G. E. Hutchinson, his students and others intrigued by the opportunities for a pioneer existence on the intellectual frontier, the colonization of ecology occupied at least the decade from 1955 to 1965.

A source of colonists was stated by Shugart, Klopatek, and Emanuel (1981), although they were thinking of systems ecologists: "Ecology has been colonized by scientists from methodologically rich disciplines." In either case, the metaphor, in ecological terms, implies occupation of a relatively barren area, an influx of new talent and skills, and it is explicit that the skill was mathematics, the "rich disciplines" being physics, chemistry, and engineering. Patil and Rosenzweig extended the metaphor to include niche theory by having the colonists feeding on an unused resource of accumulated ecological data. For some of the new generation of ecologists theoretical ecology and mathematical ecology occupied the identical domain.

The stress on "new" overlooked the extended history of mathematics in ecology from an earlier "colonization" and its impact on ecology. Theoretical ecology, in this restricted sense, began, as Leigh (1968) and May (1974a) asserted, in the 1920s. What is not entirely clear is whether the "new" mathematical theoretical ecology of the 1960s was a true pioneer colonizer or a "poor quality duplication" of the "Golden Age of theoretical ecology" associated with the earlier colonizers from "rich disciplines," among them Alfred Lotka, who was concerned with physics and physical chemistry, and Vito Volterra, a mathematician (Scudo 1982 pers. commun.). Lotka and Volterra focused on the "biological association" or community, according to Leigh, although subsequent efforts in population theory were largely limited to consideration of one or two species, which formed the bulwark of the early colonization by theoretical mathematical ecology. Theoretical mathematical ecology began in the 1920s as (1) a consequence of interest in economic problems of fisheries, fur trade, and pest control; and (2) an interest in developing an abstract theory modeled on physics and applicable to evolution and biology at large. Much of theoretical insect ecology, for example, stemmed from the interest of insect ecologists in pest populations (Andrewartha and Birch 1973). Theoretical population ecology was concerned with population dynamics. The intrinsically quantitative nature of populations and their dynamics and the studies of populations of fish, insects, and a few terrestrial vertebrates supplied a mass of empirical observations. During the 1920s and 1930s a number of biologists, ecologists, and nonbiologists explored ways of analyzing populations mathematically. Scudo (1971), Scudo and Ziegler (1978), and Kingsland (1981, 1982, 1983, 1985) provided the first detailed historical analyses of the development of this phase of mathematical ecology. Some ecologists, such as Chapman (1931), were assured that mathematical theory was "going to form a very firm part of the foundation for our future science." Ecologists, notably insect ecologists such as A. J. Nicholson, adopted theoretical mathematical ecology as a major part of population studies (Nicholson 1933). Others, like W. R. Thompson, although he was a pioneer user of mathematical approaches in host-parasite studies, became increasingly doubtful of the merit of mathematics in biology (Kingsland 1983). During the 1930s and 1940s, however, mathematical theory and experiments designed to test it continued, although Scudo and Ziegler said the Golden Age ended in 1940. If, indeed, the Golden Age ended in 1940, it ended with a rhetorical bang, not a whimper, although there is little indication that it was heard in either case. Haskell (1940) called for "mathematical systematization" of "environment," "organism," and "habitat." Haskell wrote that for ecology to become an "exact science . . . all its basic notions will have to be redefined in such ways as to be fairly functionally constant and amenable to progressive regulation." He deplored the extremely low state of ecological theory and its inability to predict. Although ecology had little predictive capacity, Haskell was at least prescient in urging ecologists to adopt the second law of thermodynamics, entropy, and $n$-dimensional geometry, preferably non-Euclidean – all of which appeared in force in ecology in the 1960s and 1970s.

The progress of theoretical mathematical ecology was not, however, linear or its success unquestioned. Thomas Park (1946), a notable experimental population ecologist, who had worked in the laboratory of Raymond Pearl, the major proponent of the logistic equation, wrote of the mathematical theory of populations:

> Whatever the merits of this attack it is fair to conclude at this time it has not been nearly as productive for population ecology as the statistical probability attack has been for population genetics.

G. E. Hutchinson and E. S. Deevey (1949) took a more positive view than Park of mathematical theory and wrote, "Perhaps the most important theoretical development in general ecology has been the application of the logistic by Volterra, Gause and Lotka to two species cases." Hutchinson (1947) showed effects of modifications of the classic logistic and competition equations. F. E. Smith (1952) reviewed the utility of deterministic population theory and its experimental testing and commented on the general failure of experiment to support the logistic equation. He suggested that the future of mathematical theory lay in stochastic theory and concluded, "Up to the present little of the experimental work is at all conclusive. Most of the ideas in this field should be regarded as hypotheses not theories." Slobodkin (1965) wrote, "The simple models of population growth, beloved of the mathematician and ideally amenable to grandiose theory formation, simply do not hold." Peculiarly, Oster (1981) claimed that "for a long time most ecologists took these equations quite seriously – as if there were hidden in them some great, but subtle truth about nature." In fact, ecologists like Park, Smith, and Slobodkin questioned the worth of those equations, and some doubted the easy assumptions about the application of mathematical theory in ecology. Krebs and Myers (1974) wrote that theories of population control did not apply to voles or lemmings, and Richmond et al. (1975) stated that the Lotka-Volterra model was inadequate to explain the dynamics of two species of *Drosophila*. Slobodkin (1975) provided a list of caveats to mathematicians entering ecology. They were little heeded. Contrary to Oster's understanding, Levandowsky (1977) wrote:

> Few ecologists are interested now in these misleading equations but mathematicians are always trying to foist them off on us – a classical case of the drunkard who loses his watch in the dark but looks for it under the lamppost because that's where the light is.

Kingsland (1982) noted the persistence of the logistic curve in population ecology and suggested that it was due to psychological or historical reasons more than to its much questioned applicability to population research. Kingsland attributed the significance attached to the logistic curve to a determined campaign by Raymond Pearl, who had resurrected it. The significance attached to its descendants, the two-species equations, by Volterra, Gause, and many subsequent ecologists was not shared by most ecologists. Some ecologists suggested that mathematical models had attracted interest in ecology on the basis of psychological and sociological focus rather than demonstrated utility in addressing ecological questions (Simberloff 1983). In fact, latter-day proponents of mathematical theoretical ecology in the 1950s deplored the lack of belief in the utility of this approach by most ecologists.

In spite of Scudo and Ziegler's view of the end of the Golden Age in

1940 and the doubts expressed by many ecologists of the success of mathematical population ecology, theoretical ecology flourished in the 1960s and 1970s. Some commentators attributed this resurgence to Robert MacArthur (Cody and Diamond 1975; Fretwell 1975; Hutchinson 1978). Clearly, G. E. Hutchinson spanned much of the period between the first "colonization" of ecology by mathematical theoreticians and the more recent one and was on the beach to welcome the new colonists. Hutchinson was influential in the careers of many of the ecologists, mathematical and otherwise, who were significant contributors to diverse aspects of ecology (Edmondson 1971; Kohn 1971). Undoubtedly, MacArthur gave theoretical ecology a new look and revived interest in animal community ecology. Krebs (1977) wrote that because of MacArthur's influence, "the study of communities and ecosystems was raised from the doldrums of ecological energetics to become an intellectually challenging branch of ecology." It is clearly too early to evaluate the contributions of MacArthur to theoretical ecology. It is apparent that he attracted many people to ecology and that his work precipitated a small flood of work which his admirers described as a revolution or new paradigm in ecology. MacArthur advanced ideas in a number of areas of key concern to ecology since its earliest days. Moreover, he advocated, and his work exemplified, a "new" theoretical approach to ecology commonly designated as the MacArthur "school." The crux of this approach was described as "powerful quantitative theories" coupled with "recognition of widespread patterns in nature" producing a "predictive science" of ecology (Cody and Diamond 1975). It is perhaps unfair to judge MacArthur's work against the inflated claims advanced in a memorial volume, but this somewhat evangelical tone concerning the MacArthur school of theoretical ecology was common in the 1970s and persists today, although somewhat chastened by ecological reality. MacArthur contributed ideas and mathematical models embodying those ideas in several aspects of ecology, especially species diversity, relative abundances of species, competition and species packing as components of niche theory and, borrowing from classical logistic notation, $r$ and $K$ selection theory. Transcending ecology, he formulated island biogeography theory with E. O. Wilson and developed ideas concerning species and area which also had repercussions in ecology. Island biogeography theory was variously described as a revolution, as nomothetic, or as fairyland (McIntosh 1980a). It had a difficult time living up to the promise seen by Christiansen and Fenchel (1977:128):

In addition to being a predictive theory for the faunas of isolates, it has generated new insight into the nature of biotic communities by integrating concepts of competitive interactions and fugitive equilibria into a general theory of communities. MacArthur's sadly truncated publishing career began in 1955 with a measure of community stability based on the number of links in the food web and a mathematical demonstration that these were related. This was followed by what Cody and Diamond (1975) described as the "classical" broken-stick model. These first essays by MacArthur into ecological theory were subsequently tested and falsified in good Popperian fashion. The broken-stick model was even vilified but proved difficult to destroy (McIntosh 1980a). Perhaps this illustrates H. C. Cowles's maxim that a theory need not be true, even better if it is false, as long as it stimulates work and is fruitful.

It is not entirely clear at this time if the new ecology associated with the MacArthur school was the beginning of a predictive theoretical ecology, as described by its proponents, or a "public relations web," as suggested by one of its critics (Mitchell 1974). Mathematical theory is plagued by the absence of dependable regularities, even in the classic deterministic mathematical models which can produce dynamic trajectories indistinguishable from a random process (May and Oster 1976). L. B. Slobodkin (1965) described experiments on predator-prey interaction in which the prey grew spines in the presence of the predator and commented, "No respectable mathematical theory can be expected to forecast anything like that nor should it be expected to." A major stimulus to the rejuvenated interest in animal community and ecological theory had been Hutchinson's (1957a) set theory formulation of the niche. This venerable concept of each organism having its unique "place" in the scheme of things included not only the physical place but the set of habitat conditions and relations with other organisms. Hutchinson's formulation led animal theorists into $n$-dimensional hyperspace, where Haskell (1940) and Lewontin (1969a) agreed they should be. Animal ecologists joined plant ecologists in the use of multivariate analysis and the concept of the multidimensional space or hypervolume and efforts to reduce it to comprehensible, manageable dimensions. Niche theory is an effort to establish quantitative relations among competing species, their distribution in respect to available resources, and the ways in which species may evolve and coexist. It was intensely pursued by ecologists concentrating on ecological and evolutionary relations among species, with mixed results described as both "useful" (Pianka 1980) and "a disappointment" (Brown 1981). Attempts to link diversity and stability by use of quantitative mathematical theory were also seen as disappointing (Goodman 1975).

A criterion of the new theoretical ecology was very self-conscious and formal attention to using mathematical models. May (1981a), however, recognized that "a lot of useful theory takes the form of verbal models," and traditional ecology was rife with verbal and graphic models. Clements's (1905) basic descriptive model of succession became many years later, although still verbal, the "facilitation" model in which the earlier plants prepare the site for occupation by later occupants (McIntosh 1980b). Hedgpeth (1977) described Möbius's biocenosis as the "first model in marine ecology . . . conceived as a self-contained box limited by a finite food resource." Early ecology books were full of graphic models of succession and trophic organization of communities (Clements 1905; Shelford 1913) showing chronological sequences of seres and nutritional sequences of organisms, respectively. Many such models coexisted with the first generation of mathematical models in the 1920s, although the coexistence may have been a form of displacement, as suggested by competitive exclusion and niche theory. However, the relatively manageable era of succession models, the trophic model of Raymond Lindeman, the mathematical models of one- or two-species populations of Lotka and Volterra, and the experimental population or community models of Gause, Chapman, Park, and Nicholson mushroomed in the 1960s and 1970s into what Schoener (1972) described as a "constipating accumulation of models." Kadlec (1971) provided a bibliography of ecological models very broadly construed. Jeffers (1972) was accused of stretching the term *mathematical model* "to embrace a variety of activities that are certainly not included by it" (Pielou 1972). Ecological models themselves became an object of study independent of organisms (May 1973; Smith 1975b).

Mathematical models were described as an integral part of theoretical ecology, and the IBP instituted the position of ecological modeler. Models were created for populations, aggregates of populations or communities, individual processes, and whole ecosystems. Fisheries models were developed for individual species populations, and the concept of maximum sustainable yield and models thereof were the basis of the fishing industry (Graham 1935; Beverton and Holt 1957; Gulland 1977). Some models achieved substantial success – for example, the JABOWA model of forest growth (Botkin, Janak, and Wallis 1972). Others, such as the ELM model of the Grassland Biome of the IBP, were widely discussed but never lived up to their advanced billing. Like many aspects of theoretical ecology, mathematical models were viewed variously. The modeling efforts of the several IBP biomes were reviewed (Patten 1975c), and Shugart (1976) saw the hope of the future in each. Rigler (1976), however, commented that they read "like an advertising brochure for a product that has not been invented." Watt (1975), an early proponent of mathematics in ecology, commented that in 40 years of model building the vast majority of ecological models did not describe the phenomena they purported to describe or had internal mathematical problems, or both. O'Neill (1976) argued that future ecosystem studies should nevertheless "infuse modeling into every facet of the research program." May (1974b), although he recognized the relative unfruitfulness of models in ecology, was similarly optimistic:

> But in the long run, once the "perfect crystals" of ecology are established it's likely that a future ecological engineering will draw upon the entire spectrum of theoretical models, from the very abstract to the very particular, just as the more conventional (and more mature) branches of science and engineering do today.

A widespread problem in the use of ecological models is the difficulty of identification of "perfect crystals" at population and community levels. Another concern about use of ecological models is the "validation problem" (Caswell 1976). Caswell was critical of the validation of models as an outmoded, verificationist approach to science in contrast to a falsificationist approach as advocated by Popper. Schaffer and Leigh (1976) considered mathematical models largely developed by animal ecologists inappropriate for plants. Pielou (1981) took stock of ecological models and questioned the utility of most.

The expansion of theoretical ecology following World War II produced a large body of theory superimposed on, but hardly integrated with, prewar ecological theory. The need to bring order to this growth and to increase communication among various subgroups of ecologists is manifest in a number of recent efforts to sort out the several approaches to ecology. The Institute of Ecology attempted to bridge the deepest chasm and convened a workshop on "Ecological Theory and Ecosystem Models" (Levin 1976). Levin commented, "It would be fruitless to differentiate the many subgroups within ecology" and stated that the diversity among the participants raised "nearly insuperable obstacles." Although Levin sought unity, the workshop effectively demonstrated the split between theoretical population ecologists and systems ecologists and the barriers to communication between them. The Division of Ecology of the American Society of Zoologists organized a symposium on "Theoretical Ecology" in 1980 which brought together a range of theoretical population and community ecologists, with one systems ecologist included. The editor of the proceedings wrote that empirical ecologists believed theoretical ecology was not coping with the real complexity of nature, theoretical ecologists believed that emphasis on complexity impeded progress, and there was a "deep gap" in communication between them (Gordon 1981). In the same year, the Ecological Research Committee of the Swedish Natural Science Research Council arranged for a conference on "Theories in Population and Community Ecology" (Brinck 1980). A central concern of this conference was theoretical ecology related to applied concerns about the environment. The contributions to these several publications range the length and breadth of current theoretical ecology. Perhaps the principal problem to be faced by theoretical ecologists is the requirement that ecology develop a unified ecology (MacFadyen 1975) or a predictive ecology (Peters 1980). Ecology has typically been described as immature, with the implication that there was a mature mold which it should fit. Failing to do so, ecology was damned to second-class citizenship in the scientific polity. In the recent symposia on theoretical ecology some authors recognized classes of theory, which complicates things for ecologists. Oster (1981) described general theory and special theory, and Grant and Price (1981) recognized pure theory and operational theory. General theory and pure theory seem to be theory for theory's sake, without direct association with actual data or real-world situations. Special or operational theory is directed at a particular problem or experiment. The implication in either case is that ecology is doomed to immaturity and that general theory may well be pursued without reference to ordinary ecological concerns. May (1981a), a leading proponent of mathematical theory in ecology, arrived at a more eclectic view of theoretical ecology than in his earlier publications on the subject. He eschewed unduly simple formulations of the way to do science, whether it be by the H-D model or an ideal of mathematical prediction. May suggested, as a model, Charles Darwin's more catch-as-catch-can style as a model of scientific inquiry. Since Darwin's model of scientific inquiry has provided material for what has been called the "Darwin industry" and occupies a legion of philosophers and historians attempting to explain it, this seems like excellent advice for ecologists.

The prospect for anything like a general or pure theory of ecology seems remote. Perusal of the several efforts to examine theoretical ecology suggested broad conceptual and methodological gaps. Connell (1980), for example, wrote that origin of species by coevolution seems unlikely. Patten (1981) described coevolution as already understood in terms of group selection, and, he said, evolution of whole systems by coevolution is closing the gap between ecosystem and evolutionary ecology. Brown (1981) took a rather gloomy view of the contributions to community ecology of ecological theory based on populations. He examined the dichotomy between the new ecosystem ecology and the new theoretical population ecology, tracing each to its traditional sources. He assessed the failure of theoretical population ecology to deliver the predictive quantitative theory some ecologists and "colonizers" of ecology had promised. He particularly noted the failure of population ecologists to follow G. E. Hutchinson's emphasis on energetics. Brown does not comment on population ecologists such as L. B. Slobodkin who pursued energy transfers between species experimentally and makes no mention of the extended literature on energetics to be found in the literature of ecosystem ecology. In fact, he urges a beginning which has been under way for some decades.

Perhaps the most interesting aspect of recent commentary on ecological theory is the lack of the ebullience of the 1960s. Stearns (1980) questioned if life history "tactics" exist, contrary to earlier confident assertions about such tactics. Harper (1980) reviewed six ecological theories to illustrate the controversy and suggested that classic Lotka-Volterra theory and its derivatives are unsuitable for plants and many colonial animals. Lomnicki (1980) made suggestions to ecologists that are drawn from theoretical models which tell the ecologist what he has long known. Jackson (1981) cautioned against the "arrogance of the present." Werner and Mittelbach (1981) urged the interplay of theory and experiment, and Grant and Price (1981) suggested the need to avoid the weakness of single theory testing. Brown (1981) described competition theory as "a disappointment" and detected widespread pessimism among community ecologists. He pointed to the excitement of the last two decades but noted that the answers have eluded an entire generation of bright, dedicated, and ambitious ecologists. He summarized his analysis with a familiar refrain:

Perhaps the lack of immediate success should not be surprising. Ecological communities are perhaps the most complex of biological structures. Who ever thought it would be easy to find out why there are so many species?

Most recently Paine (1981) in his address as past president of the Ecological Society of America spoke on "Truth in Ecology." He addressed the problem of uncertainty in ecological predictions and argued that natural communities are constantly changing and accurate prediction is not to be achieved. He stated that, rather than assuming ecology is a failure if it does not follow the model of the physical sciences, it should be compared quite favorably with meteorology or economics, which have achieved notable success although their predictive capabilities may be questioned. Considering the expenditures on these and the amount of resources available to them for data gathering and analysis as compared to ecology, ecological capacity for prediction does not compare unfavorably.

The complexity of natural systems had been recognized since the early days of ecology, and after nearly a century of self-conscious ecological work they still appear dauntingly complex and unpredictable in the large and not readily subject to a reductionist approach. Ecology is frequently derogated as being "immature" or "nascent" because it has not approached the idealized concept of mathematization, axiomatization, or methodology that some philosophers have suggested a science should possess. Ecology is commonly compared unfavorably with the physical sciences which have more formal theoretical structure based on properties of matter with well-established constants, laws, and regularities which allow for "general" or "pure" theory and predictability within the domains those sciences claim. Ecology is also sometimes contrasted with the engineering sciences in failing to provide sufficiently precise guidance and prediction for management of natural and seminatural ecosystems. Such criticisms seem unwarranted. Engineers provide excellent guidance for construction of mechanical devices and even the operation of sewage plants, but clearly they do not resolve the problems of natural ecosystems, on which engineers have major impact but about which they provide little prediction or management.

The view of philosophy of science from which critics of ecology derive their assessment of its failings has not been effectively extended to biology (Hull 1974; Mayr 1982; Niven 1982). Some ecologists have questioned whether an ideal concept of how to do science expressed by universal covering laws or global mathematical models is appropriate as a measure to judge the maturity of ecology. It may be simply that ecology has not as yet had its Galileo or Newton to reduce its more intractable problems to a general theory to explain and predict a broad range of ecological phenomena. It may also be that the classic and continued success of physical science was achieved in a limited domain of natural phenomena and is not readily extended to other types of natural phenomena such as earthquakes, weather, or ecological systems. Physicists, mathematicians, and ecologists borrowing from them have consistently attempted to reframe ecology in terms of thermodynamics, dissipative systems, information, or other bodies of knowledge, which work extremely well in appropriate contexts. It may be that ecology is not simply an immature form of physics or biochemistry and that ecologists will have to create a new type of theoretical framework to match the complexity and heterogeneity of ecological phenomena. Ecologists have advanced such ideas, not as counsels of despair or admission of failure, but as a statement of the needs of ecological science. Slobodkin (1965) denied the analogy to physics and wrote, "The simple models of population growth, beloved of the mathematician and ideally amenable to grandiose theory formation, simply do not hold." Slobodkin suggested as alternatives (1) relatively inelegant mathematics, (2) new types of mathematics, (3) radically new insights identifying new variables. According to Slobodkin:

> The normal criteria of scientific quality which we use as biologists are not the same as those of the physicist and mathematician. . . . Empirical sciences must develop their own standard of quality and cannot take refuge from the necessity of thought in the shadow of Newton or Euclid. (Slobodkin 1965)

Whittaker and Levin (1977) suggested that the desire of ecologists for a general theory of ecology may be frustrated by absence of a master plan and the diversity and complexity of ecological relations. Hutchinson (1975), the acknowledged fountain of much theoretical ecology, attempted to redress an imbalance in ecology.

> Many ecologists of the present generation have great ability to handle the mathematical basis of the subject. Modern biological education may let us down as ecologists if it does not insist, and it still shows too few signs of insistence, that a wide and quite deep understanding of organisms, past and present, is as basic a requirement as anything else in ecological education.

Oster (1981) wrote that "inflated hopes" of "understanding ecology like physicists understand physics" should have been approached with "more modest" claims by theorists. Oster noted a turn from the "seduction" of "General Theory" and a trend back to "Special Theory" in connection with particular experiments. He contributed to the trend to "more modest" claims of theorists in ecological research: "Theory, providing you are not too dogmatic, can actually facilitate the process." Levin (1981) took a significantly different view of the theorist's role. For the theorist, he said, the theory is a systematic statement of principles and methods, and it is "this perception of theory which guides him rather than that of an hypothesis requiring testing." According to Levin, theory development is "closely tied to" but "separate and independent in its objectives and perspective from . . . field observation and experimentation." Falsifiability as a criterion of theory is "based on a subordinate and derivative definition of theory." The problem for the practising ecologist is, as May stated, "Ecological theory comes in many forms." In addition, it is not always clearly stated. Margalef's (1968) *Perspectives in Ecological Theory* was described as leaving "a feeling that sometimes the introspective conviction becomes more poetic than scientific" (Slobodkin 1969). E. O. Wilson (1969) wrote that reading Richard Levin's (1968a) exposition of theory of niche and fitness sets gives "one . . . the feeling that he is receiving secrets of the universe from a space visitor anxious to be on his way." Coupling the population explosion of theorists with multitudinous and often unclear or contradictory versions of theory, "general" or otherwise, has confused both empirical and theoretical ecologists.

There is currently a healthy retrenchment in ecological circles from extravagant claims and a more realistic view by theorists about the phenomena about which they are proposing theories. There is also a desirable skepticism among field and experimental ecologists about the latest form of model or mathematics thrust upon them. Still to be achieved is better understanding, if not sympathy, between the proponents of "theoretical ecology" and "systems theory." How, or if, that will be achieved is beyond the scope of this chapter and its author.

# 8

## Ecology and environment

All definitions of ecology agree that it has to do with the interrelationships of organisms and environment. The organism of greatest concern is *Homo sapiens*. Glacken (1967) commented that every thinker from the 5th century B.C. to the end of the 18th century A.D. had something to say about the earthly environment and humans' relation to it. There has been no letup in the 19th and 20th centuries. Indeed, concern with the environment, or broadly speaking nature, became central to human concerns (Ekirch 1963; Nash 1967; Passmore 1974; Sheail 1976). Ekirch (1963:1) wrote, "Man and nature is the basic fundamental fact of history." Although the concept of nature has a long history and many diverse interpretations (Hepburn 1967; Kormondy 1974, 1978; Hausman 1975), the antithesis implied in Ekirch's phrase is characteristic of most traditional Western environmental thought. Nature is commonly thought of as that part of the physical world other than humanity and its constructions, and *natural* commonly implies phenomena taking place without human involvement. Some, like Kormondy, question the distinction but retain it as useful. Passmore wished he could avoid the word *nature,* describing it as "ambiguous" but also "indispensable." In familiar usage, nature is "man's" environment and clearly has shaped "his" biological and cultural history. Stilgoe (1982) contrasted the *landscape* as the environment created by humans with wilderness as a threatening, evil area beyond human control, a contrast to the romantic view of wilderness. Although ecologists have sometimes been stereotyped as seeking to deal only with nature in a pristine or virgin condition, in "a state of nature," unsullied by human effects (Egler 1964; Welch 1972), they have since the earliest days of ecology wrestled with problems of the relationship of humans to, and their effects on, their environment. Fraser Darling (1967) recognized a persistent difficulty of ecology when he wrote:

> Ecology, as the science of the organism in relation to its environment and of the relations between communities of like or different kinds, was a bigger idea than the initiators grasped.

The real import of Darling's observation was not fully apparent to ecologists until the 1960s, when other professions, the general public, and even political leaders became aware of what was commonly called the environmental crisis. *Ecology* became a popular catchword (Nelkin 1976). Ecology and its approaches to organisms, including humans, and environment was, in the 20th century, a late arrival among various groups which had views on humans and their environment. Passmore (1974) reviewed the cultural traditions of East and West and, in each, the several expressions of different religious faiths. The relationship of humanity to nature characteristic of Eastern religions (and the religions of American Indians) as a harmonious integration with nature is seen by some modern ecologists and many nonecologists as a more desirable and a more "ecological" view. The ecologist may even be described as "Zen master" (Barash 1973). Western Christianity was described as having a very different concept of the relation of humankind and nature. Aldo Leopold (1949:viii) wrote succinctly, "Conservation is getting nowhere because of our Abrahamic concept of land." A historian of science and technology, Lynn White (1967), placed the blame for the ecologic crisis on Christian attitudes toward nature and received the Mercer Award of the Ecological Society of America for his article. The fault was ascribed to the widespread application of passages of Genesis giving humanity dominion over the earth and its other inhabitants and the right to subdue and use these to serve human ends. The ecologist W. P. Cottam (1947), in the context of a conflict over excessive grazing, had found it useful to interpret another Old Testament source as offering a different interpretation of divine guidance. He quoted Leviticus (25:23): "The land is mine; for ye are strangers and sojourners with me." Passmore recognized these divergent interpretations of the Old Testament but agreed with White that the one which apparently justified arrogant and despotic action by humans in their maltreatment of nature was predominant in Western culture.

Apart from folk traditions, myths, and theological and philosophical interpretations of the relations of humanity to nature, myriads of writers and artists had their say in the 18th and 19th centuries. Idealizations of nature wild and nature tamed, or how it ought to be, are prominent in literature and art. The myth of a past or a reestablished Eden was widespread (Sanford 1961). British writers such as William Wordsworth and the other Lake poets stimulated and shared the romantic view of nature of the American favorites William Cullen Bryant and Walt Whitman. Wordsworth wrote in *The Tables Turned:* "Come forth into the light of things, Let nature be your teacher." Bryant echoed in *Thanatopsis:* "To him who in the love of Nature holds communion with her visible forms, she speaks a various language." Whitman followed the Bible and anticipated Aldo Leopold's (1949) "Odyssey of an Atom" in *Leaves of Grass:* "I bequeathe myself to the dirt to grow from the grass I love; If you want me again, look for me under your boot-soles."

Nineteenth-century landscape painting shared with its literature links with nature, aesthetics, and morality. J. M. W. Turner was described as the Byron of painting in his interpretation of nature (Cheney 1946). Thomas Cole and others of the Hudson River School painted the romantic images of nature described verbally by Bryant (Sanford 1957).

Writers, artists, clerics, and political figures shared the Arcadian ideal of nature and the "agrarian dream" of the 18th and 19th centuries, even as the conflicts with the hard realities of nature and with human technological progress emerged (Marsh 1864; Ekirch 1963; Worster 1977). The transition from theological, philosophical, aesthetic, romantic, and transcendental commentaries on nature and environment to an ecological outlook is, as the course of this volume shows, not simple, linear, or even unidirectional. Gilbert White's (1789) *Natural History and Antiquities of Selborne* is perhaps the distillation of a reverential yet tentatively scientific view of nature which represents the best of the great British tradition of natural history, which is sometimes despised as "birdwatching" by past and current critics of ecology, who forget that some things are only learned that way. White's influence is evident in the 90 editions of his book before 1901 and in the pilgrimages to Selborne of the American nature writer John Burroughs, nearly a century after White's death, and of Edwin Way Teale, another naturalist-author, nearly a century after Burroughs. Ralph Waldo Emerson said in his lecture "The Uses of Natural History" that nature could be approached through science and that it offered lessons for humans (Ekirch 1963). Henry David Thoreau is the classic example of the writer as observer, and also as measurer and recorder of nature, learning from it yet split between poetry and science. He was among those who came to deplore the impact of commerce on nature and on human society. His famous dictum "Simplify, simplify" and the social vision it suggests are evident in the recent appeal to ecology as a guide to a simpler way of life and in such works as E. F. Schumacher's (1973) *Small Is Beautiful.*

Many scientists, notably geologists such as Hutton, Lyell, T. C. Chamberlain, and V. S. Shaler and geographers (professional or not) such as Humboldt, A. P. DeCandolle, and G. P. Marsh, made salient comments about the environment and humans. A most significant turning point in the view of the natural world in the 19th century was the work of the American diplomat turned geographer George Perkins Marsh (Marsh 1864; Thomas 1956; Lowenthal 1958; Ekirch 1963). Marsh's thesis was in sharp contrast to the familiar concerns of how nature affected people, their crops, animals, or health. He argued that human actions had a profound, reciprocal, and commonly destructive effect upon the environment. Marsh recognized that transformation of natural productivity was necessary, but he said that the appropriate measure was being exceeded in the destructive propensity of developing human cultures. Marsh advanced the basic thesis of most modern conservationists, environmentalists, and ecologists: Humans depend on soil, water, plants, and animals. In using them to support human life, humans may destroy the fabric of nature on which they depend. The lesson was that humans must learn to understand their environment and must maintain and where necessary restore its productive capacity. Marsh's was the first real synthesis of human effects on the earth and was a transition between the romantic or transcendental view of nature and the conservation movement and ecology of the turn of the century.

## Ecology and the conservation movement

The last third of the nineteenth century, following the Civil War in the United States, brought forth many of the significant figures and institutions which fortified the tradition of interest in nature and laid the groundwork for the conservation movement. The young naturalist John Muir was stimulated by the efforts of Increase A. Lapham, a pioneer naturalist and conservationist, to save the trees of Wisconsin, and he studied carefully Marsh's *Man and Nature* (1864). The American West was, in the 1870s and 1880s, a Mecca for Muir and many others concerned with nature and the presumably limitless resources of the barely explored lands. John Wesley Powell forsook the limited scope offered by Illinois in order, in his view, to finish the exploration of the West, and in the process he discovered the Grand Canyon. The concern for land and water resources was evident in the establishment in 1870 of the American Fisheries Society and in 1872 of the United States Fish Commission and the designation of Yellowstone as the first national park. The American Forestry Association was formed in 1875, and in 1886 B. F. Fernow, a Prussian-trained forester, was named head of a new Division of Forestry of the United States government. In 1876 G. B. Grinnell founded the Audubon Society. In 1885 the Ornithologist's Union was formed, New York State established as "forever wild" its Adirondack Forest Preserve, and the United States government established a Division of Economic Ornithology and Mammalogy in the Department of Agriculture under the direction of C. H. Merriam. This became the Bureau of Biological Survey in 1940 and was transferred to the Department of Interior as the Fish and Wildlife Service, continuing and complicating the inchoate response of government to the environmental problems then being discerned. In 1892 the Sierra Club was founded by John Muir, just in time to help defeat the first of many attacks on Yosemite National Park by commercial interests. In this same interval several states had established natural history surveys, and local natural history societies flourished, particularly in Britain.

Concern about encroachment of development on the countryside was widespread in Britain (Sheail 1976, 1981). In 1860 the Commons, Open Spaces, and Footpaths Preservation Society was formed to protect open space and access to it. In 1866 a Board of Conservators was established for fisheries. In 1878 an act was passed by Parliament to protect Epping Forest, which had been preserved from exploitation by public protest. In 1882 the Ancient Monuments Act was passed to preserve specific prehistoric sites such as Avebury and Stonehenge. Far in advance of the United States, the Society for Checking the Abuses of Public Advertising was formed in 1883. In 1894 the National Trust for the Preservation of Places of Historic Interest and Natural Beauty was formed to preserve lands and buildings. Subsequently these sites were declared inalienable, only to be disposed of by act of Parliament. In 1898 a Royal Commission on Stream Pollution was formed. In both Britain and America, public concern for natural beauty was evident in interest in parks and planning well before 1900. Frederick Law Olmsted had instituted a new era of urban planning and park development in America. In Britain, Patrick Geddes followed a long tradition of planning of gardens and parks in applying his botanical training to town planning (Stalley 1972). Geddes deplored the restriction of botany to the taxonomic herbarium and transformed it into "ecology at its best" (Sears 1956). Tansley (1905) noted Geddes's influence on an ecological study of the Scottish Highlands, and Sears recognized his influence on later geographers like Dudley Stamp, planners such as Lewis Mumford, and the ecologist C. C. Adams.

The 1890s were, according to the historian Henry Steele Commager (1950), "a watershed" in many aspects of American history. It is a nice coincidence that at Madison, Wisconsin, in 1893, the Botanical Congress selected the term *ecology* for the newly emerging science and, in the same location and year, Frederick Jackson Turner read his famous paper on the closing of the American frontier. The widespread concern for the environment and natural resources was evident in the rise of the conservation movement and its impact on the political scene. The notable figure of Gifford Pinchot (like Fernow, trained in forestry in Prussia) arrived on the Washington scene in 1898 as head of the Forestry Division of the Department of Agriculture, and fortuitously, Theodore Roosevelt, an avid hunter, fisherman, outdoorsman, and nature buff, was elected president in 1901. It was a remarkable era that brought together in the wilderness, in apparent amity, nature lovers and writers like John Burroughs, nature lovers and writers with a more scientific bent like John Muir, scientifically trained and politically sensitive men like Pinchot, inventors like Thomas Edison, industrial magnates such as Henry Ford and E. H. Harriman, and President Theodore Roosevelt, sometimes in the same camp. *Camp* has to be read literally in this case, for the conservation movement was very diverse, and figuratively its adherents were often in very different camps. Ekirch (1963) divided turn-of-the-century conservationists into those who advocated scientific management of natural resources and lovers of nature who wanted nature to remain as unspoiled as possible. This is perhaps too facile a dichotomy, giving rise to the sexist image of little old ladies in tennis shoes holding up progress. L. M. Wolfe (1947), in her biography of John Muir, recounted a confrontation between Muir and Pinchot. Muir read a newspaper account quoting Pinchot as stating that sheep grazing in forest reserves did no harm. It so happened that Pinchot was attending a meeting in the same hotel. Muir accosted him in the presence of a group of newspapermen and asked Pinchot if the newspaper quoted him correctly, which it had. Muir then accused Pinchot of contradicting a statement made to Muir the previous summer that sheep did a great deal of harm. Muir angrily declared, "I don't want anything more to do with you." Wolfe saw the rift as between those, like Pinchot, who advocated a utilitarian-commercial conservation and those, like Muir, who advocated an aesthetic-utilitarian conservation. Muir was, of course, a farmer as well as a wanderer in the mountains. The dispute about the proper use of the earth continued from Muir and Pinchot to later conservationists and ecologists – and politicians. It was evident in the furor over Secretary of the Interior James Watt in the Reagan administration, but President Reagan is no Theodore Roosevelt. The belief of many turn-of-the-century conservationists and ecologists was clearly voiced by the geologist N. S. Shaler (1910:1) in his book *Man and the Earth:*

> They will date the end of barbarism from the time when the generations began to feel that they rightfully had no more than a life estate in this sphere, with no right to squander the inheritance of their kind.

In addition to the ethical concerns about the relation of humanity to the earth, there were problems of how to deal with a nature largely, as Marsh and Shaler showed, under the influence of human technology and its increasingly destructive potential. Carl Schurz, secretary of the interior under President Hayes, made this clear in an address to the Forestry Association in 1889 (Commager 1967:89):

> The laws of nature are the same everywhere. Whoever violates them must always pay the penalty. No country ever so great and rich, no country ever so powerful, inventive and enterprising can violate them with impunity.

Schurz touched on the key distinction between many conservationists, environmentalists, and ecologists who argued that human activity is in fact limited by nature and many social scientists (notably economists), industralists, and politicians who argued that humanity is sufficiently inventive and enterprising that it need not be limited by ecological or environmental restrictions. Little worth is attached by the latter to the strictures of conservationists and ecologists such as Aldo Leopold (1934), who wrote, "The only reality is an intelligent respect for, and adjustment to, the inherent tendency to produce life."

The problem of ecology, as it emerged at the turn of the century into an existing maelstrom of conflicts about the conservation of natural resources, was to meld the knowledge of individual organisms and of the way they function in the aggregate by combining natural history insights with newer scientific approaches to the functioning of populations and communities in relation to their environment. Much of the widespread interest in the environment in the 19th century was a mixture of romantic and aesthetic idealism about nature. Such ideas were often held by persons unfamiliar with the hardships of pastoral or frontier life and with conflicting economic or exploitive interests in the natural resources then being surveyed with little aesthetic concern. The image of nature as a cornucopia everflowing for the benefit of human society was hit hard by the recognition in the last quarter of the 19th century that the frontier was closed, fisheries were being depleted, prairie agriculture was impeded by weeds and drought, forests overexploited, soils becoming less productive, and farms abandoned, destroying the agrarian dream. The worst fruits of urbanization and industralization were not yet realized, although urban decay and encroachment on rural areas were matters of concern. Scientific knowledge to address these problems was limited.

Many early self-conscious ecologists were explicitly aware of the human and economic concerns of ecology in the sense of applied ecology. S. A. Forbes (1896) said ecology is to the economic entomologist what physiology is to the physician. Human interference with nature gives rise to reactions corresponding to disease. Hence, the problem was to use the processes of nature to restore the environment to a healthful state, not necessarily to a putative state of nature. Arthur (1895) and Spalding (1903) agreed that agriculture and horticulture are practical applications of ecology and expected that ecology would occupy a prominent place in the curricula of these disciplines. The tradition of plant ecology inspired by C. E. Bessey at the University of Nebraska was initiated as a response to the technological needs of grassland agriculture, weed control, drought, and grazing pressures (Tobey 1981). F. E. Clements and J. E. Weaver were, during their long careers, deeply involved in practical matters of grazing, land use, soil erosion, and shelter belt planting. This was not unexpected, for Pound (1896) noted in a review of a book by Oscar Drude, an acknowledged source of the Nebraska school, that he included plants of cultivated places and weeds of waste places. An unsigned review ("A new book . . ." 1905) of Clements's *Research Methods in Ecology* commented cryptically, if not ironically, "It analyzes critically the problems which confront the practical ecologist (theoretical ecologists seem to have no such difficulties)." Ecologists were often practical, or practical biologists became ecologists. H. L. Shantz (1911) studied natural vegetation as an indicator of the usefulness of land for crops. The New Zealand ecologist Leonard Cockayne (1918) wrote, "Agriculture is neither more nor less than applied plant and animal ecology." Barrington Moore (1920), the first editor of *Ecology,* agreed, although he excepted breeding. Clements (1920) continued Shantz's work on plant indicators, and he and his associate J. E. Weaver studied plant roots, including those of crop plants (Weaver, Jean, and Crist 1922). Although some early ecologists may have measured their observations against a putative pristine balance of nature, most were aware of the significance of ecology in respect to human activity. British ecologists certainly had few illusions about pristine states in a landscape abounding with standing stones, flint quarries, and reminders of Roman, Arthurian, Saxon, and Norman life. Moss, Rankin, and Tansley (1909) recognized little if any virgin forest in Britain, and Clements (1912), commenting on the International Phytogeographical Excursion in the British Isles, contrasted the disturbed forests of Britain with the virgin forests of North America. Tansley (1913–14), however, in his comments on the famous excursion in North America two years later, noted that Warren's Woods in Michigan was one of the few remnants of the virgin deciduous forest remaining in the whole of the eastern United States. By 1913, Clements's assertions about virgin forest were largely based on his experience in the Rocky Mountains, for most of the United States east of the Mississippi was grossly modified by human action, and the West was going fast.

The change in the relation of humans to nature becoming apparent to many in the late 19th century was evident in the continuing rhetoric of conservationists and ecologists in the 20th century. The 20th century was designated the "Ecological Century" by Worthington (1983). Ecologists and their institutions were allied with the conservation movement. Many ecologists believed that the real role of ecology in its self-conscious scientific sense was to respond to the issue raised by Carl Schurz – the requirement to learn the laws of nature. Ecology was sometimes described as the scientific arm of the conservation movement. One perceptive ecologist, William Vogt (1948:274), provided an excellent analogy, borrowed from T. H. Huxley, a prolific source of biological wisdom before ecology:

> Suppose it were perfectly certain that the life and fortune of each and every one of us would one day, or other, depend upon his winning or losing a game at chess. Don't you think that we should all consider it to be a primary duty to learn at least the names of the pieces, to have a notion of a gambit, and a keen eye for all the means of giving and getting out of check?. . . Yet it is a very plain and elementary truth that the life, the fortune and the happiness of everyone of us do depend upon our knowing something of the rules of a game infinitely more complicated than chess. The chessboard is the world, the pieces are the

phenomena of the universe and the rules of the game are what we call the laws of Nature. The player on the other side is hidden from us. We know that his play is always fair, just and patient. But we also know, to our cost, that he never overlooks a mistake or ignorance. . . . One who plays ill is checkmated – without haste but without remorse.

The game metaphor is very current in ecology. The point, however, of the ecological game, like the evolutionary game, is not to win but to continue to play. Huxley's chess analogy is not accurate in the respect that the pieces and moves of chess are fixed and known. The ecological game has indeterminate pieces, not clearly distinguishable, the moves are roughly known, but there is an indeterminate element of chance. The chessboard remains the earth or, in modern parlance, "Spaceship Earth." Much traditional protoecological and early ecological thought assumed that the pieces were fixed and could be defined as units and that the rules of the game were similarly fixed and could be learned, or at least that humans could impose their own rules of the game and even create their own pieces. This was suggested by the common application of "law" to some ecological phenomena and by the widespread belief in communities as units. This idea has recently been revived in the phrase *assembly rules* for species in communities. Ecology can appropriately be envisioned as the effort to learn the rules and pieces of the ecological game, not only as it is played by nature but as humans play the game *in* nature. As human influences have become paramount, it seems as if we are playing *with* nature.

## Nature preserves and surveys

Surveys of natural resources and of vegetation were closely associated with the development of ecology in Britain and America (Lowe 1976; Sheail 1976, 1981; Boyd 1983; Worthington 1983). One offshoot of these surveys was the recognition of the need to set aside areas of natural interest for scientific study, preservation of habitats, species, or, in the very useful British phrase, their amenity value. The organizer of vegetation surveys in Britain was the Committee for the Survey and Study of British Vegetation suggested by Tansley (1904b) and later redubbed the British Vegetation Committee. One of its members, F. W. Oliver, was appointed to the Executive Committee of the National Trust for the Preservation of Places of Historical Interest and Natural Beauty, which had been established in 1894 (Smith 1908).

Preservation of nature was in the air on the Continent, in Britain, and in America, and ecologists were deeply involved. Conwentz (1914) reviewed national and international efforts to protect nature, even protection of forests in an enemy country. Webb (1913) traced the early establishment of nature reserves in Britain and noted the establishment of a Society for Promotion of Nature Reserves and the Royal Society for Protection of Birds. Concern for the human environment was evident, in 1917, in the formation of a Committee for Development of Regional Survey to survey areas in relation to villages, towns, and cities. F. W. Oliver (1917), in his presidential address to the British Ecological Society, noted the importance of ecology to the rural economy in grazing studies. General Jan Christian Smuts, the South African soldier, political leader, and philosopher of holism, stimulated surveys of African lakes and reserves by British and other European biologists in the 1920s and 1930s (Worthington 1983). During the 1920s and 1930s concern for land-use planning required by urban spread and rural decay continued in Britain at local, regional, and national levels. Proposals for national parks were considered. A plan was offered in 1937 for a National Survey Commission to conduct a national survey of rural resources of soils and vegetation. The committee recommending the surveys included the ecologists C. S. Elton and A. G. Tansley, but the proposal was controversial and lost out in the context of wartime concerns (Sheail 1981). The continuing role of British ecologists in nature conservation in the work of Tansley was traced by Godwin (1977). A striking indication of the significance attached to nature preservation is the formation, during the darker days of World War II, of at least two committees to consider postwar needs (Tansley 1945). One was a quasi-official body, including prominent ecologists, to advise the government on nature preserves. The other was a special committee of the British Ecological Society, chaired by Tansley. The committees agreed on the desirability of establishing a number of national nature reserves in addition to those then held by the National Trust and private organizations. When, in 1949, the British Nature Conservancy was created by royal charter, Tansley became its first chairman. In 1959 there were some 84 nature reserves including 56,000 hectares. By 1976 this had grown to 153 reserves including 120,500 hectares. These reserves continue to serve a very useful research and educational function as well as preservation of natural areas.

One of the first actions of the newly formed Ecological Society of America in 1917 was to establish a Committee on the Preservation of

Natural Conditions for Ecological Study under the chairmanship of Victor Shelford. In 1920 the Executive Committee of the Division of Biology and Agriculture of the National Research Council voted to refer consideration of reserves of natural areas to the Ecological Society and its committee. The committee prepared the *Naturalist's Guide to the Americas* (Shelford 1925). For 26 years the committee and its successors attempted to locate and save natural areas for scientific purposes, supporting the efforts of the Okefenokee Society and the Save the Redwoods League, and urging protection of national parks. In 1946, following a disputed decision that the society should no longer directly support such activities, Shelford organized an independent group of ecologists, called the Ecologists' Union, to further nature reserves (Dexter 1978). In 1950, the Ecologists' Union was reorganized and renamed the Nature Conservancy. The American Nature Conservancy, unlike its British namesake, is a private membership organization. Following some early growing pains, it has proven markedly successful in securing natural areas using a revolving fund and arranging for their protection, usually by transferring responsibility to a stable institution, such as a university. At the time of its conversion the Ecologists' Union published a preliminary inventory of nature sanctuaries in the United States and Canada, cataloging some 691 areas in various ownerships. The Nature Conservancy by 1978 had completed 2,144 projects comprising some 1,500,000 acres in 49 states. Support for the Nature Conservancy is now very widespread, with a nationwide membership over 60,000. In this era various states undertook to establish "natural areas" for scientific research. Wisconsin, under the leadership of Albert Fuller of the Milwaukee Public Museum and John T. Curtis of the University of Wisconsin, and with the cooperation of state officials, set an excellent example (Loucks 1968). In the 1930s the University of Wisconsin, following Aldo Leopold's suggestion, established its Arboretum, which served for horticultural collections and uniquely for establishment of areas representative of natural communities (Sachse 1965). Lake Wingra, a part of the Arboretum, was the site of a major International Biological Program study in the 1970s, and its reestablished prairie and forests serve both scientific and educational purposes. The Duke University Forest, established in the 1930s, provided a protected base for forest surveys on permanent plots which are being resurveyed in the 1980s (Christensen and Peet 1980). Natural areas established by government, universities, and private foundations for various purposes have served ecologists well as areas for teaching and research, and provide much of interest for all interested in nature. Perhaps the most intensively studied natural area on the earth is Wytham Woods, Oxfordshire, from which Charles Elton gathered, since its establishment in the early 1940s, the material for *The Pattern of Animal Communities* (Elton 1966).

## Human ecology

Early self-conscious ecologists were aware of and even insistent about the relevance of their still somewhat nebulous science to humans and their activities. Ecology developed in the late 19th and early 20th centuries in parallel with the widespread increase of interest in the environment, conservation of natural resources, establishment of parks and reserves, and urban planning. It developed in a period of rising concern that not all was well with either natural or human-dominated environments and a growing suspicion, on the part of some, that humans might be making a mess of things in their ignorance and, some would add, greed. The key questions were posed in the first formal works and journals of ecology. Clements (1905:16) reviewed the activities of humans as they changed the earth and initiated succession. He wrote that sociology "is the ecology of a particular species of animal and has, in consequence, a similar close association with plant ecology." Shelford (1913:318) quoted Theodore Roosevelt and Elizabeth Barrett Browning in contrasting the wilderness with tamed or urban nature. He addressed the question of ethics in the animal world and human responsiblity toward animals and provided a diagrammatic representation of primeval and man-made communities. Shelford listed various types of communities associated with human activity and cited several studies of polluted waters. He also related ecology to human society as studied by geographers, sociologists, and psychologists who, he said, had erroneously compared structure of animals with culture in humans rather than comparing animal behavior and human culture. Adams (1913:12) noted that the studies of humans had been developed largely independently of studies of animals but suggested that they were converging to their mutual advantage, and he anticipated that animal ecology and human ecology would also converge. He illustrated his point with a quotation from T. H. Huxley, who had asserted that the province of biology included humans:

> You should not be surprised if it occasionally happens that you
> see a biologist apparently trespassing in the region of philoso-

phy or politics; or meddling with human education; because
after all, that is a part of his kingdom which he has only
voluntarily forsaken. (Quoted in Adams 1912)

Such comments hardly endeared Huxley to contemporary politicians,
like Prime Minister Gladstone, or educators, clerics, and philosophers
at large. His successors in apparent attempts to reclaim aspects of the
study of humans (e.g., E. O. Wilson, sociobiology; K. E. F. Watt,
economics; or P. A. Colinvaux, history) similarly find that they are not
entirely welcomed in this part of biology now largely claimed by
others. Adams (1913:33) readily incorporated humans into ecology:

The disturbances due to man are a problem in the adjustment
of the highest type of animal, as a member of an animal association, to its complete environment.

Elton (1933) similarly compared animal social life with community
organization of humans and argued that even humans could not be
treated as an isolated unit.

The British Ecological Society, at its first Summer Meeting in 1914,
considered ecology in the widest sense, "including human ecology,"
and its members were urged to apply in primary school and university
"the viewpoints extending from such an extension of the fundamental
principals of ecology into human affairs." The Ecological Society of
America when it was founded in 1916 (Handbook of the Ecological
Society of America 1917) included no social scientists among its
charter members but did include the climatologist Ellsworth Huntington, who became its second president. The society in its first year had
a standing committee on climatic conditions with two members, Huntington and E. C. Schneider, concerned with humans and climate. The
committee disappeared before 1920, but some elements of the environmental determinism associated with Huntington appeared in publications of the society. In 1925, a plot of the number of points relative to
population in the International Olympic Games was used as an index
of the effect of climate on human energy. It included only European
and North American countries, Norway being number one and the
United States well down the line at eleventh (Hoxmark 1925). Such a
simple view of human activity as environmentally determined largely
disappeared with other single-factor ecology, but nothing more sophisticated replaced it.

The early expositors of ecology took a broad view of ecology including its philosophical, political, and economic overtones. Adams (1917)
did not go so far as H. L. Parsons (1977) to consider *Marx and Engels*

*on Ecology*. He did, however, point out that science is a tool to aid in bettering human living and "not simply a toy for a leisure class." Adams hailed the return of biology from the laboratory and museum to create the "New Natural History–Ecology." He reminded his readers, "We must remember that the economics of man is a phase of human ecology." This seems reasonable enough given the often stated origins of *ecology* and *economics* from the same Greek root meaning "house." The recent tendency of ecologists to borrow, or perhaps recover is a better word, economic models suggests convergence of the twins of the household. However, the enormous success of economics and economists in persuading governments that their advice is sound and that their predictions reasonably follow from their theories contrasts strangely with the failure of ecologists in this respect. The Council of Economic Advisors to the president in the United States government is a force to be reckoned with, and the pronouncements of its chairman are recorded with deadly seriousness by the media. The Council of Environmental Quality, by contrast, is a recent arrival in the Executive Offices of the President. Its major figures have not been ecologists, and it has been recently all but evicted from the select circle of White House occupants. Yet there is excellent reason to believe that economic prediction is no better than ecologic prediction (McCloskey 1983).

Other ecologists broadened the reach of ecology. Barrington Moore (1920) described aspects of geography as human ecology and noted the tendency of historians to correlate historical events with the influence of the environment on humans. Forbes (1922) urged the humanizing of biology, and Adams (1935) foresaw application of general ecological ideas to human ecology. Clements (1935) quoted "Mr. Wells" (presumably H. G. Wells) as saying, "Economics is a branch of ecology," and quoted General Smuts as stating:

> Ecology must have its way; ecological methods and outlook must find a place in human government as much as in the study of man, other animals, and plants. Ecology is for mankind.

Taylor (1936) attempted to relate ecology to other sciences and quoted the chairman of the National Research Council, the geographer Isaiah Bowman, and the secretary of agriculture Henry Wallace in staking out a broad scope for ecology. The relationship of animal and human ecology was strengthened in the effort to develop a common biology, a "law" of population growth, applying to *Drosophila* and *Homo sapiens* in the demographic studies of Raymond Pearl (1925). Ecologists commonly saw their science as a synthesizer of other disparate sciences, and some, like C. C. Adams, Victor Shelford, and Arthur Tansley, stressed the relationship of humans to their environment. Tansley (1939) in his second presidential address to the British Ecologial Society commented on human ecology and said that human communities "can only be intelligently studied in their proper environmental setting." He anticipated the establishment of a worldwide ecosystem "deriving from increasing interdependence." Although he confidently asserted that "the principles of ecology are unquestionably applicable to mankind," he noted that the human ecologist required different methods. The views of ecologists were confirmed by the philosopher E. C. Lindeman (1940), who in a symposium on human ecology went beyond the ecologists. Lindeman described ecology as the middleground "where the physical and biological sciences leave off and the social sciences begin." Reflecting the views of some past and future ecologists, Lindeman wrote:

> The ecologist stands in a most advantageous position. He has already acquired the habit of dealing with wholes as well as fractions. To this extent he is a philosopher.

The urge of ecologists for a holistic view was ubiquitous when Lindeman wrote that. It is still widespread, but is deplored by some ecologists, or critics of ecology, as obscuring the understanding and predictability demanded of a "hard" science.

Ecologists did more than press the potential of their young and not widely accepted science in human affairs. Many ecologists, as we have noted, were involved in aspects of agriculture, grazing, forestry, and weed and insect control. In the second quarter of the 20th century, ecologists argued the consequences for humanity of ignoring an ecological outlook and laid the groundwork for its later description as "the subversive subject" by Sears (1964). The problems and promise of the American West in the 19th century had been documented by the historian W. P. Webb (1931) in his book *The Great Plains*. Another historian, James Malin (1961), related the ecological and historical development of the grasslands. Paul B. Sears (1935c), perhaps the most articulate plant ecologist in relating ecology to human affairs, examined the ecological consequences of misunderstanding the Great Plains in his book *Deserts on the March*. Sears followed in the footsteps of his eminent predecessor C. E. Bessey (Overfield 1975, 1979) in scientific and ecological consideration of the American grassland and grassland agriculture. Both shared the conviction that a knowledge of the environment was essential to advance human society, although Bessey sometimes had his doubts about the merits of the upstart science of ecology. Nevertheless, it was Bessey and his students, and their influence, which created the applied science of range management and led to application of ecological techniques in range management (Dyksterhuis 1958; Tobey 1981; White in press). Sears experienced the drought years of the 1930s in Oklahoma, and he noted the effect of allowing excessive plowing of soil and of overgrazing and cultivation of marginal lands in removing the vegetative cover. The efforts of Bessey and the young U.S. Department of Agriculture to establish forested areas as windbreaks in the grassland before World War I had not ameliorated the effects of the great drought of the 1930s, when even the native grassland underwent substantial change.

It is a matter of some interest that ecologists, in the early decades of the 20th century, were much involved in matters of practical land use. C. E. Bessey had a significant role in developing federal plans for foresting areas of the grasslands, and his student F. E. Clements had consulting relationships with both the Forest Service and Department of Agriculture. Ecologists such as Homer Shantz, Forrest Shreve, Arthur Sampson, and H. C. Hanson all applied their ecological skills to the development of the grasslands, deserts, and their resource problems. During the 1930s President Franklin D. Roosevelt initiated important legislation affecting natural resources, and Bessey's earlier shelter belt work was greatly expanded. However, the formalization of ecology and the development of professional organizations, albeit with some overlap, of foresters, range scientists, fisheries managers, agronomists, and game managers resulted in a tendency to withdraw into special spheres of interest which divide ecology and limit its effect as a force in environmental concerns. The course of empire wended its way in the Middle East and Africa, and British ecologists were involved with similar problems of land use, agriculture in unaccustomed places, and their environmental consequences, desertification and soil erosion among them (Worthington 1983). The ecologist W. P. Cottam (1947) raised the desertification concerns expressed earlier by Paul Sears. Cottam was concerned with the same effect of overgrazing by sheep which had outraged John Muir and asked, "Is Utah Sahara Bound?" His stand got him into trouble with the Mormon Church, which sent a deputation to the president of the University of Utah to seek his dismissal (G. Cottam 1983 pers. commun). Apart from quoting biblical passages in criticism of the grazing practices widespread in Utah, Cottam asserted the "social wickedness" of passing on to their descendants "land impaired by selfish exploitation." "Social wickedness" and "barbarism" (Shaler 1910) are associated with squandering of resources – an evil that is the focal point of many now writing about the environmental crisis.

In this same era, before the environmental crisis was generally perceived, ecologists were earning the name "Cassandra" by examining the consequences of large-scale human activity on the environment (Schmidt 1948). William Vogt (1948) published one of the early warnings by ecologists of the impending environmental crisis. Leopold (1949) provided a prose-poem plea for a shift of values in his now famous book, *Sand County Almanac.* It was well known in 1949, but largely among the already converted. Not until the environmental crisis became widely apparent in the late 1960s was Leopold's plea familiar everywhere. He merged ecology and ethics to touch one aspect of human ecology:

> That land is a community is the basic concept of ecology, but that land is to be loved and respected is an extension of ethics. (Leopold 1949:VIII)

He touched on another sensitive area of human behavior in his comment (1949:VII), "We of the minority see a law of diminishing returns in progress." That the early warnings and pleas went unheeded is evident by a flood of articles and volumes in the 1960s and 1970s concerning the ecocrisis, ecocatastrophe, collision between society and environment, *Titanic* effect, and the Fifth Horseman – pollution – as if famine, war, pestilence and death were not enough. Rachel Carson (1962) was both vilified and hailed for dramatically, and correctly, demonstrating the hazards of pesticides. Numerous ecologists and others speaking in the name of ecology expressed concern about the state of the environment. All these formed what were lumped together as the "Doomsday syndrome" by one of those who complained that the threats to the environment and humanity were exaggerated and argued that they ignored the potential of science and technology to resolve the various aspects of the environmental or ecological crisis (Maddox 1972). In fact, some ecologists and many others claimed that the crisis was a product of unbridled science and technology in the grip of a questionable economics neither offering effective solutions and not, sometimes, even admitting the problems of overpopulation, pollution, and environmental decay. Maddox, however, made a useful point in noting that ecology was all too often used as a slogan rather than the name of a science with claims to a substantial body of information concerning the environment, including that of humans.

During the 1920s and 1930s, human ecology, at least in name, had been adopted as a synonym of the social sciences, individually or collectively. The hope of J. F. V. Phillips (1934–35), Sears (1932, 1937), and Adams (1935) that ecology would contribute to human well-being was not, however, well represented in the extensive literature on "human ecology." Shepard (1967) suggested that the gratification ecologists might have felt by the "vigor with which the sociologists embraced ecology" was dispelled when they came to read the resultant literature. Some saw geography as human ecology (Barrows 1923). Hawley (1950) attributed the use of the phrase *human ecology* to sociologists in 1921, although it was familiar to ecologists certainly by 1914. Human ecology was perpetuated in an extension of ecology to the human community. Ophuls (1934) provided at least a prolog to a political theory of the ecological steady state, McKenzie (1934) offered readings in human ecology, and Bews (1935) a book on human ecology. Alihan (1938), in a book entitled *Social Ecology,* used some of Clements's ideas and placed heavy emphasis on competition in contrast to the animal ecologist Allee (1931), who emphasized cooperation among animals. University of Chicago ecologists, such as Allee, were much influenced by contemporary sociology. Human ecology never quite crystallized as a discipline in ecology or the social sciences, although it appeared frequently enough in titles of articles and books having little in common except a focus on humans. The Ecological Society of America contributed a Symposium on Human Ecology in 1940. Paul Sears (1954) described human ecology, aptly, as "a problem in synthesis." And so it has largely remained.

In 1955 a Committee on Human Ecology was formed in the Ecological Society of America. Its first report in 1956 indicated that it was not clear just how such a committee should be organized but that the effort should continue. The committee (Committee on Human Ecology 1957) arranged a symposium, "Advances in Human Ecology," in which the four participants considered (1) the problem of establishing the limits of human ecology, (2) the nefarious effects of Judeo-Christian religious concepts, (3) new levels of behavioral and cultural concerns introduced, and (4) factors controlling population densities. This symposium suggested to some the desirability of creating a section of the society on human ecology, but interest and support waned and it was not formed. In 1958 only a brief verbal report was given, and in 1959 and 1960 the committee was described as being reorganized. In fact, the Committee on Human Ecology was moribund. Six years later it was resurrected under new leadership (Committee on Human Ecology 1967). It was then said that the revised committee would include anthropologists, economists, political scientists, and physicians–"ecology in its broad aspect." Such a committee was formed but again was short-lived, although programs on human ecology appeared in meetings of the Ecological Society of America. Shepard (1967) wondered, "Whatever happened to human ecology?"

It was a good question. In spite of the familiar assertions by ecologists that ecology had much to contribute to human affairs, prior to the 1960s ecology was little recognized outside its professional sphere. The several uses of the word in the social sciences were largely window dressing, with little reference to ecologists and their ideas. Geography, sociology, and other disciplines concerned with humans, their cultures, and their relations to the environment sometimes adopted the name but rarely the substance of ecology. The unfortunate suggestion by some of simplistic environmental determinism and a belief that science was irrelevant to understanding human cultures may have contributed to the lack of understanding. The several efforts to bring together ecologists and social scientists failed to integrate them or to produce really significant moves toward interdisciplinary approaches.

## Ecology and the environmental movement

The long-term concern of ecologists with the environment and the relations of humans to its diverse components, physical and biotic, is evident in the actions of their societies. Both the British and American ecological societies were, however, reluctant to engage in overt advocacy of particular positions or in lobbying. This is formalized in a constitutional provision of the Ecological Society of America prohibiting lobbying. Peter Greig-Smith (1978), president of the British Ecological Society, said the society "cannot have a corporate opinion on practical affairs and if it appears to do so its credibility over scientific aspects will be damaged." The conflict between the image of science as objective and value-free and that of ecology as intrinsically value-laden and a guide to ethics for humans, animals, and even trees is difficult to reconcile. Segregation of strictly scientific concerns from matters of public policy is not easy, as atomic scientists had found. Ecologists and their societies often feared that political and social issues were beyond their competence or that their credibility as impartial consultants would suffer.

The minutes, committee reports, and discussions of both British and American ecological societies in the post-World War II era are replete with such problems, and individual ecologists devoted large amounts of time to environmental concerns. The Applied Ecology Committee of the Ecological Society of America lamented much land use and management policy in the United States. It frequently cited the need for ecological analysis and noted the absence of an effective means of getting ecological ideas heard at national administrative and congressional levels. The society also created a Committee on Effects of Radionuclides in the aftermath of World War II, just as the U.S. Atomic Energy Commission was being pressed by ecologists to study radiological effects on the environment as well as clinical effects on humans. The effects of large-scale, unstudied, and often ineffectual applications of pesticides were a frequent target. There was even a specific vote in opposition to the use of Mirex in attempts to control the fire ant. Decisions by government agencies concerning natural resources in the absence of, or even in the face of, scientific advice and commonly based on political expediency were a common concern. The negligible concern for the environment at national political levels during the 1950s was evident in one report (Committee on Applied Ecology 1958) which expressed concern about pollution. It quoted President Eisenhower in a news conference to the effect that pollution was not a proper federal function–"It is strictly local in its character and I think it belongs to local government." In its next report (Committee on Applied Ecology 1960) the committee reviewed numerous problems subject to ecological insights and summarized:

> It is evident that there are endless possibilities for the application of ecological knowledge to the management of wildlife resources. It is likewise evident that scientific knowledge can be a basis for public policy only if implemented by a strong public demand. This situation emphasizes again the key importance of using every available means to spread factual information on natural relationships.

The Ecology Study Committee (Miller 1965) declared its purpose was "to review and formulate so far as possible . . . the function and status of ecology in science and society." It noted the imbalance between basic and applied ecological research and stressed the need for funds for long-term research. It particularly urged, "There are clearly areas of public interest which ecologists can no longer avoid, either as individuals or as a Society."

British ecologists similarly continued their concern with application of ecological ideas to maintain and improve the human environment. In 1964 a proposal was made that the British Ecological Society become involved in problems resulting from urban industrial life. When in 1969 a Commonwealth Human Ecology Council was formed, the society was represented on it (Worthington 1983). Some years later (Report of the Annual General Meeting 1973) the society was still considering and formally debating its role in human ecology. A new magazine concerned with the human environment, *The Ecologist,* had published a popular article concerning ecology entitled "Blueprint for Survival." Opinions on the merits of the article were divided. The afternoon session was a debate on the motion "The Society should now abandon the blackboard in favor of the placard." Although the title was facetious, the concerns were real. In Britain, as in the United States, the late 1960s and 1970s had seen an upsurge in concern for the human environment. Committees and workshops of the society reported on derelict lands (Ranwell 1967) and planning (Holdgate and Woodman 1975). The Nature Conservancy considered conservation of wildlife (Ratcliffe 1977) and agriculture and nature conservation (Moore 1977).

In the 1970s the multiplicity of environmental problems facing humankind appeared overwhelming, and ecology, in its narrower sense as a scientific discipline and in its "broader penumbra" as a normative way of life, was thrust into the limelight. It became "Ecology – Now or Never" (Neiring 1970). Ecology was urged as a basis of American institutions by a nonecologist (Marx 1970), who phrased the now familiar dilemma:

> What confronts us is an extreme imbalance between society's hunger – the rapidly growing sum of human wants – and the limited capacities of the earth.

The new import of ecology is suggested by a publication entitled *The Role of Ecology in the Federal Government,* which asserted unequivocally, "Ecology as a Science has come of age" (Council on Environmental Quality and Federal Council for Science and Technology 1974). Ecology took on elements of "public interest" (Nelkin 1976) and "politics" (Lowe 1977). Ecology was even linked with national security (C. H. 1977).

In this interval members of the Ecological Society of America pressed for formation of a National Institute of Ecology, as a government agency with the purpose of enhancing application of ecological science to environmental and social problems (Report of the Study Committee 1968). The timing was ripe in that, in 1970, the United States government established the Environmental Protection Agency (EPA) "to conduct investigations, studies, surveys, research and analysis relating to ecological systems and environmental quality" (Carpenter 1970). This was a large order, and the problem was one of ecological credibility and what, or who, was an ecologist. American and British ecological societies produced lists of certified or consulting ecologists, respectively. Many ecologists were concerned that science and technology had gotten out of control, with deleterious effects on the environment. The hope was that a relatively unsung aspect of science which had as its essence a holistic approach to the environment and human society, as well as other organisms, could alleviate the problems widely perceived. John Cantlon (1970), the retiring president of the Ecological Society of America, emphasized the need for "ecological bridges" between science, technology, and the humanities. He suggested that the advent of an "Age of Ecology" required "more healthful couplings" between "the urban-industrial, the agricultural, and the wild systems" on which human life depends. This coupling would require "bridge building" to engineering and planning professions and to the social and political sciences. The vital and difficult requirement was to build ecological science, not only ecological rhetoric, into the process of decision making at all levels. The need was aptly stated by Carpenter (1970) in an essay "The Political Use of Ecological Information":

> Without compromising the validation processes of the scientific method, ecological information must be fed into decision-making as quickly as possible. Doom-crying and esoteric jargon are to be avoided. Although many individual scientists and research organizations will be directly involved, some central nexus with the political process is needed. Scientific data and expert opinion must be evaluated, authenticated, organized, analyzed, and interpreted for use by legislators and administrators. The Ecological Society of America through a special committee studying the feasibility of a National Institute of Ecology, has concluded that much basic ecological information already known to science is not finding its way into the decision-making process. The technology assessment mechanisms under development provide an excellent opportunity to illus-

trate the value to society of ecology as a predictive science. The government and the discipline should work together to build an efficient information transfer link, perhaps as a part of the developing National Institute of Ecology. (Copyright © 1970 by the American Institute of Biological Sciences.)

A National Institute of Ecology as a federal agency never came to fruition.

The Institute of Ecology was a unilateral response of the Ecological Society of America to the call to contribute to the solution of the manifest problems of the human environment about which ecologists had long been sensitive. Following several years of gestation it was incorporated in 1971 under the name Inter-American Institute of Ecology (Inger 1971; Deevey 1971), which was shortened to the Institute of Ecology when it was broadened to include members outside the Americas. Its first president was a distinguished ecologist, Arthur D. Hasler, and its first major effort was to hold a workshop in global ecological problems, published as *Man in the Living Environment* (Report of the Workshop on Global Ecological Problems 1972). This report was designed to provide ecological perspective to a United Nations Conference on the Human Environment. It was followed by numerous subsequent reports of diverse types. Notable among these was a *Report of a Workshop Concerning Tropical Ecology* (Farnworth and Golley 1974). These and other publications of the Institute of Ecology attempted to address the difficult problems mentioned in Carpenter's advisory. Ecologists and others involved in the institute hoped it would provide an increased flow of accurate, scientifically based information concerning environmental problems, provide some of the bridges between science and the humanities called for by Cantlon, and address the questions involved in "The Politics of Ecology" (Lowe 1977). Although the Institute of Ecology got off to a promising start, it did not enjoy the continued success of the Nature Conservancy, an earlier offspring of the Ecological Society of America. It failed to fulfill the hopes for it, due to managerial and fiscal problems stemming from its inherently diffuse organization and clientele. This effort to integrate ecology with general public policy was, if not premature, apparently beyond the scope of the capabilities of ecology as an "integrative science." The hope expressed by early ecologists such as C. C. Adams and A. G. Tansley that ecology would have a significant role in human concerns, a hope reiterated by ecologists ever since, is, however, perpetuated in continuing efforts of individual ecologists and their institutions (cf. Sears 1971).

One of the manifest difficulties in the "Age of Ecology" was that the environment, in its broadest sense, was everybody's business (Dunnett 1982). The meaning of ecology was distorted. The "Ecology" shelf at one university bookstore included seven books on solar homes, three on earth-sheltered homes, three on various forms of home heating, three on alternative energy sources, and one each on notes from an energy underground, radical agriculture, and nature and madness – none on scientific ecology. The problem for the ecologist was to retain a sense of proportion about the nature of ecology as a science and its contributions to the environmental crisis. Ecologists, as Paine (1981) put it, had to consider "Truth in Ecology" in offering scientifically based and justifiable knowledge appropriate to the myriad environmental problems besetting humanity. H. N. Southern (1970), in his presidential address to the British Ecological Society, commented that some had said that ecology is too important to be left to ecologists and asked in effect – Who else? Passmore (1974), on the other hand, said that the solution of ecological problems cannot safely be left to scientists "because the solution of ecological problems demands a moral or metaphysical revolution." The "ecological crisis" was associated with "the ecological conscience," "ecology and social institutions," and "the metaphysics of ecology" in a collection of writings concerning ecology (Disch 1970). Ecologists, in any traditional sense, faced difficult problems in integrating their ecological insights about the human environment and human society with those whose insights derived from other professional traditions which ordinarily dealt with matters of conscience, social institutions, and metaphysics independently of ecological issues (Nelkin 1976). Even those interested in and sympathetic to ecological ideas sometimes understated the interest and ability of ecologists to enter into human concerns. L. K. Caldwell (1971) commented:

> The subversive potential of ecology had been unperceived even by ecologists, this nascent science having been focused largely upon manageable microproblems from which the human animal was usually excluded.

In fact, ecology was first described explicitly as a subversive subject by Paul Sears in 1964. Granted that Sears was no run-of-the-mill ecologist, it is fair to state that he was not alone or even first among ecologists in this perception. As usual, he simply said it more effectively than other ecologists. Ecologists had frequently commented on the relatively unmanageable macroproblems in which the human animal is at the core, and they were not always welcomed. Ecologists were certainly prominent among the lonely voices crying figuratively in the wilderness and literally about the wilderness before the merit of wilderness to humans, as well as wolves, was widely apparent. Ecologists were among those who continued where George Perkins Marsh had left off in pointing out adverse effects of human actions on the earth and its continuing productive capacity. Ecologists were among those who noted the effects of areas created and dominated by humans, known as urban areas, upon other organisms and their reciprocal effects upon humans. Ecologists were emphatically among those who noted what were sometimes euphemistically described as side effects of human actions in macroscale, such as high dams, pesticides, nuclear weapons, and industrial pollution. In most instances it was ecologists who had developed the concepts and basic methods of data collection and analysis which allowed detection of more subtle reactions of populations and communities.

Certainly a number of individuals who started out as biologists and ecologists, presumably dealing with relatively manageable microproblems, continued the tradition of earlier ecologists and made major contributions to the recognition, understanding, and, it may be hoped, resolution of problems involving the human animal. Among notable British ecologists was Fraser Darling, who extended his interests from red deer to the Scottish Highland landscape and its human and economic problems and then to human environmental problems at large. E. B. Worthington expanded his limnological interests to national and international scales of land use and environmental problems (Worthington 1983). A. D. Bradshaw went from microproblems of plant genetics on ancient and medieval mine tips and modern fence rows to large-scale problems of restoration of extensive areas of derelict land using his genetic and ecological skills (Bradshaw and Chadwick 1980).

Among American ecologists, Garrett Hardin transcended his ecological interests in the competitive exclusion principle and turned to the most sensitive and difficult of human problems of who shall live and who shall die on an international scale with his ideas of triage, tragedy of the commons, and lifeboat ethics. Paul Ehrlich continued his studies of evolution and ecology of butterflies but did less of these than he might have if he had not turned to the macroproblems of population growth and resource availability. The faculty of the University of Michigan alone supplied several ecologists who took up human problems. Pierre Dansereau turned from vegetation studies to large-scale planning studies in Canada. Stanley Cain turned from vegetation studies to policy, particularly, predator policy studies in the U.S. Department of Interior. Cain is the only ecologist who ever attained a post as high as undersecretary in a department of the federal government. F. E. Smith moved up the ecological hierarchy from population theory to ecosystem problems, leaving Michigan for landscape and regional planning at Harvard University. John Wolfe, George Woodwell, E. P. Odum, H. T. Odum, Stanley Auerbach, and other ecologists advanced studies of radiation effects on the environment and the devastating potential of nuclear war. C. S. Holling turned his interest from insect populations to regional planning in Vancouver, Canada. K. E. F. Watt similarly left microecological problems for regional planning in California. Few ecologists were arrogant enough to assume that ecology or ecologists were in themselves sufficient to deal with all of the ramifications of the human dimensions of ecology. However, ecologists contributed the basic concepts and much of the detailed knowledge of what Barry Commoner aptly termed "the ecological facts of life" as related to humans. These constituted the approach to T. H. Huxley's "rules" by which the ecological game was played by organisms on earth. The crux of much of the discussion in the 1970s was whether humans played by the same rules.

An early distinction restricted biology and ecology to a concern with organisms controlled by their genetic makeup and the study of humans to other disciplines, presumably because of the cultural component of humans. The term *human ecology,* in the 1930s, was applied to a variety of ways of looking at physical and cultural responses of humans, with little integration with general ecology or effective development of a unified field of human ecology. In the aftermath of the ecological crisis and with the rise of the environmental movement in the 1960s, human ecology was rejuvenated and reappeared in institutes, symposia, and book titles (Bresler 1966; Sargeant 1974a,b; Dunlap 1980a). The continuing difficulty of identifying human ecology precisely was acknowledged by Sargeant, who provided an essay "The Nature and Scope of Human Ecology" (Sargeant 1974b). Sargeant ended by quoting K. E. Boulding, a prominent economist who had published extensively on environmental affairs:

> It is not unreasonable to look upon the present era as a chance which man has (and probably a unique chance at that, which will never be repeated) of translating his natural capital into enough knowledge that will enable him to do without it.

Sargeant's article is immediately followed by one by the ecologist E. J. Kormondy (1974) entitled "Natural and Human Ecosystems." Kormondy summarized:

> The intent here has but one specific point, the fact that human ecosystems are natural ecosystems, that man is subject to the laws of ecosystems, and that he can and does subject these laws to stress.

Kormondy crossed the line between human and natural and allowed no more options for humans to transcend the laws of natural ecosystems than for any other organism to do so. In Boulding's and presumably Sargeant's view, "man's" knowledge could relieve him of his dependency on "natural capital." Actually, the burden of most ecology has to do with humankind's use or misuse of its natural capital, its ability to maintain and increase its productivity, and the tendency to destroy its natural capital. Certainly, a persistent problem in formulating human ecology and integrating it with general ecology lies in this interdependence. It allows no option for transcending humankind's natural capital, only for making effective and indefinite use of it.

Many aspects of what is recognized as human ecology are autecology of human groups and not substantially different from autecology of other organisms. The behavioral, physiological, or anatomical results of physical or chemical effects of environment on mice and humans may differ in problems of data gathering, but neither conceptual nor methodological problems alienate those studying humans from those studying animals. The parallels in studies of animal and human demography, and even sharing of models and methods, suggest no insurmountable barriers. The environment, to paraphrase Haeckel's premier definition, includes effects of physical and biological components of the environment. Humans, like many animals, and to a greater degree than any, can avoid, mitigate, or increase adverse effects of the environment and enhance or reduce the desirable effects. They do this, however, as Lewis Mumford long ago pointed out, at a cost. Low temperatures can be increased and high temperatures decreased, at least locally, according to quite well-established principles of physics and less well-established principles of economics, ecology, and politics. Autecological effects on humans are often established, in part, by parallel studies of autecology of animals.

The effect of another organism on a human population, however, is clearly not determined solely by intensive studies of the human population but must take into account the idiosyncracies of other organisms.

Human epidemiology had early associations with animal ecology, and the study of animal vectors of disease links animal ecology effectively to aspects of human health and the ecology thereof. The effects of physical stress on susceptibility and the influence of environmental conditions in initiation and spread of disease and of amelioration of environmental stress on prevention of disease have been amply demonstrated. Thus although the medical aspects of human ecology are carried on largely by physicians, anatomists, microbiologists, and others who do not ordinarily think of themselves as ecologists, they are not usually at odds with ecologists. At worst, they just do not recognize their affinity, and the opportunity for profitable interaction may be lost.

When it comes to synecology, the relation of human ecology and general ecology becomes less clear and more controversial. Social scientists and humanists commonly think of the human population as a community by virtue of the diversity of roles (niches) of individuals. Ecologists think of a community as comprised of several species, each species having its own role or niche as a member of the community. Charles Elton, in expanding on the idea of niche, said that the ecologist must learn to think of the role of the species in the same sense that saying, "There goes the vicar" conveys an idea about an individual's role in the human community. Social scientists do not ordinarily think of the human population as simply one species, albeit probably the one with the greatest biomass, among many. There are notable and fascinating exceptions – for example, Salamun's (1952) "Social Influence of the Potato" – in which human history is shown in its relation to other species and their dependence on the environment. Anthropologists studying the use of plant and animal resources by early human cultures by examining their middens are not likely to feel estranged from animal ecologists who examine the record of prehistoric use of plant materials by the wood rat *(Neotoma)* as represented in deposits, perhaps in the same caves occupied by humans. Physical anthropologists seeking evidence among primates for human attributes of carriage and food use are concerned with environmental effects in much the same way as a zoologist making inferences about the ecological meaning of an anatomical structure. Sargeant (1974b) provided a sequence of cultural development of human societies, including gathering, hunting and fishing, herding, agricultural, to industrial and urbanized societies. The increasing complexity of environmental relations of these different stages of human culture makes formation of a unified ecology difficult.

A major difficulty of developing an effective human ecology and a reason that the social sciences have not been readily incorporated into any ecological framework is because "the social sciences have largely ignored the fact that human societies depend upon the biophysical environment for their survival" (Dunlap 1980b). In spite of earlier efforts of social scientists to formulate a human ecology, Dunlap described them as falling into the "anthropocentric Western thought" which views humans as apart from nature and has resulted in "unecological" traditions and perspectives in modern social science. Dunlap wrote:

> All of the social sciences assume that various *human* "mechanisms" – social institutions, culture, technology, and so forth, will operate to insure that a human population will adapt successfully to its biophysical environment.

Only in recent years, according to Dunlap, have social scientists accepted an ecological paradigm that *"Homo sapiens* is governed by the same physical laws that regulate growth and development of all other species."* Actually, that is not really much of an admission, for the major issue is not physical laws but whether workings of ecological processes which are much less well understood extend to human societies (Dunlap 1980a; Catton and Dunlap 1980). It is a matter of some interest that although Dunlap's article occurs in an issue of a social science journal devoted to ecology and the social sciences (Dunlap 1980a,b), only one of seven articles cited a substantial number of ecologists, and none is written by an ecologist. Lest ecologists lay the blame for the failure to develop an integrated human ecology entirely on social scientists, they should ponder the criticism of another social scientist (Rodman 1980):

> Ecology itself is not a clear and settled disciplinary paradigm even in biology, but something developing, so that social scientists who construct their alternative paradigms on the basis of "what 'ecology' is". . .risk building upon shifting sands.

It is striking that for an indication of "what ecology is" Rodman refers the reader to two references written by social scientists, one of which barely gets into the 20th century and concentrates on the 18th- and 19th-century roots of ecology. One of the barriers to ecology in responding to the demands of the environmental crisis is the compartmentalization of those who study various aspects of human organization and a similar compartmentalization among those who study ecology. Rodman's caveat has more truth in it than his sources revealed. The problem of determining "what ecology is" and extending its concepts and theories to include humans and the environments they modify or create is the responsibility of ecologists. They have the problem of arriving at an effective relationship with those social scientists who regard humans as beyond ecology. A recent example is evident in a review of a volume on desertification written from the perspective of a social scientist (Dyson-Hudson 1983). Problems of drought, desertification, and human relations to these were among the earliest concerns of ecology in the 1890s as it emerged as a self-conscious discipline. Ecologists like Paul Sears and Walter Cottam were among those who subsequently warned of desertification as a consequence of land management practices. Dyson-Hudson expressed concern that later consideration of intensification of desert conditions "allowed no role for social scientists even though desertification, as diagnosed and defined by ecologists, involves human factors that are beyond the limits of ecological explanation." If human factors are beyond ecological consideration, what, then, is human ecology? It is not clear whether ecology will expand to encompass the social sciences and develop as a metascience of ecology (Odum in press). The alternative is a more effective interdisciplinary relationship between ecology and the several social sciences.

Ecology has been credited with supplying aesthetic, ethical, moral, and even metaphysical insights for the human dilemma. All too often it has not been adequately credited with supplying scientific insights. The real contribution of ecology is that it has endeavored to understand how organisms function in nature in the aggregate as populations and communities and, latterly, in ecosystems. In some cases ecologists were concerned with organisms of remote places with minimal human effect. Charles Elton started his career with early surveys of animals on Spitzbergen, and W. S. Cooper established plots on the moraine at Glacier Bay, Alaska. Others considered landscapes, streams, lakes, forests, grasslands, or ocean areas clearly influenced by human activity past and present. Many younger ecologists have little or no experience or familiarity with wilderness areas. In the wake of the rapid increase of effects of human technology on the environment many ecologists are concerned with studying and, it may be hoped, mitigating the consequences of human actions. That these often involve injury or degradation of the environment is suggested in the appearance of "forensic ecology" (Willard 1980). Some ecologists may spend as much time in hearings or court actions as in the field (Loucks 1972; Wenner 1982; Carpenter 1983). In this case "the challenge to ecology is to ensure that the facts on which important points of law are decided are as good as they can be" (Cantlon 1980). The extensive development of environmental litigation leaves out of account the metaphysical questions sometimes posed in the name of ecology and makes it difficult to testify on the basis of ill-developed principles and theories (Willard 1980).

Ecologists share with many of their predecessors and contemporaries the appreciation of the aesthetic and value insights to be gained from nature. They contributed greatly to the effort to protect these aspects of the natural world from destruction as a matter of right as well as of expediency or economics. However, ecologists are intensely concerned with the *how-to* as well as the *ought-to* considerations. They are determined to devise appropriate techniques, concepts, and theories, as extensions of traditional natural history, the "new" biology of the 19th century, and the even newer biology following World War II, to allow improved relations of humans and a nature now largely modified by humans. Ecologists study populations of organisms clearly desired by humans and some clearly undesirable to humans. They study snail darters and louseworts and urge their interest and intrinsic significance. They study lemmings in Arctic wastes and rats in Baltimore with a core of basic techniques and ideas. The clear lesson is that no population is an island, not even, or especially, the human population.

The environment and the relation of humans to it became, with the rise of the conservation movement and, more recently, the environmental movement, a social and political issue. In the extreme this issue has been dubbed the politics of survival. Recognition of this has created a demand for sound ecological information and a market for environmental rhetoric, sound and otherwise. It has also stimulated recognition of the problem of decisions affecting the environment made in the absence of, or in the face of, sound ecological information. "Decision makers" in our society are not usually ecologists. They frequently weight scientific ecological criteria less heavily than economic, political, or other criteria. One problem in the attempt to provide ecological insight is that government agencies and policies have traditionally compartmentalized environmental problems and the agencies designed to deal with them. The holistic approach, ideally characteristic of ecology, did not traditionally appeal to government agencies. It is not easy to reverse decades of institutionalized bureaucracy in government agencies or, for that matter, in academic institutions or scientific societies.

The holistic approach is not seen equally clearly as desirable even by all ecologists, or at least their views of what constitutes holism differ. A prominent element in recent ecology, which has been intent on developing a theoretical and mathematical population-based ecology to make it a "predictive" science, has not been notably successful to date. Even the showcase island biogeography theory and its utility for planning natural areas has not produced consensus among ecologists. Theoretical approaches of this type have not proven clearly useful as a basis for applied ecology, and many applied ecologists are ignorant of them or ignore them. Systems ecologists are commonly confident that their approach is readily adaptable to application to or as a basis of ecological engineering. It is not yet clear that this merit stems from the concepts of systems theory, in its various manifestations, as introduced into ecology. The application of very-large-scale complex models of ecosystems has not produced effective guidelines for environmental decision making. Ecologists, thrust into producing environmental impact statements, have found it difficult to apply some of the products of the "rich theoretical phase" of ecology (Willard 1980; Suter 1981; Carpenter 1983). Others have argued that small- to medium-scale process models, supported by adequate empirical data, are necessary and effective elements of the application of technical ecological data in environmental litigation (Loucks 1972).

It is unfortunate that the demand for theoretical ecological insights with which to support rhetorical ecology comes at a time when ecology is in a condition sometimes described as a paradigm change or, perhaps better, paradigm confusion. The press in recent decades to produce a theoretical ecology has coincided with a multiplicity of theoretical ecologies philosophically and methodologically at odds with each other (McIntosh 1980a). Even within a group of ecologists who agree on the need for mathematical approaches to ecology, a heated and sometimes acrimonious dispute has developed (Lewin 1983).

The failure of any school of theoretical ecology to provide the hoped-for predictive capacity for ecology need not vitiate the effective use of ecological insights and expertise. A notable theoretical ecologist, J. Maynard Smith (1974:6), stated, with perhaps a slight pejorative note:

> Ecology is still a branch of science in which it is usually better to rely on the judgement of an experienced practitioner than on the predictions of a theorist.

Maynard Smith hoped for a "happy state of affairs" when ecology has "a sound theoretical basis," meaning, of course, a mathematical basis.

This hope is predicated on a conventional conception of science which may be too limiting a framework to contain ecology. It is not necessary, of course, to stand about and wait for the theoretical millennium or a merger of ecology and the social sciences in human ecology. Ecology has a large number of what Maynard-Smith aptly described as "experienced practitioners." These practitioners have in recent years, notably in the large-scale, relatively well-funded ecosystem studies (with or without benefit of systems analysis), produced extensive guidelines for effective ecological advice. The Hubbard Brook studies, as a case in point, illustrate the advantages of and critical need for long-term data collection for understanding nutrient flows in ecosystems. Ecologists have for decades been offering advice at least as soundly grounded in experience and theory as that offered by economists and medical scientists. They have been much less successful than economists in getting a hearing for their advice and having it factored into public policy in respect to environmental concerns. Ecologists certainly do not get the attention that the several "media" give to meteorologists, nor have the necessary long-term basic data required for ecological "predictions" been funded with anything like the support provided for meteorological data collection. It is only within the last decade, and at the instance of ecologists, that a network of Long Term Ecological Research (LTER) areas has been established in the United States with support from the National Science Foundation (Summary of a Workshop 1979). It is true that various federal and state agencies have supported specific mission-oriented institutions concerned with applied aspects of ecology. In some instances individuals in these agencies and institutions contributed notably to basic ecological work, and the institution contributed effectively to public awareness of diverse environmental concerns. However, the institutional arrangements, the traditional specialist training of the staffs, and funding, political, and bureaucratic limitations have often inhibited the best intentions to apply the best of ecological knowledge to environmental problems.

Sometimes lost in the recent environmental alarms which have been sounded calling upon ecology for guidance is the fact that ecology had developed a large body of empirical information and very useful concepts, if not predictive theories. Ecology was an important aspect of the widely ignored early warning system of increasing environmental degradation and a too-little-used guide to effective responses and preventive measures. However, ecology was there, "preadapted" in biological parlance, when the need for such a science became apparent to many who had been previously blind. It had grown by examining phenomena largely ignored by the more highly touted and heavily funded aspects of biology, physiology and genetics. It emphasized nonhuman populations, communities of aggregations of many populations, and the interaction of these with the physical environment and, very often, with human populations. It was sometimes described as only a point of view, not a science at all. It now suffers the hazard of being transformed back to a point of view, a sociopolitical position, or even a guide to ethics and philosophy, sometimes by ignoring its accumulated scientific insights. Ecologists have sometimes been accused, falsely I believe, of being above the battle or unconcerned with the earthy details of the environment as modified by humans. I submit that, to the contrary, they have explicitly, overtly, and in some cases unavoidably been concerned with the environment of humans as well as other organisms. Clearly ecology, even given its manifest difficulties in establishing a consensus on theory or paradigm, is the aspect of 20th-century science which has addressed the complex problems of assessing what actually happens to organisms in the "field," be it a literal field or a decayed urban center. It remains to be seen if ecology can relate to diverse social sciences in an effective way. For the moment, the answer to Professor Southern's question whether ecologists, using ecological concepts and methodologies, effectively address ecological questions remains – Who else?

# References

Adams, C. C. (1901). Base leveling and its faunal significance, with illustrations from Southeastern United States. *American Naturalist*, 35, 839-52.
– (1905). The postglacial dispersal of the North American biota. *Biological Bulletin*, 9, 53-71.
– (1908). The ecological succession of birds. *Auk*, 25, 109-53.
– (1913). *Guide to the Study of Animal Ecology*. New York: Macmillan.
– (1917). The new natural history – ecology. *American Museum Journal*, 7, 491-4.
– (1935). The relation of general ecology to human ecology. *Ecology*, 16, 316-35.
Ager, D. V. (1963). *Principles of Paleoecology*. New York: McGraw-Hill.
Alihan, M. A. (1938). *Social Ecology*. New York: Columbia University Press.
Allard, D. C., Jr. (1967). *Spencer Fullerton Baird and the U.S. Fish Commission: A Study in the History of American Science*. Ph.D. Dissertation, Washington University. Reprinted New York: Arno Press (1978).
Allee, W. C. (1927). Animal aggregations. *Quarterly Review of Biology*, 2, 367-98.
– (1931). *Animal Aggregations: A Study in General Sociology*. Chicago: University of Chicago Press.
– (1932). Animal Ecology. *Ecology*, 13, 405-7.
– (1934a). Concerning the organization of marine coastal communities. *Ecological Monographs*, 4, 541-54.
– (1934b). Some papers read at the Boston meeting of the American Association for the Advancement of Science. *Science* (suppl.), 79(2041), 5.
– (1939). An ecological audit. *Ecology*, 20, 418-21.
Allee, W. C., Emerson, A. E., Park, O., Park, T., and Schmidt, K. P. (1949). *Principles of Animal Ecology*. Philadelphia: Saunders.
Allee, W. C., and Park, T. (1939). Concerning ecological principles. *Science*, 89, 166-9.
Allen, G. E. (1979). Naturalists and experimentalists: The genotype and the phenotype. *Studies of the History of Biology*, 3, 179-210.
Allen, T. F. H. (1981). The noble art of philosophical ecology. *Ecology*, 62, 870-1.
Allen, T. F. H., and Starr, T. B. (1982). *Hierarchy: Perspectives for Ecological Complexity*. Chicago: University of Chicago Press.
Andrewartha, H. G. (1961). *Introduction to the Study of Animal Populations*. Chicago: University of Chicago Press.

Andrewartha, H. G., and Birch, L. C. (1954). *The Distribution and Abundance of Animals.* Chicago: University of Chicago Press.

– (1973). The history of insect ecology. In *History of Entomology*, ed. R. F. Smith, T. E. Mittler, and C. N. Smith, pp. 229-66. Palo Alto, Calif.: Annual Reviews.

Antonovics, J. (1976). The input from population genetics: "The new ecological genetics." *Systematic Botany*, 1, 233-45.

– (1980). The study of plant populations. *Science*, 208, 587-9.

Argen, G. I., Anderson, F., and Fagerstrom, T. (1980). Experiences of ecosystem research in the Swedish coniferous forest project. In *Structure and Function of Northern Coniferous Forests: An Ecosystem Study*, pp. 591-6. Stockholm: Ecological Bulletins, Swedish Natural Research Council.

Arnold, J., and Anderson, W. W. (1983). Density-regulated selection in a heterogeneous environment. *American Naturalist*, 121, 656-68.

Arrhenius, O. (1921). Species and area. *Journal of Ecology*, 9, 95-9.

Arthur, J. C. (1895). Development of vegetable physiology. *Science*, 44, 163-84.

Auerbach, S. I. (1965). Radionuclide cycling: Current uses and future needs. *Health Physics*, 11, 1355-61.

Auerbach, S. I., Burgess, R. L., and O'Neill, R. V. (1977). The biome programs: Evaluating an experiment. *Science*, 195, 902-4.

Ayala, F. J. (1969). Review of *Topics in Population Genetics*. *Science*, 163, 316.

– (1970). Invalidation of principle of competitive exclusion defended. *Nature*, 227, 89.

– (1974). The concept of biological progress. In *Studies in the Philosophy of Biology*, ed. F. J. Ayala and T. Dobzhansky, pp. 339-56. Berkeley: University of California Press.

Bailey, K. D. (1978). Review of *On Systems Analysis*. *Contemporary Sociology*, 7, 181-2.

Baker, F. C. (1916). *The Relation of Mollusks to Fish in Oneida Lake.* Technical Publication No. 4., New York State College of Forestry at Syracuse University.

– (1918). *The Productivity of Invertebrate Fish Food on the Bottom of Oneida Lake with Special Reference to Mollusks.* Technical Publication No. 9., New York State College of Forestry at Syracuse University.

Bakuzis, E. V. (1969). Forestry viewed in an ecosystem perspective. In *The Ecosystem Concept in Natural Resources Management*, ed. G. M. Van Dyne, pp. 189-258. New York: Academic Press.

Bancroft, W. D. (1911). A universal law. *Science*, 30, 159-79.

Barash, D. P. (1973). The ecologist as Zen master. *American Midland Naturalist*, 89, 214-17.

Barlow, N. (ed.) (1958). *The Autobiography of Charles Darwin.* New York: W. W. Norton.

Baron, W. (1966). Gedanken über der Ursprünglichen Sinn der Ausdrüche Botanik, Zoologie und Biologie. *Suddhoffs Archiv für Geschichte der Medizin und der Naturwissenshaften*, 1-10.

Barrows, H. (1923). Geography as human ecology. *Annals of the Association of American Geographers,* 13:1-14.

Battelle Columbus Laboratories (1975). *Evaluation of Three of the Biome Studies Programs Funded Under the Foundation's International Biological Program (IBP).* Final Report to the National Science Foundation. Columbus, Ohio: Battelle Columbus Laboratories.

Beebe, W. (1945). *The Book of Naturalists.* New York: Knopf.

Berg, K. (1951). The content of limnology demonstrated by F. A. Forel and August Thienemann on the shore of Lake Geneva. *International Association of Theoretical and Applied Limnology Proceedings,* 11, 41-57.

Berlinski, D. (1976). *On Systems Analysis: An Essay Concerning the Limitations of Some Mathematical Methods in the Social, Political, and Biological Sciences.* Cambridge, Mass.: MIT Press.

Bertalanffy, L. von (1951). General systems theory: A new Approach to Unity of Science, pp. 302-11. In *Problems of General Systems Theory.* Symposium of the American Philosophical Society, Toronto, December 29, 1950.

– (1968). *General Systems Theory: Foundations, Development, Applications.* New York: Braziller.

Bessey, C. E. (1902). The word ecology. *Science,* 15, 593.

Beverston, R. J. H., and Holt, S. J. (1957). *On the Dynamics of Exploited Fish Populations.* London: Ministry of Agriculture, Fisheries, and Food.

Bews, J.W. (1935). *Human Ecology.* Oxford: Oxford University Press.

Bigelow, H. B. (1931). *Oceanography: Its Scope, Problems, and Economic Importance.* Boston: Houghton-Mifflin.

Billings, W. D. (1957). Physiological ecology. *Annual Review of Plant Physiology,* 8, 375-92.

– (1974). Environment: Concept and reality. In *Vegetation and Environment,* ed. B. R. Strain and W. D. Billings, pp. 9-35. The Hague: Junk.

– (1980). *Physiological Ecology Plant. McGraw-Hill Encyclopedia of Environmental Science.* New York: McGraw-Hill.

Biological Sciences Curriculum Study (1963). *Green Version: High School Biology.* Chicago: Rand McNally.

Birch, L. C. (1960). The genetic factor in population ecology. *American Naturalist,* 94, 5-24.

Birge, E. A. (1898). Plankton studies on Lake Mendota, II: The crustacea of the plankton from July 1894 to December 1896. *Transactions of the Wisconsin Academy of Sciences, Arts, and Letters,* 11, 274-447.

Birge, E. A., and Juday, C. (1911). *The Inland Lakes of Wisconsin: The Dissolved Gases of the Water and Their Biological Significance.* Wisconsin Geological and Natural History Survey Bulletin No. 22.

– (1922). *The Inland Lakes of Wisconsin, the Plankton. 1. Its Quantity and Chemical Composition.* Wisconsin Geological and Natural History Survey Bulletin No. 64.

Blair, W. F. (1977a). *Big Biology.* Stroudsburg, Pa.: Dowden, Hutchinson and Ross.

– (1977b). The biome programs. *Science,* 195, 822.

Blair, W. F., Auerbach, S. I., Gates, D. M., Inger, R. I., and Ketchum, B. H.

(1968). The importance of ecology and the study of ecosystems. *Hearings before the Committee on Interior and Insular Affairs,* U.S. Senate and the Committee on Science and Astronautics, U.S. House of Representatives, 19th Congress, 2nd Session, July 17, 1968, pp. 154-8, No. 8.

Bodenheimer, F. S. (1957). The concept of biotic organization in synecology. I. Ecological and philosophical approach. In *Studies in Biology and Its History,* ed. F. S. Bodenheimer, pp. 75-90. Jerusalem: Biological Studies Publishers.

– (1958). *Animal Ecology Today.* The Hague: Junk.

Boerker, R. H. (1916). A historical study of forest ecology: Its development in the fields of botany and forestry. *Forestry Quarterly,* 14, 380-432.

Boffey, P. M. (1976). International Biological Program: Was it worth the cost and effort? *Science,* 193, 866-8.

Bolsche, W. (1909). *Haeckel: His Life and Work.* London: Watts.

Bormann, F. H., and Likens, G. E. (1969). The watershed-ecosystem concept and studies of nutrient cycles, In *The Ecosystem Concept in Natural Resource Management,* ed. G. M. Van Dyne, pp. 49-76. New York: Academic Press.

– (1979a). Catastrophic disturbance and the steady state in northern hardwood forests. *American Scientist,* 67, 660-9.

– (1979b). *Pattern and Process in a Forested Ecosystem.* New York: Springer-Verlag.

Botkin, D. B., Janak, J. F., and Wallis, J. R. (1972). Some ecological consequences of a computer model of forest growth. *Journal of Ecology,* 60, 849-72.

Boyd, J. M. (1983). Nature conservation. *Proceedings of the Royal Society of Edinburgh B,* 84, 295-336.

Bradshaw, A. D. (1952). Populations of *Agrostis tenius* resistant to lead and zinc poisoning. *Nature,* 169, 1098.

– (1972). Some of the evolutionary consequences of being a plant. In *Evolutionary Biology,* ed. T. Dobzhansky, M. K. Hecht, and W. C. Steere, pp. 25-47. New York: Appleton-Century-Crofts.

Bradshaw, A. D., and Chadwick, M. J. (1980). *The Restoration of Land.* Berkeley: University of California Press.

Bray, J. R. (1958). Notes toward an ecological theory. *Ecology,* 39, 770-6.

Bray, J. R., and Curtis, J. T. (1957). An ordination of the upland forest communities of southern Wisconsin. *Ecological Monographs,* 27, 325-49.

Bresler, J. B. (ed.). (1966). *Human Ecology: Collected Readings.* Reading, Mass.: Addison-Wesley.

Brewer, R. (1960). *A Brief History of Ecology. Part I – Pre-Nineteenth Century to 1919.* Occasional Papers of the C. C. Adams Center For Ecological Studies, No. 1.

Briggs, W. (1980-81). *Annual Report of the Director, Department of Plant Biology.* Washington, D.C.: Carnegie Institution of Washington Yearbook 80.

Brinck, P. (1980). Theories in population and community ecology: Preface. *Oikos,* 35, 129-30.

Brinkhurst, R. O. (1974). *The Benthos of Lakes.* New York: St. Martin's Press.

Broad, W. J. (1979). Paul Feyerabend: Science and the anarchist. *Science,* 206, 534-7.

Brookhaven Symposia in Biology (1969). *Diversity and Stability in Ecological Systems.* No. 22. Upton, N.Y.: Brookhaven National Laboratory.

Brown, J. H. (1981). Two decades of homage to Santa Rosalia: Toward a general theory of diversity. *American Zoologist,* 21, 877-88.

Browne, J. (1980). Darwin's botanical arithmetic and the "principle of divergence," 1854-1858. *Journal of the History of Biology,* 13, 53-89.

– (1983). *The Secular Ark: Studies in the History of Biogeography.* New Haven: Yale University Press.

Burdon-Sanderson, J. S. (1893). Inaugural address. *Nature,* 48, 464-72.

Burgess, R. L. (1977). The Ecological Society of America: Historical data and some preliminary analysis. In *History of American Ecology,* ed. F. N. Egerton, pp. 1-24. New York: Arno Press.

– (1981a). United States. In *Handbook of Contemporary Developments in World Ecology,* ed. E. J. Kormondy and J. F. McCormick, pp. 67-101. Westport, Conn.: Greenwood Press.

– (1981b). Sources of bibliographical information on American ecologists. *Bulletin of the Ecological Society of America,* 62, 236-55.

– (1981c). The ecology photograph, IV International Congress of Plant Sciences. *Bulletin of the Ecological Society of America,* 62(3), 203-7.

– (1983). Some commentary on distinguished ecologists. *Bulletin of the Ecological Society of America,* 64(1), 19-21.

Burk, C. J. (1973). The Kaibab deer incident: A long-persisting myth. *BioScience,* 23, 113-14.

Burns, F. J. A. (1901). A sectional bird census. *Wilson Bulletin,* 8, 84-103.

C. H. (1977). Ecology and national security. *Science,* 198, 712.

Cain, S. A. (1938). The species-area curve. *American Midland Naturalist,* 19, 573-81.

– (1939). The climax and its complexities. *American Midland Naturalist,* 21, 146-81.

Cairns, J., Jr. (1979). Academic blocks to assessing environmental impacts of water supply alternatives. In *Thames/Potomac Seminars,* ed. A. M. Blackburn, Proceedings of the Washington Seminar, Interstate Commission on the Potomac River Basin, pp. 77-79.

– (ed.) (1980). *The Recovery Process in Damaged Ecosystems.* Ann Arbor, Mich.: Ann Arbor Science.

Caldwell, L. K. (1971). New legal arena. *Science,* 171, 665-66.

Calow, P., and Townsend, C. R. (1981). Energetics, Ecology, and Evolution. In *Physiological Ecology,* ed. P. Calow, and C. R. Townsend, pp. 3-19. Oxford: Blackwell Scientific.

Cannon, S. F. (1978). *Science in Culture: The Early Victorian Period.* New York: Dawson and Science History.

Cantlon, J. E. (1970). Ecological bridges. *Bulletin of the Ecological Society of America,* 51(4), 5-10.

– (1980). The institutional challenges for ecology. In *Oak Ridge National Laboratory Environmental Sciences Laboratory Dedication, February 26-27, 1979.* No. 5666, pp. 31-42. Oak Ridge, Tenn.: Oak Ridge National Laboratory 5666.

Carpenter, J. R. (1939). The biome. *American Midland Naturalist,* 21, 75-91.

Carpenter, R. A. (1970). The political use of ecological information. *BioScience,* 20(24), 1285(15 December).

– (1976). The scientific basis of NEPA: Is it adequate? *Environmental Law Report,* 6, 50014-19.

– (1983). Ecology in court, and other disappointments of environmental science and environmental law. *Natural Resources Lawyer,* 15, 573-97.

Carpenter, S. R. (1981). Submersed vegetation: An internal factor in lake ecosystem succession. *American Naturalist,* 118, 372-83.

Carson, R. (1962). *Silent Spring.* Boston: Houghton Mifflin.

Caswell, H. (1976). The validation problem. In *Systems Analysis and Simulation in Ecology, Vol. IV,* ed. B. C. Patten, pp. 313-25. New York: Academic Press.

– (1982a). Deacon blues: Life history theory and the equilibrium status of populations and communities. Presented at a symposium, Community Ecology: Conceptual Issues and the Evidence, Tallahassee, Fla., March 1981. (Pers. commun.)

– (1982b). Life history theory and the equilibrium status of populations. *American Naturalist,* 120, 317-39.

Caswell, H., Koenig, H. E., Resh, J. A., and Ross, Q. E. (1972). An introduction to systems analysis for ecologists. In *Systems Analysis and Simulation in Ecology, Vol. 3,* ed. B. E. Patten, pp. 3-78. New York: Academic Press.

Cattell, J. M. (1906). A statistical study of American men of science. *Science,* 24, 658-65.

Catton, W. P., Jr., and Dunlap, R. E. (1980). New ecological paradigm for post-exuberant sociology. *American Behavioral Scientist,* 24, 15-47.

Caughley, G. (1970). Eruption of ungulate populations, with emphasis on Himalayan thar in New Zealand. *Ecology,* 51, 53-72.

Chamberlain, T. C. (1890). The method of multiple working hypotheses. Reprinted in *Science,* 148, 754-9 (1965).

Chandler, D. C. (1963). Michigan. In *Limnology in North America,* ed. D. G. Frey, pp. 95-116. Madison: University of Wisconsin Press.

Chapman, R. N. (1931). *Animal Ecology.* New York: McGraw-Hill.

Cheney, S. (1946). *A World History of Art.* New York: Viking Press.

Christensen, N. L., and Peet, R. K. (1980). Succession: a vegetation process. *Vegetatio,* 43, 131-40.

Christiansen, F. B., and Fenchel, T. M. (1977). *Theories of Populations in Biological Communities.* Berlin: Springer-Verlag.

Cittadino, E. (1980). Ecology and the professionalization of botany in America, 1890-1905. *Studies in the History of Biology,* 4, 171-98.

– (1981). *Plant Adaptation and Natural Selection after Darwin: Ecological Plant Physiology in the German Empire, 1880-1900.* Ph.D. Dissertation, University of Wisconsin.

Clapham, A. R., Lucas, C. E., and Pirie, N. V. (1976). A review of the United Kingdom contribution to the International Biological Programme. *Philosophical Transactions of the Royal Society of London B,* 274, 277-555.

Clarke, B. (1974). Causes of genetic variation. *Science,* 186, 524-5.

Clarke, G. (1954). *Elements of Ecology.* New York: Wiley.

Clarke, R. (1974). *Ellen Swallow: The Woman Who Founded Ecology.* Chicago: Follett.

Clausen, J. J., Keck, D. C., and Hiesey, W. M. (1940). *Experimental Studies on the Nature of Species. I. Effect of Varied Environments on Western North American Plants.* Publication No. 520. Washington, D.C.: Carnegie Institution of Washington.

Clements, F. E. (1904). *The Development and Structure of Vegetation. Botanical Survey of Nebraska 7. Studies in the Vegetation of the State.* Lincoln, Nebr.

– (1905). *Research Methods in Ecology.* Lincoln: University Publishing Company. Reprinted New York: Arno Press (1977).

– (1909). Darwin's influence upon plant geography and ecology. *American Naturalist,* 43, 143-51.

– (1912). Phytogeographical excursion in the British Isles. VIII. Some impressions and reflections. *New Phytologist,* 11, 177-9.

– (1916). *Plant Succession: An Analysis of the Development of Vegetation.* Publication No. 242. Washington, D.C.: Carnegie Institution of Washington.

– (1920). *Plant Indicators: The Relation of Plant Communities to Process and Practice.* Publication No. 290. Washington, D.C.: Carnegie Institution of Washington.

– (1924). *Methods and Principles of Paleo-ecology.* Yearbook 32. Washington, D.C.: Carnegie Institution of Washington.

– (1935). Experimental ecology in the public service. *Ecology,* 16, 342-63.

– (1936). Nature and structure of the climax. *Journal of Ecology,* 24, 252-84.

Clements, F. E., and Shelford, V. E. (1939). *Bio-Ecology.* New York: Wiley.

Clements, F. E., Weaver, J. E., and Hanson, H. C. (1929). *Plant Competition: An Analysis of Community Functions.* Publication No. 398. Washington, D.C.: Carnegie Institution of Washington. Reprinted New York: Arno Press (1977).

Cockayne, L. (1918). The importance of plant ecology with regard to agriculture. *New Zealand Journal of Science and Technology,* 1, 70-4.

Cody, M. L. (1974). *Competition and the Structure of Bird Communities.* Princeton, N.J.: Princeton University Press.

– (1981). Citation classic. *Current Contents,* 12(23), 14.

Cody, M. L., and Diamond, J. M. (eds.) (1975). *Ecology and the Evolution of Communities.* Cambridge, Mass.: Belknap Press of Harvard University.

Cole, L. C. (1949). The measurement of interspecific association. *Ecology,* 30, 411-24.

– (1954). The population consequences of life history phenomena. *Quarterly Review of Biology,* 29, 103-37.

- (1957). Sketches of general and comparative demography. *Cold Spring Harbor Symposium in Quantitative Biology*, 22, 1-15.
Coleman, W. (1977). *Biology of the Nineteenth Century*. Cambridge: Cambridge University Press.
- (1979). Bergmann's rule: Animal heat as a biological phenomenon. *Studies in History of Biology*, 3, 67-88.
Coleman, W. H. (1848). On the geographical distribution of British plants. *Phytologist*, 3, 217-21.
Colinvaux, P. A. (1982). Towards a theory of history: Fitness, niche, and clutch size of *Homo sapiens*. *Journal of Ecology*, 70, 393-412.
Colinvaux, P. A., and Barnett, B. D. (1979). Lindeman and the ecological efficiency of wolves. *American Naturalist*, 114, 707-18.
Colwell, T. B., Jr. (1970). Some implications of the ecological revolution for the reconstruction of value. In *Human Values and Natural Science*, ed. E. Lazlo and J. B. Wilbur, pp. 245-58. New York: Gordon and Breach, Science Publishing Company.
Commager, H. S. (1950). *The American Mind*. New Haven: Yale University Press.
- (ed.) (1967). *Living Ideas in America*. New York: Harper & Row.
Committee on Applied Ecology. (1958). Report. *Bulletin of the Ecological Society of America*, 39, 18-25.
- (1960). Report. *Bulletin of the Ecological Society of America*, 41, 25-9.
Committee on Human Ecology. (1957). Report. *Bulletin of the Ecological Society of America*, 38, 27-9.
- (1967). Report. *Bulletin of the Ecological Society of America*, 48, 103.
Committee on Nomenclature. (1947). *Report to Ecological Society of America, 32nd Annual Meeting*. Chicago. Revised and Resubmitted at the Cornell University Meeting, September 1952.
Conard, H. S. (1951). *The Background of Plant Ecology*. Ames: Iowa State College Press.
Connell, J. H. (1978). Diversity in tropical rain forests and coral reefs. *Science*, 199, 1302-10.
- (1980). Diversity and the coevolution of competitors; or, the ghost of competition past. *Oikos*, 35, 131-8.
Connell, J. H., and Slatyer, R. O. (1977). Mechanisms of succession in natural communities and their role in community stability and organization. *American Naturalist*, 111, 1119-44.
Connell, J. H., and Sousa, W. P. (1983). On the evidence needed to judge ecological stability or persistence. *American Naturalist*, 121, 789-824.
Connor, E. F., and McCoy, E. D. (1979). The statistics and biology of the species-area relationship. *American Naturalist*, 113, 791-833.
Conwentz, H. (1914). On national and international protection of nature. *Journal of Ecology*, 2, 109-22.
Cook, R. E. (1977). Raymond Lindeman and the trophic-dynamic concept in ecology. *Science*, 198, 22-6.
- (1979). Ecology since colonial times. *Science*, 203, 429.

Cook, S. G. (1980). *Cowles Bog, Indiana and Henry Chandler Cowles (1869-1939): A Study in Historical Geography and the History of Ecology.* Indiana Dunes National Lake Shore, National Park Services, U.S. Dept. Interior.

Cooper, W. S. (1913). The climax forest of Isle Royale, Lake Superior and its development. *Botanical Gazette,* 55, 1-44, 115-40, 189-235.

– (1923). The recent ecological history of Glacier Bay, Alaska: II. The present vegetation cycle. *Ecology,* 4, 223-46.

Cottam, G., and Curtis, J. T. (1949). A method for making rapid surveys of woodlands by means of pairs of randomly selected trees. *Ecology,* 30, 101-4.

Cottam, W. P. (1947). Is Utah Sahara bound? In *Our Renewable Wild Lands – A Challenge,* ed. W. P. Cottam, pp. 1-52. Salt Lake City: University of Utah Press.

Coulter S. (1893). The phanerogamic flora of Indiana. *Proceedings of the Indiana Academy of Sciences,* 3, 193-9.

Council on Environmental Quality and Federal Council for Science and Technology (1974). *The Role of Ecology in the Federal Government.* Report of the Committee on Ecological Research. Washington, D.C.

Cowles, H. C. (1898). The phytogeography of Nebraska. *Botanical Gazette,* 25, 370-1.

– (1899a). The ecological relations of the vegetation of the sand dunes of Lake Michigan. *Botanical Gazette,* 27, 95-117, 167-202, 281-308, 361-91.

– (1899b). A new treatise on ecology. *Botanical Gazette,* 27, 214-16.

– (1901). The physiographic ecology of Chicago and vicinity: A study of the origin, development, and classification of plant societies. *Botanical Gazette,* 31, 73-108, 145-82.

– (1904). The work of the year 1903 in ecology. *Science,* 19, 879-85.

– (1908). An ecological aspect of the conception of species. *American Naturalist,* 42, 265-71.

– (1909). Present problems in plant ecology. I. The trend of ecological philosophy. *American Naturalist,* 43, 356-68.

– (1911). The causes of vegetative cycles. *Botanical Gazette,* 51, 161-83.

– (1915). A proposed ecological society. *Science,* 42, 496.

Cox, D. L. (1979). *Charles Elton and the Emergence of Modern Ecology.* Ph.D. Dissertation, Washington University.

– (1980). A note on the queer history of "niche." *Bulletin of the Ecological Society of America,* 64, 201-2.

Cragg, J. B. (1966). Preface. *Advances in Ecological Research,* 3, vii.

Craig, R. B. (1976). Review of *Evolutionary Ecology. Ecology,* 57, 212.

Crane, D. (1972). *Invisible Colleges: Diffusion of Knowledge in Scientific Communities.* Chicago: University of Chicago Press.

Cravens, H. (1978). *The Triumph of Evolution.* Philadelphia: University of Pennsylvania Press.

Culver, D. C. (1975). The relationship between theory and experiment in community ecology. In *Ecosystems Analysis and Prediction,* ed. S. A. Levin, pp. 103-10. Proceedings SIAM-SIMS Conference on Ecosystems, Alta, Utah, July 1-5, 1974, SIAM Institute of Mathematics and Society.

Curl, H., Jr. (1968). IBP delays. *Science, 175,* 1065.

Curtis, J. T. (1959). *The Vegetation of Wisconsin.* Madison: University of Wisconsin Press.

Curtis, J. T., and Juday, C. (1937). Photosynthesis of algae in Wisconsin lakes. III. Observations of 1935. *International Review of Hydrobiology, 35,* 122-33.

Curtis, J. T., and McIntosh, R. P. (1950). The interrelations of certain analytic and synthetic phytosociological characters. *Ecology, 31,* 434-55.

– (1951). An upland forest continuum in the prairie-forest border region of Wisconsin. *Ecology, 32,* 476-96.

Dale, M. P. (1970). Systems analysis and ecology. *Ecology, 51,* 2-16.

Damkaer, D. M., and Mrozek-Dahl, T. (1980). The Plankton-expedition and the copepod studies of Friedrich and Maria Dahl. In *Oceanography: The Past,* ed. M. Sears and D. Merriman, pp. 462-73. New York: Springer-Verlag.

Dansereau, P. (1957). *Biogeography: An Ecological Perspective.* New York: Ronald Press.

Darling, F. F. (1955). *West Highland Survey: An Essay in Human Ecology.* Oxford: Oxford University Press.

– (1967). A wider environment of ecology and conservation. *Daedalus, 96,* 1003-19.

Darwin, C. R. (1859). *The Origin of Species by Means of Natural Selection; or, the Preservation of Favored Races in the Struggle for Life.* London: John Murray.

Daubenmire, R. (1966). Vegetation: Identification of typal communities. *Science, 151,* 291-8.

Davenport, C. B. (1903). The Animal Ecology of the Cold Spring Sand Spit, with remarks on the theory of adaptation. Decennial Publications of the University of Chicago, *The Biological Sciences, 10,* 155-76.

Davis, M. B. (1969). Palynology and environmental history during the Quaternary period. *American Scientist, 57,* 317-32.

Dayton, P. K. (1979). Ecology: A science and a religion. In *Ecological Processes in Coastal and Marine Ecosystems,* ed. R. J. Livingstone, pp. 3-18. New York: Plenum Press.

– (1980). Citation classic. *Current Contents,* 11(32), 18.

Deacon, M. B. (1971). *Scientists and the Sea, 1650-1900: A Study of Marine Science.* New York: Academic Press.

– (ed.) (1978). *Oceanography: Concepts and History.* Stroudsburg, Pa.: Dowden, Hutchinson and Ross.

Deam, J. R. (1966). *Down to the Sea: A Century of Oceanography.* Glasgow: Brown, Son, and Ferguson.

Dean, B. (1893). Report on the European methods of oyster-culture. *Bulletin U.S. Fish Commission,* 11, 357-406.

DeBach, P. (1966). The competitive displacement and coexistence principles. *Annual Review of Entomology,* 11, 183-212.

Deevey, E. S., Jr. (1942). Reexamination of Thoreau's Walden. *Quarterly Review of Biology,* 17, 1-11.

- (1947). Life tables for natural populations of animals. *Quarterly Review of Biology*, 22, 283-314.
- (1964). General and historical ecology. *BioScience*, 14, 33-5.
- (1970). In defense of mud. *Bulletin of Ecological Society of America*, 51(1), 5-8.
- (1971). Inter-American Institute of Ecology – Twenty questions. *Bulletin of the Ecological Society of America*, 52(1), 5-10.
Dexter, R. W. (1978). History of the Ecologist's Union – spin off from the ESA and prototype of the Nature Conservancy. *Bulletin of the Ecological Society of America*, 59, 146-7.
Diamond, J. M. (1978). Niche shifts and the rediscovery of competition: Why did field biologists so long overlook the widespread evidence for interspecific competition that had already impressed Darwin? *American Scientist*, 66, 322-31.
Dice, L. R. (1947). Effectiveness of selection by owls of deer mice *(Peromyscus maniculatus)* which contrast in colour with their background. *Contributions of the Laboratory of Vertebrate Biology of the University of Michigan*, 34, 1-20.
- (1952). *Natural Communities*. Ann Arbor: University of Michigan Press.
- (1955). What is ecology? *Scientific Monthly*, 80(6), 346-55.
Dimbleby, G. W. (1952). Soil regeneration on the north-east Yorkshire moors. *Journal of Ecology*, 40, 331-41.
Disch, R. (ed.) (1970). *The Ecological Conscience: Values for Survival*. Englewood Cliffs, N.J.: Prentice-Hall.
Dobben, van, W. H., and Lowe-McConnell, R. H. (eds.) (1975). *Unifying Concepts in Ecology*. The Hague: Junk.
Dobzhansky, T. (1968). Adaptedness and fitness. In *Population Biology and Evolution*, ed. R. C. Lewontin, pp. 109-21. Syracuse, N.Y.: Syracuse University Press.
Dogan, M., and Rokkan, S. (1969). Introduction. In *Social Ecology*, ed. M. Dogan and S. Rokkan, pp. 1-15. Cambridge, Mass.: MIT Press.
Doncaster, I. (1961). *In the Footsteps of the Naturalists*. London: Phoenix House.
Douglass, A. E. (1928). *Climatic Cycles and Tree Growth: A Study of the Annual Rings of Trees in Relation to Climate and Solar Activity*. Publication No. 289, Vol. 2. Washington, D.C.: Carnegie Institution of Washington.
Downhower, J., and Mayer, R. (1977). Biome programs. *Science*, 195, 823.
Drude, O. (1890). *Handbuch der Pflanzengeographie*. Stuttgart: Verlag von J. Engelhorn.
- (1896). *Deutschlands Planzengeographie*. Stuttgart: Verlag von J. Engelhorn.
- (1906). The position of ecology in modern science. In *Congress of Arts and Sciences, Universal Exposition, St. Louis, 1904*, Vol. V, *Biology, Anthropology, Psychology, Sociology*, ed. H. J. Rogers, pp. 179-90. Boston: Houghton Mifflin.
Duff, A. G., and Lowe, P. D. (1981). Great Britain. In *Handbook of Contem-*

*porary Developments in World Ecology*, ed. E. J. Kormondy and J. F. McCormick, pp. 141-56. Westport, Conn.: Greenwood Press.

Dunlap, R. E. (ed.) (1980a). Ecology and the social sciences: An emerging paradigm. *American Behavioral Scientist*, 24, 5-151.

– (1980b). Paradigmatic change in social sciences. *American Behavioral Scientist*, 24, 5-14.

Dunnett, G. M. (1982). Ecology and everyman. *Journal of Animal Ecology*, 51, 1-14.

Du Rietz, G. E. (1930). Classification and nomenclature of vegetation. *Svensk Botanisk Tidskrift*, 24, 489-503.

– (1957). Linnaeus as a phytogeographer. *Vegetatio*, 7, 161-8.

Dyksterhuis, E. J. (1958). Ecological principles in range evaluation. *Botanical Review*, 24, 253-72.

Dyson-Hudson, R. (1983). Desertification as a social problem. *Science*, 221, 1365-6.

Eastern Deciduous Forest Biome (1972). *U.S. IBP Analysis of Ecosystems Newsletter*, No. 9, Oak Ridge, Tenn.: Oak Ridge National Laboratory.

Ebeling, A. W. (1982). The workings of ecosystems science. *Science*, 218, 1110-11.

Ecological Society of America. (1916). *Science*, 43, 382-3.

Ecological Society of America. (1917). Abstracts of papers at a meeting New York City, Dec. 27-29, 1916. *Journal of Ecology*, 5, 119-28.

Ecologist's Union and the Ecological Society of America. (1950-1). Nature sanctuaries in the United States and Canada. *Living Wilderness*, 35, 1-45.

Ecology of closely allied species (symposium). (1944). *Journal of Animal Ecology*, 13, 176-7.

Edmondson, Y. H. (1971). Some components of the Hutchinson legend. *Limnology and Oceanography*, 16, 157-72.

Edson, M. M., Foin, T. C., and Knapp, C. M. (1981). "Emergent properties" and ecological research. *American Naturalist*, 118, 593-6.

Egerton, F. N. (1962). The scientific contributions of Francois Alphonse Forel, the founder of limnology. *Schweizerische Zeitschrift für Hydrologie*, 24, 181-99.

– (1967). *Observations and Studies of Animal Populations before 1860: A Survey Concluding with Darwin's Origin of Species*. Ph.D. Dissertation, University of Wisconsin.

– (1968a). Leeuwenhoek as a founder of animal demography. *Journal of the History of Biology*, 1, 1-22.

– (1968b). Studies of animal populations from Lamarck to Darwin. *Journal of the History of Biology*, 1, 225-59.

– (1968c). Ancient sources for animal demography. *Isis*, 59, 175-89.

– (1973). Changing concepts in the balance of nature. *Quarterly Review of Biology*, 48, 322-50.

– (1976). Ecological studies and observations before 1900. In *Issues and Ideas in America*, ed. B. J. Taylor and T. J. White, pp. 311-51. Norman: University of Oklahoma Press.

– (ed.) (1977a). *History of American Ecology*. New York: Arno Press.
– (1977b). A bibliographical guide to the history of general ecology and population ecology. *History of Science*, 15, 189-215.
– (1979a). Hewett C. Watson: Great Britain's first phytogeographer. *Huntia*, 3, 87-102.
– (1979b). Review of *Nature's Economy*. *Isis*, 70, 167-8.
– (1983). History of ecology: Achievements and opportunities, Part 1. *Journal of the History of Biology*, 16, 259-310.
Egler, F. E. (1951). A commentary on American plant ecology based on the textbooks of 1947-1949. *Ecology*, 32, 673-95.
– (1952-4). Vegetation science concepts. I. Initial floristics composition, a factor in old-field vegetation development. *Vegetatio*, 4, 412-7.
– (1964). Pesticides in our ecosystem. *American Scientist*, 52(1), 110-36.
– (1982). Environmentalism of the 1970's: Legislation and litigation. *Ecology*, 63, 1990-1.
Ehrlich, P. R., and Birch, L. C. (1967). The "balance of nature" and "population control." *American Naturalist*, 101, 97-124.
Eigenmann, C. H. (1895). Turkey Lake as a unit of environment and the variation of its inhabitants. *Proceedings of the Indiana Academy of Sciences*, 5, 204-96.
Ekirch, A. E., Jr. (1963). *Man and Nature in America*. New York: Columbia University Press.
Elster, H. J. (1974). History of limnology. *Mitteilungen Internationale Vereinigung Limnologie*, 20, 7-30.
Elton, C. (1927). *Animal Ecology*. London: Sidgwick and Jackson.
– (1930). *Animal Ecology and Evolution*. New York: Oxford University Press.
– (1933). *The Ecology of Animals*. London: Methuen.
– (1940). Scholasticism in ecology. *Journal of Animal Ecology*, 9, 151-2.
– (1942). *Voles, Mice, and Lemmings: Problems in Population Dynamics*. Oxford: Clarendon Press.
– (1966). *The Pattern of Animal Communities*. London: Methuen.
Elton, C. S., and Miller, R. S. (1954). The ecological survey of animal communities: With a practical system of classifying habitats by structural characters. *Journal of Ecology*, 42, 460-96.
Engel, J. R. (1983). *Sacred Sands: The Struggle for Community in the Indiana Dunes*. Middletown, Conn.: Wesleyan University Press.
Engelberg, J., and Boyarsky, L. L. (1979). The noncybernetic nature of ecosystems. *American Naturalist*, 114, 317-24.
Engelmann, M. D. (1966). Energetics, terrestrial field studies, and animal productivity. *Advances in Ecological Research*, 3, 73-115.
Evans, F. C. (1956). Ecosystem as the basic unit in ecology. *Science*, 123, 1127-8.
Evans, G. C. (1976). A sack of uncut diamonds: The study of ecosystems and the future of resources of mankind. *Journal of Ecology*, 64, 1-39.
Faegri, K. (1954). Some reflections on the trophic system in limnology. *Nytt Magasin für Botanik*, 3, 43-9.

Farber, P. L. (1982). The transformation of natural history in the nineteenth century. *Journal of the History of Biology*, 15, 145-52.

Farnworth, F. G., and Golley, F. B. (eds.) (1974). *Fragile Ecosystems: Evaluation of Research and Applications in the Neotropics*. New York: Springer-Verlag.

Fernow, B. E. (1903). Applied ecology. *Science*, 17, 605-7.

Flader, S. L. (1974). *Thinking Like a Mountain*. Columbia: University of Missouri Press.

Foin, T. C., and Jain, S. K. (1977). Ecosystems analysis and population biology: Lessons for the development of community ecology. *BioScience*, 27, 532-8.

Forbes, E. (1844). On the light thrown on geology by submarine researches. *New Philosophical Journal* (Edinburgh), 36, 318-27.

Forbes, E., and Godwin-Austen, R. (1859). *The Natural History of the European Seas*. London: Van Voorst.

Forbes, S. A. (1880a). On some interactions of organisms. *Bulletin Illinois State Laboratory of Natural History*, 1, 3-17.

– (1880b). The food of fishes. *Bulletin Illinois State Laboratory of Natural History*, 1,18-65.

– (1883a). The first food of the common whitefish. *Bulletin Illinois State Laboratory of Natural History*, 1, 95-109.

– (1883b). The food relations of the Carabidae and Coccindellidae. *Bulletin Illinois State Laboratory of Natural History*, 1, 33-64.

– (1887). The lake as a microcosm. *Bulletin Science Association of Peoria, Illinois*, 1887, 77-87.

– (1888). On the food relations of freshwater fishes. *Bulletin Illinois State Laboratory of Natural History*, 2, 475-538.

– (1896). *Nineteenth Report of the State Entomologist on the Noxious and Beneficial Insects of the State of Illinois*, Vol. 32. Springfield: Illinois Department Agriculture Transactions.

– (1907a). On the local distribution of certain Illinois fishes: An essay in statistical ecology. *Bulletin Illinois State Laboratory of Natural History*, 7, 273-303.

– (1907b). An ornithological cross-section of Illinois in autumn. *Bulletin Illinois State Laboratory of Natural History*, 7, 305-35.

– (1907c). History of the former state natural history societies of Illinois. *Science*, 26, 892-8.

– (1909). Aspects of progress in economic entomology. *Journal of Economic Entomology*, 2, 25-35.

– (1922). The humanizing of ecology. *Ecology*, 3, 89-92.

Ford, E. B. (1931). *Mendelism and Evolution*. London: Methuen.

– (1964). *Ecological Genetics*. London: Methuen.

– (1980). Some recollections pertaining to the evolutionary synthesis. In *The Evolutionary Synthesis*, ed. E. Mayr and W. B. Provine, pp. 334-42. Cambridge, Mass.: Harvard University Press.

Forel, F. A. (1871). Rapport à la Société vaudoise des Sciences Naturelles sur l'étude scientifique du Lac Léman. *Bulletin Société Vaudoise Sciences Naturelles*, 11.

– (1892). *Lac Léman: Monographie Limnologique.* Lausanne: Rouge.

Fretwell, S. D. (1975). The impact of Robert MacArthur on ecology. *Annual Review of Ecology and Systematics,* 6, 1-13.

Frey, D. G. (ed.) (1963a). *Limnology in North America.* Madison: University of Wisconsin Press.

– (1963b). Wisconsin: The Birge-Juday era. In *Limnology in North America,* ed. D. J. Frey, pp. 3-54. Madison: University of Wisconsin Press.

Friederichs, K. (1927). Grundsätzliches über die Lebenseinheiten höherer Ordnung und den ökologischen Einheitsfaktor. *Die Naturwissenschaften,* 15, 153-7, 182-6.

– (1958). A definition of ecology and some thoughts about basic concepts. *Ecology,* 39, 154-9.

Fritts, H. C. (1966). Growth rings of trees: Their correlation with climate. *Science,* 154, 973-9.

Fry, F. E. J. (1947). Effects of the environment on animal activity. *University of Toronto Studies Biological Series 55: Publications of the Ontario Fisheries Research Laboratory,* 68, 1-62.

Fuchs, G. (1967). Das konzept der ökologie in der Amerikanischen Geographie: Am Beispiel der Wissenschaftstheorie zwischen 1900 und 1930. *Erdkunde,* 21, 81-93.

Fuller, G. D. (1928). Origin and development of plant sociology. *Botanical Gazette,* 85, 229-32.

Gaardner, T., and Gran, H. H. (1927). Investigations of the production of plankton in the Olso Fjord. *Rapport et Proces-Verbaux des Reunions Conseil International Exploration de la Mer,* 42, 1-48.

Gallucci, V. F. (1973). On the principles of thermodynamics in ecology. *Annual Review of Ecology and Systematics,* 4, 329-57.

Ganong, W. F. (1902). The word ecology. *Science,* 15, 593-4; 792-3.

– (1903). The vegetation of the Bay of Fundy salt and diked marshes: An ecological study. *Botanical Gazette,* 36, 161-86, 280-302, 349-76, 429-555.

– (1904). The cardinal principles of ecology. *Science,* 19, 493-8.

Gates, D. M. (1968). Toward understanding ecosystems. *Advances in Ecological Research,* 5, 1-36.

Gause, G. F. (1932). Ecology of populations. *Quarterly Review of Biology,* 7, 27-46.

– (1934). *The Struggle for Existence.* Baltimore: Williams & Wilkins.

– (1936). The principles of biocœnology. *Quarterly Review of Biology,* 11, 320-36.

– (1970). Criticism of invalidation of the principle of competitive exclusion. *Nature,* 227, 89.

Gendron, V. (1961). *The Dragon Tree.* New York: Longmans, Green.

Ghiselin J. (1981). Applied ecology. In *Handbook of Contemporary Developments in World Ecology,* ed. E. J. Kormondy and J. F. McCormick, pp. 651-64. Westport, Conn.: Greenwood Press.

Ghiselin, M. T. (1969). *The Triumph of the Darwinian Method.* Berkeley: University of California Press.

– (1974). *The Economy of Nature and the Evolution of Sex.* Berkeley: University of California Press.

– (1980). The failure of morphology to assimilate Darwinism. In *The Evolutionary Synthesis,* ed. E. Mayr and W. B. Provine, pp. 180-92. Cambridge, Mass.: Harvard University Press.

Gibson, J. H. (1977). The biome programs. *Science,* 195, 822-3.

Gimingham, C. H., Spence, D. H. N., and Watson, A. (1983). Ecology. *Proceedings of the Royal Society of Edinburgh B,* 84, 85-183.

Glacken, C. J. (1967). *Traces on the Rhodian Shore.* Berkeley: University California Press.

Gleason, H. A. (1910). The vegetation of the inland sand deposits of Illinois. *Bulletin Illinois State Laboratory of Natural History,* 9, 21-174.

– (1917). The structure and development of the plant association. *Bulletin of the Torrey Botanical Club,* 43, 463-81.

– (1920). Some applications of the quadrat method. *Bulletin of the Torrey Botanical Club,* 47, 21-33.

– (1922). On the relation of species and area. *Ecology,* 3, 158-62.

– (1925). Species and area. *Ecology,* 6, 66-74.

– (1926). The individualistic concept of the plant association. *Bulletin of the Torrey Botanical Club,* 53, 1-20.

– (1936). Twenty-five years of ecology, 1910-1935. *Memoirs of the Brooklyn Botanical Garden,* 4, 41-9.

– (1939). The individualistic concept of the plant association. *American Midland Naturalist,* 21, 92-110.

– (1953). Autobiographical letter. *Bulletin of the Ecological Society of America,* 34, 40-2.

Godwin, H. (1931). Studies in the ecology of Wicken Fen. I. The groundwater level of the fen. *Journal of Ecology,* 19, 449-73.

– (1934). Pollen analysis: An outline of the problems and potentialities of the method. I. Technique and interpretation. *New Phytologist,* 33, 278-305. II. General applications of pollen analysis. *New Phytologist,* 33, 325-58.

– (1977). Sir Arthur Tansley: The man and the subject. *Journal of Ecology,* 65, 1-26.

Goldman, C. R. (ed.) (1966). *Primary Productivity in Aquatic Environments.* Berkeley: University of California Press.

Golley, F. B. (1960). Energy dynamics of a food chain of an old-field community. *Ecological Monographs,* 30, 187-206.

– (1984). Historical origins of the ecosystem concept in ecology. In *Ecosystem Concept in Ecology,* ed. E. Moran, pp. 33-49. Washington, D.C.: American Association Advancement of Science Publications.

Goodall, D. W. (1952). Quantitative aspects of plant distribution. *Biological Reviews,* 27, 194-245.

– (1954). Objective methods for the classification of vegetation. III. An essay in the use of factor analysis. *Australian Journal of Botany,* 2, 304-24.

– (1972). Building and testing ecosystem models. In *Mathematical models in ecology,* ed. J. N. R. Jeffers, pp. 173-94. Oxford: Blackwell Scientific.

Goodland, R. J. (1975). The tropical origin of ecology: Eugen Warming's jubilee. *Oikos,* 26, 240-5.

Goodman, D. (1975). The theory of diversity-stability relationships in ecology. *Quarterly Review of Biology,* 50, 237-66.

Gordon, M. S. (1981). Introduction to the symposium Theoretical ecology: To what extent has it added to our understanding of the natural world? *American Zoologist,* 21, 793.

Gorham, E. (1955). Titus Smith, a pioneer of plant ecology in North America. *Ecology,* 36, 116-23.

Gorham, E., Vitousek, P. M., and Reiners, W. A. (1979). The regulation of chemical budgets over the course of terrestrial ecosystem succession. *Annual Review of Ecology and Systematics,* 10, 53-84.

Gould, S. J., and Lewontin, R. C. (1979). The Spandrels of San Marcos and the Panglossian paradigm: A critique of the adaptationist programme. *Proceedings of the Royal Society of London B, Biological Sciences,* 205, 581-98.

Graham, G. M. (1935). Modern theory of exploiting a fishery and application to North Sea trawling. *Journal du Conseil Permanent International pour l'Exploration de la Mer,* 10, 264-74.

Grant, P. R., and Price, T. D. (1981). Population variation in continuously varying traits as an ecological genetics problem. *American Zoologist,* 21, 795-811.

Greene, E. L. (1909). *Landmarks of Botanical History.* Smithsonian Miscellaneous Collections, Vol. 54.

Greene, J. C. (1959). *The Death of Adam: Evolution and Its Impact on Western Thought.* Ames: Iowa State University Press.

Greig-Smith, P. (1957). *Quantitative Plant Ecology.* London: Butterworths Scientific.

– (1978). Presidential viewpoint. *Bulletin of the British Ecological Society,* IX(1), 2-3.

Grinnell, J. (1908). The biota of the San Bernardino Mountains. *University of California Publications in Zoology,* 5, 1-170.

– (1917). Field tests of theories concerning distributional control. *American Naturalist,* 51, 115-28.

Grisebach, A. R. H. (1872). *Die Vegetation der Erde.* 2 Vols. Leipzig: Engelman.

Gross, P. R. (1982). The interface of modern scientific research and parasitology. In *The Current Status and Future of Parasitology,* ed. K. S. Warren and E. F. Purcell, pp. 256-68. New York: The Josiah Macy, Jr. Foundation.

Gulland, J. A. (1977). *Fish Population Dynamics.* London: Wiley.

Gutierrez, L. T., and Fey, W. R. (1980). *Ecosystem Succession: A General Hypothesis and a Test Model of a Grassland.* Cambridge, Mass.: MIT Press.

Haeckel, E. (1866). *Generelle Morphologie der Organismen: Allgemeine Grundzüge der organischen Formen-wissenschaft, mechanisch begründet durch die von Charles Darwin reformirte Descendenz-Theorie.* 2 vols. Berlin: Reimer.

– (1891). Plankton Studien. *Jena Zeitschrift für Naturwissenschaft*, 25, 232-336. (Trans. G. W. Field in *Report of United States Commissioner of Fish and Fisheries*, 1889-1891, pp. 565-641.)

Haefner, J. W. (1978). Ecological theories, laws, and explanations. *Ecology*, 59, 864-5.

Haila, Y., and Järvinen, O. (1982). The role of theoretical concepts in understanding the ecological theatre: A case study in island biogeography. In *Conceptual Issues in Ecology*, ed. E. Saarinen, pp. 261-78. Dordrecht: Reidel.

Hairston, N. G. (1981). Citation classic. *Current Contents*, 12(20), 20.

Hairston, N. G., Smith, F. E., and Slobodkin, L. B. (1960). Community structure, population control, and competition. *American Naturalist*, 94, 421-5.

Haldane, J. B. S. (1956). The relation between density regulation and natural selection. *Proceedings of the Royal Society of London Series B*, 145, 306-8.

Halfon, E. (ed.) (1979). *Theoretical Systems Ecology.* New York: Academic Press.

Handbook of the Ecological Society of America. (1917). *Bulletin of the Ecological Society of America*, 1, 1-56.

Hanski, I. (1982). Dynamics of regional distribution: The core and satellite species hypothesis. *Oikos*, 38, 210-21.

Haraway, D. J. (1976). *Crystals, Fabricus, and Fields. Metaphors of Organicism in Twentieth Century Biology.* New Haven: Yale University Press.

Hardesty, D. L. (1980). The ecological perspective in anthropology. *American Behavioral Scientist*, 24, 107-24.

Hardin, G. (1960). The competitive exclusion principle. *Science*, 131, 1292-7.

Hardy, A. (1965). *The Open Sea: Its Natural History.* Boston: Houghton Mifflin.

– (1968). Charles Elton's influence in ecology. *Journal of Animal Ecology*, 37, 3-8.

Harper, J. L. (1967). A Darwinian approach to plant ecology. *Journal of Ecology*, 55, 247-70.

– (1977a). Review of *Theoretical Ecology. Journal of Ecology*, 65, 1009-12.

– (1977b). The contributions of terrestrial plant studies to the development of the theory of ecology. In *Changing Scenes in the Life Sciences, 1776-1976*, ed. C. E. Goulden, pp. 139-157. Special Publication 12. Philadelphia: Academy of Natural Sciences.

– (1977c). *Population Biology of Plants.* New York: Academic Press.

– (1980). Plant demography and ecological theory. *Oikos*, 35, 244-53.

– (1982). After description. In *The Plant Community as a Working Mechanism*, ed. E. I. Newman, pp. 11-26. Special Publications Series of the British Ecological Society, No. 1. Oxford: Blackwell Scientific.

Harper, J. L., and White, J. (1974). The demography of plants. *Annual Review of Ecology and Systematics*, 5, 419-63.

Harrisson, T. H., and Hollom, P. A. D. (1932). The great crested grebe enquiry, 1931. *British Birds,* 26, 62-92, 102-31, 142-55, 174-95.

Haskell, E. F. (1940). Mathematical systematization of "environment," "organism," and "habitat." *Ecology,* 21, 1-16.

Hasler, A. D., Brynildson, O. M., and Helm, W. T. (1951). Improving conditions for fish in brown water bog lakes by alkalization. *Journal of Wildlife Management,* 15, 347-52.

Hausman, D. B. (1975). What is natural? *Perspectives in Biology and Medicine,* 19, 92-100.

Hawley, A. (1950). *Human Ecology: A Theory of Community Structure.* New York: Ronald Press.

Hedgpeth, J. W. (1957a). Concepts of marine ecology. *Geological Society of America Memoir,* 67, 29-52.

– (ed.) (1957b). *Treatise on Marine Ecology and Paleoecology,* Vol. 1, *Ecology.* Geological Society of America Memoir 67.

– (1969). A fit home for earth's noblest inhabitant. *Science,* 164, 666-8.

– (1977). Models and muddles: Some philosophical observations. *Helgolander Wissenschaft Meeresunters,* 30, 92-104.

Hensen, V. (1884). Über die Bestimmung der Planktons oder das im Meeretreibenden Materials an Pflanzen und Thieren. *Berichte der Kommission zur Wissenschaftlichen Untersuchungen der Deutschen Meeresforsuchung Kiel,* 5, 1-107.

Hepburn, R. W. (1967). Philosophical ideas of nature. In *The Encyclopedia of Philosophy.* Vol. 5, ed. P. Edwards, pp. 454-8. New York: Macmillan, Free Press.

Herrick, F. H. (1911). *Natural History of the American Lobster.* U.S. Bureau of Fisheries Document 747. Reprinted New York: Arno Press (1977).

Heslop-Harrison, J. (1964). Forty years of genecology. *Advances in Ecological Research,* 2, 159-247.

Holdgate, M. W., and Woodman, M. J. (1975). Ecology and planning: Report of a workshop. *Bulletin of the British Ecological Society,* VI(4), 5-14.

Hollingshead, A. B. (1940). Human ecology and human society. *Ecological Monographs,* 10, 354-66.

Hopkins, A. D. (1920). The bioclimatic law. *Journal of the Washington Academy of Science,* 10, 34-40.

Horn, D. J., Stairs, G. R., and Mitchell, R. D. (eds.) (1979). *Analysis of Ecological Systems.* Columbus: Ohio State University Press.

Howard, L. O. (1932). Biographical memoir of Stephen Alfred Forbes, 1844-1930. *National Academy of Sciences of the United States of America. Biographical Memoirs,* 15, 1-25.

Howard, L. O., and Fiske, W. F. (1911). *The Importation into the United States of the Parasites of the Gipsy Moth and the Brown-tail Moth.* U.S. Department of Agriculture, Bureau of Entomology, Bulletin No. 91. Reprinted New York: Arno Press (1977).

Howell, W. H. (1906). Problems of physiology of the present time. In *Biology, Anthropology, Psychology, Sociology,* Vol. V, *Congress of Arts and Sci-*

*ences, Universal Exposition,* ed. H. S. Rogers, pp. 416-34. New York: Houghton Mifflin.

Hoxmark, G. (1925). The International Olympic Games as an index to the influence of climate on human energy. *Ecology,* 6, 199-202.

Hubbell, S. P. (1971). Of sowbugs and systems: The ecological bioenergetics of a terrestrial isopod. In *Systems Analysis and Simulation in Ecology.* Vol. I, ed. B. C. Patten, pp. 269-324. New York: Academic Press.

Hull, D. L. (1974). *Philosophy of Biological Science.* Englewood Cliffs, N.J.: Prentice-Hall.

Humboldt, A. von, and A. Bonpland. (1807). *Essai sur la Geographie des Plantes.* Paris: Librarie Lebrault Schoell.

Hutchinson, G. E. (1940). Review of Bio-Ecology. *Ecology,* 21, 267-8.

– (1947). A note on the theory of competition between two social species. *Ecology,* 28, 319-21.

– (1953). The concept of pattern in ecology. *Proceedings of the Philadelphia Academy of Natural Science,* 105, 1-12.

– (1957a). Concluding remarks. *Cold Spring Harbor Symposium on Quantitative Biology,* 22, 415-27.

– (1957b). *A Treatise on Limnology.* Vol. I. New York: Wiley.

– (1959). Homage to Santa Rosalia; or, why are there so many kinds of animals. *American Naturalist,* 93, 145-59.

– (1963). The prospect before us. In *Limnology in North America,* ed. D. G. Frey, pp. 683-90. Madison: University of Wisconsin Press.

– (1964). The lacustrine microcosm reconsidered. *American Scientist,* 52, 334-41.

– (1965). *The Ecological Theatre and the Evolutionary Play.* New Haven: Yale University Press.

– (1969). Eutrophication, Past and Present. In *Eutrophication: Causes, Consequences, Correctives,* pp. 17-26. Washington, D.C.: National Academy of Sciences.

– (1975). Variations on a theme by Robert MacArthur. In *Ecology and Evolution of Communities,* ed. M. L. Cody and J. M. Diamond, pp. 492-521. Cambridge, Mass.: Belknap Press of Harvard University.

– (1978). *An Introduction to Population Ecology.* New Haven: Yale University Press.

Hutchinson, G. E., and Bowen, N. T. (1947). A direct demonstration of the phosphorus cycle in a small lake. *Proceedings of the National Academy,* 33, 148-53.

Hutchinson, G. E., and Deevey, E. S., Jr. (1949). Ecological studies on populations. *Survey of Biological Progress,* 1, 325-59.

Hutchinson, G. E., and Wollack, A. (1940). Studies on Connecticut lake sediments: Chemical analysis of a core from Linsley Pond, North Branford. *American Journal of Science,* 238, 493-517.

Hynes, H. B. N. (1970). *The Ecology of Running Waters.* Toronto: University of Toronto Press.

Imbrie, J., and Newell, N. D. (1964). Introduction: The viewpoint of paleoecology. In *Approaches to Paleoecology,* ed. J. Imbrie and N. D. Newell, pp. 1-7. New York: Wiley.

Inger, R. F. (1971). Inter-American Institute of Ecology: Operational plan. *Bulletin of the Ecological Society of America,* 52(1), 2-4.

Innis, G. S. (ed.) (1975a). *New Directions in the Analysis of Ecosystems.* Simulation Council Proceedings Series Vol. 5. La Jolla, Calif.: Society for Computer Simulation.

– (1975b). The use of a systems approach in biological research. In *Study of Agricultural Systems,* ed. G. E. Dalton, pp. 369-91. London: Applied Science Publishers.

– (1976). Reductionist vs. whole system approaches to ecosystem studies. In *Ecological Theory and Ecosystem Models,* ed. S. A. Levin, pp. 31-6. Indianapolis: Institute of Ecology.

Innis, G. S., and O'Neill, R. V. (eds.) (1979). *Systems Analysis of Ecosystems,* Fairland, Md.: International Cooperative Publishing House.

Jackson, J. B. C. (1981). Interspecific competition and species' distribution: The ghosts of theories and data past. *American Zoologist,* 21, 889-901.

Jaksic, F. M. (1981). Recognition of morphological adaptations in animals: The hypothetico-deductive method. *BioScience,* 31, 667-9.

Jameson, D. A. (1970). Basic concepts in mathematical modelling of grassland ecosystems. In *Modelling and Systems Analysis in Range Science,* ed. D. A. Jameson, pp. 1-15. Science Series No. 5. Fort Collins, Colo.: Range Science Department.

Janzen, D. H. (1977). The impact of tropical studies on ecology. In *Changing Scenes in the Natural Sciences, 1779-1976,* ed. C. E. Golden, pp. 159-87. Special Publication 12. Philadelphia: Academy of Natural Sciences.

Jeffers, J. N. R. (1972). *Mathematical Models in Ecology.* Oxford: Blackwell Scientific.

– (1978). *An Introduction to Systems Analysis with Ecological Applications.* London: Edward Arnold.

Jenny, H. (1941). *Factors of Soils Formation.* New York: McGraw-Hill.

Johnson, H. A. (1970). Information theory in biology after 18 years. *Science,* 168, 1545-50.

Johnson, L. (1981). The thermodynamic origin of ecosystems. *Canadian Journal of Fisheries and Aquatic Science,* 38, 571-90.

Johnstone, J. (1908). *Conditions of Life in the Sea: A Short Account of Quantitative Marine Biological Research.* Cambridge: Cambridge University Press. Reprinted New York: Arno Press (1977).

Jones, N. S. (1950). Marine bottom communities. *Biological Reviews,* 25, 283-313.

Jordan, C. F. (1981). Do ecosystems exist? *American Naturalist,* 18, 284-7.

Jordan, D. S. (1905). The origin of species through isolation. *Science,* 22, 545-62.

Jordan, D. S., and Kellogg, V. L. (1901). *A First Book of Zoology.* New York: Appleton.

Just, T. (ed.) (1939). Plant and animal communities. *American Midland Naturalist,* 21, 1-255.

Kadlec, J. (ed.) (1971). *A Partial Annotated Bibliography of Mathematical Models in Ecology*. Ann Arbor: Analysis of Ecosystems, IBP, School of Natural Resources, Ann Arbor, University of Michigan.

Kendeigh, S. C. (1954). History and evaluation of various concepts of plant and animal communities in North America. *Ecology*, 35, 152-71.

– (1961). *Animal Ecology*. Englewood Cliffs, N.J.: Prentice-Hall.

Kennedy, C. R. (1976). *Ecological Aspects of Parasitology*. Amsterdam: North Holland.

Kerner von Marilaun, A. (1863). *Das Planzenleben der Donaulander*. Innsbruck: Wagner. Trans. H. S. Conard as *The Background of Plant Ecology*. Ames: Iowa State College Press (1950).

Kerr, S. R. (1980). Niche theory in fisheries ecology. *Transactions of the American Fisheries Society*, 109, 254-7.

Kettlewell, H. B. D. (1955). Selection experiments on industrial melanism in the Lepidoptera. *Heredity*, 9, 323-42.

Kiester, A. R. (1982). Natural kinds, natural history, and ecology. In *Conceptual Issues in Ecology*, ed. E. Saarinen, pp. 345-56. Dordrecht: D. Reidel.

King, J. E. (1981). Late quarternary vegetational history of Illinois. *Ecological Monographs*, 51, 43-62.

Kingsland, S. E. (1981). *Modelling Nature: Theoretical and Experimental Approaches to Population Ecology 1920-1950*. Ph.D. Thesis, University of Toronto.

– (1982). The refractory model: The logistic curve and the history of population ecology. *Quarterly Review of Biology*, 57, 29-52.

– (1983). *Theory and Practice in the Early Years of Population Ecology*. Symposium, Schools of Ecology in Historical Perspective, American Association for the Advancement of Science, July 31, 1983.

– (1985). *Modeling Nature*. Chicago: University of Chicago Press.

Kitching, R. L. (1983). *Systems Ecology: An Introduction to Ecological Modelling*. St. Lucia: University of Queensland Press.

Kittredge, J. (1948). *Forest Influences*. New York: McGraw-Hill.

Klaauw, C. J. Van der (1936). Oekologische Studien und Kritiken zur Geschichte der Definitionen der Oekologie besonders auf Grund der Systeme der zoologischen Disziplinen. *Sudhoffs Archiv für Geschichte der Medizin und der Naturwissenschaften*, 29, 136-77.

Knight, R. L., and Swaney, D. R. (1981). In defense of ecosystems. *American Naturalist*, 117, 991-2.

Kofoid, C. (1897). On some important sources of error in the plankton method. *Science*, 6, 829-32.

– (1903). The plankton of the Illinois River, 1894-1899. *Bulletin of the Illinois State Laboratory of Natural History*, 6, 95-635. Reprinted New York: Arno Press (1977).

Kohn, A. J. (1971). Phylogeny and biogeography of Hutchinsoniana: G. E. Hutchinson's influence through his doctoral students. *Limnology & Oceanography*, 16, 173-6.

Kolata, G. B. (1974). Theoretical ecology: Beginnings of a predictive science. *Science*, 183, 400-1.

Kolkwitz, R., and Marsson, M. (1908). Okologie des pflanzlichen Saprobien. *Berichte der Botanische Gesellschaft*, 26, 505-519.

Kormondy, E. J. (1969). *Concepts of Ecology*. Englewood Cliffs, N.J.: Prentice-Hall.

– (1974). Natural and human ecosystems. In *Human Ecology*, ed. F. Sargent II, pp. 27-43. Amsterdam: North Holland.

– (1978). Ecology/economy of nature – synonyms? *Ecology*, 59, 1292-4.

Kormondy, E. J., and McCormick, J. F. (1981). Introduction. In *Handbook of Contemporary Developments in World Ecology*, ed. E. J. Kormondy and J. F. McCormick, pp. xxii-xxvii. Westport, Conn.: Greenwood Press.

Kozlovsky, D. G. (1968). A critical evaluation of the trophic level concept. *Ecology*, 49, 48-60.

Krebs, C. J. (1979). Small mammal ecology. *Science*, 203, 350-1.

Krebs, C. J., and Myers, J. H. (1974). Population cycles in small mammals. *Advances in Ecological Research*, 8, 267-399.

Krebs, J. R. (1977). Communities: Ecology and evolution. *BioScience*, 27, 50.

Kuhn, T. (1970). *The Structure of Scientific Revolutions*, 2nd ed. Chicago: University of Chicago Press.

Lack, D. (1954). *The Natural Regulation of Animal Numbers*. Oxford: Clarendon Press.

– (1966). *Population Studies of Birds*. Oxford: Clarendon Press.

– (1973). My life as an amateur ornithologist. *Ibis*, 115, 421-34.

Ladd, H. S. (1959). Ecology, paleontology, and stratigraphy. *Science*, 129, 69-78.

Lane, P. A., Lauff, G. H., and Levins, R. (1975). The feasibility of using a holistic approach in ecosystem analysis. In *Ecosystem Analysis and Prediction*, ed. S. A. Levin, pp. 111-28. Proceedings SIAM-SIMS Conference on Ecosystems, Alta, Utah, July 1-5, 1974, SIAM Institute for Mathematics and Society.

Lankester, E. R. (1889). Zoology. *Encyclopaedia Britannica*, 9th ed., 24, 799-820.

Lauff, G. H. (1963). A history of the American Society of Limnology and Oceanography. In *Limnology in North America*, ed. D. G. Frey, pp. 667-82. Madison: University of Wisconsin Press.

Lauff, G. H., and Reichle, D. (1979). Experimental ecological reserves. *Bulletin of the Ecological Society of America*, 60, 4-11.

Lazlo, E. (ed.) (1972). *The Relevance of General Systems Theory*. New York: Brazillier.

– (1980). Some reflections on systems theory's critics. *Nature and System*, 2, 49-53.

Le Cren, E. D. (1976). The productivity of freshwater communities. *Philosophical Transactions of the Royal Society London B*, 274, 359-74.

– (1979). The first fifty years of the freshwater biological station. *Annual Report of the Freshwater Biological Association*, 47, 27-42.

Leigh, E. G., Jr. (1968). The ecological role of Volterra's equations. In *Some Mathematical Problems in Biology*, pp. 1-14. Providence, R.I.: American Mathematical Society.

– (1970). Review of *Population Genetics and Evolution*. *American Scientist*, 58, 110-1.

Lemaine, G., MacLeod, R., Mulkay, M., and Weingart, P. (eds.) (1977). *Perspective on the Emergence of Scientific Disciplines*. Chicago: Aldine.

Leopold, A. S. (1933). *Game Management*. New York: Scribner's.

– (1934). Review of *Notes on Game Management*, chiefly in Bavaria and Baden. *Journal of Forestry*, 32, 775-6.

– (1949). *Sand County Almanac*. New York: Oxford University Press.

Levandowsky, M. (1977). A white queen speculation. *Quarterly Review of Biology*, 52, 383-6.

Levene, H. (1953). Genetic equilibrium when more than one ecological niche is available. *American Naturalist*, 87, 331-3.

Levin, B. R. (1979). Rapprochements in population biology. *Science*, 205, 1254-5.

Levin, S. A. (ed.) (1975). *Ecosystem Analysis and Prediction*. Proceedings SIAM-SIMS Conference on Ecosystems, Alta, Utah, July 1-5, 1974, SIAM Institute for Mathematics and Society.

– (ed.) (1976). *Ecological Theory and Ecosystem Models*. Indianapolis: Institute of Ecology.

– (1981). The role of theoretical ecology in the description and understanding of populations in heterogeneous environments. *American Zoologist*, 21, 865-75.

Levins, R. (1968a). *Evolution in Changing Environments*. Princeton, N.J.: Princeton University Press.

– (1968b). Ecological engineering: Theory and technology. *Quarterly Review of Biology*, 43, 301-5.

Levins, R., and Lewontin, R. (1980). Dialectics and reductionism in ecology. *Synthese*, 43, 47-78.

Lewin, R. (1982). Adaptation can be a problem for evolutionists. *Science*, 216, 1212-3.

– (1983). Santa Rosalia was a goat. *Science*, 221, 636-9.

Lewis, R. W. (1982). Theories, structure, teaching, and learning. *BioScience*, 32, 734-7.

Lewontin, R. C. (1968). Introduction. In *Population Biology and Evolution*, ed. R. C. Lewontin, pp. 1-4. Syracuse, N.Y.: Syracuse University Press.

– (1969a). The meaning of stability. In *Diversity and Stability in Ecological Systems*, pp. 13-24. Upton, N.Y.: Brookhaven National Laboratory.

– (1969b). The bases of conflict in biological explanation. *Journal of the History of Biology*, 2, 35-45.

– (1983). The corpse in the elevator. *New York Review of Books*, 24 (Jan. 20), 34-7.

Lewontin, R. C., and Baker, W. K. (1970). Editor's report. *American Naturalist*, 104, 499-500.

Libby, W. F. (1952). *Radiocarbon Dating*. Chicago: University of Chicago Press.

Lidicker, W. C. (1978). History of holism and reductionism. *Pymatuning Symposia on Ecology, No. 5. Small Mammal Populations*, pp. 12-139. Pymatuning, Pa.: Pymatuning Laboratory of Ecology.

Liebetrau, S. F. (1973). *Trailblazers in Ecology: The American Ecological Consciousness, 1850-1864*. Ph.D. Thesis, University of Michigan.

Likens, G. E., Bormann, F. H., Pierce, R. S., Eaton, J. S., and Johnson, N. M. (1977). *Biogeochemistry of a Forested Ecosystem*. New York: Springer-Verlag.

Lilienfeld, R. (1978). *The Rise of Systems Theory: An Ideological Analysis*. New York: Wiley.

Limoges, C. (1971). *Economie de la Nature et Idéologie Juridique chez Linné*. Proceedings XIII International Congress History of Science, Moscow, 1971, Vol. 9, 25-30. Moscow: Nauka.

Lindeman, E. C. (1940). Ecology: An instrument for the integration of science and philosophy. *Ecological Monographs*, 10, 367-72.

Lindeman, R. L. (1942). The trophic-dynamic aspect of ecology. *Ecology*, 23, 399-418.

Livingston, B. E. (1909). Present problems of physiological plant ecology. *American Naturalist*, 43, 369-78.

Livingston, B. E., and Shreve, F. (1921). *The Distribution of Vegetation in the United States as Related to Climatic Conditions*. Publication No. 284. Washington, D.C.: Carnegie Institution of Washington.

Lloyd, B. (1925). The technique of research on marine plankton. *Journal of Ecology*, 13, 277-88.

Lomnicki, A. (1980). Regulation of population density due to individual differences and patchy environment. *Oikos*, 35, 185-93.

Lotka, A. J. (1925). *Elements of Physical Biology*. Baltimore: Williams & Wilkins.

Loucks, O. (1968). Scientific areas in Wisconsin: Fifteen years in review. *Bioscience*, 18, 396-8.

– (1972). Systems methods in environmental court actions. In *Systems Analysis and Simulation in Ecology*, Vol. II, ed. B. E. Patten, pp. 419-75. New York: Academic Press.

– (in press). The United States IBP. A perspective after 13 years. In *Ecosystem Theory and Application*, ed. G. A. Knox and N. Polunin. Sussex, U.K.: Wiley.

Lovejoy, A. O. (1936). *The Great Chain of Being*. Cambridge, Mass.: Harvard University Press.

Lowe, P. D. (1976). Amateurs and professionals: The institutional emergence of British plant ecology. *Journal of the Society of Bibliography of Natural History*, 7, 517-35.

– (1977). The politics of ecology. *Bulletin of the British Ecological Society*, VIII(3), 3-10.

Lowenthal, D. (1958). *George Perkins Marsh: Versatile Vermonter*. New York: Columbia University Press.

Lussenhop, J. (1974). Victor Hensen and the development of sampling methods in ecology. *Journal of the History of Biology*, 7, 319-37.

Luten, D. B. (1980). Ecological optimism in the social sciences. *American Behavioral Scientist*, 24, 125-51.

Lutz, F. E. (1909). The effect of environment upon animals. *American Naturalist,* 43, 248-51.

Lyon, J., and Sloan, P. R. (eds.) (1981). *From Natural History to the History of Nature: Readings from Buffon and His Critics.* Notre Dame: University of Notre Dame Press.

Macan, T. T. (1963). *Freshwater Ecology.* New York: Wiley.

– (1970). *Biological Studies of English Lakes.* Amsterdam: Elsevier.

MacArthur, R. H. (1955). Fluctuations of animal populations and a measure of community stability. *Ecology,* 36, 533-6.

– (1962). Growth and regulation of animal populations. *Ecology,* 43, 579.

– (1965). Ecological consequences of natural selection. In *Theoretical and Mathematical Biology,* ed. T. Waterman and H. Morowitz, pp. 388-97. New York: Blaisdell.

– (1972). *Geographical Ecology.* New York: Harper and Row.

MacArthur, R. H., and Wilson, E. O. (1967). *The Theory of Island Biogeography.* Princeton: Princeton University Press.

MacFadyen, A. (1957). *Animal Ecology.* London: Sir Isaac Pitman.

– (1964). Energy flow in ecosystems and its exploitation by grazing. In *Grazing in Terrestrial and Marine Environments,* ed. D. J. Crisp, pp. 3-20. Oxford: Blackwell Scientific.

– (1975). Some thoughts on the behavior of ecologists. *Journal of Animal Ecology,* 44, 351-63.

– (1978). The ecologist's role in the international scientific community. *Oikos,* 31, 1-2.

MacGinitie, G. E. (1939). Littoral marine communities. *American Midland Naturalist,* 21, 28-55.

Macklin, M., and Macklin, R. (1969). Theoretical biology: A statement and a defense. *Synthese,* 20, 261-76.

MacMahon, J. A. (1980). Ecosystems over time: Succession and other types of change. In *Forests: Fresh Perspectives from Ecosystem Analysis,* ed. R. H. Waring, pp. 27-58. Corvallis: Oregon State University Press.

MacMillan, C. (1892). *Metaspermae of the Minnesota Valley.* Reports of the Geological and Natural History Survey of Minnesota. Botanical Series, I.

– (1897). Observations on the distribution of plants along the the shore at lake of the woods. *Minnesota Botanical Studies,* 1, 949-1023.

Maddox, J. (1972). *The Doomsday Syndrome.* New York: McGraw-Hill.

Madison Botanical Congress (1894). *Proceedings.* Madison, Wisc., August 23-4, 1893.

Maelzer, D. A. (1965). Environment, semantics, and system theory in ecology. *Journal of Theoretical Biology,* 8, 395-402.

Maiorana, V. C. (1978). An explanation of ecological and developmental constants. *Nature,* 273, 375-7.

Maitland, P. S. (1983). Freshwater Science. *Proceedings of the Royal Society of Edinburgh B,* 84, 171-210.

Major, J. (1951). A functional, factorial approach to plant ecology. *Ecology,* 32, 392-412.

– (1969). Historical development of the ecosystem concept. In *The Ecosystem Concept in Natural Resource Management,* ed. G. M. Van Dyne, pp. 9-22. New York: Academic Press.

Malin, J. C. (1961). *The Grassland of North America: Prolegomena to Its History, with Addenda and Postscript.* Lawrence, Kans.

Malthus, T. R. (1798). *An Essay on the Principle of Population.* London: Johnson.

Manier, E. (1978). *The Young Darwin and His Cultural Circle.* Dordrecht: D. Reidel.

Mann, K. H. (1969). The dynamics of aquatic ecosystems. *Advances in Ecological Research,* 6, 1-83.

– (1982). *Ecology of Coastal Waters: A Systems Approach.* Berkeley: University of California Press.

Margalef, R. (1958). Information theory in ecology. *General Systems,* 3, 36-71.

– (1963). On certain unifying principles in ecology. *American Naturalist,* 97, 357-74.

– (1968). *Perspectives in Ecological Theory.* Chicago: University of Chicago Press.

Marks, P. L., and Bormann, F. H. (1972). Revegetation following forest cutting: Mechanisms for return to steady-state nutrient cycling. *Science,* 176, 914-5.

Marsh, G. P. (1864). *Man and Nature; or, Physical Geography as Modified by Human Action.* New York: Scribner's.

Martin, G. W. (1922). Food resources of the sea. *Scientific Monthly,* 15, 455-67.

Martin, P. S. (1963). *The Last 10,000 Years: A Fossil Pollen Record of the American Southwest.* Tucson: University of Arizona Press.

Marx, L. (1970). American institutions and ecological ideals. *Science,* 170, 945-52.

Mason, H. L., and Langenheim, J. H. (1957). Language analysis and the concept environment. *Ecology,* 38, 325-40.

May, J., and May, R. M. (1976). The ecology of the ecological literature. *Nature,* 259, 446-7.

May, R. M. (1973). *Stability and Complexity in Model Ecosystems.* Princeton: Princeton University Press.

– (1974a). Ecological simulations. *Science,* 184, 682-3.

– (1974b). Scaling in ecology. *Science,* 184, 1131.

– (ed.) (1976). *Theoretical Ecology: Principles and Applications.* Philadelphia: Saunders.

– (1977). Mathematical models and ecology: Past and future. In *Changing Scenes in Natural Sciences, 1776-1976,* ed. C. E. Goulden, pp. 189-202. Special Publication 12. Philadelphia: Academy of Natural Sciences.

– (1981a). The role of theory in ecology. *American Zoologist,* 21, 903-10.

– (1981b). Patterns in multispecies communities. In *Theoretical Ecology,* 2nd ed., ed. R. M. May, pp. 197-227. Sunderland, Mass.: Sinauer Associates.

May, R., and Oster, G. F. (1976). Bifractions and dynamic complexity in simple ecological models. *American Naturalist,* 110, 573-99.

Maycock, P. F. (1967) Jozef Paczoski: Founder of the science of phytosociology. *Ecology*, 48, 1031-4.

Maynard-Smith, J. (1974). *Models in Ecology*. Cambridge: Cambridge University Press.

Mayr, E. (1982). *The Growth of Biological Thought*. Cambridge, Mass.: Belknap Press of Harvard University.

McAtee, W. L. (1907). Census of four square feet. *Science*, 26, 447-9.

McCloskey, D. N. (1983). The rhetoric of economics. *Journal of Economic Literature*, 21, 481-517.

McCormick, J. F. (1978). Letter to the editor. *Bulletin of the Ecological Society of America*, 59, 162-3.

McIntosh, R. P. (1958a). Fogdrip: An anticipation of ecology. *Ecology*, 39, 159.

- (1958b). Plant communities. *Science*, 128, 115-120.

- (1960). Natural order and communities. *Biologist*, 42, 55-62.

- (1962). Raunkiaer's "law" of frequency. *Ecology*, 43, 533-5.

- (1963). Ecosystems, evolution, and relational patterns of living organisms. *American Scientist*, 51, 246-67.

- (1967). The continuum concept of vegetation. *Botanical Review*, 33, 130-87.

- (1970). Community, competition, and adaptation. *Quarterly Review of Biology*, 45, 259-80.

- (1974a). Commentary – An object lesson for the new ecology. *Ecology*, 55, 1179.

- (1974b). Plant ecology, 1947-1972. *Annals of the Missouri Botanical Garden*, 61, 132-65.

- (1975a). H. A. Gleason, "individualistic ecologist," 1882-1975: His contributions to ecological theory. *Bulletin of the Torrey Botanical Club*, 102, 253-73.

- (1975b). "Ecology": A clarification. *Science*, 188, 1158.

- (1976). Ecology since 1900. In *Issues and Ideas in America*, ed. B. J. Taylor and T. J. White, pp. 353-72. Norman: University of Oklahoma Press.

- (ed.) (1978). *Phytosociology*. Stroudsburg; Dowden, Hutchinson and Ross.

- (1980a). The background and some current problems of theoretical ecology. *Synthese*, 43, 195-255.

- (1980b). The relationship between succession and the recovery process in ecosystems. In *The Recovery Process in Damaged Ecosystems*, ed. J. Cairns, Jr., pp. 11-62. Ann Arbor, Mich.: Ann Arbor Publishers.

- (1981). Succession and ecological theory. In *Forest Succession: Concepts and Applications*, ed. D. C. West, H. H. Shugart, and D. B. Botkin, pp. 11-23. New York: Springer-Verlag.

- (1983a). Pioneer support for ecology. *BioScience*, 33, 107-12.

- (1983b). Excerpts from the work of L. G. Ramensky. *Bulletin of the Ecological Society of America*, 64, 7-12.

- (1983c). Edward Lee Greene: The man. In *Landmarks in the History of Botany*, ed. F. N. Egerton, pp. 18-53. Stanford, Calif.: Stanford University Press.

McKenzie, R. D. (ed.) (1934). *Readings in Human Ecology*. Ann Arbor: Wahr.

McMillan, C. (1959). The role of ecotypic variation in the distribution of the central grassland of North America. *Ecological Monographs,* 29, 285-308.

McMullin, E. (1976). The fertility of theory and the unit for appraisal in science. In *Essays in Memory of Imre Lakatos,* ed. R. S. Cohen et al., pp. 681-718. Dordrecht: D. Reidel.

McNaughton, S. J., and Coughenour, M. B. (1981). The cybernetic nature of ecosystems. *American Naturalist,* 117, 985-92.

Merriam, C. H. (1894). Laws of temperature control of the geographic distribution of terrestrial plants and animals. *National Geographic Magazine,* 6, 229-38.

Mesarovic, M. D. (1968). Systems theory and biology – View of a theoretician. In *Systems Theory and Biology,* ed. M. D. Mesarovic, pp. 59-87. New York: Springer-Verlag.

Michael, E. L. (1921). Marine ecology and the coefficient of association: A plea in behalf of quantitative biology. *Journal of Ecology,* 8, 54-9.

Miller, R. S. (ed.) (1965). Summary report of the ecology study committee with recommendations for the future of ecology and the Ecological Society of America. *Bulletin of the Ecological Society of America,* 46, 61-82.

– (1973). Letter to the editor. *BioScience,* 23, 458.

Mills, E. L. (1969). The community concept in marine zoology with comments on continua and instability in some marine communities: A review. *Journal of the Fisheries Research Board of Canada,* 26, 1415-28.

Mills, H. B. (1958). From 1858 to 1958. *Illinois Natural History Survey Bulletin,* 27, 85-103.

– (1964). Stephen Alfred Forbes. *Systematic Zoology,* 13, 208-14.

Milne, A. (1957). Theories of natural control of insect populations. *Cold Spring Harbor Symposia on Quantitative Biology,* 22, 253-71.

Mitchell, R. (1974). Scaling in ecology. *Science,* 184, 1131.

Mitchell, R., Mayer, R. A., and Downhower, J. (1976). An evaluation of three biome programs. *Science,* 192, 859-65.

Mitchell, R. D., and Williams, M. P. (1979). Darwinian analysis: The new natural history. In *Analysis of Ecological Systems,* ed. D. J. Horn, G. R. Stairs, and R. D. Mitchell, pp. 23-50. Columbus: Ohio State University Press.

Möbius, K. (1877). *Die Auster und die Austernwirtschaft.* Berlin: Verlag von Wiegandt, Hempel and Pary. Trans. by H. J. Rice, pp. 683-751, in *Report of the Commissioner for 1880,* Part VIII, U.S. Commission of Fish and Fisheries.

Moore, B. (1920). The scope of ecology. *Ecology,* 1, 3-5.

– (1938). The beginnings of ecology. *Ecology,* 19, 502.

Moore, N. W. (1977). Agriculture and nature conservation. *Bulletin of the British Ecological Society,* VIII(2), 2-4.

Morales, R. (1975). A philosophical approach to mathematical approaches to ecology. In *Ecosystem Analysis and Prediction,* ed. S. A. Levin, pp. 334-7. Proceedings SIAM-SIMS Conference on Ecosystems, Alta, Utah, July 1-5, 1974, SIAM Institute for Mathematics and Society.

Morowitz, H. (1965). The historical background. In *Theoretical and Mathe-*

*matical Biology*, ed. T. Waterman and H. Morowitz, pp. 2-35. New York: Blaisdell.

Mortimer, C. H. (1941-2). The exchange of dissolved substances between mud and water in lakes. *Journal of Ecology*, 29, 280-329.

– (1956). E. A. Birge, an explorer of lakes. In *E. A. Birge: A Memoir*, ed. G. C. Sellery, pp. 163-211. Madison: University of Wisconsin Press.

Morton, A. C. (1981). *History of Botanical Science*. New York: Academic Press.

Moss, C. E. (1910). The fundamental units of vegetation. Historical development of the concepts of the plant association and the plant formation. *New Phytologist*, 9, 18-22, 26-41, 44-53.

– (1913). Evolutionary aspects of ecology. *Journal of Ecology*, 1, 292-3.

Moss, C. E., Rankin, W. M., and Tansley, A. G. (1909). The woodlands of England. *New Phytologist*, 9, 113-49.

Mueller-Dombois, D., and Ellenberg, H. (1974). *Aims and Methods of Vegetation Ecology*. New York: Wiley.

Mulholland, R. J. (1975). Stability and analysis of the response of ecosystems to perturbations. In *Ecosystem Analysis and Prediction*, ed. S. A. Levin, pp. 166-81. Proceedings SIAM-SIMS Conference on Ecosystems, Alta, Utah, July 1-5, 1974, SIAM Institute for Mathematics and Society.

Muller, C. H. (1982). Citation classic. *Current Contents*, 13(45), 20.

Murie, A. (1944). The wolves of Mount McKinley. *Fauna of the National Parks of the United States*, 5, 1-238.

Murray, J., and Pullar, L. (1910). *Bathymetrical Survey of the Scottish Fresh-Water Lochs*. Edinburgh: Challenger Office. Reprinted New York: Arno Press (1977).

Nash, R. (1967). *Wilderness and the American Mind*. New Haven: Yale University Press.

National Academy of Sciences (1969). *Eutrophication: Causes, Consequences, Correctives*. Washington, D.C.: National Academy of Sciences.

– (1974). *U.S. Participation in the International Biological Program*. Report No. 6, U.S. National Committee for the International Biological Program. Washington, D.C.: National Academy of Sciences.

– (1975). *An Evaluation of the International Biological Program*. Contract C3 10. Washington, D.C.: National Science Foundation.

Naumann, E. (1919). Nagra synpunkter angående limnoplanktons ökologi med särskild hänsyn till fytoplankton. *Svensk Botanisk Tiddskrift*, 13, 129-63.

Needham, J. G. (1941). Fragments of the history of hydrobiology. In *A Symposium on Hydrobiology*, pp. 3-11. Madison: University of Wisconsin Press.

Needham, J. G., and Lloyd, J. T. (1916). *The Life of Inland Waters*. Ithaca, N.Y.: The Comstock Publishing Company.

Neel, R. B., and Olson, J. S. (1962). *Use of Analog Computers for Simulating the Movements of Isotopes in Ecological Systems*. No. 3172. Oak Ridge, Tenn.: Oak Ridge National Laboratory.

Neiring, W. A. (1970). Ecology–Now or never. *Bulletin of the Ecological Society of America*, 51(1), 2-3.

Nelkin, D. (1976). Ecologists and the public interest. *Hastings Center Report*, 6, 38-44.

Nelson, G. (1978). From Candolle to Croizat: Comments on the history of biogeography. *Journal of the History of Biology*, 11, 269-305.

Neuhold, J. M. (1975). Introduction to modeling in the biomes. In *Systems Analysis and Simulation in Ecology*, ed. B. C. Patten, pp. 7-12. New York: Academic Press.

New book on ecology. (1905). *Science*, 21, 963.

Nice, M. M. (1937). *Studies in the Life History of the Song Sparrow*. New York: Dover.

Nicholson, A. J. (1933). The balance of animal populations. *Journal of Animal Ecology*, 2, 132-78.

Nicholson, A. J., and Bailey, V. A. (1935). The balance of animal populations. *Proceedings of the Zoological Society of London*, Part 3, 551-98.

Nicolson, M. (1982a). Was there a Linnean ecology?–A comment on some recent literature. (Pers. commun.)

– (1982b). Divergent classifications–A case study from the history of ecology. (Pers. commun.)

– (1983). J. T. Curtis enters ecology. (Pers. commun.)

Niven, B. S. (1982). Formalization of the basic concepts of ecology. *Erkenntnis*, 17, 307-20.

Odum, E. P. (1953). *Fundamentals of Ecology*, 1st ed. Philadelphia: Saunders. (2nd ed., 1959; 3rd ed. 1971.)

– (1964). The new ecology. *BioScience*, 14, 14-16.

– (1968). Energy flow in ecosystems: A historical review. *American Zoologist*, 8, 11-18.

– (1969). The strategy of ecosystem development. *Science*, 164, 260-70.

– (1971). *Fundamentals of Ecology*, 3rd ed., Philadelphia: Saunders.

– (1972). Ecosystems theory in relation to man. In *Ecosystems: Structure and Function*, ed. J. Wiens, pp. 11-24. Corvallis: Oregon State University Press.

– (1977). The emergence of ecology as a new integrative discipline. *Science*, 195, 1289-93.

– (in press). Introductory review: Perspectives of ecosystem theory. In *Ecosystem Theory and Application*, ed. G. A. Knox and N. Polunin. Sussex, U.K.: Wiley.

Odum, H. T. (1957). Trophic structure and productivity of Silver Springs, Florida. *Ecological Monographs*, 27, 55-112.

– (1971). *Environment, power, and society*. New York: Wiley-Interscience.

– (1983). *Systems Ecology: An Introduction*. New York: Wiley.

Odum, H. T., and Odum, E. P. (1955). Trophic structure and productivity of a windward coral reef community on Eniwetok Atoll. *Ecological Monographs*, 25, 291-320.

Odum, H. T., and Pinkerton, R. C. (1955). Times speed regulator, the optimum efficiency for maximum output in physical and biological systems. *American Scientist*, 43, 331-43.

Ohta, K. (1981). A historical note on three pioneer works in population biology. *Journal of Humanities and Natural Sciences* (Tokyo), 59, 65-71.

Okubo, H. (1980). *Diffusion and Ecology Problems: Mathematical Models.* Berlin: Springer-Verlag.

Oldroyd, D. R. (1980). *Darwinian Impacts.* Atlantic Highlands, N.J.: Humanities Press.

Oliver, F. W. (1917). President's address. *Journal of Ecology*, 5, 56-60.

Olson, J. S. (1958). Rates of succession and soil changes on southern Lake Michigan sand dunes. *Botanical Gazette*, 119, 125-70.

– (1964). Advances in radiation ecology. *Nuclear Safety*, 6, 78-81.

– (1966). Progress in radiation ecology: Radionuclide movement in major environments. *Nuclear Safety*, 8, 53-7.

– (1983). "Present at the Creation": The Development of Systems Ecology in the 1960's and its Impact on Ecology Today. (Pers. commun.)

O'Neill, R. V. (1976). Paradigms of ecosystems analysis. In *Ecological Theory and Ecosystems Models*, ed. S. A. Levin, pp. 16-19. Indianapolis: Institute of Ecology.

O'Neill, R. V., and Giddings, J. M. (1979). Population interactions and ecosystem function, phytoplankton competition, and community production. In *Systems Analysis of Ecosystems*, ed. G. S. Innis and R. V. O'Neill, pp. 103-23. Fairland, Md.: International Cooperative Publishing House.

O'Neill, R. V., Hett, J. M., and Sollins, N. F. (eds.) (1970). *A Preliminary Bibliography of Mathematical Modeling in Ecology.* ORNL-IBP-70-3. Oak Ridge, Tenn.: Oak Ridge National Laboratory.

O'Neill, R. V., and Reichle, D. E. (1979). Dimensions of ecosystem theory. In *Forests: Fresh Perspectives from Ecosystem Analysis*, Proceedings of the 40th Annual Biology Colloquium, ed. R. H. Waring, pp. 11-26. Covallis: Oregon State University Press.

Oosting, H. J. (1948). *The Study of Plant Communities.* San Francisco: Freeman.

Ophuls, W. (1934). *Ecology and the Politics of Scarcity: Prologue to a Political Theory of the Steady State.* San Francisco: Freeman.

Orians, G. H. (1962). Natural selection and ecological theory. *American Naturalist*, 96, 257-64.

– (1980). Micro and macro in ecological theory. *BioScience*, 30, 79.

Osmond, C. B., Bjorkman, D., and Anderson, D. J. (1980). *Physiological Process in Plant Ecology: Towards a Synthesis with Atriplex.* Berlin: Springer-Verlag.

Oster, G. (1981). Predicting populations. *American Zoologist*, 21, 831-44.

Otto, R. A. (1979). Poor Richard's population biology. *BioScience*, 29, 242-3.

Overfield, R. A. (1975). Charles E. Bessey: The impact of the "new botany" on American agriculture. *Technology and Culture*, 16, 162-81.

– (1979). Trees for the Great Plains: Charles E. Bessey and forestry. *Journal of Forest History*, 77, 18-31.

Paine, R. T. (1981). Truth in ecology. *Bulletin of the Ecological Society of America*, 62, 256-8.

Pammel, L. H. (1893). *Flower Ecology.* Carroll, Iowa: Hungerford.

Park, O. (1941). Concerning community symmetry. *Ecology*, 22, 164-7.

Park, T. (1939). Ecology looks homeward. *Quarterly Review of Biology*, 14, 332-6.

– (1945). Ecological aspects of population biology. *Scientific Monthly*, 60, 311-3.

– (1946). Some observations on the history and scope of population ecology. *Ecological Monographs*, 16, 313-20.

– (1962). Beetles, competition, and populations. *Science*, 138, 1369-75.

Parkhurst, D. F., and Loucks, O. L. (1972). Optimal leaf size in relation to environment. *Journal of Ecology*, 60, 505-38.

Parsons, H. L. (ed.) (1977). *Marx and Engels on Ecology*. Contribution in Philosophy No. 8. Westport, Conn.: Greenwood Press.

Parsons, T. R. (1980). The development of biological studies in the ocean environment. In *Oceanography: The Past*, ed. M. Sears and D. Merriam, pp. 540-50. New York: Springer-Verlag.

Passmore, I. (1974). *Man's Responsibility for Nature: Problems and Western Traditions*. New York: Scribner's.

Patil, G. P., and Rosenzweig, M. L. (eds.) (1979). *Contemporary Quantitative Ecology and Related Econometrics*. Fairland, Md.: International Cooperative Publishing House.

Patrick, R. (1977). The changing scene in aquatic ecology. In *Changing Scenes in Natural Science*, ed. C. E. Goulden, pp. 205-22. Special Publication 12. Philadelphia: Academy of Natural Sciences.

Patten, B. C. (1959). An introduction to the cybernetics of the ecosystem: The trophic dynamic aspect. *Ecology*, 40, 221-31.

– (1966). Systems ecology: A course sequence in mathematical ecology. *BioScience*, 16, 593-8.

– (ed.) (1971). *Systems Analysis and Simulation in Ecology*, Vol. 1. New York: Academic Press.

– (ed.) (1972). *Systems Analysis and Simulation in Ecology*, Vol. 2. New York: Academic Press.

– (ed.) (1975a). *Systems Analysis and Simulation in Ecology*, Vol. 3. New York: Academic Press.

– (1975b). Ecosystem linearization: An evolutionary design problem. *American Naturalist*, 109, 529-39.

– (1975c). Ecosystem as a coevolutionary unit: A theme for teaching systems ecology. In *New Directions in the Analysis of Ecological Systems*, ed. G. S. Innis, pp. 1-8. Simulation Council Proceedings, Vol. 5. No. 1. La Jolla, Calif.: Society for Computer Simulation.

– (1976). Afterthoughts on the Cornell TIE workshop. In *Ecosystem Theory and Ecosystem Models*, ed. S. A. Levin, pp. 63-6. Indianapolis: Institute of Ecology.

– (1981). Environs: The superniches of ecosystems. *American Zoologist*, 21, 845-52.

Pearl, R. (1914). The service and importance of statistics to biology. *Quarterly Publication of the American Statistics Association*, 1914, 40-88.

– (1925). *The Biology of Population Growth*. New York: Knopf.

– (1927). The growth of populations. *Quarterly Review of Biology*, 2, 532-48.

Pearl, R., and Reed, L. J. (1920). On the rate of growth of the population of the United States since 1970 and its mathematical representation. *Proceedings of the National Academy of Sciences*, 6, 275-88.

Pearsall, W. H. (1917). The aquatic and marsh vegetation of Esthwaite Water, Part I. *Journal of Ecology*, 5, 180-202.

– (1921). The development of vegetation in the English lakes considered in relation to the general evolution of glacial lakes and rock basins. *Proceedings of the Royal Society B.*, 92, 259-84.

– (1932). Phytoplankton in the English lakes. II. The composition of the phytoplankton in relation to dissolved substances. *Journal of Ecology*, 20, 241-62.

– (1964). The development of ecology in Britain. *Journal of Ecology* (suppl.), 52, 1-12.

Peters, R. H. (1976). Tautology in evolution and ecology. *American Naturalist*, 110, 1-12.

– (1980). From natural history to ecology. *Perspectives in Biology and Medicine*, 23, 191-203.

Petersen, C. G. J. (1913). *Valuation of the Sea. II. The Animal Communities of the Sea Bottom and Their Importance for Marine Zoogeography.* Reports of the Danish Biological Station No. 21, 1-44.

– (1918). *The Sea Bottom and Its Production of Fish Food.* Reports of the Danish Biological Station No. 25, pp. 1-62.

Petersen, C. G. J., and Jensen, P. B. (1911). *Valuation of the Sea. I. Animal Life of the Sea Bottom, Its Food and Quantity.* Report of the Danish Biological Station to Board of Agriculture No. 10, 1-76.

Peterson, C. H. (1975). Stability of species and of community for the benthos of two lagoons. *Ecology*, 56, 958-65.

Phillips, J. F. V. (1934-35). Succession, development, the climax, and the complex organism, Parts I-III. *Journal of Ecology*, 22, 554-71; 23, 210-43, 488-508.

Phillipson, J. (1966). *Ecological Energetics.* London: Edward Arnold.

Pianka, E. (1980). Guild structure in desert lizards. *Oikos*, 35, 194-201.

Pielou, E. C. (1969). *An Introduction to Mathematical Ecology.* New York: Wiley.

– (1972). On kinds of models. *Science*, 177, 981-2.

– (1975). *Ecological Diversity.* New York: Wiley.

– (1981). The usefulness of ecological models: A stocktaking. *Quarterly Review of Biology*, 56, 17-31.

Ponyatovskaya, V. M. (1961). On two trends in phytocoenology. *Vegetatio*, 10, 373-85.

Pound, R. (1896). The plant-geography of Germany. *American Naturalist*, 30, 465-8.

Pound, R., and Clements, F. E. (1897). Review of "Observations on the Distributions of Plants along the Shore at Lake of the Woods." *American Naturalist*, 31, 980-4.

– (1898a). A method of determining the abundance of secondary species. *Minnesota Botanical Studies*, 2, 19-24.

– (1898b). *The Phytogeography of Nebraska,* 1st ed. Lincoln, Nebr. (2nd ed., 1900.) Reprinted New York: Arno Press (1977).

Preston, F. W. (1948). The commonness and rarity of species. *Ecology,* 29, 254-83.

– (1962). The canonical distribution of commonness and rarity, Parts I and II. *Ecology,* 43, 185-215, 410-32.

Quinn, J. A. (1978). Plant ecotypes: Ecological or evolutionary unit. *Bulletin of the Torrey Botanical Club,* 105, 58-64.

Ramaley, R. (1940). The growth of a science. *University of Colorado Studies, General Series A,* 26, 3-14.

Ramensky, L. G. (1924). Basic regularities of vegetation covers and their study. (In Russian.) *Věstnik Opytnogo děla Stredne-Chernoz. Ob., Voronezh,* 37-73.

Ranwell, D. S. (ed.) (1967). Sub-committee report on landscape improvement advice and research. *Journal of Ecology,* 55, 1P-8P.

Ratcliffe, D. A. (1977). The conservation of important wildlife areas in Great Britain. *Bulletin of the British Ecological Society,* VIII(1), 5-11.

Raunkaier, C. (1904). Biological types with reference to the adaptation of plants to survive the unfavorable season. *Botanisk Tidsskrift,* 26. (Trans. in C. Raunkaier 1934.)

– (1908). The statistics of life-forms as a basis for biological plant geography. *Botanisk Tidsskrift,* 29. (Trans. in C. Raunkaier 1934.)

– (1910). Investigations and statistics of plant formations. *Botanisk Tidsskrift,* 30. (Trans. in C. Raunkaier 1934.)

– (1918). *Statistical Researches on Plant Formations.* Kgl. Danske Videnskabernes Selskab. Biologiske Meddelelser 1.3. (Trans. in C. Raunkaier 1934.)

– (1934). *The Life Forms of Plants and Statistical Plant Geography.* Oxford: Clarendon Press.

Redfield, A. C. (1945). The Marine Biological Laboratory. *Ecology,* 26, 208.

– (1958). The inadequacy of experiment in marine biology. In *Perspectives in Marine Biology,* ed. A. A. Buzzati-Traverso, pp. 17-26. Berkeley: University of California Press.

Reed, H. S. (1905). A brief history of ecological work in botany. *Plant World,* 8, 163-70, 198-208.

Reeve, M. R. (1979). The problem of patchiness. *Science,* 204, 943.

Regier, H. A., and Rapport, D. J. (1978). Ecological paradigms, once again. *Bulletin of the Ecological Society,* 59, 2-6.

Rehbock, P. F. (1979). The early dredgers: Naturalizing in British seas, 1830-1850. *Journal of the History of Biology,* 12, 293-368.

– (1983). *The Philosophical Naturalists: Themes in Early Nineteenth Century British Biology.* Madison: University of Wisconsin Press.

Reichle, D. E., and Auerbach, S. I. (1972). Analysis of Ecosystems. In *Challenging Biological Problems: Directions toward Their Solution,* ed. J. A. Behnke, pp. 260-80. New York: Academic Press.

Reid, G. K., and Wood, R. D. (1976). *Ecology of Inland Waters and Estuaries.* New York: Van Nostrand.

Report of Committee on Nature Conservation and Nature Reserves (1944). Nature conservation and nature reserves. *Journal of Ecology*, 32, 45-82.

Report for the National Science Foundation (1977). *Experimental Ecological Reserves: A Proposed National Network*. Indianapolis: Institute of Ecology.

Report of the Study Committee (1968). A National Institute of Ecology: Synopsis of the plans of the Ecological Society of America: History and status. *Bulletin of the Ecological Society of America*, 49, 48-54.

Report of the Workshop on Global Ecological Problems (1972). *Man in the Living Environment*. Indianapolis: Institute of Ecology.

Rice, A. L., and Wilson, J. B. (1980). The British Dredging Committee. In *Oceanography: The Past*, ed. M. Sears and D. Merriam, pp. 373-83. New York: Springer-Verlag.

Richards, O. W. (1926). Studies on the ecology of English heaths. III. Animal communities of the felling and burn succession at Oxshott Heath, Surrey. *Journal of Ecology*, 14, 244-81.

Richards, P. W. (1952). *The Tropical Rainforest*. Cambridge: Cambridge University Press.

Richardson, J. L. (1980). The organismic community: Resilience of an embattled ecological concept. *BioScience*, 30, 465-471.

Richman, S. (1958). The transformation of energy by *Daphnia pulex*. *Ecological Monographs*, 28, 273-91.

Richmond, R. C., Gilpin, M. E., Salsa, S. P., and Ayala, F. J. (1975). A search for emergent competitive phenomena: The dynamics of multi-species *Drosophila* systems. *Ecology*, 56, 709-14.

Ricker, W. E. (1954). Stock and recruitment. *Journal of the Fisheries Research Board of Canada*, 11, 559-623.

– (1977). The historical development. In *Fish Population Dynamics*, ed. J. A. Gulland, pp. 1-26. London: Wiley.

Rider, R. E. (1981). Two mathematicians. *Science*, 217, 1496.

Rigler, F. H. (1975a). Lakes 2: Chemical limnology, nutrient kinetics, and the new topology. *Verhandlungen Internationale Vereins Limnologie*, 19, 197-210.

– (1975b). The concept of energy flow and nutrient flow between trophic levels. In *Unifying Concepts in Ecology*, ed. W. H. van Dobben and R. H. Lowe-McConnell, pp. 15-26. The Hague: Junk.

– (1976). Review of *Systems Analysis and Simulation in Ecology*, Vol. 3. *Limnology and Oceanography*, 21, 481-3.

– (1982). The relation between fisheries management and limnology. *Transactions of the American Fisheries Society*, 111, 121-32.

Ripley, S. D. (1968). *Testimony on The International Biological Programs*. Report of the Subcommittee on Science Research and Development of the Committee on Science Astronautics, U.S. House of Representatives, 90th Congress, 2nd Session, March 11, 1968.

Robertson, C. (1906). Ecological adaptation and ecological selection. *Science*, 23, 307-10.

Rodhe, W. (1975). The SIL foundation and our fundament. *Verhandlungen Internationale Vereinigung Limnologie*, 19, 16-25.

– (1979). The life of lakes. *Archiv für Hydrobiologie Beihefte Ergebenknisse Limnologie,* 13, 5-9.

Rodman, J. (1980). Paradigm change in political science: An ecological perspective. *American Behavioral Scientist,* 24, 49-78.

Roe, K. F., and Frederick, R. G. (1981). *Dictionary of Theoretical Concepts in Biology.* Metuchen, N.J.: Scarecrow Press.

Romesburg, H. C. (1981). Wildlife science: Gaining reliable knowledge. *Journal of Wildlife Management,* 45, 293-313.

Rosen, R. (1972). Review of *Trends in General Systems Theory. Science,* 177, 508-9.

Rosenzweig, M. L. (1976). Review of *Small Mammals. Science,* 192, 778-9.

Ross, R. (1911). Some quantitative studies in epidemiology. *Nature,* 87, 466-7.

Roth, V. L. (1981). Constancy in the size ratios of sympatric species. *American Naturalist,* 118, 394-404.

Roughgarden, J. (1983). Competition and theory in community ecology. *American Naturalist,* 122, 583-601.

Rowe, J. S. (1961). The level-of-integration concept and ecology. *Ecology,* 42, 420-7.

Rubel, E. (1927). Ecology, plant geography, and geobotany: Their history and aim. *Botanical Gazette,* 84, 428-39.

Ruse, M. (1973). *The Philosophy of Biology.* London: Hutchinson.

Rutter, A. J. (1972). Summary and assessment: An ecologist's point of view. In *Mathematical Models in Ecology,* ed. J. N. R. Jeffers, pp. 375-80. Oxford: Blackwell Scientific.

Saarinen, E. (1982). *Conceptual Issues in Biology.* Dordrecht: D. Reidel.

Sachs, J. (1874). *Lehrbuch der Botanik, nach dem gegenwortigen Stand der Wissenschaft, Leipzig,* 4th ed. Trans. A. W. Bennet and W. T. Thiselton Dyer, as *Textbook of Botany: Morphological and Physiological.* Oxford: Clarendon Press (1875).

Sachse, N. D. (1965). *A Thousand Ages.* Madison: University of Wisconsin Arboretum.

Salamun, R. N. (1952). The social influence of the potato. *Scientific American,* 187(6), 50-6.

Sale, P. F. (1977). Maintenance of high diversity in coral reef fish communities. *American Naturalist,* 11, 337-59.

Salisbury, E. J. (1942). *The Reproductive Capacity of Plants.* London: Bell.

– (1964). The origin and early years of the British Ecological Society. *Journal of Ecology* (suppl.), 52, 13-18.

Salt, G. W. (1979). A comment on the use of the term emergent properties. *American Naturalist,* 113, 145-8.

Sanders, H. L. (1960). Benthic studies in Buzzards Bay. III. The structure of the soft bottom community. *Limnology and Oceanography,* 5, 138-53.

– (1968). Marine benthic diversity: A comparative study. *American Naturalist,* 102, 243-82.

Sanders, H. L., and Hessler, R. R (1969). Ecology of the deep sea benthos. *Science,* 163, 1419-24.

Sanford, C. L. (1957). The concept of the sublime in the works of Thomas Cole and William Cullen Bryant. *American Literature,* 28, 434-48.

– (1961). *The Quest for Paradise.* Urbana: University of Illinois Press.

Sargent, F., II (ed.) (1974a). *Human Ecology.* Amsterdam: North Holland.

– (1974b). Nature and scope of human ecology. In *Human Ecology*, ed. F. Sargent II, pp. 1-25. Amsterdam: North Holland.

Sarukhán, J., and Harper, J. L. (1973). Studies on plant demography, *Ranunculus repens* L., *R. Bulbosus* L., and *R. acris* L. 1. Population flux and survivorship. *Journal of Ecology*, 61, 675-716.

Schaffer, W. M., and Leigh, E. G. (1976). The prospective role of mathematical theory in plant ecology. *Systematic Botany*, 1, 209-32.

Schimper, A. F. W. (1898). *Pflanzen-Geographie auf physiologischer Grundlage.* Jena: Fischer. Translated (1903) as *Plant Ecology upon a Physiological Basis.* Oxford: Clarendon Press.

Schlee, S. (1973). *The Edge of an Unfamiliar World: A History of Oceanography.* London: Robert Hale.

Schmidt, K. P. (1948). Cassandra in Latin America. *Ecology*, 29, 221.

Schoener, T. W. (1972). Mathematical ecology and its place among the sciences. *Science*, 178, 389-91.

– (1982). The controversy over interspecific competition. *American Scientist*, 70, 586-95.

Schouw, J. F. (1822). *Grundraek til en almindelig Plantegeografie.* Copenhagen: Gyldendalske. German Trans. *Grundzuge einer allegemeinen Pfanzengeographie.* Berlin: Reimer (1823).

Schröter, C., and Kirchner, O. (1896). Die Vegetation des Bodensees. *Schriften: Vereins für Geschichte des Bodensees und seiner Umgebung*, 25, 1-119.

Schröter, C., and Kirchner, O. (1902). Die Vegetation des Bodensees. *Schriften: Vereins für Geschichte des Bodensees und seiner Umgebung*, 31, 1-86.

Schumacher, E. F. (1973). *Small Is Beautiful.* New York: Harper & Row.

Schurz, C. (1889). Address to Forestry Association. In *Living Ideas in America*, ed. H. S. Commager, pp. 88-91. New York: Harper & Row.

Sclater, P. L. (1858). On the general geographical distribution of the members of the class *Aves. Journal of the Proceedings of the Linnaean Society of London (Zoology)*, 2, 130-45.

Scudo, F. M. (1971). Vito Volterra and theoretical ecology. *Theoretical Population Ecology*, 2, 1-23.

– (1982). The roots of theoretical ecology. IV. Theoretical ecology in the 1930s and in the 1960s – Two different philosophies. (Pers. commun.)

Scudo, F., and Ziegler, J. R. (1978). *The Golden Age of Theoretical Ecology, 1923-1940.* New York: Springer-Verlag.

Sears, M., and Merriam, D. (eds.) (1980). *Oceanography: The Past.* New York: Springer-Verlag.

Sears, P. B. (1932). *Life and Environment.* New York: Bureau of Publications, Teachers College, Columbia University.

– (1935a). Types of North American pollen profiles. *Ecology*, 16, 488-99.

– (1935b). Glacial and postglacial vegetation. *Botanical Review*, 1, 37-51.

– (1935c). *Deserts on the March.* Norman: University of Oklahoma Press.

– (1937). *This Is Our World.* Norman: University of Oklahoma Press.

## 362     References

- (1954). Human ecology: A problem in synthesis. *Science,* 120, 959-63.
- (1956). Some notes on the ecology of ecologists. *Scientific Monthly,* 83, 22-7.
- (1964). Ecology – A subversive subject. *BioScience,* 14, 11-13.
- (1971). Toward design for the future. *Bulletin of the Ecological Society of America,* 52(3), 5-7.
Second decennial of the Botanical Seminar of the University of Nebraska. (1906). *Science,* 24, 629-631.
Seddon, G. (1974). Xerophytes, xeromorphs, and sclerophylls: The history of some concepts in ecology. *Linnaean Society of London Biological Journal,* 6, 65-87.
Sellery, G. G. (1956). E. A. Birge, a memoir. In *An Explorer of Lakes,* ed. C. H. Mortimer, pp. 165-211. Madison: University of Wisconsin Press.
Semper, K. (1881). *Animal Life as Affected by the Natural Conditions of Existence.* New York: Appleton.
Shaler, N. S. (1910). *Man and the Earth.* New York: Duffield.
Shantz, H. L. (1911). *Natural Vegetation as an Indicator of the Capabilities of Land for Crop Production in the Great Plains Area.* Bureau of Plant Industry Bulletin No. 201.
Shaw, C. H. (1909). Present problems in plant ecology. III. Vegetation and altitude. *American Naturalist,* 43, 420-31.
Sheail, J. (1976). *Nature in Trust: A History of Nature Conservation in Britain.* Glasgow: Blackie.
- (1981). *Rural Conservation in Inter-War Britain.* Oxford: Clarendon Press.
Shelford, V. E. (1911). Physiological animal geography. *Journal of Morphology,* 22, 551-618.
- (1913). *Animal Communities in Temperate America as Illustrated in the Chicago Region.* No. 5. Chicago: Bulletin of the Geographical Society of Chicago. Reprinted New York: Arno Press (1977).
- (1915). Principles and problems of ecology as illustrated by animals. *Journal of Ecology,* 3, 1-23.
- (ed.) (1917). Handbook of the Ecological Society of America. *Bulletin of the Ecological Society of America,* 1(3), 1-57.
- (ed.) (1925). *Naturalist's Guide to the Americas.* Baltimore: Williams & Wilkins.
- (1929). *Laboratory and Field Ecology.* Baltimore: Williams & Wilkins.
- (1932). Basic principles of the classification of communities and habitats and the use of terms. *Ecology,* 13, 105-20.
Shepard, P. (1967). Whatever happened to human ecology? *BioScience,* 17, 891-4.
Shimwell, D. W. (1971). *The Description and Classification of Vegetation.* Seattle: University of Washington Press.
Shreve, F. (1914). *A Montane Rain-forest: A Contribution to the Physiological Plant Geography of Jamaica.* Publication No. 199. Washington, D.C.: Carnegie Institution of Washington.
Shugart, H. H. (1976). Review of B. C. Patten (ed.), *Systems Analysis and Simulation in Ecology. Quarterly Review of Biology,* 51, 456-7.
Shugart, H. H., Klopatek, J. M., and Emanuel, W. R. (1981). Ecosystems

analysis and land use planning. In *Handbook of Contemporary Developments in World Ecology*, ed. E. J. Kormondy and J. F. McCormick, pp. 665-99. Westport, Conn.: Greenwood Press.

Shugart, H. H. and O'Neill, R. V. (eds.) (1979). *Systems Ecology*. Stroudsburg, Pa.: Dowden, Hutchinson & Ross.

Simberloff, D. S. (1974). Equilibrium theory of island biogeography and ecology. *Annual Review of Ecology and Systematics*, 5, 161-82.

– (1980). A succession of paradigms in ecology: Essentialism to materialism and probabalism. *Synthese*, 43, 3-39.

– (1983). Competition theory, hypothesis testing, and other community ecological buzzwords. *American Naturalist*, 122, 626-35.

Simberloff, D. S., and Boecklen, W. (1981). Santa Rosalia reconsidered: Size ratios and competition. *Evolution*, 35, 1206-28.

Simon, M. A. (1971). *The Matter of Life: Philosophical Problems of Biology*. New Haven: Yale University Press.

Sjors, H. (1955). Remarks on ecosystems. *Svensk Botanisk Tidsskrift*, 49, 155-69.

Slobodkin, L. B. (1955). Conditions for population equilibrium. *Ecology*, 36, 530-3.

– (1959). Energetics in *Daphnia pulex* populations. *Ecology*, 40, 232-43.

– (1961). Preliminary ideas for a predictive theory of ecology. *American Naturalist*, 95, 147-53.

– (1962). *Growth and Regulation of Animal Populations*. New York: Holt, Rinehart and Winston.

– (1965). On the present incompleteness of mathematical ecology. *American Scientist*, 53, 347-57.

– (1968). Aspects of the future of ecology. *BioScience*, 18, 16-23.

– (1969). Pathfinding in ecology. *Science*, 164, 817.

– (1972). On the inconstancy of ecological efficiency and the form of ecological theories. *Transactions of the Connecticut Academy of Arts and Sciences*, 44, 293-305.

– (1975). Comments from a biologist to a mathematician. In *Ecosystem Analysis and Prediction*, ed. S. A. Levin, pp. 318-29. Proceedings SIAM-SIMS Conference on Ecosystems, Alta, Utah, July 1-5, 1974, SIAM Institute for Mathematics and Society.

Smit, P. (1967). Ernst Haeckel and his Generelle Morphologie: An evaluation. *Janus*, 54, 236-52.

Smith, F. E. (1952). Experimental methods in population dynamics. *Ecology*, 33, 441-50.

– (1967). *First Annual Report of the Analysis of Ecosystems*. An Integrated Research Program of the U.S. IBP. Nov. 11, 1967.

– (1968). The International Biological Progam and the science of ecology. *Proceedings of the National Academy of Sciences*, 60, 5-11.

– (1969). *Termination of the Central Program, Analysis of Ecosystems*. Analysis of Ecosystems Programs, U.S. IBP.

– (1975a). Ecosystems and evolution. *Bulletin of the Ecological Society of America*, 56(4), 2-6.

– (1975b). Comments revised; or, What I wish I had said. In *New Directions in the Analysis of Ecological Systems*, ed. J. S. Innis, pp. 231-34. Simulation Councils Proceedings Series, Vol. 5, No. 2. La Jolla, Calif.: Society for Computer Simulation.

– (1976). Ecology: Progress and self-criticism. *Science*, 192, 546.

– (1978). Episodes in ecology. *Science*, 200, 526-7.

Smith, H. S. (1939). Insect populations in relation to biological control. *Ecological Monographs*, 9, 311-20.

Smith, R. (1899). On the study of plant associations. *Natural Science*, 14, 109-20.

Smith, R. L. (1980). *Ecology and Field Biology*, 3rd ed. New York: Harper & Row.

Smith, S. H. (1968). Species succession and fishery exploitation in the Great Lakes. *Journal of the Fisheries Research Board of Canada*, 25, 667-93.

Smith, W. G. (1908). The British Vegetation Committee. *New Phytologist*, 8, 203-6.

Southern, H. N. (1970). Ecology at the crossroads. *Journal of Ecology*, 58, 1-11.

Southwood, T. R. E. (1966). *Ecological Methods, with Particular Reference to the Study of Insect Populations*. London: Methuen.

Spalding, V. M. (1903). The rise and progress of ecology. *Science*, 17, 201-10.

Sprugel, D. G. (1980). A "pedagogical genealogy" of American plant ecologists. *Bulletin of the Ecological Society of America*, 61, 197-200.

Spurr, S. H. (1952). Origin of the concept of forest succession. *Ecology*, 33, 426-7.

– (1964). *Forest Ecology*. New York: Ronald Press.

Stalley, M. (ed.) (1972). *Patrick Geddes, Spokesman for Man and the Environment*. New Brunswick, N.J.: Rutgers University Press.

Stanley J. (1932). A mathematical theory of the growth of populations of the flour beetle *Tribolium confusum*, Duv. *Canadian Journal of Research*, 6, 632-71.

Stauffer, R. C. (1957). Haeckel, Darwin, and ecology. *Quarterly Review of Biology*, 32, 138-44.

– (1960). Ecology in the long manuscript version of Darwin's *Origin of Species* and Linnaeus' *Œconomy of Nature. Proceedings of the American Philosophical Society*, 104, 235-41.

Stearns, F., and Montag, T. (1974). *The Urban Ecosystem: A Holistic Approach*. Stroudsburg, Pa.: Dowden, Hutchinson and Ross.

Stearns, S. C. (1980). A new view of life-history evolution. *Oikos*, 35, 266-81.

Stebbins, G. L. (1980). Botany and the synthetic theory of evolution. In *The Evolutionary Synthesis*, ed. E. Mayr and W. B. Provine, pp. 139-52. Cambridge, Mass.: Harvard University Press.

Steere, J. B. (1894). On the distribution of genera and species of nonmigratory land-birds in the Phillipines. *Ibis*, 1894, 411-20.

Stephen, A. C. (1933). Studies on the Scottish marine fauna: The natural faunistic divisions of the North Sea illustrated by the quantitative distribution of the molluscs. *Transactions of the Royal Society of Edinburgh*, 57, 391.

Stephenson, W. (1973). The validity of the community concept in marine biology. *Proceedings of the Royal Society of Queensland*, 84, 73-86.

Stephenson, W., Williams, W. T., and Cook, S. D. (1972). Computer analysis of Petersen's original data on bottom communities. *Ecological Monographs*, 42, 387-415.

Stieber, M. (1980). Delectus Huntiana 2. (Photograph and comments on botanical seminar, 1896.) *Bulletin of the Hunt Institute of Botanical Documentation*, 2(2), 3-5.

Stilgoe, J. R. (1982). *Common landscapes in America, 1580 to 1845*. New Haven, Conn.: Yale University Press.

Stoddard, H. L. (1932). *The Bobwhite Quail: Its Habits, Preservation, and Increase*. New York: Scribner's.

Stout, B. B. (ed.) (1981). *Forests in the Here and Now*. Missoula: Montana Forest and Conservation Experiment Station, School of Forestry, University of Montana.

Strong, D. R., Jr., Simberhoff, D., Abele, L. G., and Thistle, A. B. (eds.) (1984), *Ecological Communities: Conceptual Issues and the Evidence*. Princeton, N.J.: Princeton University Press.

Subcommittee on Science Research and Development (1968). *The International Biological Program: Its Meaning and Needs*. Committee on Science and Astronautics, U.S. House of Representatives, 90th Congress, 2nd Session, Serial N. Washington, D.C.: U.S. Government Printing Office.

Suess, H. E. (1973). Natural radiocarbon. *Endeavour*, 32, 34-8.

Sukachev, V. N. (1945). Biogeocœnology and phytocœnology. *Doklady Akademica Nauk USSR*, 47, 447-9.

Summary of a Workshop (1979). *Long-term Ecological Research*. Indianapolis: Institute of Ecology.

Sussman, H. J. (1977). Review of *On Systems Analysis*. *Human Ecology*, 5, 383-5.

Suter, G. E., II (1981). Ecosystem theory and NEPA assessment. *Bulletin of the Ecological Society of America*, 62, 186-92.

Tansley, A. G. (1904a). The problems of ecology. *New Phytologist*, 3, 191-204.

– (1904b). Formation of a committee for the survey and study of British vegetation. *New Phytologist*, 4, 23-6.

– (1905). The vegetation of the Scottish Highlands. *New Phytologist*, 5, 98-100.

– (ed.) (1911). *Types of British Vegetation*. Cambridge: Cambridge University Press.

– (1913-14). International phytogeographic excursion (I.P.E.) in America, 1913. *New Phytologist*, 12, 322-6; 13, 268-75, 325-33.

– (1914a). Presidential address. *Journal of Ecology*, 2, 194-202.

– (1914b). The British Ecological Society. Summer Meeting, July 1914. *Journal of Ecology*, 2, 202-4.

– (1920). The classification of vegetation and the concept of development. *Journal of Ecology*, 8, 118-48.

– (1923). *Practical Plant Ecology*. New York: Dodd, Mead.

– (1929). *Succession: The Concept and Its Values.* Proceedings of the International Congress of Plant Sciences, 1, 677-86.
– (1935). The use and abuse of vegetational concepts and terms. *Ecology,* 16, 284-307.
– (1939). British ecology during the past quarter century: The plant community and the ecosystem. *Journal of Ecology,* 27, 513-30.
– (1945). *Our Heritage of Wild Nature: A Plea for Organized Nature Conservation.* Cambridge: Cambridge University Press.
– (1947). The early history of modern plant ecology in Britain. *Journal of Ecology,* 35, 130-7.
Taylor, F. J. R. (1980). Phytoplankton ecology before 1900: Supplementary notes to the "Depths of the Ocean." In *Oceanography: The Past,* ed. M. Sears and D. Merriman, pp. 509-21. New York: Springer-Verlag.
Taylor, L. R., and Elliott, J. M. (1981). The first fifty years of the Journal of Animal Ecology. *Journal of Animal Ecology,* 50, 951-71.
Taylor, N. (1912). Some modern trends in ecology. *Torreya,* 12, 110-17.
– (1938). The beginning of ecology. *Ecology,* 19, 352.
Taylor, W. P. (1927). Ecology or bioecology. *Ecology,* 8, 280-1.
– (1935). Significance of the biotic community in ecological studies. *Quarterly Review of Biology,* 10, 291-307.
– (1936). What is ecology and what good is it? *Ecology,* 17, 333-46.
Teal, J. M. (1957). Community metabolism in a temperate cold spring. *Ecological Monographs,* 27, 283-302.
Thienemann, A. (1918). Lebengemeinschaft und Lebensraum. *Naturwissenschaft Wocheschrift,* N.F., 17, 282-90, 297-303.
– (1925). Die Binnengewässer Mitteleuropas: Eine limnologischer Einfürung. *Die Binnengewässer,* 1, 1-225.
Thomas, W. L., Jr. (1956). Introduction. In *Man's Role in Changing the Face of the Earth,* ed. W. L. Thomas, Jr., pp. xii-xxviii. Chicago: University of Chicago Press.
Thorson, G. (1957). Bottom communities (sublittoral or shallow shelf). *Geological Society of America Memoir,* 67, 461-534.
Tinkle, D. W. (1979). Long term field studies. *BioScience,* 29, 717.
Tobey, R. (1976). Theoretical science and technology in American ecology. *Technology and Culture,* 17, 718-28.
– (1981). *Saving the Prairies: The Life Cycle of the Founding School of American Plant Ecology, 1895-1955.* Berkeley: University of California Press.
"Tongue-in-cheek" representation of the biome effort. (1972). *Eastern Deciduous Forest Biome, U.S. IBP Analysis of Ecosystems IBP Newsletter,* 9, 6.
Tonn, W. M., and Magnuson, J. J. (1982). Pattern in the species composition and richness of fish assemblages in Northern Wisconsin Lakes. *Ecology,* 63, 1149-66.
Tracy, C. R., and Turner, J. S. (1982). What is physiological ecology? *Bulletin of the Ecological Society of America,* 63, 340-7.
Trass, H. (1976). *Vegetation Science: History and Contemporary Trends of Development.* Leningrad: Nauka Press.

Traverse, A. (1974). Paleopalynology. *Annals of the Missouri Botanical Garden*, 61, 203-36.

Turesson, G. (1922). The genotypical response of the plant species to the habitat. *Hereditas*, 3, 211-350.

Tutin, T. G. (1941). The hydrosere and current concepts of the climax. *Journal of Ecology*, 29, 268-79.

Udvardy, M. D. F. (1969). *Dynamic Zoogeography*. New York: Van Nostrand Reinhold.

*U. S. Participation in the International Biological Program*. (1974). Report No. 6 of the U.S. National Committee for the International Biological Program. Washington, D.C.: National Academy of Sciences.

Uvarov, B. P. (1931). Insects and climate. *Transactions of the Entomological Society of London*, 79, 1-249.

Van der Maarel, E. (1975). The Braun-Blanquet approach in perspective. *Vegetatio*, 30, 213-9.

Vandermeer, J. H. (1972). Niche theory. *Annual Review of Ecology and Systematics*, 3, 107-32.

Van Dyne, G. M. (1966). *Ecosystems, Systems Ecology, and Systems Ecologists*. ORNL-3957. Oak Ridge, Tenn.

– (ed.). (1969). *The Ecosystem Concept in Natural Resource Management*. New York: Academic Press.

– (1972). Organization and management of an integrated ecological research program. In *Mathematical Models in Ecology*, ed. J. N. R. Jeffers, pp. 111-72. Oxford: Blackwell Scientific.

– (1980). Systems ecology: The state of the art. In *Oak Ridge National Laboratory Environmental Sciences Laboratory Dedication, February 26-27, 1979*, No. 5666, pp. 81-103. Oak Ridge, Tenn.: Oak Ridge National Laboratory.

Van Valen, L., and Pitelka, F. (1974). Commentary: Intellectual censorship in ecology. *Ecology*, 55, 925-6.

Vernadsky, W. I. (1944). Problems of biogeochemistry II. The fundamental matter-energy difference between the living and inert bodies of the biosphere. *Transactions of the Connecticut Academy of Arts and Sciences*, 35, 483-517.

Verrill, A. E. (1873). Report upon the invertebrate animals of Vineyard Sound and adjacent waters. *Report of the U.S. Commission of Fish and Fisheries, 1871-1872*, 295-778.

Vitousek, P. M., and Reiners, W. A. (1975). Ecosystem succession and nutrient retention: A hypothesis. *BioScience*, 25, 376-81.

Vogt, W. (1948). *Road to Survival*. New York: William Sloane Associates.

Voorhees, D. W. (ed.) (1983). *Concise Dictionary of American Science*. New York: Scribner's.

Vorzimmer, P. (1965). Darwin's ecology and its influence on his theory. *Isis*, 56, 148-55.

Vuillemeer, B. S. (1971). Pleistocene changes in the fauna and flora of South America. *Science*, 173, 771-80.

Walker, D. (1970). Direction and rate in some British post-glacial hydroseres.

In *Studies in the Vegetational History of the British Isles,* ed. D. Walker and R. G. West, pp. 117-39. Cambridge: Cambridge University Press.

Waller, A. E. (1947). Daniel Drake as a pioneer in modern ecology. *Ohio State Archeological and Historical Quarterly,* Oct. 1947, 362-73.

Ward, H. B. (1899a). *The freshwater biological stations of the world.* Report of the Smithsonian Institution of Washington, 1897-98, 499.

– (1899b). Freshwater investigations during the last five years. *Transactions American Microscopical Society,* 20, 261-336.

Warming E. (1895). *Plantesamfund: Grundträk af den Ökologiska Plantegeografi.* Copenhagen: Philipsen. German trans. E. Knoblauch, as *Lehrbuch der Okologischen: Pflanzengeographie: Ein Einfürung in die Kenntniss der Pflanzenvereine.* Berlin: Borntraeger (1896). English version (modified), as *Oecology of Plants: An Introduction to the Study of Plant Communities.* Oxford: Clarendon Press (1909).

Waterman, T. H., and Morowitz, H. J. (eds.) (1965). *Theoretical and Mathematical Biology.* New York: Blaisdell.

Watson, H. C. (1847). *Cybele Britannica; or, British Plants and Their Geographical Relations.* London: Longman.

Watt, A. S. (1924). On the ecology of British beechwoods with special reference to their regeneration. II. The development and structure of beech communities on the Sussex Downs. *Journal of Ecology,* 12, 145-204.

– (1947). Pattern and process in the plant community. *Journal of Ecology,* 35, 1-22.

– (1964). The community and the individual. *Journal of Ecology,* (suppl.), 52, 203-11.

Watt, K. E. F. (1962). Use of mathematics in population ecology. *Annual Review of Entomology,* 7, 243-60.

– (ed.) (1966). *Systems Analysis in Ecology.* New York: Academic Press.

– (1968). *Ecology and Resource Management.* New York: McGraw-Hill.

– (1971). Dynamics of populations: A synthesis. In *Dynamics of Populations,* ed. P.J. den Boer and G. R. Gradwell, pp. 568-80. Wageningen: Centre for Agricultural Publication and Documentation.

– (1973). *Principles of Environmental Science.* New York: McGraw-Hill.

– (1975). Critique and comparison of biome ecosystem modeling. In *Systems Analysis and Simulation in Ecology,* Vol. III, ed. B. C. Patten, pp. 139-52. New York: Academic Press.

Weadock, V., and Dansereau, P. (1960). The SIGMA papers. *Sarracenia,* 3, 1-47.

Weaver, J. E. (1924). Plant production as a measurement of environment. *Journal of Ecology,* 12, 205-37.

Weaver, J. E., and Clements, F. E. (1938). *Plant Ecology.* New York: McGraw-Hill.

Weaver, J. E., Jean, F. G., and Crist, J. W. (1922). *Development and Activities of the Roots of Crop Plants: A Study in Crop Ecology.* Publication No. 316. Washington, D.C.: Carnegie Institution of Washington.

Webb, W. M. (1913). The nature reserve movement in Britain. *Journal of Ecology,* 1, 46.

Webb, W. P. (1931). *The Great Plains.* New York: Ginn.

Welch, B. L. (1972). Ecologists. *Science,* 177, 115.

Welch, P. S. (1935). *Limnology.* New York: McGraw-Hill.

Wenner, L. B. (1982). *The Environmental Decade in Court.* Bloomington: Indiana University Press.

Werner, E. E. (1977). Review of R. H. Whittaker and S. A. Levin (eds.), *Niche: Theory and Application. Transactions of the American Fisheries Society,* 106, 649-50.

– (1980). Niche theory in fisheries ecology. *Transactions of the American Fisheries Society,* 109, 257-60.

Werner, E. E., and Mittelbach, G. G. (1981). Optimal foraging: Field tests of diet choice and habitat switching. *American Zoologist,* 21, 813-29.

West, D. C., Shugart, H. H., and Botkin, D. B. (1981). *Forest Succession: Concepts and Applications.* New York: Springer-Verlag.

West, R. G. (1964). Inter-relations of ecology and quaternary paleobotany. *Journal of Ecology,* (suppl.), 52, 47-57.

Westhoff, V. (1970). Vegetation study as a branch of biological science. In *Vegetatiekunde als synthetische Wetinschap,* ed. H. J. Venema, I. H. Doing, and I. S. Zonneveld, pp. 11-58. Wageningen, The Netherlands: H. Veenman.

Wheeler, W. M. (1902). "Natural history": "œcology" or "ethology"? *Science,* 15, 971-6.

– (1926). A new word for an old thing. *Quarterly Review of Biology,* 1, 439-43.

Whicker, F. W., and Schultz, V. (1982). *Radioecology: Nuclear Energy and the Environment,* Vol. 1. Boca Raton, Fla.: CRC Press.

White, G. (1789). *The Natural History and Antiquities of Selborne in the County of Southampton.* Reprinted London: Macmillan (1900).

White, J. (1982). A history of Irish vegetation studies. *Journal of Life Sciences, Royal Dublin Society,* 3, 15-42.

– (in press). The census of plants in vegetation. In *The Population Structure of Vegetation,* ed. J. White. The Hague: Junk.

White, L., Jr. (1967). The historical roots of our ecological crisis. *Science,* 155, 1203-6.

Whitford, P. B., and Whitford, K. (1951). Thoreau: Pioneer ecologist and conservationist. *Scientific Monthly,* 73, 291-6.

Whittaker, R. H. (1951). A criticism of the plant association and climatic climax concepts. *Northwest Science,* 25, 18-31.

– (1953). A consideration of climax theory: The climax as a population and pattern. *Ecological Monographs,* 23, 41-78.

– (1957). Recent evolution of ecological concepts in relation to the eastern forests of North America. *American Journal of Botany,* 44, 197-206.

– (1962). Classification of natural communities. *Botanical Review,* 28, 1-239.

– (1967). Gradient analysis of vegetation. *Biological Reviews,* 42, 207-64.

– (ed.) (1973). *Ordination and Classification of Communities.* The Hague: Junk.

Whittaker, R. H., and Levin, S. H. (1977). The role of mosaic phenomena in natural communities. *Theoretical Population Biology,* 12, 117-39.

Whittaker, R. H., and Woodwell, G. M. (1972). Evolution of natural communities. In *Ecosystem Structure and Function,* ed. J. A. Wiens, pp. 137-59, Corvallis: Oregon State University Press.

Wiegert, R. C. (1975). Mathematical representation of ecological interaction. In *Ecosystem Analysis and Prediction,* ed. S. A. Levin, pp. 43-55. Proceedings SIAM-SIMS Conference on Ecosystems, Alta, Utah, July 1-5, 1974, SIAM Institute for Mathematics and Society.

– (1976). Developing theory at the ecosystem level. In *Ecological Theory and Ecosystems Models,* ed. S. A. Levin, pp. 29-30. Indianapolis: Institute of Ecology.

Wiens, J. A. (1977). On competition and variable environments. *American Scientist,* 65, 590-7.

– (1983). Avian community ecology: An iconoclastic view. In *Perspectives in Ornithology,* ed. A. H. Brush and G. A. Clark, Jr., pp. 355-403. Cambridge: Cambridge University Press.

– (1984). On understanding a non-equilibrium world: Myth and reality in community patterns and processes. In *Ecological Communities: Conceptual Issues and the Evidence,* ed. D. R. Strong, D. Simberloff, L. G. Abele, and A. B. Thistle, pp. 439-58. Princeton, N.J.: Princeton University Press.

Willard, D. E. (1980). Ecologists, environmental litigation, and forensic ecology. *Bulletin of the Ecological Society of America,* 61, 14-18.

Williams, G. C. (1966). *Adaptation and Natural Selection.* Princeton, N.J.: Princeton University Press.

Willson, M. F. (1981). Ecology and science. *Bulletin of the Ecological Society of America,* 62, 4-12.

Wilson, E. O. (1969). The new population biology. *Science,* 163, 1184-5.

– (1978). Introduction: What is sociobiology? In *Sociobiology and Human Nature,* ed. M. S. Gregory, A. Silius, and D. Sutch, pp. 1-12. San Francisco: Jossey-Bass.

Wolfe, J. (1969). Radioecology: Retrospection and future. In *Symposium on Radioecology,* ed. D. J. Nelson and F. C. Evans, pp. xi-xii. Rept. CONF-670503. Washington, D.C.: U.S. Atomic Energy Commission.

Wolfe, L. M. (1947). *Son of the Wilderness: The Life of John Muir.* New York: Knopf.

Woodmansee, R. G. (1978). Additions and losses of nitrogen in grassland ecosystems. *BioScience,* 28, 448-53.

Woodwell, G. M. (1976). A confusion of paradigms (musings of a president-elect). *Bulletin of the Ecological Society of America,* 57(4), 8-10.

– (1978). Paradigms lost. *Bulletin of the Ecological Society of America,* 59, 136-40.

– (1980). Bravo plus 25 years. In *Oak Ridge National Laboratory Environmental Sciences Laboratory Dedication, February 26-27, 1979,* No. 5666, pp. 61-64. Oak Ridge, Tenn.: Oak Ridge National Laboratory.

– (1981). A postscript for the old boys of the subversive science. *BioScience,* 31, 518-22.

Woodwell, G. M., and Botkin, D. B. (1970). Metabolism of terrestrial ecosystems by gas exchange techniques. In *Analysis of Temperate Forest Ecosystems,* ed. D. E. Reichle, pp. 73-85. Berlin: Springer-Verlag.

Woodwell, G. M., and Whittaker, R. H. (1968). Effects of chronic gamma irradiation on plant communities. *Quarterly Review of Biology*, 43, 42-55.

Worster, D. (1977). *Nature's Economy: The Roots of Ecology*. San Francisco: Sierra Club Books.

Worthington, E. B. (ed.) (1975). *The Evolution of IBP*. Cambridge: Cambridge University Press.

– (1983). *The Ecological Century: A Personal Appraisal*. Oxford: Clarendon Press.

Young, O. R. (1956). A survey of general systems theory. *General Systems*, 1, 61-80.

# Name index

# Subject index